They Called It Pilot Error

They Called It Pilot Error

True Stories behind General Aviation Accidents

Robert L. Cohn

TAB Books

Division of McGraw-Hill, Inc.

New York   San Francisco   Washington, D.C.   Auckland   Bogotá
Caracas   Lisbon   London   Madrid   Mexico City   Milan
Montreal   New Delhi   San Juan   Singapore
Sydney   Tokyo   Toronto

Published by Tab Books, a division of McGraw-Hill, Inc.

1 2 3 4 5 6 7 8 9 0 DOC/DOC 9 9 8 7 6 5 4

Library of Congress Cataloging-in-Publication Data
Cohn, Robert L., 1930-
    They called it pilot error : true stories behind general aviation
accidents / by Robert L. Cohn.
        p.   cm.
    Includes index.
    ISBN 0-8306-4463-6 (p)   ISBN 0-8306-4464-4 (h)
    1. Aeronautics—United States—Accidents—Human factors.   2. Air
pilots—Training of—United States.   I. Title.
TL553.5.C49   1993
363.12'41'0973—dc20   93-8267
                                                                    CIP

Acquistions editor: Jeff Worsinger
Editorial team: Robert E. Ostrander, Executive Editor
                Norval G. Kennedy, Book Editor
Production team: Katherine G. Brown, Director
                Rhonda E. Baker, Layout
                Linda L. King, Proofreading
                Stacey Spurlock, Indexer
Design team: Jaclyn J. Boone, Designer
                Brian Allison, Associate Designer   GEN1
Cover design: Craig Reese, Hanover, Pa.   4433

94-2118

To Sylvia
for her critique and encouragement

To all of the contributors
for their cooperation and confidence

Contents

Introduction

Aircraft and the three-dimensional environment in which they operate are not user-friendly for human beings. As a result, developing and maintaining the proficiencies necessary to safely and efficiently fly an airplane or helicopter are difficult, time-consuming, and costly.

Flight training has barely progressed beyond the basics, perhaps because of a typical pilot's limited time and money. Training remains a sort of crash course in not crashing, with almost exclusive concentration on physically coordinating, maneuvering, and manually handling—not manhandling—an aircraft. In that limited mind-set, in fixed-wing training, considerable time is spent on things such as steep turns, S-turns, turns about a point, slow flight, stall entries and recoveries, and short field takeoffs and landings—all things that should be scrupulously avoided in safe, efficient flying.

In my 6,400 hours of business and personal flying, I never made a short field takeoff or landing, or slow-flighted an airplane to anywhere near the point of stalling, or made an S-turn or a turn steeper than 60°, or ever deliberately put an airplane into a stall or any other out-of-control condition, except in training, for a biennial flight review, or for a checkride. In other words, a substantial part of my training was meant to prepare me for more training and had nothing at all to do with my real-world use of an airplane.

In retrospect, I was short-changed. And so is every pilot who, because it is still required by the FAA, undergoes flight training that way. When I thought more about it, I realized that I had never been taught or even made aware of many of the things that are truly crucial to the safe and proper use of an airplane. I had to learn those the hard way.

For instance, I never had any training—not even in ground school—on most of the physiological, mental, and purely human factors that can seriously detract from or materially contribute to safe flying. Some examples: I never even saw an oxygen mask or oxygen tank until I had been flying for more than five years. I never knew that the effects of alcohol and medications could remain in my body for 24 hours or more until I read about it in a newspaper article about drunk driving—after I had been flying for more than 20 years as a casual drinker. And I never had any formal preparation whatsoever for dealing with icing, or severe turbulence, or night flying and navigating, or spatial disorientation, or vertigo, or ear problems, or optical illusions.

As my list of voids kept growing, something happened at one of my pilot workshop/seminars that triggered a compulsion in me to begin writing down those missing items, and then watching for them in the accident reports I was studying: A brand new pilot complained to me that the first checkride was a failure because stall entries were not adequately demonstrated. The stall recoveries were just fine, according to the pilot.

That bothered me because the last thing you ever want to do as the pilot of an airplane is a stall entry. It would be like deliberately swerving and slamming on the brakes of your car in expressway traffic just to get the feel of its skid and rollover characteristics. But I checked on it and sure enough improperly executed stall entry is a bustable item on an FAA checkride.

On the other hand, according to the checkride standards, an applicant does not have to demonstrate an understanding of numerous safety topics: use of oxygen, icing conditions, severe turbulence, snowy runways, and other real problems that a pilot is going to eventually encounter with enough hours. Also, beyond an instructor's endorsement, an applicant is not required to conduct any portion of any checkride at night, even though most pilots will eventually fly at night, and even though night flying demands different skills and orientations and is statistically more dangerous than day flying.

Rather than pick a fight with city hall, or try to change those inbred flight training procedures by writing letters or standing in picket lines, I decided to write this expanded sequel to my first book *Aviahomosapionics*; it was my first investigative exposure to the human factors in general aviation accidents.

In doing so, I must acknowledge the splendid, unrestrained cooperation of the FAA, the NTSB, air traffic controllers, flight service station specialists, the Air Force School of Aerospace Medicine, NASA's Technical Utilization and Space Medicine & Biology groups, NASA's Aviation Safety Reporting System team, and every aviation manufacturer and fixed-base operator that I contacted. They all contributed more than what was requested, put forth extra time and effort to be sure I understood everything they were imparting—much of it new technology—and gave me innumerable suggestions that improved the format and content of this book.

The Aviation Safety Reporting System (ASRS) at NASA is exceptional in concept, straightforward in performance, and useful beyond measure. Recall that the ASRS is a clearinghouse wherein pilots are guaranteed absolute immunity and complete confidentiality if they will report incidents that compromised or threatened air safety. ASRS headquarters is adjacent to Moffett Field U.S. Naval Air Station at Mountain View, California. Approximately 3000 written reports are received monthly and analyzed by experts, primarily former airline captains and air traffic controllers. Nearly 80 percent of the reports are from airline pilots.

Without much fanfare, ASRS pipelines its salient findings directly to NASA and the appropriate airlines, manufacturers, and government agencies. A newsletter that highlights ASRS activities and the pilot reports—anonymously—is available to anyone. As a result, significant changes have evolved that have improved airline safety without much fanfare. General aviation pilots would help their own cause with better participation in the ASRS program.

A couple of startling facts came front-and-center early in the research process:

- The need for and the use of oxygen is dangerously misunderstood and poorly administered in general aviation—to a lesser degree by many airlines but not by the military where standards and procedures have reduced the potential for hypoxia (lack-of-oxygen sickness) to a nonfactor. NASA's space program recognizes the significance of properly administered oxygen; nominal oxygen concentration is earth normal, worst-case environment is a 4000–6000-foot equivalent, and anything exceeding 10,000 feet is a life-threatening emergency. NASA's standards are based upon the results of exhaustive study and experience. Yet general aviation, as regulated by the FAA, persists in allowing continuous flight without supplemental oxygen as high as 12,500 feet, and for up to 30 minutes at 14,000 feet, even at night when oxygen concentration levels might be much lower than daytime. NASA's data needs to be shared with the FAA.

- Many of the FAA's flight standards and Federal Aviation Regulations (FARs) as applied to general aviation are poorly written, outdated, misunderstood, and misleading. Regulations urgently need revision, but most shocking of all is that none of the FARs contain any provisions for meaningful enforcement. You can fly drunk or drugged,

without a medical, license, or type rating and not be subject
to any fines or imprisonment except in a very few states.
Doing any or all of those things might adversely affect your
insurance premiums, but it won't threaten your freedom. It
would, however, endanger you and the rest of us. The NTSB
is studying enforcement possibilities and driving records are
subject to review when applying for a medical certificate.

When I began interviewing the people who were involved in
pertinent accidents and incidents, all of which had been fully documented by the NTSB, I ran into some stonewallers. Pilots, passengers, family members, friends, insurance companies, and lawyers
refused to elaborate or comment primarily for legal reasons and fear
of reprisals.

Fortunately, most of the barriers came down following my persistent assurances of total confidentiality. Many of the people then became anxious to clear the air and relieve their harbored misgivings
about what had really taken place versus what was in the official reports. They shared facts, previously suppressed information, suggestions, ideas, and especially their own admitted speculations. It was an
enlightening experience that gave me a deeper understanding of the
pain and suffering these accidents have caused.

Official confidentiality of a few complex cases precluded any
possible follow-up or further investigation. In most of those instances, however, the involved government agencies willingly provided expert insights into the most likely causes and remedies of the
accidents, even though none of the confirmed findings were made
available.

Occasionally, local police, fire, and hospital reports were coupled
with confirmations by local airport personnel and other eyewitnesses
to fill in the material gaps that had been left in the officially released
conclusions.

As a result, all anecdotes, names, places, and events described in
this book have been de-identified and modified enough to preserve
the absolute confidentiality promised to the contributors.

The glossary might be helpful for nonpilots because the language
of general aviation vocabulary has evolved into numerous terms, abbreviations, acronyms, and verbal shorthand based upon convenience and common usage. Ideally the definitions will clear up some
of the apparently opaque technical aspects of the terminology that
might cloud a better understanding.

This book is a work of fiction that is based upon carefully researched and thoroughly documented facts and enhanced with con-

tributions from aviation experts. It is written to entertain and educate, to provoke thought and better flight safety through personal self-discipline, and to spotlight the real underlying causes of accidents attributed to "pilot error."

Pilot error has become an insidious dumping ground classification that is still officially attributed to more than 90 percent of all general aviation accidents and incidents. The NTSB classifies nearly every accident as pilot error when the cause cannot be otherwise attributed to provable and confirmable physical causes; if it isn't black and white, it's pilot error—no gray or maybe areas.

Even the board's use of the term *probable cause* when rendering a conclusion is limited almost entirely to things such as engine failures and broken components that can be documented or photographed without rebuttal.

When it comes to the analysis of any number of factors that can cause an aircraft accident—human, weather, operational, training, regulatory factors—the final answer is too often pilot error with little or no effort put forth to explain, discover, or even ask why the pilot made that particular error.

The "pilot error" accidents described in this book, even in their fictionalized form, are intended to provoke thought about why the qualified pilots made the mistakes. One disturbing common thread tends to be present in all of these accidents: genuine causal factors that could have been—should have been—prevented. But in nearly all of the instances those factors were completely unknown to each pilot either due to ignorance, lack of training, misleading regulations, inexperience, bad luck, or typically all of the above.

One other prevalent attitude that I found particularly unsettling was an almost cavalier indifference toward pilot and passenger safety by many of the support forces in aviation. You will notice it in the accounts of several of the interviews. FBOs, ground personnel, mechanics, even some flight instructors and government operatives still seem to embrace the idea that: "Flying is not for the timid, the squeamish, or the nonadventurous; it's a do-it-at-your-own-risk elite activity, and if you can't handle the danger, stay on the ground." Unfortunately, as long as a macho mind-set rules the domain, general aviation will continue to stifle itself and deny the exhilaration, utility, and convenience of private flying to hundreds of thousands of would-be participants.

I learned more about flying in the 18 months that it took to research, assemble, and prepare this book than I had learned in approximately 40 years of being involved in aviation. I especially learned more about human factors: how they are manifested, how they affect safety, and how easily they can be controlled by awareness and understanding.

I sincerely hope you find this subject matter to be as enlightening and as helpful to your flying as I did. I also hope our government and the aviation industry will finally begin to do something meaningful about updating and modernizing age-old procedures and technologies before general aviation goes from being an endangered species to extinction.

1

High and high don't mix

Preliminary report: October; Beech A-36; private pilot single-engine land, instrument rating, 2,260 hours. The aircraft crashed in an open field 35 minutes after departing on an IFR trip from Duluth, Minnesota to Kansas City, Missouri, that should have taken more than 3 hours. The pilot reported having trouble controlling the aircraft while climbing through 10,000 feet to a flight-planned altitude of 12,000 feet. The pilot and his passenger were killed.

Further investigation revealed:

- The aircraft behaved erratically after entering the clouds at 1,800 feet. Light to moderate turbulence had been forecast in the clouds. Also, ATC advised the pilot of a PIREP from a 727 at 10,000 feet, slightly south of his flight path, reporting moderate chop while descending from 11,000 through 9,500 feet, and tops at just above 11,000 feet.
- The private pilot, an anesthesiologist, and his wife were returning home from a wedding the night before, which ended 13 hours prior to takeoff.
- An autopsy of the pilot's body revealed a residual blood alcohol level of 0.05 percent. Safe driving in nearly all states is 0.08–0.10 percent maximum. The FAA maximum is 0.04 percent.
- Although there was a complete oxygen system on the Bonanza, there was no oxygen on board at the time of the crash.

Official conclusion: Pilot error. Loss of control due to probable spatial disorientation and/or vertigo caused by alcohol impairment. Pilot's residual blood alcohol level was 0.05 percent, 25 percent above the maximum safe level of 0.04 percent.

ERIC DRUCKER WAS A BY-THE-NUMBERS PILOT. At 56, he had been flying for 30 years, the last 10 of which were in his pride and joy, a Beech A-36 Bonanza purchased with low time, in mint condition, and kept that way ever since.

From the time Eric and the Bonanza came together, neither had been spared any expense in striving for complete perfection. The Bonanza had every toy that could be packed safely into an airplane, redundancy of every possible system and a host of creature comfort accessories.

Eric was meticulous about maintaining his IFR proficiency, with a continuous regimen of recurrent training and ground school classes and videos. He also qualified for the Wings Program for eight running years and read most of the leading aviation periodicals regularly. He was especially into accident reports and often became quite vocal about ". . . those (pilots) who give aviation a black eye."

Merritt Drucker, Eric's 27-year-old son "I guess you could call my dad a Type-A pilot. He did everything in flying with the same intensity as he did in his anesthesiology practice. He checked, double-checked and triple-checked every detail. As a result, he was the best, most careful pilot I ever flew with.

"I'm an instrument pilot myself but I've never been as dedicated as my dad was. I used to tell him he was a classic nitpicker. But it never fazed him. He'd just spout off on some story about an accident he'd read about and then usually give me a parting shot with his favorite flying bromide: 'Stay with it, or stay out of the sky.' He was always saving my life."

It was a 48° cloudy Saturday morning in Kansas City, pretty typical for west-central Missouri in late October. Eric and Frieda, his wife of 39 years, arrived at the airport 2½ hours before takeoff, giving themselves plenty of time for breakfast with the airport gang, preceded by a short call to flight service for a "lay-of-the-land" report, as Eric always called it.

After breakfast, a lengthy conversation with flight service ended with an IFR flight plan for a 10:35 a.m. departure, 9,000 feet initial altitude with 11,000 requested when available, 3:05 time enroute to Duluth, Minnesota, for his nephew's wedding the next day. Most of the flight would be between layers with only a slight chance of some light icing in the clouds at 6–7,000 feet. All in all, a nice tailwind and a smooth uneventful ride. Eric was relaxed and matter-of-fact as he loaded the luggage and checked every inch and orifice on his Beechcraft beauty.

Frieda busied herself in the pilot's lounge, putting ice in the portable cooler, checking the cockpit lunch she had prepared and then heading for the ladies' room—her always last stop before take-off. Frieda had become a seasoned general aviation traveler since the Bonanza entered their lives. She and Eric planned most of their time off together to where the Bonanza could take them. They had both grown to love the excitement and convenience of it.

Despite her complete comfort and confidence in the Bonanza with Eric, plus two pinch-hitter courses and a couple of stabs at learning to fly, Frieda could not master the demands of the three-dimensional sky or the fear of being alone in an airplane. Eric's urging and coaching brought her as far as straight-and-level flight, shallow turns using just the wheel, and gradual climbs and descents using both throttle and control pressure. She was also fairly proficient with the radio, because Eric had taught her how to find and dial in the frequencies and then communicate with ATC, responding to hand-offs, during their always-IFR cross-country trips.

But in the vicinity of an airport, Frieda was a basket case. While she marveled at Eric's cool, self-confident mastery of approaches and landings, her own attempts at approaching a runway always left her frustrated and shaken. Eric was patient and reassuring, anxious for her to become a reliable backstop. He was certain she would be, given enough time and practice. But she never shared his confidence.

Merrit Drucker "Dad was absolutely certain that my mother could get the airplane to an airport and land it safely if anything happened to him. She never believed it, but I think she could have. The few times I flew backseat with them and watched dad force her to shoot a landing—with plenty of adjustments and back-up from him—she did okay. Not exactly uneventful or a greaser landing, but never to the point of breaking up the airplane.

"The one time when she did really well, she seemed to feel pretty pleased with herself about it. Dad insisted he hadn't helped her very much, and she didn't argue with him. But I remember her telling him that he'd better stay healthy or my sister and I would be early inheritors.

"(Long pause) I still think she could have handled it."

The flight to Duluth was exactly as had been predicted, on-time, a trace of ice climbing through 6,500 feet, smooth as silk at 9,000 feet between cloud layers, and Frieda's almost-by-herself landing was on the money. During their 2 hours and 30 minutes at 9,000 feet, Eric

and Frieda used their oxygen masks periodically, as was Eric's usual
practice anytime he was above 7,000 feet for any length of time.

After they landed, Eric signed in at the FBO service counter and
ordered full tanks, oil to just below the full mark (but not checked until the next morning) and the nearly-empty oxygen bottle refilled.

Merrit Drucker "Dad used oxygen routinely. After all, he was an
anesthesiologist. So he understood all there was to know about hypoxia. In fact, he was kind of a crusader about oxygen in airplanes.
He wrote lots of letters to the flying magazines and the FAA. Some of
his stuff got printed, and he got some nice 'thank-you's' from the government once in awhile. But nothing much ever came of it.

"He did get his local FBO to always have oxygen available, but
he may have been their only regular customer for it.

"A couple of his flying buddies put masks and bottles on their airplanes, and dad taught them how to use it, but I'm not sure if they
ever really did use it.

"It used to frustrate him because he knew how serious a problem
it is. He used to say, 'Those damned bureaucrats at the FAA won't listen because it's almost impossible to prove that lack of oxygen was a
factor in an accident. And the aircraft industry doesn't want to talk
about it because they're afraid it will up the cost of their already over-
priced machines and further scare the hell out of prospective pilots
and their terrified families and friends.

"He'd go on and on about it, but that's all it was. Mostly just
talk. He never changed anything very much. He'd just get himself
all riled up and then give me heat about it and remind me to never
take off without a full bottle, which I'm still careful about. It's one
of my preflight items, and I think about them every time I check
that damned bottle."

Eric and Frieda spent a hectic weekend in Duluth, attending parties,
visiting with Eric's brother, Walter, and his wife and family, and finally
enjoying a lovely wedding thrown by one of Duluth's most prominent
families. Food and especially drink were plentiful and continuous.

Walter Drucker, Eric's 58-year old brother "We had one helluva
weekend, maybe the best we ever had as a family. Even Eric, who
usually acted like a teetotaler because of his damned flying. He and
Frieda just got caught up in all the partying and really loosened up. It
was great to see them having such a good time. (Pause)

"But right after we left the church, Eric went right back into his nondrinking mode. I doubt if he had more than one small glass of wine and maybe a sip or two of champagne during the whole reception.

"After the reception was over, most of our family came back to our place for a farewell cordial. You know, 'One for the road'? Anyway, Eric was a good sport about it. But then he bawled me out for screwing up his flying schedule with my 'lousy after-dinner drink'. He was kidding, of course, but we did change our plans to see them off from 8–10:30 a.m. Eric said that if he was going to have to miss one of his meetings, the least I could do was reciprocate by missing one or two of mine."

At 8 on Monday morning, Walter Drucker and his wife met Eric and Frieda at their motel for breakfast. Right after they ordered, Eric excused himself to call flight service.

Reaching a briefer turned out to be a marathon wait, not unusual for a Monday morning, so Eric decided to file his flight plan right then and there, rather than risk another long delay at 10, which he figured could be even more of a rush hour than at 8.

The briefing was complete, straightforward and with only one surprise: The winds aloft were more favorable at 12,000 feet than at 9,000 feet.

According to the briefing: "Local ceilings holding at 1,500–2,000 feet, solid through 10,500 this area. Several PIREPs over Minneapolis have tops at just under 11,000. Ceilings lowering en route to 800 and 4 miles in the Kansas City area. Expect some rain and possibly a few widely scattered thunderstorms through most of northern Missouri. Conditions improving after 1800 Greenwich (1 p.m. central time). Winds aloft at 9,000—240° at 40K; at 12,000—260° at 40K; and at 18,000—270° at 55K. At time of departure freezing level will be between 7 and 9,000 feet. No icing reported at this time by any departing aircraft."

Eric did his usual quick time enroute calculations and filed his flight plan: Departure at 1530 Greenwich (10:30 a.m. local time), 12,000 feet, time enroute 3:35 with 5½ hours of fuel on board. He also told the briefer he would pick up his clearance airborne rather than call in for a release time. He figured, probably correctly, that flight service might be hard to reach by phone at that hour. He also did not like rushing his run-up or takeoff to stay within short release times. Besides, the local ceiling and visibility were forecast to be comfortable VFR.

Walter Drucker "When we met them for breakfast, Eric seemed okay. He complained of a slight headache and said he needed some strong coffee and some extra time to help him shake off the weekend and my 'goddamned farewell cordial' which, in retrospect, I wish he'd never had. That one lousy drink must have been what caused his residual blood alcohol to show up a tenth of a point over the limit. None of us believe that such a tiny overage by itself could have caused the accident. We think the oxygen problem was the primary cause, or at least a major contributor, but we couldn't prove that. So, we wound up accepting a terrible settlement from the insurance company that cost his kids a fortune.

"And, as the family lawyer, I and my firm spent a pile of money running back and forth to depositions and hearings in Kansas City. I even went to Washington myself to try to get the FAA and the NTSB to amend their findings due to the kind of guy and pilot Eric was. (Pause) It was like talking to that wall. (Another longer pause)

"Anyway, Eric ordered his breakfast and then left us to go file his flight plan. When he came back to the table almost twenty minutes later, his breakfast was already cold. He didn't seem to care much, though, because he was mostly interested in telling Frieda and us about how their flight was going to be. I think he called it 'Easy IFR,' or something to that effect.

"About two bites into his breakfast, he said he was feeling a little punk and was going to call back and move their takeoff time back by an hour or so, after he finished breakfast. I guess Frieda was kind of anxious to get home because she suggested he wait until around 10 or 10:15 to make that decision. I'm sure she felt he would start feeling better after another couple of hours.

"I had blocked out the whole morning, so it didn't matter much to me. It was a little more time with my brother, who I only saw a couple of times a year. (Pause) It was nice. We talked about a lot of things just because we had nothing else to do."

Eric walked up to the FBO service counter at 9:45, laid down his credit card and told Frieda to look over the bill and sign for it while he called flight service to move their departure time back to 12. He still had his slight headache, and the three bites of the cold omelet that was his breakfast weren't sitting too well. He didn't feel like he had a hangover, just a bit frazzled from the long weekend with not enough time to relax.

Getting through to flight service was the same hassle as it had been earlier. They had one small bit of disturbing news: the Howard

East and West MOAs were both going active at 2:30 p.m. for the rest of the afternoon. It hadn't been a factor with the 10:30 departure but could be with 12.

Eric did another quick calculation and decided to file for an 11:30 departure. He would be just past the southernmost boundary of the MOA with about 15 minutes to spare, and the extra half-hour wouldn't matter that much. He wasn't feeling any worse, maybe even a tad better.

Meanwhile, Frieda looked over the service bill: 38 gallons of 100 LL and 2 quarts of multi-grade for $86.80. It looked about right to her, so she signed it, not noticing that there was no price or extension adjacent to the notation to refill the oxygen bottle.

Melissa Sanders, manager of the Duluth FBO "It was kind of an unusual request for us, especially coming in on a Saturday. We mostly sell oxygen to corporate pilots, or sometimes by special request with advance notice to people based here. But even at that, we don't sell very much of it since we're flat country here.

"The line boy either overlooked it or expected the Sunday crew to take care of it when they checked the oil. How it got past the counter girl I can't say. Maybe because it was so busy. But whatever, it couldn't have made any difference in what happened. The accident inspectors from the government told us they never got above 10,000 feet, so they wouldn't have needed the oxygen anyway."

Eric rejoined his party, took his credit card and the folded service receipt from Frieda, never looking at it, and sat down to rest for the hour or so they had to kill.

Forty minutes later, Eric was feeling better. He decided to load the airplane a little early and take some extra time doing his preflight. He was glad he did. He found the oil on the dipstick above the full line by nearly half a quart, enough to cause the engine to throw oil in flight.

A hasty and annoyed but subdued visit to the service counter brought an even hastier response from the embarrassed line boy and the field manager. In fewer than 10 minutes the situation was being corrected by a mechanic who also brought along a portable air tank because he thought the Bonanza's nose wheel looked "a bit puffy," but very likely to further appease what he might have thought was a justifiably angry customer.

Eric rechecked the loading of the baggage while the oil was being drained and continued a much-interrupted preflight. The mechanic was a friendly talker. So was the field manager. After at least three starts and stops, the preflight was completed with the oxygen bottle never having been checked.

At 11:10 sharp, Eric and Frieda bade farewell to their relatives, fired up the Bonanza and taxied out. The run-up was normal, Eric was feeling better, especially sensing that Frieda was relieved to finally be going home, and the Bonanza was off the ground two minutes ahead of their 11:30 departure time.

Climbing through 1,000 feet, Eric contacted center after three tries—it was a busy morning—and picked up his clearance: "As filed," with some instructions and new advisories: "Expect moderate turbulence in the clouds, light rime ice reported by several aircraft between 7,000 and 9,000 feet, tops at 10,800 your vicinity, please report the bases upon entering the clouds. You are cleared to 10,000, expect further clearance to 12,000 in about 20 minutes."

Eric scribbled his notes, checked his gauges carefully and sat back comfortably, looking out the window so he could report the cloud bases. He told Frieda to tighten her shoulder harness in anticipation of the expected turbulence. She had already done so as he pulled his own harness to almost uncomfortably tight.

Passing through 1,700 feet, the first light jolts of turbulence greeted the airplane, and Eric reported the bases at 1,800 feet, just as they went full IMC. The next three jolts of turbulence were more than moderate and Eric immediately focused his attention on the bouncing silhouette in his HSI. Keeping the airplane under control was his trained first priority and he gave it his full attention.

Noticing that the DG had drifted 15° right while he was concentrating on the HSI, Eric began a correcting left turn just as another sudden jolt of turbulence hit the Bonanza, throwing the HSI up and to the left. Eric reacted with down right pressure on the yoke, which caused an overcorrection just in time for the next jolt, followed by several more.

Eric found himself fighting the turbulence, not noticing his altimeter racing up, his airspeed deteriorating quickly, the DG now 25° left of his intended heading and the #1 CDI needle in a full right deflection. To make matters worse, he suddenly felt a spinning sensation and a heaviness in the pit of his stomach.

Recognizing the onset of vertigo, Eric reflexively loosened his grip on the yoke, covered one eye (as he had demonstrated to dozens of pilots in lectures he had given) and took two deep breaths. The Bonanza began to slowly level itself off, despite the continuing but now lighter turbulence. Eric's sensation of spinning eased also. His nausea had abated, somewhat.

Center had been tracking the Bonanza's errant flight along with those of several other aircraft. It was an unusually blustery October day. By the time they reached him, Eric was sure he and the airplane were "A-okay and climbing through 5,000, turning back on course now. That turbulence was a lot worse than moderate." Center acknowledged, cleared him back to on course and turned their attention to another aircraft.

Frieda, who was badly shaken by their wild ride, also took a couple of deep breaths to compose herself. She had noticed Eric struggling, in a cold sweat and obviously unable to control the aircraft. With the turbulence subsided, she began attending to Eric, dabbing his forehead with a soft handkerchief and trying to settle him down. It worked.

Now feeling better, but still quite upset over his bout with vertigo, Eric began preparing for their next encounter—the rime ice reported between 7,000 and 9,000 feet—as they passed through 5,500 feet. He reached around back for his oxygen mask, put it on and opened the valve on the bottle a half turn, by feel as he had done dozens of times before. Frieda knew the routine well and casually took her own mask from the pocket in back of her seat and put it on.

Neither of them noticed that, after only a few breaths, very little oxygen was coming into their masks. The bottle was almost empty. They were concentrating on other things—Eric on the icing, Frieda on Eric.

Passing through 7,500 feet, and no ice on the airplane, Eric relaxed. It didn't last long. Center called with another disturbing advisory: "Bonanza 24 Bravo, we just had a report of moderate to severe chop at 10,000 feet from a descending 727 25 miles south of you, about 10 miles east of your flight path. You can stay at 8,000 for now until we can clear you to 12,000. Tops still reporting at just under 11,000."

Eric glanced out his side window and saw the first traces of the rime ice beginning to form on the wing. He reflexively checked the hot prop switch, which he had turned on earlier, and responded to center: "We're starting to pick up some ice here at 8,000, so I think we'll continue climbing. We'll appreciate your expediting that clearance to 12,000, and I'll let you know if we run into that turbulence."

Center acknowledged but was now monitoring the flight more carefully. The aircraft was 13 minutes behind its flight plan. Some fast calculations by the controller caused serious enough concern for her to call her supervisor. There was now a strong probability that the Bonanza would not be clear of the Howard MOA ahead by 2:30 and would have to be diverted. Any further erosion of the flight plan, plus a diversion, could leave the aircraft with inadequate IFR fuel reserves. And conditions in Kansas City were not improving, as had been expected. Fortunately, they were not getting worse.

The supervisor rechecked the calculations and glanced at the controller's scope just in time to see the target once again drifting off course, then suddenly climbing and going through 10,000 feet without clearance.

The controller saw it, too, and immediately called: "Bonanza . . ., you're 20° right of course and above your assigned altitude. Please advise."

There was no reply. The call was repeated with urgency. The aircraft had leveled off at 10,600 feet, and was starting to descend slowly. It was also turning left and passing back through its on-course heading. Then it reversed course and began climbing again.

Finally, after an eternal 20 seconds, Eric responded in an unsteady voice: "I'm having a control problem. Heavy turbulence. Need that clearance to 12—NOW!"

The supervisor grabbed the mike: "You're cleared to 12,000. Say your condition."

In the cockpit, Eric was having more than a control problem. He and Frieda were breathing stale air from the now empty oxygen bottle, and his head was starting to spin again. The vertigo was coming back. This time like a tidal wave.

He tried to reply to center but he was being overwhelmed by the severe dizziness. Realizing that he was in trouble and that something was wrong with his breathing, Eric flailed at his mask, trying to remove it.

He was too late. With his hand gripping the mask, Eric passed out and fell forward against the yoke. The airplane lurched into a diving spiral.

Frieda never had a chance. It all happened too quickly. In her own weakened condition, and with the sudden lurch of the airplane, she tried to reach Eric but passed out on top of him. That was a blessing.

Center watched helplessly as the target disappeared from its scopes. Twenty-one seconds later, the aircraft crashed into an open field. Neither occupant survived.

Merritt Drucker "The accident investigators said that both dad and mother apparently had their masks on before they went down. They also said they had determined that there was no oxygen on board. The FBO in Duluth never filled the bottle, even though it was marked on dad's fuel order. But they didn't consider oxygen to be a factor in the accident because the highest they got was about ten-five, and they were there for only a few minutes at most.

"But I and every doctor I've talked to agrees that the stale, thinner air that dad and mother were breathing, because the damn bottle went empty, definitely could have aggravated the effects of the residual blood alcohol.

"What I can't figure is how the oxygen screwup got past everyone, what with dad being such a fanatic about it. I know that my mother signed the fuel order, and that there was some kind of a problem during the preflight. All of that came out in the investigation in Duluth. But I just can't imagine dad not checking his bottle, especially since he had filed for 12,000 feet.

"Another thing I can't understand is how dad could have had any residual blood alcohol in his body from the little bit of wine and champagne he had at the wedding. I know that he had one small after-dinner drink later on with my uncle, Walter, but that was at least 13 hours before they took off.

"I know it sounds like sour grapes, because we had to make a very unfair settlement with the insurance company, but the FAA, the NTSB and all of their so-called experts will never convince me, or any members of our family, or anyone who knew dad and the way he was about flying, that alcohol was the sole cause of the accident. It had to be because the stale air and the lack of oxygen intensified the problem.

"I'm sorry to sound like such a jerk about it, but that FBO should have been held responsible. And the FAA, or someone, should come up with a better set of rules or guidelines for knowing what your blood alcohol level is when you climb into an airplane. Dad waited over 13 hours. That sure as hell should have been long enough!"

NTSB representative "The Drucker family was understandably upset with our findings. But we consider them to be clear-cut. The autopsy confirmed that the pilot's blood alcohol level was 0.05, or 0.01 over the FAA limit, which is 25 percent too high.

"The finding was absolute, and it was reconfirmed by the pathologists who were hired by the pilot's brother, who is a lawyer. He acted on behalf of the Drucker family. Very intensely, I might add.

"Their claim that the lack of oxygen and the problem with the masks contributed to the accident is entirely possible. But there's no way to prove it, especially considering the very short time they were at altitude.

"It's certainly unfortunate that this very conscientious pilot's first and obviously inadvertent encounter with residual blood alcohol happened under such worst-case circumstances—the turbulence when he first entered the clouds followed by the much more severe turbulence at the higher altitude was very unusual for that time of the year. And the likelihood that he was never much of a drinker could have been an aggravating factor, because he may have had a very low tolerance for alcohol.

"What many pilots don't seem to grasp is the fact that a point zero four alcohol level is plenty of alcohol. We have a file cabinet full of reports of vertigo encounters where there was only half that much blood alcohol."

NASA representative "The NTSB's findings in this case are conclusive, and we don't dispute them. The blood alcohol and the circumstances were sufficient to cause spatial disorientation and vertigo, which appear to have been the reasons the aircraft went out of control.

"Whether or not the oxygen deficiency was a factor is speculation at best. Unofficially, I would say that supplemental oxygen could have helped alleviate the vertigo. I would also say that the stale air in their masks definitely did not help the situation at all. But there is no way that we have found to measure or be absolutely sure of the effect that lack of oxygen has on residual blood alcohol, especially in the very short time the airplane was at a higher altitude in this case.

"One of our space medicine specialists had a theory about this case. Based on the transcripts, she thought that there was probably a short, partial bout with vertigo, or at least some spatial disorientation when the aircraft first entered the clouds. The radio transmissions and the tapes of the center radar seemed to verify that. Then, after recovering from the vertigo and climbing on course, the pilot would have started using oxygen at 7,500 or 8,000 feet, based upon his reported usual procedures. After that it was just terribly bad luck. He probably hit the higher altitude turbulence just as he, being an anesthesiologist, realized that he wasn't getting any oxygen. He may have panicked, or at the very least was distracted by it, and then went into full blown vertigo.

"Anyway, her theory is only that. We can't prove any of it conclusively. So the report goes into the record book as 'Loss of control due to excessive residual blood alcohol.' End of report.

"But that's a shame—and please keep in mind that all of my comments from this point on are strictly unofficial—because much more than what's in that report can be learned from this accident. First of all, vertigo is a whole lot more dangerous to pilots than it's given credit for. The worst thing that pilot did was continue his flight if, as we suspect, he did have some vertigo when he first went IMC. He should have immediately descended back into VFR conditions, turned that airplane toward the nearest airport and landed as soon as possible.

"There are a few things we do know about vertigo. Firstly, we do not know of a single case of a pilot surviving after two encounters with severe vertigo in the same flight. And our ground tests confirm positively that the second shot of it is always much worse than the first, and completely debilitating. Vertigo is just not something for pilots to be messing with.

"That's why we agree with the NTSB findings in this case. The pilot was a doctor—an anesthesiologist no less—and also a highly vocal advocate of oxygen usage at much lower altitudes than is required by the FAA. So he must have known all about spatial disorientation and vertigo. Perhaps even more than most other doctors, and certainly more than most laymen or pilots.

"But he did exactly the wrong thing. He continued the flight after experiencing vertigo because . . . judgment was impaired by the alcohol. Judgment is always the first thing to go in cases of alcohol impairment, and hypoxia, too."

Author comment Perhaps on its own, but quite likely at least partially because of the Drucker tragedy, NASA soon afterward expanded its studies of the effects of oxygen and lack of oxygen on residual blood alcohol impairment, especially as it relates to three-dimensional orientation. Neither the NTSB nor the FAA has undertaken any new action relating to this subject. They will undoubtedly require confirmed direction from medical and scientific sources before doing so.

2

Long, high slam dunk

Preliminary report: January; Piper Arrow; private pilot, single-engine land, instrument rating, 510 hours. With four people on board, the Arrow was ditched in a lake ¼ mile short of Orlando Executive Airport, after a 4½ hour IFR/VFR flight from Gastonia, North Carolina. The pilot was approaching to land and had previously advised the tower that he was low on fuel. Soon after, the engine quit. All four people were able to exit the aircraft and swim to shore before the Arrow sank.

Further investigation revealed:
- The Arrow was at least 130 pounds over gross departing from its home base airport.
- Weather en route was VFR, but the flight plan was filed IFR for 11,000 feet, about 2,000 feet above the tops of the broken clouds forecast.
- After 3 hours in the air and 160 miles from Orlando, Jacksonville Center advised the pilot, a 46-year-old business owner, to land for fuel. But the pilot said he had recalculated his remaining fuel and fuel flow and would be able to make Orlando with about 30 minutes remaining. When further advised that he would need 45 minutes reserve to be legal IFR, he replied that he intended to cancel IFR after letting down through the clouds about 25 miles out of Orlando, and that his 30 minutes would then be legal.
- When the pilot reported to Orlando Approach that he was low on fuel, the Arrow was 20 miles northeast of its destination, Orlando Executive Airport. Two minutes later, it directly overflew the Sanford, Florida Airport, approximately 16 miles from Orlando.

Official conclusion: Pilot error. Loss of power due to fuel exhaustion.

GLENN HUGHES IS A SECOND GENERATION OWNER of a success-ful family construction business in Gastonia, North Carolina. He learned to fly four years before the accident and bought a brand new Piper Arrow while he was working on his instrument rating. Since then he has flown about 130–150 hours a year for business and plea-sure. The accident occurred during a pleasure trip to the family's re-sort home in the Orlando area. Glenn and his wife, Sally, had made the trip many times, alone, or with their two children, or with rela-tives and friends.

Glenn treats his flying as he does everything else in his success-ful business and well-run household. The Arrow was well-equipped and well-maintained. (After the accident, Glenn sold the salvaged Ar-row and now flies a Piper Navajo.) His flying skills and knowledge are superior. He is considered by fellow pilots, instructors and airport personnel to be a sharp pilot. His family and friends still fly with him without any second thoughts about it.

Glenn Hughes "The trip was routine. The weather was forecast to be good, except for turbulence below the clouds. Tops were a little higher than usual for that time of the year, but only by a thousand feet or so. I filed for 11,000 feet to stay on top, expecting to come down to 9 or 7 after about an hour. But the tops never got any lower, so we just stayed at 11,000. It was smooth as North Carolina cotton up there.

"After awhile, my wife and my wife's sister, Suzie, and her hus-band, Billie, were all asleep. Flying high always puts Sally to sleep. She doesn't seem to have much tolerance for the lower oxygen at higher altitudes. But she never gets a headache or anything from it. She just dozes off. Flying is kind of boring for her anyway.

"Anyhow, the winds up there were a little stronger than I had flight planned for, but I figured it wouldn't be much of a problem. Gastonia to Orlando was always 4 hours, give or take 10 minutes. And we left Gastonia with 4½ hours plus in the tanks. With the weather in Orlando as good as it was, I wasn't worried about it.

"We usually made that trip in the Arrow nonstop only when Sally and I were alone. With the kids along, or with other passengers, we would always land in Savannah or Brunswick for a pit stop. But Bil-lie and Suzie had no problems using the relief tube, so I filed 3:50 to Orlando with 4:45 fuel on board.

"Over Jacksonville, the center guy thought I might be into my re-serves if I stayed IFR all the way. But we both agreed that if I can-celed right after my descent under the clouds there'd be no problem.

My tanks were showing about a quarter full on both sides, and I figured I'd have at least 25 or 30 minutes left when I arrived.

"For the rest of the trip and the letdown, the winds didn't cooperate much. I guess we were running about 10 minutes behind when I canceled. Coming over Sanford, my gauges were just starting to hit the pegs, so I figured another 10 or 15 minutes was in the bag. That was a bad assumption. But I didn't know it then. We hit the water only a couple hundred yards short of the runway.

"I'd sum the whole thing up as bad luck, bad fuel gauges, and some bad judgment on my part."

Author "The official report indicates that you were more than 130 pounds over gross leaving Gastonia. Do you dispute that?"

Glenn "The Arrow was a real hard-working, hard-flying airplane. It handled an extra 150 pounds with little or no effort. We had a 15-knot headwind coming right down the runway and I needed the extra fuel because the winds aloft weren't going to be helpful. But I don't think we were more than 80 or 90 pounds over, even with my 220-pound brother-in-law. Over gross in that Arrow was never a big deal; in my Navajo it is and I never do it."

The morning of the flight was blustery but clear with cloud bases at 4,500 and tops at 9,500. Glenn's fuel order the evening before had requested topping both tanks to just below the tabs. The fuel attendant who handled the fueling followed the request to the letter because, "Mr. Hughes always loaded up his airplane, and my boss was worried that he'd maybe not get off the ground. So, he told me that a little less than the order would be better when it came to Mr. Hughes."

Glenn and Sally Hughes, with their passengers, Billie and Suzie Crawford, arrived at the Gastonia airport with enough luggage for their planned five days in Orlando. It was a cool morning, so they all wore sweaters and jackets. Sally had also brought along a picnic basket and a cooler full of ice and cans of soda.

Loading the airplane turned out to be tricky with all the luggage and jackets. Glenn finally settled for some cramming of jackets in the rear seat and the picnic basket on the floor under Suzie's feet. She was the shortest of the group and could rest her feet on it comfortably.

The preflight was normal, as was Glenn's call to flight service, and the Arrow was taxiing out right on schedule. After his usual careful but accelerated run-up, Glenn taxied up to the runway, waited for another airplane to clear, and then began his takeoff roll.

With a considerable amount of runway behind them, the Arrow finally labored into the air, despite a 15–20 knot headwind. Glenn prided himself on his "good wheel feel" and kept the airspeed 5 or 6 knots into the green while the Arrow gained initial altitude sluggishly. At 400 feet he settled into a normal cruise climb airspeed that yielded a rate of climb about 200 feet per minute lower than normal, due to their excess weight. Reaching 11,000 feet 25 minutes later, they were already 7 or 8 minutes behind their flight plan.

A.J. Buffett, fuel attendant at Gastonia "Mr. Hughes was in his usual hurry that morning. But it took him a lot of time to load up. Seemed like they had more'n ever to pack on that airplane. When he got done, they had stuff in the cabin, on the floor, and everywhere.

"I told him how I'd topped the tanks to just below the tabs like he'd ordered it, and he took my word for it. I remember him sayin' that I could've put a little more in, 'cause he didn't want to have to land gettin' to Orlando. But I had actually put in a little less, like my boss had told me.

"When I saw 'em takin' off, I was glad I'd listened to my boss, 'cause man, I sure didn't think they was goin' to make it that time. It looked like he was goin' to take some'a them runway lights with him. But Mr. Hughes is some kind'a pilot. He got off okay and never had any problem clearin' everythin' else out there.

"As soon as I heard what happened to 'em in Orlando, I was kind'a sorry about that fuel. Like it was my fault 'n all. But my boss, and even Mr. Hughes, have been real nice about it.

"I guess we all learned a lesson, 'cause Mr. Hughes is real careful now about what goes into his Navajo. And I always listen to what the pilots want."

Shortly after the Piper was handed off to Jacksonville Center, the controller alerted Glenn that he was then about 15 minutes behind his flight plan. He asked Glenn if he would like to land in Brunswick, suggesting that he file a continuation flight plan right then so he wouldn't lose any extra time making a short fuel stop.

By that time, the airplane had been aloft for over 2½ hours and at 11,000 feet for all but half an hour of it. With his three passengers sound asleep, Glenn had the following conversation with the Jacksonville controller:

Controller "November . . ., if you'd like to land in Brunswick or here in Jacksonville, we can take a flight plan now to get you back out without delay."

Glenn "Uh, thanks Jacksonville. But I've got three sleeping passengers up here, and plenty of fuel to make Orlando. Should have better than 30 minutes left when we get there. I always carry a little more than I file."

Controller "Sorry sir, but you'll need 45 minutes to stay legal. Unless you land, sir, I'll have to terminate your IFR to Orlando."

Glenn "No problem, sir. How about changing my destination to Daytona. I'll be letting down about there anyway. As soon as I'm clear of the clouds, I can cancel and be legal VFR going into Orlando. Any problem with that?"

Controller "Okay . . ., you're cleared to Daytona Beach, Victor 51 after Jacksonville, maintain one one thousand."

Glenn "Uh, hold on a second. How about us staying on Victor 267 to BARBS and then over? I can cancel there."

Controller "Okay . . . cleared to BARBS, flight plan, maintain 11. Stand by one while we work up a time en route for you."

Glenn ". . . Roger."

Controller (45 seconds later) "Arrow November . . ., this is Jacksonville."

Glenn "Go ahead Jacksonville . . . ready to copy."

Controller "We calculate an hour and five to Daytona. How much extra fuel do you have? We're going to need some to keep you legal to Daytona."

Glenn "I figure about an extra 20 minutes, and my fuel burn is low. I'm only flying 60 percent. Let's say I've got 2 hours left from here. That should do it."

Twenty-five minutes later, Glenn was handed off to the southern sector of Jacksonville Center. He was another 6 minutes behind his new flight plan to Daytona, and the controller was concerned that he would be arriving in the Daytona area short of fuel. Having been alerted by the previous controller and the supervisor, she doubted that Glenn really had the extra fuel he had claimed:

Controller "November . . ., say again your remaining fuel."

Glenn (Annoyed and curt) "Jacksonville, (I have) enough fuel to get to Daytona and Orlando, which is our real destination. We'll be canceling as soon as we get to BARBS."

Controller ". . . Descend to four thousand. Report reaching and advise when ready to cancel."

Glenn (Nine minutes later) "Jacksonville, Arrow . . . is VFR at 4,200. Like to cancel now."

Controller "Roger . . . .. IFR is canceled. Maintain VFR. You can remain this frequency for flight following, if you'd like, or switch over to 134.0 after you pass BARBS. They should be able to help you."

Glenn (Still sounding annoyed) "(I am) leaving the frequency. Thanks for your help. Good day."

Controller (three seconds later) "Arrow November . . ., if you're still on, please advise."

Glenn (Now more annoyed) "Still here, Jacksonville. Go ahead."

Controller ". . . If you're continuing on to Orlando, we calculate your reserves at or slightly below VFR minimums arriving Orlando. The winds have been picking up. They're now 190° at 20, gusting to 25. You'll be passing right by De Land and Sanford airports, if you'd like to stop for some extra fuel."

Glenn "Thanks again. We'll watch it closely. You have a nice day."

Controller "Good day, sir. Have a nice flight."

Reaching GUAVA intersection, 33 miles north of Orlando and 4 miles west of De Land airport, Glenn turned slightly east so he would directly overfly the Sanford Airport, 16 miles northeast of Orlando. He studied both fuel gauges carefully, noting that they were just above EMPTY, and reassured himself that he had at least 20 minutes of fuel remaining.

With Sanford in sight and the fuel gauge needles now touching the EMPTY line, Glenn decided he would have about five minutes of fuel in the tanks as he rolled up to the tie-down area at Executive Airport in Orlando. Closer than he liked, but better than killing an extra 20 or 30 minutes in Sanford.

As a precaution, Glenn called Executive tower, telling them he was 20 miles out, low on fuel, and would appreciate their help by expediting his landing. He was advised that there would be no delay and to report a 2-mile right base for Runway 25.

Eight minutes later, Glenn reported that he was on the right base. The tower had been waiting for him and cleared him to land. By then, both fuel needles were at the bottom of their EMPTY lines.

Glenn acknowledged that he was cleared to land and began a smooth right turn to final. But before he completed the turn, the engine started coughing and sputtering and then quit cold. At two miles from the runway and 800 feet agl, the Arrow was a glider without enough glide range to reach the runway.

Glenn's heart sank. His passengers experienced instant panic. And the Arrow headed for the small lake near Orlando's Executive

Airport. Luckily, Glenn didn't panic or lose control of the airplane. He never thought to retract the gear but he did execute a perfect flair 8 feet above the water.

The Arrow, because it was brought in nose high, hit the water cleanly and didn't flip, despite the extended gear. It settled on top of the water, giving its occupants time to exit, which they did as the airplane began to take water and sink slowly.

Fortunately, everyone on board was a swimmer and they were only 150 yards from shore. Although it seemed like an eternity, and there was plenty of cursing among the fully clothed swimmers, they were all safely on dry ground about 15 minutes later.

Airport security and the Orlando Police were there to greet the foursome. Ignoring their protests, and especially Glenn's insistence that someone begin attending to his sinking Arrow, they were all taken to the local hospital for observation.

Two hours later, back from the hospital and dried off but disgusted, Glenn began filling out papers and answering questions for the FAA accident investigator. It was a long afternoon.

FAA Report "The pilot was still showing signs of shock from the accident. It was clear that he knew the airplane was low on fuel long before the accident, and yet he overflew two airports less than 50 miles from his destination airport. The airplane had been in the air with two women and two men aboard for a total of 4 hours and 50 minutes, according to the best calculations available. The pilot acknowledged his time aloft and verified that he had departed his home base airport with approximately 4¾ hours of fuel. He also admitted that he had violated both the IFR and VFR fuel reserve requirements, but he did not seem to care.

"When questioned about the above deliberate violations, the pilot was vague and not sure of himself. He did offer that he did not think his fuel situation was that serious because he was sure that, even though the fuel gauges were reading EMPTY, there was still sufficient usable fuel in the tanks.

"Further questioning revealed that the pilot had limited familiarity with the airplane's fuel system, and that he had read the section about fuel systems and management in the Arrow's operations manual only once—when he bought the airplane about fours years prior to the accident.

"At the beginning of the interview, the pilot seemed more annoyed with the post-accident procedures than he was upset over, or even aware of, their very close call. He also complained of a headache and fatigue from his long flight and the ordeal of ditching the aircraft. But by the end of the 2½ hour session, he seemed to be feeling better. In fact, he expressed real surprise with himself over his conduct and was very apologetic when he left the interview."

Glenn "The guy from the FAA was a real pain at first, but then he got nicer. After all, I had been flying for nearly 5 hours, ditched an airplane in the lake and swam almost two hundred yards with my clothes on. What the hell did he expect?"

Author "Did you have the opportunity to see the FAA report?"

Glenn "I saw a report because I insisted on getting a copy of whatever they were putting in their file on me. I didn't want a black mark on my record, or anything that would affect my license. I also wanted to be damned sure they put everything in it, like the fact that the fuel attendant in Gastonia had been told to underfill my tanks. I thought I had almost 5 full hours of fuel when I left Gastonia but I didn't [know] because nobody bothered to tell me about it."

Author "But even at that, you knew you had fewer than 30 minutes of reserve coming up on two airports. You could have landed at either airport, picked up a few gallons and still been just about on time for whatever your plans were in Orlando. Or was it your usual practice to bust reserve requirements like you routinely overloaded the Arrow?"

Glenn "I already told you how much weight that Arrow could handle and I never said that I routinely loaded up over gross. You and Charlie Hopkins, who owns the Gastonia FBO, said that. And Charlie told the FAA, which caused me no end of grief at the time."

Author "You didn't answer my question about busting fuel minimums."

Glenn "That was a mistake I won't make again. Okay?"

Charlie Hopkins, FBO owner at Gastonia, N.C "I felt pretty terrible about the whole affair with Glenn Hughes. But I never thought a guy like him would ever run his tanks all the way to dry. Except for his bad habit of overloading his Arrow, Glenn did everything else better than right. He was and still is one of the best pilots around here.

"Since the accident, I think he's changed a lot. He's got himself a Navajo now and he treats it and flies it a whole lot different than he did the Arrow. He's never as rushed. He checks everything real carefully. And he's a fanatic about maintenance. Oh, and his fuel orders. He makes us plenty crazy with those. But I guess that's understandable."

NASA space medicine specialist "This is one of those accidents that makes you scratch your head and wonder how a guy as smart as that did something as dumb as that. But we suspect that there was more involved than just an apparently arrogant, overly aggressive pilot who pushed his luck too far.

"To begin with, his overloading the aircraft had no bearing on the accident. But it did convince all of the investigators that he was a pusher and a stretcher with too little regard for the rules. I'd buy off on that myself. And his conduct when he was dealing with Jacksonville Center certainly indicated a wise guy, don't-tell-me-what-to-do attitude. All of which made it an easy read. Or was it too easy?

"What I'm getting at is that arrogance or aggressiveness or being a wise guy isn't necessarily suicidal or stupid. This pilot began exhibiting bizarre behavior, at least that we can track, just about the time he was handed off to Jacksonville. The question, of course, is why?

"A closer look at the circumstances is quite revealing. To begin with, they had been at 11,000 feet for well over 2 hours without any supplemental oxygen. In fact, all three of the passengers were asleep for more than two thirds of the entire trip. Under those conditions, if he wasn't very tired and lethargic, that pilot was certainly not as sharp as when he first took off. His series of terrible judgments and foolish decisions seems to verify that conclusively.

"What's so disturbing about accidents like this is that the officially released 'probable causes' never mention that lack of oxygen might be the real culprit that is causing these otherwise competent, careful pilots to make such mistakes.

"We at NASA understand the problem that the NTSB and the FAA have with this issue—when it can't be proven, it can't be the probable cause. But in not dealing with lack of oxygen as even a *possible* cause in so many of the accidents that are obviously hypoxia related, they are actually misleading pilots as to its importance and the dangers it represents.

"In our space medicine studies, we have found innumerable variables in the effects of altitude on pilots and their ability to function. Some people handle high altitude easily most of the time. They don't feel any adverse effects from it at all. But the vast majority get strong signals that they are having some kind of trouble as their oxygen is reduced at the higher altitudes. They are the lucky ones. Because the pilots who don't get those signals are the ones who eventually get in trouble. They're the ones who tend to make those dumb and stupid mistakes. And it seems to be inevitable.

"I hate to sound like a crusader over this issue, but it is causing a high percentage of what are routinely classified as 'pilot error' accidents.

"Take this accident we're talking about. Every single thing that pilot did points to full-blown hypoxia, right down to his headache and being tired and grumpy at the beginning of his post-accident interview, and then feeling revived 2½ hours later. That grueling interview couldn't have revived him. If anything, it should have made him worse. No, it had to be that his body was recovering because it was then ingesting sufficient oxygen.

"But what did anybody learn from the official 'probable cause,' report? I leave that to your own conclusion."

Author "Are you implying that nobody should ever fly high without supplemental oxygen?

NASA specialist "Absolutely. And why not? We have proven conclusively that lack of oxygen is debilitating to the human body. Every human body. When you significantly reduce the amount of oxygen you are getting, you are bringing on hypoxia. Period. No further discussion. And that is dangerous when you're dealing with a three-dimensional environment and the demands being made on a pilot.

"So, would it be unreasonable to require oxygen for the same reasons that shoulder harnesses and seat belts are required? You're more likely to die in an airplane from the spatial disorientation brought on by hypoxia than you are from a bump on the head. So, yes, oxygen very definitely should be required."

Author "Even in training aircraft? Or on flights at very low altitudes?"

NASA specialist "Absolutely. You may use an ADF only once in a blue moon, but if it's on the airplane it has to be working or the airplane isn't airworthy. Oxygen should be treated the same way as every other system or piece of equipment on an airplane. Whether or not you're going to use it for any particular flight, it should be there and in good working order."

A transcript of the NASA interview was sent to Glenn. His response is enlightening:

Glenn "When I first saw the NASA report, I was angry because I realized that I was a victim, not just some jerk who ran out of gas and drowned his airplane.

"But the more I thought about it, the more I realized what a problem the various agencies are facing. I'm a businessman and I deal with Catch-22 situations all the time. There are lots of times when I know what the best solution is to some problem. But convincing my customer is something else. So, I just have to sit back and watch him make a mess of things that I'll get paid for to clean up later. It's like the guy who refuses to call a plumber to fix a small leak and winds up paying for a whole new bathroom.

"I can definitely sympathize with NASA and the safety board. They're stuck with the rules that the FAA makes. But the FAA has its own kinds of problems because they're dealing with so many variables. I mean, how do you convince a pilot to put on an uncomfortable oxygen mask when he's feeling fine and hasn't the slightest clue that he needs it? And even more so, how do you require an airplane owner at a seacoast airport to put an oxygen system in a trainer that's never gonna see 5,000 feet? In today's economy, and with economic conditions as bad as they are in aviation, I'd say it would be close to impossible."

Author "Are you saying there's no solution? That the FAA should continue to let pilots keep hurting themselves because oxygen is expensive or inconvenient?"

Glenn "Well, that's exactly what I'm getting at. None of the scientific gurus can precisely nail down when, where and who needs oxygen. And they can't demonstrate to the masses what hypoxia feels like when it's coming on because it's just too subtle. But they could at least begin to make a major issue of it. They can start with ground schools, the flying magazines and so forth. And they can require that every student pilot at least knows how to use oxygen, and when he or she is most likely to need it." [High altitude training chambers are located at several locations across the United States. Consult the *Airman's Information Manual* for additional information.]

"It's a frustrating subject, especially for a guy like me who had a run-in with it. I could've killed all four of us. Anyway, I hope somebody's life gets saved because they read this.

"By the way, they were able to get the airplane out of the lake with very little damage. But I never flew it again. I've since bought a Navajo with two fans, a six-hour fuel capacity, and the best oxygen system I could find.

"As you can probably tell, my brush with death has changed me and my attitudes about flying. Now I'm worrying about my cholesterol!"

Author's final comment Glenn said all he could on the subject of hypoxia and his ideas for doing something about it. Which he is now following through on. He joined a growing cadre of pilots who have been involved in hypoxia related incidents, many of which had to do with fuel exhaustion.

3

Too high, too far, too bad

Preliminary report: May; Cessna T210N Centurion; commercial pilot, single-engine land, 450 hours. The aircraft was substantially damaged while attempting a forced landing in a field after running out of fuel during a flight from Eugene, Oregon, to Malad City, Idaho. The commercial pilot and her passenger were not seriously injured. She said she had flown far off course and was unable to find the airport, which was her fuel stop on a trip to Fort Collins, Colorado.

Further investigation revealed:

- The aircraft left Eugene with full tanks, about 5 hours of fuel, for the planned 3½ hour flight.
- A full oxygen bottle and masks were on board but the pilot never used the oxygen because she did not fly above 13,500 feet. Most of the flight was at 11,500 feet.
- The pilot, a native of a sea-level town in southwestern Oregon, did not realize she was lost until nearly 4 hours had elapsed. Her remedial action was to head northeast for 10 minutes, then southeast for 10 minutes, and finally straight east for another 10 minutes looking for an airport.
- The forced landing site was less than 5 miles from an easily identifiable airport.
- Weather for the entire flight was CAVU, except for some fairly high broken clouds over eastern Oregon, which the Centurion overflew.

Official conclusion: Pilot error. Improper planning and navigating. Poorly selected landing sight. Loss of power due to fuel exhaustion.

THE DAY BEGAN IN HIGH SPIRITS for Betty Jean and Frank Lewis. They had been planning for this first major trip in their newly bought Centurion, ever since they had signed the papers for it ten weeks earlier.

It was 0715 when they left their home in Coos Bay, Oregon, a picturesque seacoast town where Betty and Frank were a husband and wife real estate team, and headed for the North Bend Airport. The Centurion was waiting for them, spic and span, having just been rolled out of the hangar. They had cleaned it, fueled it, and done a complete preflight the afternoon and evening before. Betty was a nut on detail. Frank was a neat-nik. They were both pilots, and they flew with the same professionalism that they applied to their successful real estate business, number one in the Coos Bay area.

Betty had 450 hours and a commercial rating. She had started on her instrument rating a couple of times but hadn't stuck with it. Now that they owned Lady-Luck, however, she was determined to get her ticket as soon as time permitted. That would begin soon after this trip to Fort Collins, Colorado, to visit their new granddaughter.

Frank was still a student pilot. His interest in aviation came after Betty's and was originally to appease her. But his enthusiasm was intensifying with each flight they took in the Centurion. He planned to take his instrument training along with Betty and get his rating as soon as he added 115 more hours to the 45 he then had.

The first leg of the trip was to Eugene, Oregon, to pick up the new Scott oxygen system they had ordered. This was to be their first of many trips over the mountains, and the Centurion had a 20,000 feet service ceiling. When they arrived in Eugene, the system was ready and waiting for them. But the FBO manager who had promised to demonstrate it for them was late.

A mechanic mounted the bottle in a convenient spot in the cabin and connected two of the four masks. The other two were stowed in the pockets behind the back seats. He also gave Frank the instruction manual from Scott, the manufacturer of the system, and Frank began glancing through it while Betty did a thorough recheck of everything else. It was going to be a long ride to Fort Collins with a fuel stop at Malad City, Idaho. She was being her meticulous self.

The call to flight service elated the first-time mountaineers: "Ceilings and visibilities unlimited except for a few broken clouds over eastern Oregon. Bases at 7,000 feet and tops at 10,000. Winds aloft at niner thousand—190° at 35, at twelve—200° at 40, and at eighteen—230° at 55." Not exactly a monster tailwind but enough of a push to keep the fuel reserve ample.

Betty did a final preflight after checking the fuel bill carefully. She wanted to be sure that the tanks had been filled to "the top of the top," as she had ordered it. She thanked the line boy after he reassured her that he couldn't have gotten one more drop in either tank.

Frank and Betty waited impatiently for the FBO manager to show up. Betty hadn't read the Scott manual and had never before used oxygen. She wanted that demonstration before leaving on the highest altitude flight they had ever attempted. Frank was more confident about the oxygen system and tried to explain what he had read in the manual.

The manager turned up just as Betty and Frank had given up waiting for him. Betty had just finished activating her VFR flight plan for 1030, which then gave them a total of 15 minutes to be in the air. She watched attentively and listened to the 3-minute quickie demo the manager was rushing through, noting that Frank seemed to already know everything they were being told and shown. He did. The Scott manual was excellent, the system was uncomplicated and the valve and gauge were easy to operate. Betty settled down.

Off the ground on time with Betty in left seat, the Centurion eased its way to 11,500 feet in 16 minutes. They were nearly 300 pounds under gross. The visibility was unlimited in all directions, the air was cool and refreshing, and the ride was "severe smooth," as Betty loved to call it. It was truly a perfect day to fly.

Their first real checkpoint was Bend Airport, 90 miles east of Eugene and a few miles south of the Redmond VOR. Tracking slightly south of Victor 121 kept them legal below 13,000 feet, the minimum clearing altitude on the airway. Betty was too busy finding her checkpoints from so high up to worry about trying out the new oxygen system. Frank was even busier calculating their time en route for the rest of the trip after they arrived in the Bend area 4 minutes late and nearly five miles south of their intended course.

Betty Jean Lewis "I don't remember if it was the excitement over being up so high for the first time, or if it was because I was having trouble finding some of my checkpoints. Things like railroad tracks, power lines, and water towers look very different from way up there. But I sure got a jolt when we showed up way south of the Redmond VOR and almost missed the Bend Airport. I had made a small correction about 15 miles west of there and I was sure I was going to be right on. After that, Frank and I navigated together.

Frank Lewis "It was such a beautiful day! We never had more than a few light bumps on the way up. And when we got to eleven-five and leveled off, it was like a dream. The air was so smooth. It was so clear. And it felt so clean to breathe. I really got carried away and found myself sitting there like a zombie, not helping Betty at all.

"We got quite a surprise coming up on our first real checkpoint late and off course by over 5 miles. Betty couldn't figure out what had happened, and I could hardly remember how we had even gotten there. I was so totally distracted by the scenery. For me, at the time, it was really spectacular. Anyway, right after that, we really started concentrating on our flying."

Passing south of Bend Airport, the Centurion continued southeast, heading toward the Wild Horse VOR, and penetrated the northern-most sector of the Juniper A MOA 500 feet above its floor. Betty had been listening on 119.65 MHz and was surprised to hear her number called. After a terse advisory, she turned to a heading of 060, as in-structed, and was clear of the MOA within 10 minutes.

But now some confusion began. The Wild Horse VOR was com-ing in okay, but neither Betty nor Frank could locate any of their care-fully preselected checkpoints. A glance at the DME told them that they were 61 miles from Wild Horse, but the CDI was moving toward a full right deflection. A minute later it was pegged.

Frank turned the CDI selector to the right until the needle was centered and told Betty to fly toward it. She turned right to 115°, the corresponding heading on the indicator, and began studying her map in the hope of finding something on the ground that related to some-thing on the map. Nothing matched. Frank tried to help but didn't have any more luck than she did.

Meanwhile, because neither of them was watching the CDI, the southerly wind was blowing them to the left of their intended course. Nearly 10 minutes went by before Betty noticed that the needle had again pegged itself to the right. She turned the selector to center the needle, looked again at the DME and, for the first time in 100 miles, had a pretty good idea of where they were: about 15 miles north of course.

At that point, she and Frank had their first of many subsequent consultations. Betty showed him exactly where on the map the CDI and the DME said they were. They both looked in every direction, fi-nally spotting the town of Burns off in the distance to their right, right where the map said it was supposed to be according to its proximity to the Wild Horse VOR. They were both immediately relieved.

Betty "I remember what a relief it was to find that little town of Burns and the airport sitting right under the VOR on our sectional. You'd have thought Frank and I had arrived at Mecca or something.

"Anyway, we decided not to fly toward Burns, which would have put us back on our route of flight because it was by then too far out of the way. Instead, we took up a heading toward Boise so we could pick up Victor 4 there and fly it all the way to Malad City. If I remember correctly, that was where Frank took over so I could rest. Including the trip to Eugene, I had been flying for more than 2 hours by then."

Passing 16 miles north of the Wild Horse VOR, the Centurion continued on a heading of 80°, the Lewis's guess as the one that would take them to Boise, wind and all. It wasn't a good guess. And Frank wasn't very good at tracking VORs. He was still a student pilot.

Betty watched Frank for a very few minutes and then drifted off into a happy nap. With the help of the autopilot, Frank had little trouble holding his heading and maintaining their altitude at 11,500 feet. They were soon north of course again while Frank continued looking for checkpoints. He didn't find any that he could identify. And Betty slept on.

By the time she awoke, over an hour later, the Lewis's were nearly 50 miles northeast of Boise and looking ahead at mountains that were higher than they were.

Betty "When Frank finally woke me up, we were in the middle of nowhere. There weren't supposed to be any real high mountains on our route of flight, so I knew immediately that something was very wrong. I asked Frank about it, and he told me where he thought we were. But neither of us could pinpoint anything.

"I centered the VOR needle on Boise and couldn't believe we were so far away from it, and with a FROM reading, no less. That's when I decided to call flight watch to see if they could give me a frequency to get some flight following and find out for sure where we actually were. But the only flight watch I could reach was Salt Lake. They suggested I call Salt Lake Center, but I knew they wouldn't be of much help. Salt Lake was just too far away."

Betty's call to flight watch could have been answered by Boise, but Salt Lake heard it loud and clear and responded. It was the first radio communication Betty had made since being shooed away from the Juniper A MOA.

The flight watch operator knew immediately that the pilot was lost. He questioned Betty about her instrument readings and quickly determined that the airplane was in high mountain country somewhere in the vicinity of Ryan Peak and Hyndman Peak, the two highest mountains in the Pioneer Range. Pointing that out to her, he suggested she call Salt Lake Center on 118.05 MHz or 134.5 MHz. But he didn't think to tell her that those two frequencies served the general area she was in, even though they were part of Salt Lake Center. It never occurred to him that Betty might presume that because the frequencies were apparently at Salt Lake, that the controllers would be too far away to assist her. She never called.

Frank and Betty began pouring over their sectionals, trying to relate something on a chart with a visible ground point. Frank thought the two high peaks on either side of them would be on one of the maps, but neither of them could find anything.

The Centurion continued on its easterly heading, still drifting slightly north from the southerly wind. Betty decided to climb to 13,500 feet as they got closer to Ryan's Peak, which also gave her and Frank a better vantage point in their quest for a known landmark, preferably an airport. A look at the fuel gauges told her she needed to land reasonably soon. Another look at Frank told her it should be very soon. He was ashen.

Frank was coming to the same conclusions. Betty's face was drawn and waxy. They had been flying for over 3 hours with nothing to eat or drink and they were dehydrated. The fact that they were also seriously hypoxic from the high altitude was not apparent to either one of them. Had it been, they would have used the oxygen system they had just bought.

Frank "I had recently learned all the rules on oxygen in my ground school course. And the FBO who sold us the system told us essentially the same things: that it's required above 14,000 feet, and for any sustained flight of over 30 minutes above 12,500 feet. We never flew above 11,500 feet, except for that brief stint when we came to those real high mountains. And that couldn't have been for more than 10 minutes or so.

"I realize now that we were both badly affected by the altitude that day. Maybe because it was so clear and the pressure was so high because neither one of us had ever been bothered by it before. Not even when we were snow skiing. We also never felt anything but good. As a matter of fact, from what I've learned about it since, I'd say that we both felt too good. Too light headed. Too spacey. To the point of not being able to even figure out where we were, let alone handle the airplane properly.

"In that regard, considering the condition we apparently were in, Betty did a super job of bringing Lady Luck into that field without killing both of us. She's some kind of pilot. She made a better forced landing than I've ever seen demonstrated in my flight training. Unfortunately, the only place we could land didn't cooperate, and the airplane got badly damaged. But we came out okay. We were luckier than Lady Luck."

Betty and Frank stayed at 13,500 feet for only long enough to be clear of the high terrain. While they were up there, they scanned the horizon from end to end looking for something recognizable. Anything. A few prominent landmarks came into view, but they couldn't identify any of them, not even the few small towns that were within eyeshot. Unfortunately, they never saw any of the widely spread out airports.

Descending from 13,500 feet back to 11,500 feet, they decided on a new strategy. From the 80° heading they had been holding for more than an hour, they would head 35° for 10 minutes or so, then 125° for the next 10 minutes and then back on the 80° heading for the same amount of time. They reasoned that they would be panning the entire area in a way that would eventually help them find a place to land.

It turned out to be an incredibly unlucky game plan. In the next entire hour plus, every highway they spotted and tried to follow took them not toward but away from any of the few airports they could have reached. And they were still at 11,500 feet.

But not for long. As the fuel gauges neared empty, Betty decided it was time to look for a place to land—any place before the Centurion ran dry. She did not want to make a real forced landing in the rough terrain beneath them. It was her first sensible choice but not, as it turned out, realistic.

While Betty concentrated on the terrain directly in front of her, Frank continued panning the right side of the airplane. Finally, he saw a road ahead and to the right of them and pointed it out to Betty. With a sense of relief in that barren area, she turned 20° right and eased back on the power. They had already agreed that it would be safer landing anywhere along a roadway, because it had to lead to somewhere, and would improve their chances of being found and picked up quickly. Despite the amply provisioned emergency kit they had brought along, neither of them had any desire to test it in the Wyoming wilderness, although they had no idea that they were in Wyoming.

Frank's lucky find turned out to be the unluckiest cut of all. At the moment he spotted the road, the Riverton, Wyoming, Airport was at their 10 o'clock position and less than 10 miles away. But Betty never saw it. And Frank never looked in that direction. They were both too elated over having found State Road 789, their salvation of the moment.

Betty overflew the two-lane road, then turned northeast in a downwind leg, carefully noting the terrain below. The highway seemed to be her best bet. But fewer than 10 seconds into the down-wind, the Cessna ran out of fuel.

From only about 500 feet above the ground, Betty spotted what looked to her to be a flat area running alongside the roadway. Her reflex was to head for an easy gliding distance landing rather than risking a try for the pavement, an attempt that might have failed. It was the best choice she had made all day.

The Centurion touched down with Betty's feather touch and rolled smoothly until it encountered a tiny rivulet that was hidden from their view. Hitting it dumped the right wing enough to strike the ground and spoil what could have been a damage-free forced landing. The Centurion had flipped and was badly broken. Fortunately, there was no fire because there was no fuel.

Betty and Frank were jostled and bruised, but nothing more. Dazed and addled best describe their condition as they exited the airplane.

Help arrived in seconds. A military convoy of four vehicles was driving north on the roadway less than a mile from the site of the accident. The Wyoming State Police report contains the following report:

M. Sgt. Anton Jones   "We seen 'em turnin' toward us 'bout a mile to our right and up ahead. We couldn't figger out what they was gonna do, so we slowed up so's we wouldn't run into 'em if they was fixin' to land on the road. They kept on comin' toward the road but then they went down in the scrub grass along the side. Looked for a minute like they was gonna be okay, but then the airplane hit somethin', flipped over and got all messed up.

"We was there before the dust settled and helped the folks inside get out. They was shakin' pretty good and bruised up some, but nothin' serious. We got 'em to the hospital in Riverton real quick, and they was okay. Guess they were pretty lucky . . . comin' out of that with nothin' more'n some bumps 'n bruises."

Riverton, Wyoming Airport manager "The Lewis's spent a lot of time with us because we arranged to get the airplane over here from where it crashed. That scrub field was about the unluckiest spot you could find over in that area. The little stream that caught them came off of Beaver Creek, and it was the only one around. Any other place they could have picked would have been just fine. Then they probably could have just gotten some avgas and flown right out of there.

"When the police brought them here from the hospital, they were still in shock and, of course, dog tired. They'd been flying for most of the day. Especially Mrs. Lewis. She was really out of it. Kept complaining about how much the airplane was going to cost to put back together, and she was all upset about how were they going to get to Colorado to see their daughter and new granddaughter. Come to think of it, neither one of them seemed to realize how close they came to being killed.

"But that all changed the next day. When we all went over to get the airplane on a flat bed, and they got a good look at it, that's when it hit them. That's when they realized how lucky they were to have walked away with all of their parts still connected."

Betty "All hell broke loose when we hit that ditch, or whatever it was. Up to then, I thought we had it made. But I guess it just wasn't our day. Some soldiers helped us get out of the airplane. They happened to be coming up the road just as we were setting down. It all happened so fast, but I do remember them hustling Frank and me off to the hospital there in Riverton.

"Everything else is still fuzzy for both of us. There were soldiers and doctors and nurses and police and what must have been the whole town running around, but we were just trying to get our bearings, figure out how we were going to get to Fort Collins and, as we almost forgot, get in touch with our daughter. Thank God Frank thought of that. She would have been a nervous wreck.

"As it was, Frank and I were both wrecks and didn't know it. So much was going on. So much had happened. And there were so many things to take care of. It was a real nightmare. In some ways, I'm glad I can't remember all of it because I'm sure it would be haunting me worse than it has been ever since. (Pause)

"By the next morning we thought we were fine. But with so much to deal with, like the airplane and deciding whether to go on to Fort Collins or head back home, we were both out of it again before midday. I can't explain it. Riverton isn't any higher than Fort Collins. And I've never been bothered by the altitude there. But I sure was in Riverton. It must have been the excitement and the tension and all."

FAA representative "These people were looking to blame someone or something for what happened to them when, in reality, they just didn't use common sense. They had oxygen on board. Our rules don't say *not* to use it below 12,500 or 14,000 feet. They were also on a trip that was poorly planned, or at the very least poorly mapped out.

"As I understand it from the report I read, they had only been able to find two or three of their checkpoints in the whole 5 hours they were in the air. And that plan they followed to scan the area—

flying left, then right, then straight ahead—that was an unrealistic course of action. Hell, they had a full IFR panel. Why didn't they use it? And why, for heaven's sake, didn't they call someone? They had a Mode C transponder and they were up over 11,000 feet. Any radar within 200 miles would have picked them up.

"If you want an opinion about this accident, I'd say they just plain panicked and forgot all they ever knew about flying. I'm sure the lack of oxygen played some part in it. But I'm much more sure that they were way over their heads in a sophisticated airplane that they were not totally familiar with and on a trip that was beyond their capabilities. That's my personal opinion.

"Officially, this is a fuel exhaustion accident caused by pilot error. You couldn't call it anything else."

NASA representative "If ever there was a classic case of hypoxia, this had to be it. What's alarming, though, is the indifferent attitude about oxygen by nearly everyone in general aviation, including the people making the rules.

"From what I understand, the FBO who sold them the oxygen system never really explained to them how to use it. And before that, the second pilot swore that he had just studied oxygen requirements in ground school. Then they just came to the wrong assumption, which is exactly what happens to hundreds of pilots from coast to coast every day of the week, because nobody ever tells anybody the real facts about oxygen.

"As a matter of fact, the whole subject of oxygen is a damned can of worms. Nobody from the airlines, or from ski resorts, or from any other high altitude attraction wants to talk about it, let alone deal with it or, God forbid, tell the general public about it.

"I guess they all figure that publicizing it would create a worse set of problems than exists now. It would be bad for business, alarm a completely reactionary population, and cause more problems than could be handled in a short time. Can you see the headlines? 'FAA admits oxygen needed at much lower altitudes.' Or, 'United Airlines says jet lag made worse by lack of oxygen.' Or, 'Surgeon General advises ski lift operators to provide oxygen.' There would be chaos. It would scare the daylights out of the whole country. The prevailing attitude for years has been 'Better to kill a few hundred pilots every year and bang up a few thousand airplanes at the same time. Who needs all those little airplanes around anyway?' Even the gurus of general aviation aren't doing anything about it.

"As a result, there isn't a decent education effort in place for general aviation pilots. It's as if the industry and the FAA feel that knowing about oxygen will hurt people when, of course, the exact opposite is true. But because it could dissuade a lot of people from ever becoming pilots, I can see their point. Again, it could be bad for business. And from what I've seen of the course material at some of the aviation academies and universities, I'd say they feel the same way about it. After all, they're in business, too!"

NTSB representative "In a case like this there are so many possible and probable contributing causes that it's hard to blame it on any single thing. Certainly, those people should have used the oxygen they had on board. Why not? But even more certainly, they should have been much better prepared for the trip they undertook. They missed nearly all of their checkpoints. They apparently never used their navigating equipment properly and they never even called anyone except flight watch.

"My personal conclusion is that they never should have been there in the first place. They were an accident deciding when and where to happen. It's lucky for them that they weren't killed or hurt. In the minds of some people, general aviation's image has been hurt, though.

"They should both go back and get some flight training and ground school. And this time, they should pay attention and do their homework as if their lives depended upon it. Because that's how it is. And that's how it is for all of us. Enough said.

"I'm sorry if I sound unsympathetic about this one, but some accidents really rile me. Everyone wants to blame the FAA and us and the system when, most of the time, it's their own damned fault. We only report what we see and find out, impartially and from the facts."

Betty "I never saw so much finger pointing in my life. Frank and I never looked to blame anyone for what happened to us. We're just amazed that no one seems to want to do anything about it. I mean, would it be so terrible to tell pilots about something that can kill them? What's everybody so afraid of?

"Since the accident, we've really tried to learn as much as we could about oxygen and hypoxia. It hasn't been easy. We've talked to doctors, we've talked to the FAA, and Frank even had a meeting with a guy from Scott, the company that made the oxygen system we bought. We have lots of opinions, plenty of suggestions, and answers all over the place. But still nothing concrete. I mean, it varies all over the map, depending on who you're talking to and what they're either selling or defending themselves from.

"I can tell you this: Frank and I never felt anything. We never knew what was happening to us. And we especially never knew how dangerous it was. Now, that shouldn't be. Every pilot is entitled to know about something like that.

"And one more thing. Some of the government people we talked to were downright nasty. They probably decided in advance that because I'm a woman and because Frank was a student pilot at the time, that we didn't know what we were doing up there in an airplane like a Centurion. Well, I resent that . . . we both *really* resent that. Frank and I aren't stupid. We're professional, successful businesspeople and at least as smart as all of those FAA people.

"I can tell you that I did then and I still fly Lady Luck just fine. And so does Frank. We both have our instrument ratings now and we've made the trip to see our daughter more times than I can remember. All without incident. And all *with* oxygen. That's one mistake we'll never make again! We even carry an extra full bottle with us on the airplane and we won't leave home without it."

Author comment Every government, industry and medical source contacted for information about oxygen, lack of oxygen, and hypoxia had the same attitude: "It's something we don't know enough about; it's something we can't nail down; it's something we can't take responsibility for; it's something somebody should be doing something about."

Every pilot contacted who has had a run in with hypoxia, or an accident because of it, feels that they had been had. They were. The present situation is inexcusable.

4

The cattle show calamity

Preliminary report: August; Mooney 231; private pilot, multi-and single-engine land, 1,690 hours. The aircraft was extensively damaged in an uncontrolled descent and subsequent landing short of a runway. The noninstrument rated pilot lost control at 9,500 feet upon entering IMC after flying 4 hours on a trip from El Paso, Texas, to Wichita, Kansas. The pilot regained control at about 3,000 feet and was given radar vectors by ATC to his destination airport, where he landed just short of the runway. The pilot and his passenger were not hurt. Investigators found that 20 inches of the right-side stabilator was missing.

Further investigation revealed:
- Weather at the destination airport had been forecast to be 4,500 broken, tops at 8,500–9,000 feet. The en route forecast called for broken to overcast, with tops to 10,000. Both forecasts were accurate.
- The pilot was recovering from a head cold at the time the flight began. He had taken four cold tablets the day before, plus a sedative cough suppressant about 10 hours prior to takeoff.
- The pilot seldom flew above 7,000 feet because he was bothered by higher altitudes. His attempts to rent or borrow oxygen equipment for the trip were unsuccessful.

Official conclusion: Inadvertent VMC into IMC. Loss of control due to partial structural failure and failure to maintain flying speed. Pilot error.

THE MORNING OF THE FLIGHT BEGAN with anxiety and uncertainty. Axel and Vera Johnson were not sure that they would be able to leave their ranch on the outskirts of El Paso, Texas, and fly to Wichita,

Kansas, for a cattle buying exposition because Axel had been nursing a bad cold for the past five days.

They had been planning the trip for nearly a month. This particular exposition was going to be more important to them than expected because they had been able to sell most of their cattle in early June at windfall high prices. Now they were hoping to replenish their herd in a down market and make a substantial paper profit.

At 0600, Axel awoke feeling better, or at least that's what he told his wife. For the past five days he had been taking two different cold remedies, one an antihistamine, both in full doses. And the night before, at about 2230, he took a sedative cough suppressant to help him get a good night's rest. It worked. He had a full night of uninterrupted sleep.

By the time Vera rolled out of bed at 0620, Axel was just hanging up from his call to flight service. He wasn't happy. The weather was VFR all the way, but there was light to moderate turbulence below the clouds up to 6,500 feet and tops ranging from 8,500 to 10,000 feet. He was muttering to himself and to Vera as he sat down for coffee and a muffin. He was trying to decide on an altitude en route, realizing that a 4-hour very bumpy ride would be terrible for Vera. But to go on top, which would not be a problem as far as staying VFR was concerned, would be difficult for him. He was a smoker, and high altitude for any length of time made him uncomfortable.

A short conversation with Vera put Axel back on the phone, this time to the airport. He gave his request to pull the airplane at 0800—and check the oil—to the counter girl and asked her to locate an oxygen bottle and some masks that he could buy, rent, or borrow. This trip was too important to put off. And he had no intention of turning Vera off on flying forever, which is what he feared would happen if they sat in moderate turbulence for almost 600 miles.

Arriving at the airport at 0745, the oil had already been checked, and the fuel attendants were moving airplanes around so they could roll the Mooney out of the hangar. But the cashier had bad news. She could not locate either an oxygen system or the FBO manager to help her find one. Several calls to possible sources followed. Nothing. On 45 minutes notice, it just wasn't available.

Axel pondered his options and decided to call flight service again for a weather update and some advice. They didn't help much. Their jurisdiction ends with facts and information boiled down to go-no-go recommendations. They are not prepared or equipped to offer technical advice about an airplane or how to fly one. Axel was on his own. But, thanks to the weather update, he had one constant to work with: The turbulence was now expected to ease up closer to Wichita, and the weather was expected to hold, maybe even improve somewhat—a nice forecast for that part of the country in late summer.

Vera Johnson "After we got to the airport and Axel spoke to the flight service folks, he and I had a conversation about how high we should fly. He said it was going to be very bumpy if we stayed under the clouds and a problem for him if we went above them.

"I suppose, in hindsight, that our best decision would have been to stay home. But we never really considered it. The opportunity in Wichita was just too good. And we had no other way of getting there in time except in our airplane. So, it was really only a matter of two choices: I suffer or he suffers. That decision was easy for me. I voted for Axel's comfort, because he was flying the plane. I also knew we could always land if it got too bad, and I would be able to get myself put back together.

"We agreed that we would live through the turbulence, because it would be safer. But just as soon as we took off, Axel went straight up through the open spaces between the clouds. When we finally leveled off, we were well above them. That's how Axel is. He's always worrying about me liking flying. He knows I've never been crazy about it, and I've never been able to convince him that I really don't mind it all that much either. So he always tries as hard as he can to make sure I have a good ride. (Pause) Even more so since the accident."

At 9,500 feet, VFR on top and perfectly smooth, Axel settled back to enjoy the ride and exert as little energy as possible. He never liked the breathless feeling at high altitude. And even though he lived at nearly 4,000 feet above sea level, perhaps because he had always been a fairly heavy smoker, going up another 5 or 6,000 feet bothered him, usually noticeably.

But not today. The air was very clear. Visibility above the clouds was truly unlimited, at least a hundred miles or more in all directions. And not a bump anywhere. Axel and Vera sat in splendorous comfort drinking in the vista all around them.

Axel Johnson "I don't think I ever remember a time before or since that flight when the weather was as good as that. I'd been worrying about staying up there at 9,500 feet for so long. But it was so pretty, and actually quite easy to breathe, that I just forgot about why I didn't like being up so high. And it seemed to relieve the lingering effects of my cold, too. The thinner, cleaner air can do that.

"By the time we got to within a hundred miles or so of Wichita, the cloud tops were starting to get higher. Pretty soon they were higher than we were, and I figured it was time to find some breaks and get down out of there. Besides, we'd been listening to the radio and hadn't heard any reports about the turbulence being bad below the clouds.

"But getting down turned into a major deal. There were way fewer breaks than there had been, or than were forecast, and those puffy cotton balls were starting to close ranks and come after us. Seeing that happening, I decided to dump the power and get us down in a hurry, before we wound up in the stuff.

"That's when the real problem hit us. I mean hit me. Because I was getting over a bad cold, my ears filled up and I couldn't clear them. I tried everything. But it kept on getting worse and within a minute or two I lost it. Vera told me I never passed out or anything. But I couldn't fly the airplane. And for sure, I couldn't keep us out of those clouds. I may not have been able to stay VFR anyway, because they were closing up pretty fast, at least where we were.

"When we hit the first cloud bank, we were suddenly being thrown all over the place. I found myself worrying that the airplane might come apart. It almost did.

"But I don't really remember much about what was going on. My head felt like it was being split wide open, and I got very dizzy. From the pain in my head and the spinning sensation, I was completely nonfunctional. When I think back on it, I might have been better off had I passed out for a couple of minutes. I might have been more relaxed and able to recover quicker when we came charging out of those clouds at only about 4,500 feet msl. We were all the way down to 3,300 feet before the Mooney finally started to right itself. With no help from me or Vera, by the way."

During the 10 minutes Axel was pondering whether or not the cloud tops in the distance ahead of them were as high or higher than he and Vera were, the Mooney overflew an area where the cloud density was less than 25 percent. It would have been easy to descend all the way to below the bases and never come within 1,000 feet of a cloud. The ideal conditions that VFR pilots who fly on top pray for.

Axel's indecision put him in 80 percent broken cloud density. Not the best circumstances for a 4,000-foot VFR letdown. He thought for a moment or two about turning around, even consulted with Vera about it, but then dismissed the idea because it would have taken too much time and fuel. Besides, Axel had made more semi-VFR descents than he cared to remember or talk about, and never had a problem, at least not as far as he was concerned.

What Axel did not realize was that the clouds building all around them were doing so at an active rate, typical for central Kansas on a warm summer day. They were also bunching up, getting ready to turn into nasty thunderheads, unforecast but not surprising in that part of the country. And they were ready to pack a terrific wallop on the unsuspecting pilot who would dare to venture in or near them.

Mooneys are known to have as much bounce to the ounce of turbulence as any airplane flying. The airplanes handle turbulence well enough, but they seem to reach out for extra bumps and grinds, especially in cumulus clouds.

The first cloud encounter came at just under 9,000 feet. Axel had set up a 500-foot-per-minute descent and thought he had found a good hole for at least their initial letdown. Surprise. It was a sucker hole. The cloud was waiting just around the bend for them.

A quick look at the altimeter gave Axel quite a jolt. They were losing 1,400 feet per minute for the first 20 seconds. Then it got worse, but Axel never knew it because his ears filled up and his head began exploding with pain. The cold or flu that he thought was over had been reawakened by the suddenness of the descent. And then spatial disorientation and vertigo set in just as suddenly. Axel was now a very sick passenger. No one was flying the airplane.

Less than a minute later, now at 7,700 feet, the Mooney was thrown out of the first cloud and hit the clear blue in a 75° right bank. Axel was helpless. But once out of the raging turbulence, the Mooney quickly righted and resumed the 500-foot-per-minute descent that it had been trimmed for.

Vera and Axel were badly shaken. Vera realized it; Axel was in too much pain and too disoriented to care. But the respite was not long enough to help them; it lasted only 2½ minutes.

The next cloud was waiting with a strong updraft. In less than 15 seconds they were climbing, and so was the airspeed. Up to and past redline in a wink. Axel, badly shaken from the sudden jolt of the updraft but somewhat awakened by it, reduced the power and neutralized the trim. It might have saved their lives.

Four more shocks of alternating downdrafts and updrafts followed. The Mooney and its partially impaired pilot and passenger were not doing well. The turbulence was as severe as Axel had ever experienced. Vera, hanging on for dear life, would have agreed. But Axel hardly noticed it. His ear pain and the dizziness had him on the verge of passing out. Together the two conditions were much worse for him than the turbulence. So bad that he never heard or felt the sickening sound of several inches of the right stabilator cracking off the airplane. Vera did but wasn't able to relate the sensations to the problem.

When the Mooney finally came out of the final unwelcoming cloud at just under 4,500 feet, it was in a steep left bank, diving and dangerously exceeding redline. Axel, who had been trying to fly the airplane, saw the ground, regained some of his senses, and then let go of the yoke. Releasing the pressure enabled the forgiving but now slightly bent Mooney to recover by itself. Axel thought that it was a brilliant recovery. The Mooney did it, but not without losing another 1,500 feet.

Compared to the roller coaster turbulence in the clouds, the bumps underneath and in the clear were actually refreshing and reviving to the Johnsons. Within minutes, Axel's ear pain was subsiding and he was once again pilot in command. Maybe not fully in command, but at least able to fly. Vera breathed several happy sighs of relief. She was sure the worst was over.

Axel waited several minutes before calling Wichita Approach. When he finally felt enough in control of himself and the Mooney to also handle a radio conversation, he advised the controller that he was now low on fuel and had just been through a terrible ride. When asked if he wanted to declare an emergency, Axel declined but requested an expedited straight in approach to Wichita's Mid-Continent Airport.

Traffic was heavier than usual, but the controller sensed that Axel was in trouble. She gave the Mooney a discreet transponder code, found them quickly and gave Axel a vector to the airport plus instructions to descend to 2,500 feet.

Axel acknowledged and began to comply. That's when he noticed that something was wrong. The yoke didn't feel right. The airplane wasn't responding correctly. He instinctively looked outside at both wings and as much of the tail as he could see but didn't spot anything wrong. Had he asked Vera to also check, she might have noticed that a substantial portion of the right stabilator was missing. But he didn't ask, and she never looked.

When the Mooney's heading began to vary because Axel was experimenting with the controls, trying to regain some feel, the controller noticed it quickly and called:

Wichita Approach Control "Mooney . . ., turn left heading one-one-zero. Are you having some kind of a problem sir?"

Axel "Yes ma'am. Mooney . . . is having a control problem. We may have gotten something bent up from that severe turbulence we came through."

Approach "Mooney . . ., understand you are having a control problem. Are you able to maintain a heading sir?"

Axel "I think so, ma'am. We'll know in a minute. That was a one-ten heading?"

Approach "Yes, sir. And maintain 2,500. The airport will be at ten o'clock and 15 miles after you make your turn. Let me know when you have it in sight."

Axel (Twenty seconds later) "Mooney . . . has the airport."

Approach "Understand in sight . . . .. Stay on your present heading. You're on a left base for Runway One Right. At your discretion, descend to 2,300 and let me know when you start your turn to final. We'll be landing two other airplanes ahead of you, and the rest of the traffic for that runway will be diverted. Right now there's a 150 at 12 o'clock and six miles, and another one at ten-thirty and eight miles. They're both on the approach. Let me know when you have them in sight."

Axel "(Two minutes later) Wichita Approach, Mooney . . . is starting a left turn to final. Never did see that traffic, ma'am."

Approach "One of the 150s is now on a one-mile final. Won't be a factor. As soon as you're established on final, call the tower on 118.2. Suggest you keep your airspeed up, sir. (The controller was a pilot.) You'll be landing on a 7,300-foot runway. If there's something damaged on the airplane, your stall speed may be elevated and a much faster approach speed would then be recommended. Good luck, sir."

Axel "Coming up on final. Thanks for your help, ma'am. We'll be switching to 118.2 now."

Approach "Tell them you're 5½ miles. Good day, sir."

Axel dutifully switched to the tower frequency and told the controller his position, plus the fact that he was having a problem controlling the aircraft, which the controller already knew about. He was immediately cleared to land and told to keep his speed up on the approach. There was a Baron 4½ miles in trail overtaking the Mooney.

Proceeding on the approach, Axel wasn't doing well at all. The airplane was wavering from side to side. When the tower controller finally spotted the Mooney, they were at least 100 yards to the left of the approach, and possibly posing a threat to the airline traffic that was on an 8-mile final to Runway 1 Left.

The call from the controller was immediate and urgent. Axel's response was a sharp right turn followed by a left turn that almost lined the Mooney up with the runway. Then it lurched again to the right, the nose dropped, then rose. There was a surge of power followed by another lurch and a raised nose. The Mooney seemed to be help-lessly suspended.

The Mooney mushed in from 120 feet in the air. Its nosewheel hit the ground first with a crunching thud. The right main gear impacted next and collapsed, leaving the unprotected right wing at the mercy of the flat but rocky terrain 1,000 feet short of the runway.

Miraculously the Mooney stayed together. There was no fire. Its propeller was gone except for the cone and chopped off pieces of the blades. Smoke was coming from the engine. The airplane and its occupants sat quietly, suspended, grateful to be all in one piece. Almost.

The fire department and airport security arrived just as the John-sons were settled down enough to begin thinking of exiting the Mooney. The controller had declared an emergency; thus, the crash equipment and personnel had been waiting. They helped Axel and Vera out and away from the airplane, then began a quick assessment of the damage. It was extensive. They also noticed that part of the tail was missing. A cursory look around the general area told them it must have come off somewhere else, before the crash.

Merle Corcoran, Wichita Mid-Continent Airport security "It was a wonder they were still alive, let alone not even scratched. When we got Mr. and Mrs. Johnson out of the airplane, we noticed right away that he was in real trouble. He had tears in his eyes. He was very sweaty, much more than he should have been, even though it was a warm day. And he could hardly stand up or walk by himself. We thought he might have had some bad internal injuries.

"But at the hospital they did all kinds of tests on him and couldn't come up with anything. They said he was fine. Just getting over a flu. Probably shouldn't have been flying that day. Maybe still in shock from the accident. That's all they put in their report. Nothing more.

"All of us who saw him, though, I mean at the scene of the acci-dent, we were sure it was more than that. He was suffering from something, and it wasn't from just shock. I've seen guys in shock be-fore, and this was much more than that. He could hardly talk. Like he had a bad concussion, or something. We couldn't believe that hospi-tal report.

"By the next morning, when Mr. Johnson came in to work with the folks from the FAA, he was just fine. Like it never happened. Like he was a completely different person, in looks and everything. He even made arrangements to have his airplane looked at by his insur-ance company, then took care of having it moved out of the field it was in, all while he was filling out a bunch of papers for the FAA. I'd say he was one real sharp guy, but he sure was a mess when we first saw him. And that was just the afternoon before."

NTSB representative "All of the information we have confirms that this was clearly a case of a VFR pilot getting tangled up with some very active cumulus clouds on a warm summer day. It goes in the record book as VMC into IMC, and there's nothing to refute that finding.

"The fact that the pilot had a cold, or an illness of some sort, undoubtedly made his situation as bad as possible. But it didn't cause the accident. And as far as we know, the medications he took were pretty much out of his system before he took off, except for maybe the cough medicine he took just before he went to sleep the night before. But even that would only have left him a little down. It wouldn't have disabled him in any way.

"He also got a bad break. The weather changed very suddenly, which it will do around here. And he decided not to make a 180 and go back to those real good conditions for his letdown that he had passed only 10 or 15 minutes earlier because he figured it wouldn't get too bad that quickly. You could call that a coin flip that lost.

"Then, when he got close to the airport and discovered that he had part of his tail missing, he just never figured out how to handle his airplane. We're trying to get some information from Mooney about how the kind of damage he had would affect the ability to control the aircraft. But he did pretty well, considering he and his wife were all beat up from their bronco ride in those clouds, and with him losing it and all. If he'd had a little more time to put himself back together before attempting a landing in that turbulent air, he more than likely would have made it. They went in only 1,000 feet short of the runway.

Axel "Since the accident, Vera and I have been trying to pin down exactly what happened to me up there. We've been in touch with the drug companies who make the cold medicines I'd been taking, and a couple of doctors to see if maybe the combination of all of them might have done me in. So far, nothing concrete. But we're still working on it.

"What the FAA told us didn't help at all. I know the probable cause, according to their official report, was VMC into IMC. But that's baloney. I've been in clouds more often than I'll admit to anyone, and I've never had a problem with it. And I've had clogged ears before, but never like that. That was the worst pain I ever had in my whole life. I can't even describe it.

"No, something else, or a combination of things, caused that accident. Maybe we'll never know for sure, but it won't be because we haven't tried to find out.

"I've told you everything Vera and I can remember about what happened. If you come up with anything, please promise that you'll let us know about it right away. We sure wouldn't want to go through anything like that again.

"By the way, Vera has agreed to start taking some flying lessons. So, maybe some good has come from all of this after all."

NASA representative "The causes of this accident may be so complicated and complex that a good set of answers may never emerge. We could spend a hundred years on a case like this and not be able to test all of the possible combinations. Speculation is the best we can do, beyond the official findings that I agree with.

"For starters, our data base on over-the-counter drugs is growing every day and it's beginning to look like a nightmare. We're finding some pretty unusual effects that can last much longer than anyone ever suspected. Like four and five days in some cases. And the combinations of two or several drugs, and even with foods and beverages, can muster up some strange reactions. Add smoking, a nip or two like the alcohol that cough medicine the pilot took probably had in it—and the side effects can start ganging up on each other.

"So, let's look at the known combinations in this case. Start with the antihistamine he took about 16–18 hours prior to takeoff. Probably innocuous by itself. Then add the 40 or 50 proof cough suppressant he took to help him get some sleep. Remember that he took the cough medicine about 10 hours before takeoff, or 6–8 hours after having taken the antihistamine. Now you've got chemical warfare in progress that can linger much longer than either of the individual substances are programmed for.

"Next, throw in the remnants of his head cold, or flu, or whatever his 5-day illness was. The plot thickens. Now mix in who knows how many cigarettes he had before and during the flight, keeping in mind that nicotine is a drug. And finally, give it the final shot with that enticing, clear, clean, thin air. I stress thin because this pilot had had problems, or at least noticeable discomfort, with high altitude before.

"With this much of a known quantity—not that we know much about the quantity, but at least we know what ingredients the ingredients were—let's examine the external circumstances and see how everything worked together to put those people down.

"The airplane flew at 9,500 feet for nearly 4 hours. The pilot and his wife felt fine, probably because the air was so smooth. It can be intoxicating, you know, which is one of the first manifestations of hypoxia. His first questionable judgment to not turn back to the easy letdown conditions is a definite indication of hypoxia.

"When the airplane entered the first cloud and was slammed by the heavy turbulence and the severe downdraft, we don't know what came first—the ear problem or the apparent vertigo. I say 'apparent' because vertigo is never officially reported unless a surviving pilot offers that he or she experienced it. And I would venture that only a small fraction of the active pilots know what vertigo is or feels like, and even less of a fraction of those would ever admit it to the FAA or the NTSB because they'd be afraid that alcohol or drugs would be suspected of having caused it. We get reports of vertigo here at NASA because of our promise of perfect confidentiality. Many of them would scare the daylights out of you. It's a shame they can't be shared with the entire pilot population because they would be very informative and maybe save some lives.

"Anyway, I was talking about what came first, the ear problem or the vertigo. My guess would be the vertigo, but it wouldn't have made much difference. The sudden downdraft caused his ears to explode, or implode, which is really what was happening. The pressure increased quickly on the outside of his ears during the rapid descent, causing the locked-in fluids in his ears to become compressed. It's one of the worst, most debilitating pains of all.

"But whichever came first hardly mattered. Because either condition would have disabled him. The two together had to be devastating. It's a wonder he didn't pass out.

"After that, it's all unprovable conjecture. But we can reliably presume that his ability to fly was impaired, even though he was able to get a disabled airplane to an airport. The one of his choice, no less. Why he lost it on a close up final is, at best, a guess. Mine would be fatigue. The aftermath of all he had been through. I think he simply ran out of gas, physically and mentally. He had nothing left, and the airplane got ahead of him, especially when the tower controller reacted to his being off course and put some pressure on him. I certainly wouldn't point to that as a probable cause, but it might have been the straw that broke this camel's back.

"By the way, if you ever get a chance to communicate with these people, you might mention to the pilot that his severe ear problem could have been easily fixed right on the spot with a simple menthol inhaler. It works like a miracle by opening up the ear passages, which, of course, relieves the pressure. Then it's good-bye pain and suffering quicker than you can snap your fingers. I think every pilot should carry one or two of those small inhalers in their flight cases, or with their maps and charts. You can fly for years and never need that inhaler, but if you ever do, it can save your life."

Author comment A copy of the NASA transcript was sent to the Johnsons, as promised. The following letter was received about three weeks later:

Dear Bob,

Vera and I want to thank you for the NASA transcript. It contains more information than we have been able to dig up since the accident. It also answered many of our questions and, for sure, has given us plenty to think about.

For instance, we had no idea whatsoever that the altitude and lack of oxygen could have caused my vertigo, if that is, in fact, what I experienced. As a result, I have been studying up on hypoxia quite intensely.

What I found out has convinced me that I can live without my cigarettes while I'm flying. We have also purchased a complete oxygen system for our new Mooney, another 231, but a later model. And anytime we are above 7,000 feet, night or day, we use it. It's a simple discipline that's working well for us so far.

NASA's advice about menthol inhalers may be a godsend. After reading that part of the transcript, Vera ran to the drugstore and bought half a dozen inhalers, two of each kind they had. We now have them in my flight case, in the glove compartment, and one is taped to the left side of the panel. That may sound like overkill to you, but if you've ever had an ear problem in an airplane, you can understand our overreaction. It's a great relief having those inhalers, knowing they can instantly control a pain like that.

As you can probably imagine, we are eternally grateful to you and the folks at NASA for all of the above.

Axel

5

The alternate airport that wasn't

Preliminary report: April; Cessna 172N; private pilot, single-engine land, 550 hours. The aircraft crashed during a forced landing after running out of fuel on a 400+ mile trip from Birmingham, Alabama, to White Sulphur Springs, West Virginia. The pilot and his passenger suffered minor injuries. The pilot said fuel exhaustion resulted from extra time spent correcting a navigational error and unexpected lowering weather at his destination, which required diverting to the nearest available alternate airport 50 miles away.

Further investigation revealed:

- The pilot deviated from his flight plan to show his passenger the Lookout Mountain Resort area. The diversion took about 15 minutes.
- A VFR flight plan had been filed for either White Sulphur Springs or Lewisburg, West Virginia, but it was never activated. It called for 3:30 time to either destination and 40 minutes of reserve fuel.
- A slight navigational error occurred after the sightseeing excursion but went unnoticed for nearly half an hour.
- The two destination airports were in an isolated area 32 miles from the closest available alternate and 51 miles from the last airport on the flight plan route.

Official conclusion: Fuel exhaustion due to pilot error. Poor planning. Insufficient VFR fuel reserves after intentional deviation from the flight plan.

NEARLY A MONTH HAD GONE INTO THE PLANNING of a trip to a medical administrator's symposium in White Sulphur Springs, West Virginia. Mark Morrison, 36, a senior staff officer at the University of

Alabama Medical Center, was the owner of a Skyhawk. His passenger to the symposium was Lisa McGregor, 32, assistant director of patient services at the medical center. They had been dating for seven months, having met at the Birmingham Municipal Airport, where Lisa had just started taking flying lessons. It was sort of a love at first flight romance. This was to be their longest trip together.

Mark and Lisa had spent nearly a week on their flight plan, setting up no less than six separate routings. If the weather cooperated, they intended to do some sightseeing and make a stop or two en route. They had the time and the inclination.

But as luck would have it, the weather on the morning of the flight was just a little better than marginal. Not conducive for meandering in mountainous terrain. Flight Service was calling for 2,500-foot ceilings initially, lowering to 1,500 after Knoxville, holding or improving for the rest of the day. Visibility ranging from 5–8 miles, with some light precip possible. There was a band of weather 50–100 miles north of the destination area that was expected to move directly east or northeast. Call it "ugh" VFR.

After a short conference, the decision was made to go back to Plan A, the direct nonstop route. Mark called flight service back and filed his VFR flight plan: Victor 115E to Chattanooga, Victor 115 to Knoxville, Victor 519 to Bluefield, direct White Sulphur Springs or Lewisburg; altitude—"We'll stay below the clouds"; time en route 3:30 with 4:10 fuel; two people on board; white with red and black stripes.

Mark usually flight planned 110 knots for the Skyhawk. With the winds aloft at 6,000 forecast to be 300° at 30, he added 10 knots of push and came up with 3:30 time en route for the 407-mile trip, give or take a half inch error measuring and drawing lines on four sectionals. His 4:10 fuel estimate was exactly that. Just a qualified guess, taken from the Skyhawk's operating manual. Mark had never run the tanks completely dry to see where the fuel gauge needle would be, or calculated his fuel burn, or kept accurate time, or done any number of tests to determine precisely how much flying time he had on a full load of fuel. Which makes him a typical VFR pilot, but not necessarily a typical aircraft owner, VFR or IFR.

Flight plan in hand and plenty of time, since the weather was expected to stay the same or improve, Mark and Lisa had a leisurely breakfast at the airport restaurant. At 1030, they preflighted the Skyhawk carefully and unhurriedly, made their usual preflight pit stop, and checked all of their charts and gear. Their runup and radio check were also thorough and unrushed. The Skyhawk was ready to fly. At 1057, they were cleared for takeoff and rolling down the runway. But their flight plan was not activated.

Climbing to 3,200 feet and still below the clouds, Mark and Lisa relaxed as he leveled off in the smooth, hazy air. Their first checkpoint was Gadsden, and everything around them was familiar. He didn't bother unfolding his sectional. More than two-thirds of his 550 hours of flying time had been in or through this general area.

After Gadsden, it was on to Chattanooga, where Lisa had never been by air. Lookout Mountain was easy to spot coming from the southwest with the visibility better than the 8 miles forecast. It was tempting, and Lisa looked anxious. Mark felt he had to show her something on this 3½ hour airway excursion over nameless hills. Besides, the weather was much better than expected.

The Lookout Mountain resort area was easy to find and worth the short deviation to see it. After 5 or 6 minutes of pointing and finding, it was time to get back on the airway. Mark checked the sectional carefully and decided to stay north and west of Chattanooga. They could get back on the airway farther up and save some time and gas. Besides, he had just calculated that they were getting a bit more help from the wind than anticipated.

Eyeballing the sectional and calculating the wind to still be at 300°, Mark decided on a 45° heading as they headed off into less familiar territory. He had been to Knoxville a few times in the past four years but never at such a low altitude. Nothing looked the same as what he recalled from higher up. No problem. Knoxville is a big city, easy to find and only 80 some miles from the Chattanooga area.

Ten minutes later they were stone cold lost. Lisa had tuned in the Knoxville VOR. But they were more than 60 miles from the station and too low to get a good signal. To stay under the cloud ceiling, they were now at 2,500 msl. With the visibility at least 8 miles, they turned their attention to the terrain, the landmarks—which were few—and the sectional. No luck. They could see and identify the Watts Barr Reservoir beneath and literally all around them but they couldn't get a fix on exactly where they were.

After an eternity of about 8 more minutes, the Knoxville VOR finally started to come in. Lisa centered the needle on a 65° reading. With several sighs of relief, kept discreetly to himself, Mark turned to a heading of 60° and watched the needle stay centered. They were 11 or 12 miles northwest of course and had lost about 5 or 6 minutes. Only 5 or 6 minutes.

Mark Morrison "When we came away from Lookout Mountain, we were just a little behind our flight plan. So I figured the wind must have been helping us more than the 10 knots I had planned on. Then, since we were north and west of the airway, I figured it would be foolish to head back southeast to the Chattanooga VOR. We could get back on the airway farther up, probably 10 or 15 miles northeast of Chattanooga.

"Rather than bother with Chattanooga at all at that point, Lisa dialed up the Knoxville VOR. But we couldn't get it from that far away, especially since we were lower by then. We had to come down some to stay out of the clouds when we were passing Chattanooga.

"Being so low, everything looked different to me. I got the Tennessee River okay and the reservoir and I knew I had to keep it on my left and it would take me to Knoxville. But then, later on, I realized there was a big fork in the river up ahead, and the heading we were on was actually taking us to Oak Ridge. By the time Lisa and I got it all unscrambled, the VOR started coming in so we just followed it to the station.

"When we passed over the Knoxville VOR, we were exactly 18 minutes behind our original flight plan. Not bad when you figure in the deviation to Lookout Mountain and the fact that we were lost for awhile. Couldn't have been more than 5 or 10 minutes altogether that we were lost. And the wind was being good to us, so Lisa and I both figured we'd make up some of that time if we stayed smack on the airway for the rest of the trip. And that's about what we did."

The Skyhawk started out approximately on the airway leaving Knoxville but was really following Interstate 81, keeping it 3 or 4 miles off the right wing, and Cherokee Lake about the same distance off to the left.

When the Glade Spring VOR came in, they already had the city of Kingsport, Tennessee, in sight. Lisa centered the needle and came up with bearing of 60° to the station. Mark spotted Hawkins County Airport right under the Skyhawk's nose, then on the map, and sat back confidently. As far as he was concerned they were right on course. Not quite the airway, but close enough. They were also another minute behind their flight plan.

Crossing the Glade VOR at 3,200 feet, all was well. They took up a 58° track off of Glade and headed toward Bluefield, 51 miles away. Mark did a quick calculation of their fuel and determined that they had about 1:15 remaining, just enough to go the 100 miles or so to White Sulphur Springs and still have reserves of about 20 or 25 minutes when they rolled up to the ramp. He was off by 15 minutes. The wrong way, unfortunately.

They had already been flying for 3 hours, and Mark was relying on Cessna's operating manual for his fuel burn rate. An unwise thing to do because the manual figures always reflect optimum performance from a brand new airplane. He also forgot to factor in the unusable fuel, another common error.

From where they were at that moment, they actually had 1:05 of fuel left, nearly 20 minutes less than the 30-minute reserve required by the FAA. The gauges showed a tad less than ¼ full, which turned out to be accurate.

Mark "When I did my fuel calculation coming out of Glade, I was sure I was dead on. I had owned the airplane nearly 4 years by then, and my fuel burn had always been right to the book numbers. Why it was off on that trip I'll never know. But it had to be by about a half-gallon per hour.

"The fuel gauges were also right on, which was unusual because they had never been right before. In fact, they usually showed unbalanced amounts of fuel, sometimes as soon as 5 minutes after take-off. Why they were giving true readings that day is, I suppose, another mystery we won't be able to solve.

"Before we reached the Bluefield VOR, which sits right at Mercer County Airport, I tried unsuccessfully to get in touch with flight watch. When that didn't work, probably because we were too low in mountainous terrain, I tried 123.6 and got flight service. That's when I got the bad news about the weather at Lewisburg. The report, by the way, was almost 50 minutes old when I got it. It said that the weather system up in the Wheeling area that had been expected to move out via the east and northeast had begun moving straight south. If it continued on its present course, it would be 20 to 30 miles north of both of our destination airports at about the time we would be arriving. Talk about lousy breaks.

"In hindsight, I know now that we should have landed right there at Bluefield. And, so help me, I don't know why we didn't. We weren't in any hurry. Our first meetings weren't until later that evening. I guess Lisa and I had given ourselves a mind-set that we were A-okay after I did those final fuel calculations. We were so sure we had more than enough left that we never gave it a second thought."

Leaving Bluefield, Mark and Lisa stayed on the 58° radial off the VOR and began paying close attention to the cloud ceiling less than 200 feet above them. They scanned the hilltops ahead making sure that none of them were obscured. Scud-running was not something either one of them relished or would ever contemplate doing deliberately. And certainly not in mountainous terrain. But everything was fine. They still had the same 7–8 miles of visibility they had started out with and they could see the top of every hill and mountain in sight.

They reached the halfway point between the Bluefield VOR and White Sulphur Springs almost a minute faster than they had expected to. The wind had become a little more favorable, giving them a ground speed of about 130 knots. They didn't notice it.

Mark saw it first and pointed it out to Lisa. The hilltops in the distance at their 9, 10 and 11 o'clock positions were no longer visible. There was also a distinct stream of rain coming from a darker cloud area about 5 miles off to their left. It startled both of them. First, because it was there. Secondly, because it had happened so suddenly.

Lisa had already dialed in 118.9 on the radio, the tower frequency at Lewisburg. It wasn't their first choice to land, because the Greenbrier Airport at White Sulphur Springs was right at the lodge where their symposium was being held. But Lewisburg had a tower and was a much better equipped airport. They had decided in advance that at the first sign of a problem they would divert to Lewisburg. The lodge could pick them up.

Mark got an immediate reply from Lewisburg tower:

Lewisburg "Say your position, this is Lewisburg."

Mark "(We are) 18 to 20 miles southwest at 3,100 feet, landing Lewisburg."

Lewisburg "Lewisburg went IFR about ten minutes ago. We're now 800 and 2½ in light to moderate rain. We don't expect any improvement for at least an hour. Suggest you try Roanoke or Bluefield. The weather system that's affecting us has been moving in from the north."

Mark (Looking at the fuel gauges, now just above the EMPTY line) "Uh, Lewisburg, any chance for a special VFR, sir? We're low on fuel."

Lewisburg "Sorry, this is mountain country, sir, and our conditions are getting worse, not better. Suggest you head for an alternate immediately."

Mark "Lewisburg, we're *very* low on fuel. We really need that special VFR."

Lewisburg (A different voice, very condescending but also very authoritative) "The way this weather's coming in, we might be below IFR minimums by the time you get here. Roanoke's weather is fine and you'll have a tailwind getting there. That's your best choice, sir. You can give them a call on 126.9. That's Roanoke Approach. I'm sure they can help you."

Mark and Lisa quickly checked their sectional. The route back to Bluefield was clearly marked, and they had just come from there. Getting to Roanoke and finding the airport might pose a problem.

They chose Bluefield and did a 180. It was the wrong choice. And they never called Roanoke Approach.

Completing the turn, Mark noticed immediately that their ground speed was much slower. A 40-mile-an-hour difference is quite obvious in a Skyhawk. He checked the fuel gauges again—still just above the EMPTY line—and told Lisa to dial up 123.6 on the radio. They were 32 miles from Bluefield, and Mark wanted to talk to someone. Those fuel gauges were creeping down while the hills all around them were creeping up.

Ten minutes later Bluefield radio answered. By then, the fuel gauges were both settling fully on EMPTY. They had just passed over the Bluestone Reservoir, about 18 miles northeast of the Mercer County Airport. Mark reported their position and their condition—fuel critical. But before the controller could respond, the Skyhawk's engine started sputtering. It was getting ready to quit, 20 minutes sooner than Mark and Lisa thought it would.

Mark handed Lisa the mike and started looking for a place to land. Lisa told the controller their approximate position, based on what she was looking at, and told him they were losing power and landing—somewhere.

A fairly flat area was at the Skyhawk's 11 o'clock position about a mile away. Mark turned toward it, at the same time looking for a road or a landmark of some sort. Lisa was also looking. But luck wasn't with them. There wasn't anything in sight range that they could identify.

Mark did a good job of mushing the Skyhawk in slowly. It would have been a perfect forced landing had it not been for the rocky ground. As hard and as well as he tried, the rocks finally won and the Skyhawk was dumped on its nose.

Lisa, holding onto just her seat, was thrown forward against the yoke and the panel, banging both shoulders and her left knee. Nothing broke, but she was hurt. Mark, who was flying and holding onto the control wheel, injured his right arm as he was hurled forward. The eerie silence was deafening as they sat for several moments waiting for something else to happen, waiting for something else to hurt.

They were okay. Battered and bruised, but okay. The Skyhawk fared less well. Its nosewheel was up in the cowling. Its propeller was impaled in the rocky soil. Its tail was up in the air where it didn't belong. But they were okay.

Almost 3 minutes went by before they began figuring out how to exit the airplane. Lisa was able to get the door open on her side. Mark's door was jammed, but he was more concerned about turning off all of his switches, making sure there wouldn't be any fire or further damage to the airplane. Funny the things you do when you're hurt and in shock.

It took Lisa several tries, plus an assist from Mark, to get his door open. Then they both had to wrestle back his seat, which had been dislodged from the impact and locked in its forward-most position. In the process, Mark twisted his back.

Finally out of the airplane and resting on the ground, the two survivors contemplated their predicament and their options. They didn't know where they were. Lisa didn't think she could walk very far. Mark was sure he couldn't carry her and even less sure that he could take more than a few painful steps with his back in spasm. So they sat. Taking their time. Waiting.

Back in Bluefield, the flight service radio operator sprang into action, calling for police and fire assistance, alerting everyone he could that a Cessna 172 Skyhawk was down somewhere southwest of Bluestone Lake. Within 30 minutes 100 people from different jurisdictions were combing the West Virginia hillsides looking for Lisa, Mark and the Skyhawk.

It took more than 4 hours to find them and would have taken longer had Lisa not thought to try the radio; 123.6 answered in a flash and began giving her instructions that would help the authorities find them. She keyed the mike and counted to 10 every minute for 10 minutes, as instructed. The state police had a fix on their position after the sixth minute and found them fewer than 40 minutes later.

Lisa McGregor Morrison "While I was sitting on that rocky ground beside the airplane with its nose in the dirt and its tail stuck up in the air like that, I kept thinking to myself: 'What am I doing here? What am I doing here with this jerk who is now part of my life who just ran his airplane out of gas and almost killed us?' The whole scene was so unreal. Like a fantasy or an illusion that you expect to go away when you blink your eyes. But it didn't. That was me. It was us, Mark and me. That was his Skyhawk and this really did happen to us. The pain in my shoulders and my leg confirmed it.

"After I settled down, I began worrying about Mark. He was in worse shape than I was. I mean psychologically as well as physically. And then I began reconstructing all of what had taken place: the flight plan that we worked up so meticulously together, the decisions we made together when the weather changed so suddenly, the bad breaks we got. But the worst part of it was realizing that we got in trouble because of what we didn't know.

"We followed every rule, or at least we thought we did. Our speed calculations were conservative. We had more than the required 30-minute fuel reserve when we started out. We used the fuel burn figure right out of the manual and added a little to it, even though in all the time Mark owned the airplane its actual fuel consumption had been at or slightly below the manual's number. I mean, what else could we do since we were doing everything right according to the FAA's rule book and according to what we had both been taught?"

FAA representative "Every time there's a fuel exhaustion accident—which, by the way, is the cause of one out of every 12 general aviation fatalities—we hear the same stories: 'The airplane had a higher fuel consumption rate than it ever had before. The engine quit the very second the needle in the fuel gauge read EMPTY. We planned our ground speed conservatively. Our navigating was close to perfect and couldn't have been off by more than 10 minutes or so. The weather changed on us very suddenly.'

"There might be a couple more I've forgotten, but to every story I say 'baloney,' and I'm not trying to be a wise guy or a Monday morning quarterback. Whenever we do some further checking into one of these cases, we invariably find wishful thinking, carelessness, negligence, and rationalization, which in my book is all baloney.

"Take the case of this Skyhawk and these two very nice, intelligent, and conscientious pilots. They flew for more than 4 hours knowing full well what that airplane's maximum range and time-in-the-air was. All they had to do was look at a wristwatch or clock to know that when they got to the Bluefield VOR they didn't have enough fuel to get to White Sulphur Springs or Lewisburg and then to an alternate, if that turned out to be necessary. Let me repeat that last part: 'If that turned out to be necessary.' That's the problem. Nobody who ever ran an airplane out of gas ever thought it would be necessary to fly to an alternate.

"In this particular accident, the alternate they used in their flight plan—which they never activated, by the way—was Mercer County Airport 51 miles away from their two destination airports. With the 20-knot headwind they faced flying toward Mercer County, their 30-minute reserve wasn't enough to get them there. It's just simple mathematics.

"One of the commonest of all errors is this business of the 30- or 45-minute fuel reserve requirement that's in the FARs. Those figures are only minimums and are so stated. Furthermore, they apply to all sizes and speeds of aircraft. So the same reserve in minutes means different things to different aircraft. Let me give you an example. An average jet can go 250 nautical miles in 30 minutes. But a Skyhawk can only go about 55 miles. The jet can outrun almost any weather surprise. The Skyhawk can hardly outrun anything.

"And the Skyhawk is limited to that 55-mile range. But what if the alternate is 60 or more miles away? We see lots of those, with pilots wondering what went wrong when they glide in 5 miles short. They just blindly use that 30- or 45-minute figure and think they're covered when mathematically they aren't. It all goes back to the fact that they never really expect to need their alternate.

"Another thing that has to be a preprogrammed misconception is the idea that when the fuel gauges read EMPTY they're only kidding. Because our automobiles always give us some extra go power beyond the EMPTY mark, we all think the same is true of airplanes. Well, it isn't. In fact, in my personal experience, the only time an airplane fuel gauge is accurate is when it's on EMPTY. The rest of the time it can be all over the place. But the instant that needle hits the EMPTY mark, the engine is going to quit.

"I always feel sorry for the people who have been involved in fuel exhaustion accidents, because the accidents were always avoidable and the people always feel stupid or victimized, or both. And then they try to lay the blame off on the FAA, or the airplane manufacturer, or the refueler, or on anything other than where it belongs . . . on themselves."

Mark "I was so shook up by what happened and the way it happened that I thought seriously about giving up flying. But Lisa and I talked it over and decided that it was really our own fault. That was hard to admit.

"Oh, we started out mad at Cessna for not making it clear that EMPTY meant EMPTY, for real. And we complained to the FAA that the FARs in general and the fuel reserve requirements in particular were written by people who have no understanding of who reads them and how the regs might be misinterpreted. But that was all grousing. We know how to read. We know how to count. We're both pilots and we should have used our heads and landed at Mercer County. After all, we had all the time in the world.

"After the airplane was put back together three months later, we made some simple rules for ourselves that will keep us out of trouble forever: Our fuel reserve is always at least a full hour, and we usually try for an hour and a half. We flight plan at 100 knots, which is 10 or 20 knots slower than the Skyhawk's true airspeed. It's nice to be early. And we check weather at regular intervals on every cross-country trip. If we had done that before we had already crossed the Bluefield VOR, we would have known that the weather at Lewisburg was stinko, and we would then have landed at Mercer County Airport. The result would have been no accident.

"Speaking of 'no accident,' Lisa and I were married 6 months ago and we're expecting. And if the baby is born on the exact anniversary of the accident, that will be 'no accident,' too."

Author comment Contrary to the well-intentioned advice from the FAA spokesperson, and the life preserving disciplines put in place by the Morrisons, some fuel exhaustion situations can be avoided *only* by not taking off.

The key is in the flight planning and dealing objectively with every factor, which must be known and understood. Example: A non-stop VFR trip to Yellowstone Airport in West Yellowstone, Montana, in a reasonably well-equipped Cessna 172 with four people on board and some luggage cannot be legally flight planned from anywhere farther than 125 miles away. And if the wind is from the southwest or west at any more than 30 knots, scrub it altogether.

Another example: A nonstop IFR trip in any piston-powered single or twin into weather covering an area of 400 miles or more in all directions from the destination airport cannot be legally filed from anywhere. It happens not infrequently in the late fall, winter and early spring. Ask any seasoned IFR pilot about the times he or she was unable to find a legal alternate within reachable distance and had to cancel an important trip.

A third example: Your calculator tells you that the combination of all of the factors adds up to "go": usable fuel, distance to alternate, weather, and wind, all okay. But you've never been there before and your alternate is not in all capital letters on your sectional—meaning it doesn't have a published approach. Your head should tell you to give yourself a more generous margin of safety because you might have trouble locating the alternate, even in good weather.

Assessment Of all the pilots I have met or interviewed who survived fuel exhaustion accidents, I never dealt with one I felt was stupid or who I wouldn't fly with. And, without exception, all of their accidents were the result of inadequate training, misunderstood rules, or forces completely beyond their control. Labeling all fuel exhaustion accidents "pilot error" is probably unfair. From an informational standpoint, it is a disservice because much more could be learned by communicating the real causes of these accidents to the general aviation pilot population. It would save some lives.

6

Tale of the lost tail

Preliminary report: November; Beech V35B Bonanza; private pilot, single-engine land, instrument rating, 1,700 hours. Partial in-flight breakup occurred and the airplane crashed during an instrument approach to Omaha's Eppley Field. The private pilot and one passenger were killed. A second passenger was seriously injured. The aircraft was on an IFR flight plan from Santa Fe, New Mexico, and had been in the air for about 4 hours. Preliminary report said the Bonanza experienced partial tail separation at 11:05 p.m. as the pilot was attempting a sharp turn to intercept the approach course at the outer marker. Weather was 700 overcast, 6 miles visibility with light snow.

Further investigation revealed:
- The flight plan had been filed "direct" from Santa Fe at 13,000 feet initial altitude, 9,000 after clearing the mountains, 3:55 time en route, 5 hrs. fuel.
- Weather at Santa Fe was CAVU. En route was forecast to be deteriorating after Garden City, Kansas, to 600 and 5 at Omaha. Chance for light rain or snow. Winds aloft at 9,000—280° at 30 kts., and at 12,000—300° at 45 kts.
- The pilot and his wife and daughter had spent three days in Albuquerque and Santa Fe. They were returning home to Omaha's Eppley Field, where the airplane was based.
- There was a full oxygen system aboard the aircraft.

Official conclusion: Loss of control due to partial structural failure caused by overstressing of the aircraft's controls. Improper instrument approach procedures. Pilot error.

A LONG ART-FAIR WEEKEND started in Albuquerque and ended in Santa Fe, New Mexico. Warren Sinclair, 46, his wife, Margaret, 42, and

Allison Sinclair, 18, their daughter and youngest child, were heading home in the family's Bonanza.

They had a relaxed supper, filed a flight plan for a 7 p.m. departure and arrived at Santa Fe County Municipal Airport at 6:15. The airplane had been serviced, with tanks topped off and two oxygen bottles filled.

Warren and Allison were both instrument pilots, as was Bob Sinclair, Allison's 20-year-old brother who did not make the trip because of school commitments. Margaret was a happy passenger and efficient helper who had no interest in learning to fly.

After paying their bill and checking again with flight service, Warren and Allison did a more-than-thorough preflight (Dad's way of setting a proper example for his daughter.), and just as carefully loaded their luggage and gear. Bonanza's have some critical CG characteristics, especially at or near gross, and the Sinclairs were aware of them.

It was a beautiful evening in Santa Fe for their takeoff from Runway 2. They maintained runway heading on the Poake One Departure, intersected the 354° radial off the Santa Fe VOR and followed it out toward the Poake intersection, 22 DME north of the station.

With their oxygen masks on at 9,000 feet, they reached 13,000, their initial altitude, in less than 10 minutes and were turned on course—Loran direct Omaha, with a heading of 030° to compensate for the 90° crosswind that wouldn't be of any help at this altitude. After the mountains, they could descend to 9,000 and get a little push, maybe 10 knots or so. Almost unfair considering the 40-knot dead-on headwind they had on their trip to Albuquerque three days before.

An hour later, crossing Victor 81, Warren descended to 9,000 feet, shut off the oxygen system, and they all removed and stowed their masks. They were three minutes ahead of their flight plan, enjoying a smooth and beautiful ride, watching the rising three-quarter moon. At this point, Allison took over so that Warren could get some rest. It was going to be an interesting approach and landing at Omaha in light snow or freezing rain.

The Bonanza had prop and windshield deicing but no boots. It handled light icing well because of its high power-to-weight ratio, and would be well under gross in another three hours. But Warren never pushed his luck. If Omaha was reporting or even hinting at icing anytime before their arrival, they would divert to Manhattan, Kansas, south of the weather system, for a surprise visit to Margaret's parents. Her father was still an active professor at Kansas State University, where Warren and Margaret met 27 years ago.

Warren's catnap turned into sound sleep of nearly an hour, twice as long as he had intended. He awoke with a heavy head and still very tired. But he stretched and shook it off and told his daughter it was her turn for some rest so they would both be refreshed and ready for Omaha.

Allison was not a sit-up-straight sleeper. So she did the Bonanza shuffle and switched places with her mother. Within two minutes she was stretched across the two back seats and sound asleep. Warren adjusted the autopilot, checked their course and airspeed—about 5 knots faster than expected—and called flight watch. All okay. The weather at Omaha was holding and not expected to get any worse. And there were no reports of any ice. Grandma and grandpa were not going to get a surprise visit on this trip.

Allison Sinclair "Dad and mom never woke me up for the approach into Omaha. I guess dad figured he could handle it okay without my help. I must have been sleeping very soundly because I didn't wake up until dad was being given a vector to GERFI, the outer marker for Runway 14 Right at Eppley.

"We were about 15 miles out at that point, and I heard the controller tell dad that there was another aircraft inbound on the localizer about 25 miles from the marker. I think he said it was a 727.

"Dad told him he would be able to make the turn onto the localizer right at GERFI so we could beat that 727 in. The controller gave him a heading—I think it was 050°—and told dad to check his speed. It was just about then that I looked out at the left wing and saw that it was snowing and that ice was beginning to build up on the wing. When I told dad about it, he just nodded. I saw that the prop-ice and windshield heater switches were both turned on and realized that he already knew about it.

"When I looked closer at dad, I saw that he was real uptight. We Sinclairs have always been afraid of ice. I also looked at the airspeed indicator and saw that it was just under the redline. When I asked dad about it, he said he was watching it and wanted it up there so we could get to the marker well ahead of that airliner on the approach. He didn't want to be up in those icing conditions any longer than necessary.

"From 2 miles out, the controller cleared us for the approach and told dad that the 727 would be about 8 miles behind us when we reached GERFI, and that we could slow down and get set up for landing. The 14 Right approach is a tight one—the marker is only 3.6 miles from the runway and you don't have much time to get your flaps and wheels down after you're on the glideslope.

"But dad never slowed down and he never put the flaps down at that point. I guess he wanted to be extra sure of beating that 727, and I think he might have felt some mushiness in the controls with the ice that was building on the wings. That would explain why he was keeping the airspeed up so high. (Pause) (She cleared her throat).

"(Then another pause and her voice softened noticeably) But I never got to ask him why. Everything happened so fast. As soon as the needle started to come in on the localizer, dad swung the airplane into a steep right turn, pulled up the nose, and reached for the switch to lower the gear. He never got there. Something cracked violently in the back of the airplane that ran a shudder right through the cabin.

"The next thing I remember is waking up in the hospital with my brother telling me I was going to be all right. Later on he told me that dad and mom were both killed."

At a mile from the marker, the controller called Warren and told him that the aircraft in trail had slowed down and would not be a factor. He also told him to slow down or he would fly through the localizer course.

Warren acknowledged the call. But if he did slow down, the controller didn't notice it. At the marker, the Bonanza started a sharp right turn, flew through the localizer course, continued around and came back through it again. A sharp left turn was then initiated but never completed as the Bonanza disappeared from the controller's scope.

It crashed 2½ miles short of the runway and 1 mile to the right of the localizer course. There was no fire. But the front seat occupants, Warren and Margaret, were crushed against the panel and killed instantly. The nose had impacted the ground in a high speed dive, driving the propeller and the engine back into and through the firewall. Allison, in the back seat, was seriously injured and unconscious when the Iowa State Police arrived at the scene. The Bonanza had come to rest 50 yards from the east bank of the Missouri River after nearly taking off the top of a semitrailer as it dove across the I-680 bypass. Several motorists saw the airplane overfly the highway and were at the crash sight before the police arrived. An eerie silence prevailed.

Eppley Approach controller "Everyone around here knew the Sinclairs. Warren was a prominent lawyer in town and a big supporter of the airport. He and his kids flew in and out of here in their Bonanza like they were out to break the record on shooting approaches. I'll bet Warren himself must have shot at least 200 a year and knew every approach better than anyone flying here.

"When he first called in that night, I didn't recognize his voice, and believe me, I knew his voice. But he called in like he always did: 'Eppley, Bonanza 42 Whiskey.' He'd never give his full description like everybody else, but we all knew it was him. Anyway, he didn't sound right to me, and he wasn't responding right either. But things were happening so quickly, and so all-of-a-sudden, that I never did ask him if he was okay. He obviously wasn't.

"I was expecting him, of course, and when his target first showed up on my scope, about 45 miles out, I knew something wasn't right. He was moving almost as fast as a jet. And he didn't call in from as far out as usual. I was about to call him when he finally did call me.

"By then he was only 18 or 20 miles southwest of the marker. We were busier than usual that night with freight and corporate stuff, and I told him we had a 727 a long way out on the localizer and a couple of other high speed aircraft inbound. Thinking back on it, I wish I hadn't, because he seemed to speed up even more. Then he asked for a vector right to the marker, even though he always asked for 3 miles outside so he could get the airplane set up to land and on the glide slope. I asked him if he wouldn't like some cushion, but he said he wanted to get down in a hurry before that 727 beat him to the approach. He didn't respond when I told him the 727 wouldn't be any closer than 8 miles even if he took the 3 miles. He just kept on coming.

"I knew he was going to blow his entry and I told him so. At the speed he was going, Bonanza's can't turn that fast. He mumbled something that sounded like, 'We'll be fine,' and 20 seconds later he was through that localizer course and back again in a flash. From that point on, he lost it. The airplane started a left turn back but then went back to straight ahead. That's when they went off my scope."

Bob Sinclair "We seldom flew the Bonanza cross-country at night. So I was surprised when dad called and asked me to pick them up at 11 p.m. He said something about having a court date in the morning and somebody sick at his office. I don't remember exactly. I told him I had heard that the weather might be turning bad, but he said he already knew about it and that if there was a problem, they'd drop in on grandma and grandpa in Manhattan. He said the weather wasn't supposed to get as far south as Manhattan before the next morning.

"As you can imagine, Allison and I have gone over every detail of the flight with the FAA, the safety board and with Burt Stewart, who was on approach control duty that night. About the best we can all figure is that they got caught with too much ice on the airplane. Dad's comments to Burt and to Allison, and the way he was flying, pretty much confirm that.

"Then he just over stressed the airplane when he made the sharp turn at the marker. But who would ever have dreamed that you could literally pull the tail off an airplane, especially a solidly built one like a Bonanza? None of us ever did, or you can be sure we never would have owned or flown that airplane. I still think it had to be something else, and so does our FBO and Beechcraft, who we also talked to.

"They think it was a combination of probable factors: The airspeed was at or over the redline; there was clear ice on the stabilators; there was some turbulence, although it wasn't reported; and then heavy and sudden back pressure was applied to keep the nose from dropping in the unusually sharp turn. The experts tell us that the combination of all of those forces would be enough to tear the tail off of any general aviation aircraft, even one built for aerobatics.

"Since we got that report that any airplane can come apart under those conditions Allison and I haven't flown since. This is Nebraska, and ice can happen here eight months out of the year. So, until we can afford a twin with full deice, we'll just stay on the ground."

NTSB representative "We don't subscribe to the position that any aircraft can come apart in an over stressed situation. There are many that won't. We also don't agree with the survivors, or any of the other agencies reporting on this accident, that it was anything but 'pilot error.'

"Let me explain that position in more human terms because we believe with absolute certainty that this accident should have been avoided. For starters, we do agree with the manufacturer as to what happened mechanically to the airplane: it was going too fast; it was turned too fast; and it was seriously over stressed when heavy back pressure was applied to the yoke. That combination could have taken the tail off of that Bonanza on that flight.

"Discounting the ice and the turbulence, neither of which we can prove—and please remember that proof is what this organization is all about—we have left the pilot who was flying the airplane. We know that he seldom flew long distances at night but had some compelling reason to do so on this flight. That tells us he was in a hurry.

"Next, we know that he was told of possible traffic, a 727, that has an approach speed substantially faster than a Bonanza. That tells us there was extra pressure on him.

"And finally we know from his daughter, who survived by a miracle—there wasn't much left of that airplane—that there was ice on the wings. We'll certainly take her word for it, even though our report can only include known findings and there was no ice on the airplane after it impacted, according to the police report and statements from airport security people who arrived at the crash sight only a few minutes after the accident. So, assuming there was ice, at least while the airplane was flying, we know from the daughter and son, who also flies, that the pilot had a healthy respect for and an outright fear of ice, and usually avoided it at all cost. That gives us a strong clue that there was possibly panic or, at the very least, extreme stress and tension.

"Putting the human equation together, then, this pilot should not have been there. He should have flown to his alternate—where he would have been able to make an uneventful landing—just as soon as ice began accumulating fast enough to make him want to keep up a dangerously high airspeed to prevent the airplane from stalling. He had plenty of fuel and knew that the weather at his alternate was fine.

"But he decided to go for it and left himself in conditions he just wasn't capable of dealing with. That, by any definition, is 'pilot error,' not any different from a VFR pilot taking off into known IFR conditions, or a qualified IFR pilot deliberately busting minimums.

"We don't officially speculate on why pilots make many of the mistakes they do. In this case, we can only assume that the pilot had a very compelling reason to get to Omaha on that particular evening and at that precise time."

NASA representative "Having a survivor of an in-flight breakup of an aircraft, partial or otherwise, is a rare opportunity to get some insights as to the causes and circumstances of these catastrophic accidents. They are almost always fatal to everyone on board. The fact that Allison Sinclair is also a pilot adds considerably to her ability to qualify what took place. We are deeply grateful to her and her brother for sharing with us virtually every memory, thought and observation they could.

"Since there has been a substantial amount of publicity about the unusual number of Bonanzas that have suffered catastrophic in-flight failure, the first thought that comes to mind in studying a case like this is: Did the pilot over stress the airplane, or did the airplane simply fall apart on the pilot? Either possibility raises several other questions: Was it a case of both—too much stress by the pilot but also some structural weakness in the airframe? Were there other human, mechanical, and environmental factors that contributed to the breakup? Which then leads to the ultimate quest: Can something be done to prevent these killer accidents?

"Because we have the Sinclairs, and especially Allison, of course, we can begin to direct our studies based on a known sequence of human and mechanical factors. And that gives us hope that the best single answer to those wide-ranging questions will be: 'Yes' to all of the above.

"Let's first dispense with the mechanical factors, those relating to the aircraft itself, by acknowledging that both the FAA and the manufacturer are already working on and have completed ADs and corrective changes in the aircraft's structure as a result of the information gleaned from this and several prior accidents. To my knowledge, whatever problem might have formally existed with Bonanzas has been solved.

"Our main thrust here at NASA is human factors, so let's concentrate on those and separate them into two parts: actions and causes. And since we have eyewitness data to work with, we'll start with the actions because they are easiest to bring into focus; they are also black-and-white definite, whereas the causes are less so.

"We know that about 2 hours into the flight the pilot took a cat-nap that turned into a continuous deeper sleep of nearly a full hour. Awakening from that, he was still quite tired and had to stretch and move around in order to shake off a heavy head. It indicates that his resting position was probably poor, leaving him slightly disoriented and somewhat lightheaded. His rather abrupt suggestion to his daughter that she get some rest so she could help him with the difficult approach ahead seems to confirm that he was thinking about his and her physical condition.

"Then, after an hour had gone by and his daughter was still in deep slumber in the back seat, the pilot and his wife made a rather irresponsible decision to let her continue sleeping, instead of awakening her and getting her back into the front seat as a useful copilot. Conditions hadn't changed any in Omaha, but the pilot was now confident that he wouldn't need any help. We can address the 'why' of that when we look at 'causes.' But for now, keep in mind that this same pilot had shown some signs of mild disorientation an hour earlier. It's safe to assume that his condition did not improve, with no further rest or food or liquid intake. If anything, it would have deteriorated somewhat. Thus the poor decision.

"Arriving into Omaha airspace, the pilot was now exhibiting visible stress. His daughter described him as uptight. The airspeed was elevated. There was ice on the wings. When she asked him why he was flying so close to redline, his answer was innocuous. And when she pointed out that there was ice building up, he didn't answer at all. Those are signs of extreme tension in a person who has been described as well-disciplined, cool under pressure, and always in command of his situation, which, in this case, was certainly a familiar one since he had shot so many real and practice approaches into Eppley Field.

"The approach controller also sensed that something was wrong with the pilot. The Bonanza's speed was excessive. The pilot's radio responses weren't completely logical and his decision to intercept the localizer right at the marker made no sense at all.

"Then it got worse. He didn't slow down when advised to do so. He never put his flaps down—How could he with his speed up so high?—and he didn't think to lower the gear until he was already into the violent turn that tore the tail loose. Those actions are all definite signs of panic of a pilot who had lost control of himself and his airplane.

"What took place, then, was a deteriorating mental and physical state, aggravated by worsening weather conditions, including unexpected icing, and then further complicated by real or imagined traffic pressures. That's the formula for an airplane getting ahead of a pilot and finding the ground by itself.

"Now let's go back as far as possible and see if we can come up with any probable causes. I don't mean the direct ones that the FAA and the NTSB identify. At NASA, we deal with the *causes* of the 'probable causes.' In other words, the 'why's': Why did the pilot exceed the redline? Why did he exhibit such unusual behavior for him? What caused him to panic? And so forth. We don't disagree with any of the official conclusions in this case. The pilot definitely over stressed the airplane. And he definitely should have diverted to his alternate the instant the ice showed up.

"But our interest is in finding out why he made those mistakes in the hope that broader, more introspective knowledge will lead us to ways that can prevent similar recurrences.

"The sequence of events leading up to this tragedy might actually have begun as far back as when the Bonanza first arrived in Albuquerque. The family came from Omaha, approximately 1,000 feet above sea level, and landed at an elevation of 5,352 feet. That much difference usually makes people a bit lethargic, and takes them a few days to get used to. But the time it takes to fully adapt varies all over the map, depending on their age, their general health, the weather, the time of the year, and so forth.

"These people spent two days in Albuquerque and then went on to Santa Fe, another 1,000 feet higher. For sure, that didn't help them. In fact, it might have played a part in their first questionable decision: to make a 4-hour night flight home—something they had never done before. The son and daughter emphasized that they seldom flew cross-country at night, not even VFR. Yet, this was to be IFR and over mountainous terrain. It brings to mind that, in situations of temporary declining mental capability, judgment is the first thing to go.

"On the evening of the flight, everything seemed normal. They had a leisurely dinner, filed a correct flight plan, did a thorough preflight and took off without incident. Then, as they were climbing out, they all put on their oxygen masks and, as far as we know, were using the oxygen system correctly.

"For over an hour, all of the time they were at 13,000 feet, they continued using oxygen. When they descended to 9,000 feet, however, they shut off the system and removed their masks. Not because they were low on oxygen—they had a spare bottle—but because it was their usual practice to not use oxygen below 10,000 feet. Besides, those masks were uncomfortable and too much oxygen wasn't ideal either.

"So, for whatever their reasons, they sat for the next 2½ hours at 9,000 feet steadily becoming hypoxic. I say that without reservation because we know with certainty that the oxygen content of the air at 9,000 feet at night is the same as the oxygen level at 14 or 15,000 feet during daylight hours. The difference is even more pronounced during the winter months, and this accident occurred in November.

"Everything after they stopped taking oxygen points to classic hypoxia: the pilot's longer than intended nap; his lightheadedness after awakening; his euphoric feelings of self-confidence that resulted in the decision to let his copilot daughter continue sleeping because he felt he could handle the approach by himself; and finally his complete lack of judgment and loss of control under the pressures of the more-difficult-than-expected approach.

"Unfortunately, all of these known findings and the conclusions we draw from them are still in the realm of supposition. We can't prove by any tests or autopsies the physical presence of hypoxia or the lack of oxygen in the human body. It's all circumstantial, based on the best knowledge available. But that knowledge can't even be cited. Because to do so, without hard data, would create a field day for insurance companies who are dodging claims, and for opportunistic lawyers who are trying to nail them.

"So, even though thousands of cause-and-effect studies have been made that verify conclusively the damage done by hypoxia, until someone comes up with an accurate mechanical way of measuring blood oxygen levels, hypoxia will continue to be a silent killer of pilots. And we, the FAA and the NTSB can't do a thing about it."

Bob and Allison Sinclair (Conference call interview) "To say that we are upset over what we have learned since the accident would be a gross understatement, at best. We are angry, disgusted with the system and sick over the way we lost our parents.

"How could anyone, government or otherwise, deliberately withhold information that is so vital to general aviation safety?

"In our last conversation with the people at NASA, which was after they had processed the data Allison had given them, they told us why they were so sure it had to be hypoxia that was actually responsible for all of the official 'probable causes.' What a thing to find out!

"Since then, we have both done plenty of checking, including going through our old ground school course materials. Let me read you a quote from our latest workbook on the subject of oxygen usage: Quote—'At night, oxygen may be needed at lower altitudes for sustained flight' Period. End of quote. Then in an entirely different section, the one on FARs, there's a somewhat broader explanation. But to interpret all of it to learn that you for sure need oxygen at or above 5,000 feet at night is next to impossible.

"Now why is that? I mean, why can't there just be a clearly written set of rules—definite rules—that simply says in plain English: 'For sustained flight at night, use oxygen above 5,000 feet. For sustained flight during the day, use oxygen above 12,000 feet?'

"And then, there should be a whole chapter devoted to hypoxia and spatial disorientation so that unsuspecting pilots will at least know what it is and how dangerous it can be."

7

Night flight to nowhere

Preliminary report: April; Beech Baron; private pilot, multi- and single-engine land, instrument rating, 3,100 hours. The aircraft was destroyed in a forced landing after losing power during an IFR night flight from Hilton Head, South Carolina, to Poughkeepsie, New York. Investigators said the Baron and the pilot had made the flight "numerous times," but only once or twice before at night. The aircraft was at 2,000 feet, near Peekskill, New York, when the pilot reported the power loss. He was given radar vectors toward Danbury Municipal Airport in Danbury, Connecticut. The pilot reported the field in sight after descending below the clouds. Witnesses saw the Baron flying low about 4 miles west of the airport but heard no sound from the engines. They lost sight of the aircraft as it entered a right turn. The Baron crashed into the southern bank of the Titicus Reservoir, and the pilot and his two passengers were killed. Investigators said there was no evidence of any fuel spillage at the crash site. Only 1 gallon was found remaining in the right main tank, and less than ½ gallon in the left.

Further investigation revealed:
- The pilot filed his flight plan with "5½ hours of fuel on board" but, a short time before the flight, had 35 gallons drained from his full tanks to stay under gross.
- On the morning of the flight, a major weather system had begun moving toward the eastern seaboard from the west, much faster than forecast. In order to beat the weather, the pilot decided to leave Hilton Head in the late afternoon, instead of waiting for his originally planned departure the next morning.
- An extra passenger and substantial additional luggage were added to the flight. The decision to do so was made only a few hours before the earlier departure time.

- Although the pilot had made this trip several times each year, this was the first time in four years that it was scheduled at night.
- Departure was delayed 1½ hours by the pilot about an hour before the scheduled takeoff time.
- Winds aloft were less favorable than had been forecast, and the flight was 16 minutes behind its flight plan arriving in the destination area.
- Just before beginning his letdown, the pilot said he was behind his flight plan schedule and would like to descend to below the overcast so he could make a fuel stop, if necessary.

Official conclusion: Fuel exhaustion. Deliberately misfiled flight plan. Pilot error.

WEATHER NEWS WAS BAD when Dale Harrington, 58, and his wife, Pauline, 57, awoke on a late April morning. A major system, stretching all the way from a low-pressure hub centered over Toronto to the Gulf of Mexico, had begun moving east much faster than expected. Instead of arriving late the next day in the Hilton Head area, where the Harringtons were staying at the condo they had owned for the past 12 years, it would be there shortly after midnight—about 14 hours sooner than forecast. Worst yet, the long-range forecasts for the area were for continued wetter-than-normal and colder-than-normal weather, with no end in sight for the 5–10 day outlook period.

Dale and Pauline began making phone calls and decisions. It had been their plan to fly home to Poughkeepsie, New York, for a weekend wedding. Following that and one major business appointment, they would fly back to close up the condo for the season and then fly home with their housekeeper, Maria, who usually spent most of the winter with them in Hilton Head. The prospect of doing all of that in bad weather was not a happy one; thus, their fairly quick decision to close up the condo and leave that same evening. The need to rush and combine two trips in one was overshadowed by the direness of the impending weather and influenced by Maria, who wanted to return to New York early. Their plan had been to take a portion of their summer things home on the first trip and everything else on the next one. Now they also faced a weight and balance problem loading the Baron.

The departing threesome worked diligently. By midafternoon they had completed their packing. An hour later, they had turned everything off, contacted the condo management company, double-checked every item on their shutdown list and were out the door.

Dale had also taken the time to file a flight plan, his usual: IFR; 180 knots; 9,000 feet; Romeo equipped; Victor 1 to Coyle, direct Colts Neck, Victor 157 to Nyack, direct Papa Oscar Uniform; time en route 4 hours; fuel 5 hours and 30 minutes; three on board; light blue with black and white stripes.

Arriving at the airport after a somewhat hurried light supper, Dale eyeballed their more-than-ample luggage—nine pieces in all—and calculated the weight of three people, the luggage, and the fuel with full tanks. Whoops. Too much weight for a Baron, by about 200 pounds. The solution to the problem wasn't good because the airplane had been serviced and fully fueled the night before. But Dale wasn't about to take off 200 pounds over gross.

As soon as the fuel draining order was made to remove about 35 gallons, Dale amended his flight plan for a 1-hour later departure. But he did not change the fuel notation. He then loaded the luggage with extreme care, utilizing much of the backseat area—making sure that Maria would be comfortable—and did a thorough preflight. He had the time. Draining fuel on Friday afternoon at a resort area airport isn't something an FBO assigns his highest priority to.

Takeoff was at dusk, about half-an-hour later than Dale had hoped, but otherwise uneventful. The flight was also uneventful until it reached the Atlantic City, New Jersey, area where Dale got the news from flight watch that Poughkeepsie was now forecasting 500 overcast and 4. Not a problem, even though it had been only a possibility, but certainly not welcome. Dale didn't need a tight approach at 11:30 p.m. after a 4-hour flight and a very long day of packing and closing up the house in Hilton Head.

Another bit of bad news became apparent when Dale realized that they were 15 minutes or so behind schedule. He did a fast compute of his fuel and came up with 1:15 remaining, with about 50–55 minutes to go. A long way from an adequate fuel reserve. But Dale was going to his home airport and knew the approach and the surrounding terrain cold. And he had fudged before.

Crossing the Colts Neck VOR and turning onto Victor 157, Dale called New York Center with a request:

Dale "(Requesting descent) to underneath the overcast early, if possible."

Center (Bewildered by the request) "No can do . . . .. The whole New York area is running 5–700-foot ceilings, and you'll be practically overflying Newark and Teterboro Airports. Do you have a problem, sir?"

Dale "Negative on the problem. But our fuel burn has been higher than usual, and our tailwind wasn't as good as forecast. We may need to stop at Teterboro."

Center "Okay . . .. Descend to 4,000 and call Newark Approach now on 128.55. We'll leave you on file for Poughkeepsie. You can change your destination with approach.

Dale (On 128.55) "Newark Approach, . . . out of niner thousand descending to 4,000."

Newark Approach "Good evening . . .. Understand you may be landing Newark. Maintain 2,000. The altimeter is 29.89 inches and falling. You can plan on the 4 Right approach, sir. You're only 14 miles from GRITY. You can turn left now, if you'd like, and we can get you in right away."

Dale "We'll have too much trouble getting back out of Newark, sir. Teterboro's a better choice, but I'm not sure we'll need to land there, either. I'll have a better idea after we're level 2,000. Thanks anyway."

Newark Approach "Okay . . .. Stay with me for now. We'll be switching you to Teterboro as soon as you pass Newark. Let me know if you change your mind before then."

Dale "Wilco, Newark, and thanks again."

Newark Approach (Five minutes later) "Baron . . ., call Teterboro Approach now on 127.6. They're expecting you. Good evening, sir."

Dale (With both fuel gauges just beginning to brush the EMPTY marks) "Teterboro Approach, Baron . . . (at) 2,000."

Teterboro Approach "Baron . . ., this is Teterboro. Turn left heading 320 for the runway 6 ILS. That will take you right to DANDY. Cross DANDY at 2,000. Altimeter is 29.88 and holding."

Dale "Uh, we don't really need to land at Teterboro, sir. Our fuel should be fine. I'd appreciate a turn about 10 degrees left, though. That will take us to just outside the marker at Poughkeepsie and save us a few minutes."

Teterboro Approach "Okay on the turn . . .. You're cleared RNAV to the marker at Poughkeepsie. Please say your remaining fuel . . .."

Dale "Oh, about an hour, give or take 5 minutes. We'll be able to make Poughkeepsie and put this bird to bed with 45 minutes of petrol in the tanks."

Teterboro Approach "You're 60 miles from Poughkeepsie, sir. That's playing it pretty close."

Dale (Sounding disturbed) "We'll be okay, Teterboro. Thanks for worrying about us. And thanks for that turn."

Immediately after the controller cleared him RNAV to MEIER, the outer marker at Poughkeepsie, Dale entered the waypoint data while their conversation continued. After signing off, Dale began tracking the CDI needle, but he had forgotten to hit the waypoint mode ON button. Without realizing it, he was actually headed straight for the Kingston VOR.

Thirteen minutes later, with a 24-mile DME reading off Kingston, the Baron's right engine began sputtering. Dale sprang into action. He checked the fuel gauge first—the needle was in the middle of the EMPTY line—and then began working the throttle and mixture just as the engine coughed emphatically, twice, and quit. He feathered the prop first and then pulled the throttle and mixture levers all the way back.

While the engine was in the quitting process, and commanding all of Dale's attention, the airplane drifted off course to the right. Dale, of course, didn't notice it. But, the controller did. He had been keeping an eye on the Baron.

Approach "Baron . . ., this is Teterboro."

Dale (Very busy) "Stand by one, Teterboro. We've got an engine down."

Approach (Doing a fast assessment of Dale's situation) "Baron . . .., your closest airport is Danbury. If you turn right heading 085°, that will put your nose right on the active there. Stay with me for now. Danbury tower is closed."

Dale (After an interminable 15 seconds.) "Uh, okay, uh, turning 085°. Descending. How low did you say that ceiling was?"

Approach "Last report at Danbury was 700 feet, visibility 6 in haze, and the altimeter is 29.86 inches and steady. The airport is now 12 o'clock and 14 miles. Let me know when you have it in sight. We'll call ahead on the monitoring frequency to clear the traffic for you." (He immediately called on 119.4) "Attention all aircraft. There's a disabled Baron inbound to Danbury. Repeat: There's a disabled Baron inbound to Danbury, now 12 miles for runway 8."

Dale never acknowledged. He was busy flying his now single-engine airplane, reducing power on the remaining left engine for a 300 feet-per-minute descent, and looking out the window for a first glimpse of the ground.

It came as the Baron was coming through 1,200 feet, first out of the side window. Three seconds later, Dale had the runway—12 o'clock, about 8 or 9 miles. A sigh of relief.

Too soon. Just as he called approach to let them know of his sighting, the left engine began sputtering. 5 seconds and two quick pops later, it was dead. Dale's notification to the controller was terse: "We're going in."

The controller froze in his seat. He was speechless. He calmed himself as best he could. Finally, after several seconds, he responded in a choked voice: "Good luck . . .." Twelve seconds later, the Baron was off his screen.

Dale was frantic. He turned the gliding, descending Baron to the left and right hoping its landing lights would locate a suitable, flat piece of treeless terrain. It was not to be. At 200 feet above the rolling hills, he thought he spotted a stream or brook to the right and initiated a right turn to put his lights on it. He couldn't stop the turn.

The Baron kept on rotating and slammed into the southwestern bank of the Titicus Reservoir. That was the water Dale saw as he was lurching the Baron back and forth looking for a flat place to land. It was a good try, but the Baron didn't cooperate with one propeller feathered and the other windmilling. No one survived when the airplane impacted the ground.

Tom Bates, New York center "The whole center watched this airplane go down. We knew something was wrong when the first contact was made. The pilot's request made no sense. He was IFR, flying into known low-ceiling conditions, and yet he asked for permission to descend below the clouds.

"Then both Newark and Teterboro approach controllers tried to coax him to land. His tracking slip showed enough fuel, so they didn't think that was a problem. He just sounded confused, disoriented, and unable to continue the flight. They were handling him accordingly, in both cases giving him turns toward the ILS approach courses, which he refused.

"When he drifted slightly to the right of his requested RNAV course, the controller spotted it several minutes later but never had a chance to tell him about it. That was when he called in with his first engine out. At that point, it was a toss-up between several nearby airports that he could reach without a lot of maneuvering. Danbury fit the bill from where he was. The controller made the right choice.

"What we can't figure out is why this pilot apparently lied to everyone about his remaining fuel. He had to know he wouldn't make Poughkeepsie from where he was. I mean, three of our people practically sent up skyhooks after him, and he still persisted in it. Now I can understand why he might not have wanted to land at Newark. It's a busy airline airport, and private pilots don't tend to want to get mixed up with all that heavy metal.

"But this guy had been to Teterboro many times. And he was a very experienced pilot. So, it just doesn't add up. We think there must have been something wrong with him . . .. There's just no other way to account for his off-the-wall behavior."

NTSB representative "Accidents like this one never make any sense to us or anyone. An experienced pilot. Easy IFR. A well-equipped airplane in perfect condition. Familiar territory. Not much traffic. Ideal airports practically under his nose. Helpful on-the-ball controllers. Talk about nonaccident circumstances. It doesn't get any better than that.

"And yet, a tragic waste of three lives and a fine airplane. We couldn't find a thing. No alcohol. No drugs. No medications of any kind. Current medical. Current BFR. No restrictions on his ticket. Over 800 hours in his Baron. Plenty of actual IFR time. About as close to perfect as you could ask for.

"He wasn't even in a hurry. We found out later that they were just going home to bed. Whatever it was they had to do—a wedding or something—it wasn't till late the next day. So, we draw a blank. Another no-answer accident. It goes in the book as 'pilot error, fuel exhaustion,' with no further explanation available or required.

"But it's frustrating as hell. Here's a perfectly sound pilot who's been flying for years, on a trip he's made dozens of times, who suddenly goes bonkers for no apparent reason. That's scary. It makes you wonder if anyone is ever completely safe in an airplane."

Amy Harrington Bell, the Harrington's married daughter "We're still soul searching what could have happened. Dad was a very good and careful pilot who just didn't make mistakes like that. And from what we were told, that wasn't just a mistake!

"I mean, he lied to all of the controllers, starting with when he first filed his flight plan. He had no reason to do that. He wasn't rushing anywhere. He wasn't rushing to beat any weather or anything. But he did lie. The people who investigated the accident verified that. I mean, they had tapes of his conversations with the controllers. And the fuel gauges in the airplane were both on EMPTY and there wasn't any gasoline on the ground or in the airplane when they found it the next day. I mean, there just wasn't any doubt at all.

"But we can't figure out why he did it. He never did anything like that before. Something had to be wrong. But we and the experts don't know what it was. (Pause)

"It's such a shame that their lives have been wasted without an answer. I guess all we can hope for is that someone will find one eventually."

Mitch Greer, line manager, Poughkeepsie FBO "I'm not all that surprised it happened. Dale Harrington always ran that Baron down to damn near empty. Especially when he'd come back from South Carolina. That was where he went most of the time when he was going on a long trip. They owned a place down there.

"There were times I'd swear he was dead-sticking it up to the ramp. Then when we'd top his tanks, we'd think we were filling a corporate job or a commuter. I can't even remember him taking less than 50 or 60 gallons ever. Seemed like he always knew exactly how much he had left and played a game with himself over it. Like he was trying to see how close he could come without hitting bottom. I don't think he ever did. Until the last time. I guess that's all it takes.

"Other than that, he was careful. His airplane got good maintenance. It was always in the hangar and washed and waxed regularly. And he flew all the time. Sometimes just pattern work and approaches. Most of his cross-country stuff was to his home down south. He'd fly up and back from there at least a dozen times a year.

"If you asked me to rate Dale up against our other twin pilots here, I'd have to say he was one of the better ones. But I'm not a pilot, so I'm really not in a position to know for sure. I just know everybody liked him a lot, and things haven't been the same around here without him."

NTSB representative "We spent a bit more time and effort on this accident than we normally do. It was clearly fuel exhaustion, but under strange circumstances. This was no low-time, inexperienced pilot in a rented airplane.

"The toxicology tests came up negative on everything. Not even a trace of alcohol or drugs or any medications. He wasn't a smoker, either. So, we interviewed a lot of people from his family, from the airport—you know, people who knew him, or flew with him. Really, anyone who could give us a clue as to why he acted so crazy that night.

"What we came up with is a sort of dual personality. On the one hand, he was a good IFR twin pilot who took his flying seriously. But he also had some quirks. Like never filling his tanks until they were under a quarter full. Or always filing his flight plans with more or less fuel than there actually was—sometimes much more. And even bragging about it when he'd bring his Baron home almost on fumes. That certainly wasn't consistent with the kind of pilot he was when it came to flight proficiency and discipline.

"When we got all through, we kind of threw our hands up in the air because nothing about this accident made any sense at all. Here was a wealthy, conservative, healthy man in his late fifties who had everything to live for. He was a proficient pilot with a high-performance airplane all paid for, by the way—a happy marriage and successful children. And with dozens of close friends and business associates. He was active in his church, too. So, why he did something as utterly stupid as he did—and persisted in it the way he did, actually continuing the lie to three different controllers who were trying to help him—well, I can't think of any reason or explanation, and neither can anyone else we've talked to. Whatever secret he had is buried with him, and now it's between him and his maker. I doubt if we will ever know."

John Harrington, Dale's younger brother and business partner

"We got so many conflicting reports after the accident that we didn't know who to believe. Especially from that manager at the airport.

"They were able to show us that his fuel orders were always for 60 or more gallons, but I understand that's not so unusual for the kind of airplane Dale flew. I think they said it held well over 100 gallons.

"Then those reports from the FAA. They only showed that he was being offered help he didn't think he needed. I don't see anything so unusual about that. I'm sure he had more flying experience than any of those controllers he was talking to. And he'd certainly know if he was in trouble of any kind.

"One of the things we're not so sure of is the fuel gauges. The investigators said they were both on EMPTY. But that airplane was such a mess, there was no way on earth for them to prove that those needles weren't knocked that way from the crash. They also said there wasn't any fuel on the ground or in the fuel tanks. But, hell, they didn't find them until the next day. By then, any fuel there was would have all run into the ground and evaporated. That many hours later, you wouldn't even be able to smell it.

"Then there's the possibility that something broke in one or both of the engines, or in the fuel lines or something. They can't prove that either. Those engines must have looked like scrambled eggs after a crash like that.

"So, what have you got? A thorough investigation that winds up in a damnation of my brother without any proof of anything. I call that a bureaucratic nightmare and an insult to my brother and his family."

NASA representative "This sounds like a complicated case because there are dozens of conflicting elements. Yet, it might be that all of these complex parts came unglued because of one or two factors that screwed up the machinery.

"I believe that because of the experience level and maturity of this pilot you can discount many of what seem like obvious contributors to this accident. For example, he knew exactly how many gallons he wanted drained from the airplane before takeoff. Then he had to know how much fuel reserve he would need upon arrival because he'd made the same trip as many as 100 times. And things like being rushed, or careless, or filing the wrong flight plan—even though he didn't change the fuel notation, probably because he didn't think it was important enough to bother with—none of those really made any difference.

"Then there's the issue about the fuel gauges. Our assessment would be that because he is reported to have run his tanks almost dry several times, that he knew, or thought he knew, exactly how much fuel he had remaining by looking at his fuel gauge needles. They aren't all that accurate but they usually are very consistent. And if he had run them to the brink so many times, he could relate what the needles were telling him to what was in the tanks. Close enough to satisfy himself anyway.

"As you can see, this might not be a simple fuel exhaustion, pilot error accident after all. It might be something far different. Like a broken something in the airplane that leaked fuel. Or a pilot who was confronted by an unexpected change or two in something and then found himself being badgered—in his opinion—by several well-intended but possibly overbearing controllers. A combination of both of those could have complicated what might have otherwise been a routine flight.

"And then there's the possibility that the 9,000-foot altitude for 3 plus hours at night could have had an effect. That is definitely more like a probability. For sure it had to have had some negative influence on his manual dexterity, his mental quickness and alertness and, most of all, on his judgment. It would also tend to explain his unusual, bizarre behavior, which would have been a normal by-product of hypoxia. But it can't be pinpointed as the sole cause of this accident.

"If you take everything together, though, including his strange quirk about pushing his fuel reserves to the limit, it would tend to explain why he so casually declined the offers to land at close-by, familiar airports. It was as if he had decided well in advance that he wouldn't need to.

"In conclusion then, it's obvious that this was not a simple fuel exhaustion accident by a dummy who couldn't calculate; or a pilot-error situation by some low-time, inexperienced pilot who didn't know what he was doing. This is the most disturbing kind of an accident because it happened to an ideal pilot in ideal equipment and under circumstances that were completely familiar to him.

"Perhaps because of his quirk that made him an accident waiting to happen [fuel management] or because of hypoxia—none of the overt signs of which he exhibited, by the way—or the several complications that were thrust upon him, are what caused this accident. In combination they certainly could have. But he's dead. So we'll never know for sure."

Author comment All of the interviews and reports in this case were cross-distributed to the contributing governmental parties. It would be an enlightening experience to go through the whole process again to see if any of them had now changed their opinions.

Short of that, it seems apparent that the responsible government agencies will have continuing differences in their conclusions of the probable causes of fuel exhaustion accidents. And all with reasonable justification.

8

Smoking up
a storm

Preliminary report: September; Piper Aztec; commercial pilot, multi- and single-engine land, 2,075 hours. After breaking up in a line of thunderstorms during a VFR flight, the aircraft crashed without its left wing and tail, killing the pilot. He was returning home to Shreveport, Louisiana, after dropping off two passengers in Baton Rouge, Louisiana, 180 miles away. The pilot was apparently receiving flight following from ATC. About 30 miles from home, he reported that he was descending out of 12,500. The controller issued a vector to the airport, advised of heavy precipitation ahead and instructed the pilot to maintain VFR. He also recommended a precautionary landing. Later, the controller asked the pilot about his flight conditions and (the pilot reported) IMC with rain and heavy turbulence. Radio contact was lost shortly thereafter. Witnesses said there was a severe thunderstorm in the area when they saw the Aztec crash into a farm building and burn.

Further investigation revealed:

- The pilot often bragged about making extensive use of a Stormscope in the Aztec even though he did not have an instrument rating.
- Recomputing the Aztec's fuel supply, the pilot might not have had enough to deviate around the line of thunderstorms and still make it to his destination.
- Despite the fact that he was a heavy smoker, the pilot preferred to fly at the highest VFR altitudes. There was no oxygen on board.
- The pilot had recently flunked an insurance physical due to high blood pressure. As a result, for five months prior to the flight he had been taking Tenormin, a common prescription medication that reduces elevated blood pressure. He was due for his FAA flight physical in late November.

Official conclusion: Deliberate VMC into IMC. Loss of control due to structural failure in a severe thunderstorm. Possible physical impairment due to unapproved medication. Pilot error.

A VERY PLEASANT TWO WEEKS of summer break had just ended for Bonnie Caldwell, 20, and it was time for her and her school roommate, Ellen Mack, also 20, to head back to LSU in Baton Rouge, Louisiana. Ellen had spent the last week of the break with the Caldwells. Bonnie's father, Hank, 53, had agreed to fly the girls back to school in the family's Piper Aztec.

Their departure from Shreveport Regional Airport was the usual hustle and bustle of fueling the airplane, loading the girls' luggage, checking weather, and doing a thorough preflight. Hank was extra methodical in dealing with all of the airplane items because he was also explaining everything to Ellen, who had never before flown in anything smaller than a 727. She was impressed.

She was even more impressed when Bonnie climbed into the left front seat and began turning knobs and switches. Bonnie was a multi-engine instrument pilot who had aspirations of flying for a major airline. Ellen knew that. But the sight of her roommate making preparations about to fly came as a shock; she was visibly taken aback.

Bonnie was more than a competent pilot, with nearly 700 hours of flight time—mostly in the Aztec—under her belt. She planned to have over 1,000 hours in two more years, part of which she would get by working as a charter pilot for Tom Whitney, whose company operated out of Shreveport Downtown Airport. Then she would be ready for a commuter job. In that mind-set, she was meticulous and perfectly disciplined about everything she did in an airplane.

Her mind-set was the exact opposite of her father, who flew like an old barnstormer. Hank had been flying since he was 20. He got his commercial license shortly after his private, started on his instrument rating and quit after convincing himself that he wouldn't use it enough to stay current. But he had the good sense to equip his airplane for IFR flight and knew how everything worked. Well, sort of. He took liberties with abandon and occasionally got himself close to trouble.

His ace-in-the-hole was a recently installed Stormscope that, as he loved to brag, "keeps the thunder out of my storms." It's a very useful instrument, especially in thunderstorm-prone Louisiana. But Hank, as a VFR pilot, should never have been close enough to a thunder bumper to need it. Bonnie bawled him out about that every time she heard him bragging. So, he stopped telling her.

But Bonnie knew her father. Take this flight, for instance. Hank had called flight service to get a weather briefing. But he didn't file a flight plan. He never did. Bonnie, on the other hand, knowing that her father shunned regimentation, called flight service on her own and filed an IFR flight plan for the trip to Baton Rouge. She always did. Even when it was VFR. Like today.

She also found out from flight service that there was a good possibility of some heavy weather moving into the Shreveport area later that day; thus, their morning departure so that her father would make it home before the weather did.

Taxiing out to Runway 23 for a southwest departure, Bonnie took her IFR flight plan from Shreveport Clearance: "As filed, maintain 2,000, expect 7,000 in five minutes, all the MOAs are active, fly the runway heading and call departure on 119.9."

Two minutes after takeoff and still heading 230°, Hank began complaining to his daughter about what he felt was wrong with IFR in good weather: "They take you out of the way to put you on their damned airways and waste a lot of time and gas." He wasn't any happier when departure turned them over to center and they were given a turn to 170°. Hank wanted a heading of 140°, which would have taken them more directly to Baton Rouge, but through the then active MOA. That wouldn't have bothered Hank.

But Bonnie ignored her father's grousing and flew Victor 566 all the way to MOTTO intersection, which was the initial approach fix for Baton Rouge. It was a comfortable, routine flight at 7,000 feet. Ellen loved it.

Saying goodbye to the two girls, Hank started back toward the Aztec but then changed his mind and headed instead for the restaurant in the main terminal. He had also ignored Bonnie's advice about buying some extra fuel for the trip home because it cost 11 cents more per gallon than at Shreveport. He appreciated her concern but "it ain't her money."

An hour or so later, Hank made his way back to the Aztec, started up without a preflight—he had already done one of those earlier—cranked up the engines and called the tower for clearance to go. Six minutes later he was off the ground, turning to a 300° heading and climbing to 12,500 feet, his favorite altitude. He liked to be up high.

Because he knew the MOAs were active, Hank asked for and was getting flight following service. It was always a good idea in Louisiana in the summertime. Thunderstorms could pop up faster than crocodiles. So, Hank usually used the service and appreciated it. Today was no exception.

The Aztec's ground track ran directly between two municipal airports, which meant that Hank was on a straight-line course to Shreveport Regional. He looked ahead at a formidable cloud buildup stretching from 10–2 o'clock across his field of vision. It was going to be a real banger and he confirmed it by checking his Stormscope, now a kaleidoscope of dots that kept intensifying as he flew closer to the weather ahead.

Hank looked left and right and straight ahead for a hole to head for in the looming storm system. Nothing was apparent. But checking the Stormscope showed a clearer area at his 1 o'clock position. Looking all the way left and then right, Hank realized that he would probably need to fly more than 60 miles in either direction to get around this monster. A look at his fuel gauges told him the 120-mile round trip to home wouldn't work.

He decided to call the flight following controller to get additional information before making a choice. What he really wanted was more options.

Hank "Houston Center . . .. Wonder if you can give me any updates on the buildup I'm looking at? Seems like it's 30 miles or so dead ahead."

Houston ". . . This is Houston. We don't go up quite that far, sir. We're showing some of it as far west as Lufkin and running northeast almost to Monroe. But you'll have to call Fort Worth Center on 127.7 to get a better look at it. We have a lot of airplanes doing 180s in that general vicinity, sir. Must be pretty nasty up around Shreveport."

Hank (Signing off and calling Fort Worth) "Fort Worth Center, Aztec . . . at twelve-five, coming up from the vicinity of Pineville, heading three-zero-zero and looking at a mess up ahead. Wonder if you could help me pick my way through that stuff? I'm inbound to Shreveport."

Fort Worth Center "We're showing a line of thunderstorms 100 miles long and 20 miles wide running southwest to northeast. Moving southeast at 7 with tops running over 50,000 feet. We haven't had anybody attempt to penetrate it, sir. Our jet traffic is going around it. All the rest are settin' down and waitin' it out."

Hank "(The Stormscope shows) a clear area at about 1 o'clock. Out the window looks okay, too. You got anything on it?"

Fort Worth "We have some areas opening up some, but they close up pretty quick. Suggest you head back to Pineville or, if you'd like, Natchitoches is still looking okay. That would put you closer to Shreveport."

Hank "The area I'm looking at is looking better as I get closer to it. If that system is only 20 miles wide, I think I can get through it okay. I'll have a good fix on it from my echoes."

Fort Worth "Okay . . .. Right now a heading of 320° will take you to the clearest area we're showing. That must be the one you're looking at. Maintain VFR. And we'd appreciate a PIREP, sir."

Hank "Wilco, center. We're out of twelve-five now for five grand. Thanks for your help."

Hank turned the Aztec's nose right toward the 3-mile-wide hole he was looking at. Sure enough, the DG was showing 320°. They got it right. In the meantime, the Stormscope was starting to look not quite as clear on the back side of the hole Hank was heading for. But he ignored the subtle warning and kept boring in on what looked to him to be a clear track through the storm system. Once on the other side of it, he'd be happy to give center a PIREP.

Ten miles closer, center radar began showing the northwest side of the storm line closing up. As the Aztec reached the open area, Hank's Stormscope was filling in fast. The controller called immediately:

Fort Worth "Aztec . . .. We're showing the hole you're in beginning to close up. Say your flight conditions."

Hank "Looks like we're gettin' in it. Bouncin' pretty hard." (Broken conversation) "About to do a 180 . . . holdin' on . . . trying to stay level 5 . . . can't . . .."

Hank's transmission stopped in midsentence. A violent updraft wracked the Aztec. Hank fought the controls, trying to hold the aircraft at 5,000 feet. It was a mistake. He should have let the monster storm take him wherever it wanted to. Another powerful thermal hit the Aztec broadside. Hank was fighting to keep the Aztec level and upright. It was hopeless. The storm was going to win.

A third and final bone-crushing funnel tore at the Aztec and ripped its left wing and tail. The force of it threw Hank against the left side of the cabin, then forward, putting overpowering pressure on the controls. The combination of forces tore off the left wing and half the tail. The Aztec began to tumble out of control. Down. Like a falling rock.

An ordinary farm storage building took the full brunt of the meteor-like Aztec hurtling toward the ground. Hank never saw it coming. He was either unconscious or dead from the slamming he took.

The Fort Worth Center controller noted the exact spot where the Aztec disappeared from his scope. It took him three tries to put a tiny piece of marking tape on the screen because his hands were shaking out of control.

FAA accident investigator "There wasn't much left of the airplane or the pilot. We found the left wing over a mile away. Part of the tail showed up close to the wing. So we figure they must have come loose at about the same time.

"It never burned, probably because there wasn't much fuel. Maybe 15–20 gallons at most. The panel got badly mashed up, but what we found looked normal. And the engine was running okay. The prop chewed up the wall and roof of that storage building like it was running at least at cruise. Best we could tell, wasn't a thing wrong with the airplane before it got tore up.

"People who saw it go in reported it was raining like crazy. Blowing real hard, too. Must have been one of our usual thunder blasters. We get maybe 10 or 12 of them a year. Come up out of nowhere, blow everything away, and then they're gone like they never happened.

"Funny this guy got caught in it. More often happens to someone who's not from around here. Local folks know these storms and have the good sense to stay away from them. We thought maybe something else was wrong, like he was drunk or sick or maybe on drugs. But the tests came back showing only some blood pressure medicine he was taking. Shouldn't have made him goofy enough to mess with a storm like that.

"Anyway, our report went in pretty simple: Airplane okay. Pilot questionable. Thunderstorm devastating. It got written up real official, but that was the gist of it. Nothing more to say about it. Just the same old message: Stay the hell out of thunderstorms."

Bonnie Caldwell "I knew something was wrong even before my father went down because I called home about 2½ hours after he dropped us off. At the time I didn't know he had stopped for lunch and hadn't taken off until almost 2 hours later.

"I had purposely scheduled the trip so he would get back before the thunderstorms were expected to show up. He knew that. So I can't understand why he spent so much time in Baton Rouge. We even saw him walking toward the airplane. He must have changed his mind at the last minute.

"The accident investigator from the FAA told me the radio transcripts were pretty normal. My father didn't seem to be impaired in any way. About the only thing they thought was unusual was the way he referred to his 'echoes.' I knew immediately that he had to be talking about the Stormscope. That was my father's favorite instrument. He was sure it protected him.

"I, on the other hand, was sure it was going to get him in trouble and I used to tell him so. Because he used it wrong. It is not an instrument to help you pick your way through a thunderstorm. It merely tells you where the electrical discharges are coming from so you can avoid a thunderstorm even if you can't see it visually. Like when you're IFR and the cells are embedded.

"But my father thought otherwise, like he did about a number of things. He flew too high. He flew in weather he shouldn't have. He flew like he owned the system. We used to argue about his attitude all the time and wind up calling each other names. Mine was 'Miss Prissy.' He knew it upset me but that's how he would end every argument.

"He also had some idiosyncrasies: Because he got a fuel discount from the FBO, he always left Shreveport with full tanks, even if he knew he was over gross. Then, on the way back from anywhere, if he had to buy fuel, he would buy as little as possible. Just because he would be spending a few pennies more per gallon. Can you imagine? Here was a man with a good-size business risking his life over nonsense.

"But that's how my father was. Everything in his life was always right on the edge. Getting the most out of every deal. Paying as little as possible, even by pennies. It was like a game with him. He loved the challenge and the excitement of it."

Ellen Mack "I can't tell you how surprised I was when Connie got into the pilot's seat in Shreveport. I knew she was a pilot because that's all she ever talks about, but I never thought her father would actually let her fly his airplane. He was so proud when he showed it to me that I didn't think he'd ever let another human being even touch it.

"I got over the initial shock real fast and then I was impressed that he had so much confidence in Connie. But that didn't last very long, because he started right in complaining about every single thing she did. It really upset her, what with me being there and all. Seemed like he was showing off or playing games with her. I'm not a pilot, so I wouldn't know the difference. But it wasn't right for Connie.

"After we took off, he never let up. I remember him saying that she was flying too stiff, too much by the numbers, or something like that. He said she had to loosen up or she'd never have any fun doing it. By then, she wasn't even listening to him anymore. And neither was I. I was just enjoying myself. It was a great experience.

"When we left Mr. Caldwell at the Baton Rouge Airport, Connie told me how worried she was about him flying. At first, I thought she was talking about his high blood pressure. But she made it real clear that she was concerned about the way he flew. His attitude and all. She was afraid he wasn't safe. (Pause) Maybe that was just a premonition or something."

NTSB representative "You'd think that with all the accident reports that are put in the various flying magazines that every pilot in the world would know enough to stay away from thunderstorms. But every year, we get dozens of airplanes to haul away after they were torn to pieces by these monster storms.

"It really makes you wonder how a pilot with as much experience as this one had could wind up in the middle of a squall line that big. He saw it from 50 or more miles away. The controller told him how big it was and advised to land and wait it out. But he flew into it anyway, like it wasn't going to hurt him. Like he was bigger than God.

"We came up with quite a profile on Mr. Henry Caldwell. He was a very successful businessman with a happy marriage and an abundance of friends. Sharp. Energetic. All the right adjectives. Yet, when it came to flying, he was a brinksman, a 53-year-old daredevil who got his greatest kicks making hangar talk about his close calls and near misses. Not quite a Jeckyl and Hyde, but close.

"His behavior leading up to this accident was strange, to say the least. So much so, that we spent quite a bit of time checking some things out. Like the medication he was on—Tenormin. It's a blood pressure reducer and not approved for flying without special permission from the FAA. His doctor knew that and claims he told the pilot where and how to go about getting approval. But the FAA never heard from him or the doctor, and Mr. Caldwell's wife said she was unaware of it being a problem. The doctor sent in the pilot's chart showing a detailed notation, but that could have been just to cover his backside.

"Tenormin, by the way, shouldn't have had any effect on his behavior. It's really a blood thinner that is more of a problem for IFR pilots because it can increase their susceptibility to vertigo. In this instance, he probably did experience considerable disorientation, but that wouldn't have been a factor in the accident. Just being in that thunderstorm was the problem, and the Tenormin didn't put him there.

"Next we found out that he was a heavy smoker, more than two packs a day. So we thought he might have been diagnosed with cancer or emphysema and not told his wife and family about it, and was covering up a suicide. But that never went anywhere. His doctor was a close personal friend and assured us he would have known about it.

"There were a number of other things like that: His business was fine, no problems. He owned the airplane free and clear, and his house, too. So he was in good shape financially. And, as far as we can tell, his family life was equally successful. In general then, an all around solid citizen.

"His wife and daughter told us about a couple of his peculiarities: That he was cheap as a clam, even though he had plenty of money. By the way, the Aztec was beautifully maintained and had lots of expensive equipment on it. But he also had a fetish about his fuel cost. He had a deal with the FBO at Shreveport for a bulk discount of some kind. Then he wouldn't buy fuel anywhere else unless there was no way to avoid doing so. To the point where he would fly back into Shreveport pretty close to empty because he hated the idea of spending a few cents more per gallon with another operator.

"When we got through checking out our own hunches, and all of the possibilities we could think of, we were really nowhere. We couldn't explain in any provable way how this individual's complexities could have ganged up on him and caused him to kill himself. It wasn't suicide. It wasn't stupidity. It wasn't alcohol or drugs or medications. It wasn't lack of experience or training. But with all the 'wasn'ts' we could eliminate, we still couldn't come up with any reasonable probable causes for this accident.

"You hate to give up when you think you're so close to striking gold. By that I mean a direct cause-and-effect situation where there is something important to learn. But it just wasn't meant to be. This accident goes into the record on only the facts of what happened, without any real probable causes. We know what he did. I doubt if we'll ever know why."

NASA representative "Every once in awhile we run into a set of circumstances that look like the gateway to the fountain of knowledge. Provable facts. Direct substance ingestion. Information coming from a dozen directions. What more could a researcher or accident investigator ask for?

"But when the smoke clears—zilch. One fact cancels out another. Possible conclusions lead nowhere. Clues are all blind alleys. So you take your licking in stride and give up.

"We were about ready to give up on this one. And believe me, NASA doesn't like to give up on anything. But then, as luck would have it, someone came up with the bright idea that this may have been a mental preconditioning problem complicated by an unusual blend of circumstances.

"Let me explain that a little. You have undoubtedly heard of a behavior analysis, or an aptitude profile. Those are often used for recruiting people for certain kinds of jobs. To make sure they have compatible personalities and skills for the work they will be doing. Outgoing for salespeople. Dominating and demanding for executives. Passive for administrators. And so forth.

"We used to think those traits were permanent, genetic, almost like fingerprints. But enough exceptions have been studied to disprove that theory completely. In fact, some of the most successful personality adaptations have been crossovers. In business. In science. In government.

"What that tells us is that preconditioning may be more important than inherited personality, because it can change personality—for better or for worse. In other words, it's a powerful force. Something we had better understand.

"One of the things we have learned is that preconditioning can block out other influences and distort logic. If you try something that has frightened you, and it doesn't hurt you, you are less afraid of it. Repeat it a hundred times and you're not afraid of it at all. That's preconditioning in simple terms.

"Now take something more complex than that. Like a pilot who is continuing to venture with each hurdle of proficiency in flight training and experience. Pretty soon, venturing becomes less and less frightening, and more and more challenging. The fear is replaced by the excitement, by the exhilaration of accomplishment until venturing becomes a precondition all by itself. Then, given enough successes and not enough failures, the expectation of success begins to completely overshadow the fear of failure or danger. And finally, confidence becomes overconfidence and fear is for the nonadventurous, for the guys who haven't been there before.

"If you apply this scenario to Mr. Caldwell, you can quickly identify the reasons for his seemingly dual personality. In business, at home, socially—a straitlaced, successful trendsetter. Because that was his preconditioning—what everyone had grown to expect of him, and what he consequently grew to expect of himself.

"Now put this same personality in an airplane. He obviously didn't or couldn't apply himself to flying with the same diligence as he did to other parts of his life, or he would have had an instrument rating. After all, he saw to it that his daughter did. But he wasn't the kind of person who accepted failure or nonaccomplishment easily. His preconditioned response was to compensate—to be able to fly as successfully, but another way. Without an instrument rating.

"His Stormscope was part of that process. It could bring him, a VFR pilot, as close to killer weather as radar could bring an IFR pilot.

What an equalizer! But in his mind it was more than that. It completely obliterated any fear or respect he had for thunderstorms.

"Now, having identified this loaded gun, add the other ingredients: He was on medication that loosened him up at least a little. He spent an hour at 12,500 feet. The effects of that on a heavy smoker had to be somewhat debilitating. And then the worst thing: He had just been a passenger on an IFR trip flown by his daughter and she had impressed the hell out of her roommate. Not easy for a mover and shaker like Henry Caldwell to watch and not be able to match or beat.

"Then he got some bad breaks: The storm ahead had some visible openings in it that both his Stormscope and the controller's radar confirmed. It must have made him proud and confident that his airborne instrument was showing the same readings as the government's sophisticated and very expensive radar. At that moment, his Stormscope became his security blanket. He was ready to tackle that thunderstorm.

"So much so, that when the controller suggested a precautionary landing, it was almost an insult to him. In his mind, to land would have been to back away from the same storm that every other VFR and most IFR pilots were running away from. But not him. He had his Stormscope and his opening. He was as sure of success as he was indifferent to the danger.

"The rest of this tragedy is in the record book. Hard facts. But our suppositions, all of which are the result of serious study and investigation (are never seen by pilots). That's a shame because the 'possibility' I just described is the most likely 'probable cause' of this accident. We're convinced of it because we've seen hundreds of cases where this same kind of preconditioning has led to this same kind of disaster."

Author comment The NTSB and NASA usually agree on the hard facts of any accident investigation and seldom disagree very much on their speculations and suppositions. But their communications to the public differ widely. The NTSB is limited primarily to hard facts. NASA is restrained by confidentiality.

In this case, it is interesting to note the similarities in their underlying attitudes, even though their statements are quite different. The NTSB is frustrated because they are unable to identify what caused this very experienced pilot flying a high-performance airplane to commit a mistake that even a fledgling pilot in a two-seater probably would not have made. But NASA, convinced almost beyond doubt that preconditioning was the primary culprit, is equally frustrated because they haven't been able to convince anyone else, not even the NTSB.

Thunderstorm-related accidents tend to involve fairly high-time pilots almost exclusively. Lesser pilots have apparently not yet had enough experience to develop disdain and disrespect for nature's most destructive weather phenomenon. Statistically a pilot will develop the disdain and disrespect after logging 1,500 hours, which seems to be the crossover point.

NASA hopes to head them off with documented communications about their studies into the ways that human factors lead to accidents—the "why's" behind the causes. The NTSB expects to accomplish the same thing by expanding its investigations beyond the hard facts so that pilots will be encouraged to constantly think seriously about accident prevention and make it a routine, automatic part of their flying.

Because NASA and the NTSB are probably right about their divergent approaches, both of which seem to be effective, it would undoubtedly benefit everyone greatly if they could find ways to work more closely together.

9

The bird hunters of Texas

Preliminary report: November; Cessna Skywagon; student pilot, single-engine land, 31 hours. The pilot and two passengers were killed instantly and the aircraft was destroyed after crashing in Palo Duro Canyon State Park, southeast of Amarillo, Texas. A third passenger survived the accident but died nine days later. There was no evidence of airframe or engine malfunction. A witness had reported seeing an aircraft matching the description of the Skywagon flying about 50–75 feet above the ground and maneuvering.

The flight had originally departed solo from Tradewind Airfield in Amarillo, stopped to pick up the three passengers at Rockwell Field in Canyon, Texas, and then flew directly to the state park. A full case of beer was found aboard the aircraft, 14 cans of which had apparently been consumed during the flight. Also aboard the Skywagon were four shot guns, and a large quantity of live shells and spent shell casings were scattered throughout the wreckage. Toxicology checks of the occupants noted blood alcohol levels of 0.153–0.178 percent, the pilot's being the lowest.

Further investigation revealed:

- The unlicensed student pilot discontinued his flight training 10 months prior to the accident, but was able to rent the Skywagon after an elaborate ruse involving a fictitious logbook that showed him with more than 700 hours of flight time, mostly cross-country. He had a current 3rd class medical and claimed to have lost his license certificate. He was able to pass a checkride after 3 hours of instruction by the FBO owner of the aircraft.
- Indications are that the pilot and these same passengers had flown together several times, drinking alcohol and shooting birds from the aircraft while in flight.

- The pilot's driver's license had been suspended and his car was impounded four months prior to the accident, following his third DUI arrest and conviction. Under court supervision, he was enrolled in a rehabilitation program and had not driven a motor vehicle since.
- Seconds before he lost control of the aircraft, the pilot and the left rear seat passenger fired their shotguns at a large bird. Shotgun pellets from one or both of the guns struck the outer portion of the left wing and tore open a gaping hole.

Official conclusion: Unauthorized low flight and buzzing. Poor judgment. Impairment due to alcohol. Failure to maintain flying speed. Loss of control. Pilot error.

AT THE AGE OF 29, Billie Lee Riggs could best be described as a no-account kid who refused to grow up. He and his crew of friends, all in their mid 20s, were known around Amarillo as hell-raisers. Few of them worked regular jobs. All of them drank heavily.

On the morning of the flight, three of Billie's regulars—Dexter Swift, Sonny Martin and Lonnie Brewster—loaded a case of beer and two six-packs of malt liquor, plus four shotguns and over 100 shells into Dexter's beat up panel truck. They headed south out of Amarillo toward Canyon, Texas, and stopped at Rockwell Field, a private airport with a 4,000-foot sod runway.

Meanwhile, Billie had another friend drive him to Tradewind Airport on the south side of Amarillo and drop him off at the flight office where Billie usually rented a Cessna Skywagon. He had called ahead, and the airplane was waiting for him on the ramp, right out in front of the flight office.

Unbeknown to the FBO, Billie was not a licensed pilot. He had a total of about 30 hours of on-again-off-again flight training that ended nearly a year ago when he moved from Lubbock to Amarillo, following his divorce. When he first showed up at the FBO, Billie presented a logbook that he had carefully falsified, showing himself with about 700 hours of flying time. His friends had signed off in the log for fake checkrides and even a BFR, using FAA certificate numbers that were really serial numbers from dollar bills—it had been great fun preparing the log at the Bronco Bar. Billie also had showed the FBO his valid medical from 14 months prior, but gave the excuse that he had lost his pilot license when his wallet was misplaced during his move from Lubbock. The FBO, not unhappy to rent his vintage Skywagon for $95 an hour, was more than willing to check Billie out in it—"However long it takes"—when Billie pealed off $400 in cash in advance. It took the better part of 3 hours for the checkride, after which the FBO deemed him competent to fly the Skywagon. That was almost 4 months ago.

Billie paid the cashier $500 in cash, as usual, to rent the airplane for the whole day. They would settle up for the actual hours flown and the layover time when he returned. Having made the same arrangement several times before, the cashier handed Billie the keys to the airplane and signed him out on the flight register, hardly noticing that Billie's eyes were glassy. He had already had his first two drinks earlier that morning.

Wasting no time, Billie did a cursory preflight, certain that the fuel attendant had checked everything out for him. Then he handed the attendant the usual $5 tip and climbed aboard. Less than 5 minutes later—his runup was also abbreviated—Billie was lifting off of Runway 17 and turning left to an easterly heading. He flew east until he was about 7 miles from the airport—far enough to be out of sight—and then turned southwest. Ten minutes later he made an uneventful landing at Rockwell Airport and taxied up to the remote area where Dexter's panel truck was parked. Billie's friends had arrived 10 minutes before he did. Over the past four months, this had become a well-rehearsed weekly routine.

It took 3 minutes to load the cooler of beer, the shotguns, and the shells onto the Skywagon. It took another hour to polish off the dozen cans of malt liquor. Now they were taking their time. Waiting for the strong alcohol content of the malt liquor to condition their already addled brains for the lunacy they were about to undertake: Bird hunting from a flying airplane.

Canyon, Texas police officer, Willis Fuller "Ah got called to the airport after they was there about an hour. Seems like this same group of dudes was usin' the place like an outdoor beer garden, or somethin'. Made the airport folks real nervous havin' people drinkin' out there like that.

"Ah drove up to where the airplane was parked next to their truck to shoo 'em out a there. But the pilot told me he had flown in to pick up the three guys and had to wait for the airplane to cool down before restartin' it. He said somethin' 'bout a cooler wasn't workin' right and it could blow the engine out if it was started hot. Ah checked that out with the airport folks, and they said it was possible.

"The pilot also said he never drank, 'cause you can't drink and fly.' He didn't look too good, but ah never did see him drink anythin'. But they all looked to me like they was plenty wrung out, and they acted like it, too. Even asked me to have a beer with them. Real friendly. But ah just stuck to business, told them to pick up the cans and leave the place like they found it.

"If ah'd a had a breath-o-lizer unit, ah'd a had that pilot breathe into it. But ah didn't, so he didn't, and ah guess we'll never know if he really was drunk before they took off. Sure did seem to me like he was.

"Anyway, even if ah'd a had a breath-o-lizer, it wouldn't've made no difference. We don't have jurisdiction over pilots or airplanes. Only things with wheels on 'em. So, I finally just told 'em to git. And they did."

Hurried in their departure from Rockwell Airport by an unfriendly local police officer, the foursome took off and headed straight for Palo Duro Canyon State Park, never getting higher than 200 feet agl. But rather than going directly to the state park, they made several diversions to buzz people and anything that looked occupied. Their fun had already begun.

One target was a chicken and egg farm. The Skywagon's fourth and lowest pass sent the chickens scurrying in all directions, and also sent the owner to the phone. She called the sheriff's office and the state police, who checked with the FAA in Amarillo. Because no flight plan had been filed and because the chicken farm owner hadn't been quick enough to spot the airplane's N number, no identification could be made and no action was taken.

Finally bored with buzzing, Billie turned the Skywagon's nose toward the state park. It was time for the serious insanity they had come for. And in preparation for it, Dexter in the left-rear seat and Lonnie in the right-rear seat loaded all four shotguns. When they were finished, with help from Billie and Sonny, they forced open the two front side windows and positioned the gun barrels, two on each side, so they could be fired left and right and straight out or down. Well-planned so as not to shoot off the propeller or make holes in the wings.

Finding birds in the park, large and small, was easy. Getting close enough in the airplane to shoot any of them was very difficult. It took skillful flying and precision maneuvering, neither of which Billie was capable of, drunk or sober. But shoot they did, at everything that moved. About 70 times.

Beer and buckshot don't mix well, but that did not deter the slaphappy foursome from downing another dozen or so cans of brew while they were firing, then flailing away with their shotguns. Which didn't improve their marksmanship at all. They never hit a thing. At least that they could see, because nothing fell out of the sky after they shot at it.

Disappointed at their inability to kill anything, they turned meaner and more determined. On one of their previous hunting expeditions, they had noticed a large, lazy-flying hawk near the southeast end of the state park. Sonny suggested making it their prime target, an appropriate quest to avenge their poor showing. Billie turned the Skywagon southeast.

The unsuspecting hawk was soon spotted flying low over the diverse terrain. Billie maneuvered the Skywagon so they would fly by with the hawk on their right side and slightly below them. That would give Sonny and Lonnie ideal position to "nail that sucker." It did. But they missed from less than 200 feet. Not a likely performance from experienced shooters. Except when they're too drunk to see straight.

Billie and Dexter were heartless in wreaking loud guffaws upon the distaff shooters through their uproarious laughter. It brought an immediate, angry challenge to the left side wise guys. Dexter had already reloaded his and Billie's shotguns and checked to be sure they were propped up in position as Billie turned the Skywagon back toward where the hawk was concentrating on its own quest.

Coming up for clear shots at the hawk from the left side of the Skywagon, Billie was determined not to miss. He took careful aim from 300 feet and was about to fire when the hawk started a swooping dive toward its own target on the ground. With his left hand on the trigger and his right hand on the Skywagon's yoke, Billie went after the hawk. Down. To 40 feet above the ground. Billie and Dexter both took aim. But, just as they were about to fire, the hawk started back up and turned away from them. Reflexively following the hawk in their gunsights, both shooters exerted extra force on the pried open window, opening it wider, aiming their guns higher. As they fired in unison, a hail of buckshot tore into the underside of the left wingtip, tearing it partially off and opening a gaping hole in the leading edge on the outer portion of the wing.

The sudden change in airflow dropped the left wing and the nose of the Skywagon. Billie countered it with a strong pull on the control wheel to the right and back. Too strong. The Skywagon lurched up, then to the right, then into a shaking stall buffet, then back to the left, and then the nose dropped out from under them and headed straight for the ground 80 feet below them. The accelerating impact was devastating, like a powerful explosion when it hit.

Miraculously, the ELT began sending a signal. But it was late in the afternoon before the wreckage was spotted from above. The state police removed three dead bodies from the crushed Skywagon after first rushing an unconscious, critically injured Dexter Swift by helicopter to Northwest Texas Hospital in Amarillo.

Dexter regained consciousness after undergoing extensive surgery the next day. The FAA and the NTSB were able to interview him sporadically over the next several days but were unable to complete his report. He died of internal injuries related to the accident on the ninth day.

Texas State Police representative "Two of our troopers arrived at the crash site by helicopter. The time was 4 p.m., or about 5 hours after the airplane went down. They were followed almost immediately by another helicopter bringing three people from the FAA district office in Amarillo. The area of the crash was not accessible by car, although a heavy-duty flatbed truck was able to remove the wreckage late the next day and deliver it to its owner at Tradewind Airfield in Amarillo.

"Our troopers were amazed to find one of the four occupants still alive in what was described as the obliterated remains of a high-wing airplane. The other three appeared to have died on impact. Our helicopter was used to fly the unconscious person, later identified as Dexter Swift, a white male, age 25, to the receiving hospital in Amarillo.

"Found immediately in the wreckage was a smashed cooler and several cans of light beer, most of which had been opened and apparently consumed by the occupants. There were also four heavy-gauge shotguns, a large number of empty shell casings and also a good amount of live ammunition. The shotguns were very dirty, by the way, indicating that they had been fired several times. All of them.

"A short time before the airplane's locator transmitter began sending its automatic signal, which we presume would be the time of the crash, we had a phoned-in report of an airplane buzzing an area about 10 miles northwest of the accident site. The woman who called in wasn't able to give a registration number but she did describe it as a high-wing airplane, white with red markings. She said she had seen it before. Her description pretty well matched what we found.

"When we later examined the belongings of the deceased, we were able to identify the pilot as Billie Lee Riggs, a white male, age 29. We determined that he was the pilot because his wallet contained an FAA medical certificate. We also discovered, after a routine computer check, that he was under court supervision in an alcohol rehab program. His driver's license had been pulled after three DUIs. Can you imagine that? The guy couldn't drive a car but he could fly an airplane. Makes you wonder about who's flying all those little planes.

"We sent our report over to the FAA office but they didn't send us anything back. Maybe they were embarrassed because we found out that they had no record of the pilot being an alcoholic. Hard to believe, though. His first conviction was three years ago when he lived in Lubbock. They should have picked up on it if they did any kind of a routine check. Must be it isn't part of their procedures."

Bernard (Biff) Riggs, age 48, Billie's oldest brother "When we heard that Billie got killed in an airplane, we couldn't believe it. Hell, he couldn't even drive a car. How in God's name did anyone ever let him rent and fly an airplane?

"It wasn't like Billie was some kind of a closet drunk or anything. He was a known alcoholic. Had been for the last 10 years. Don't they have rules about not giving licenses to alcoholics? I thought you couldn't drink and fly.

"No one in the family even suspected that Billie had taken flying lessons when he lived in Lubbock. I know his ex-wife and his two daughters never knew about it because they were as surprised as the rest of us were. He never said a word about it to anyone, which wasn't at all like Billie. He usually shot his mouth off over everything he did. Which wasn't much. Billie was the family's no-account. He never amounted to much after he dropped out of med school. Kind of gave up on life and quit trying.

"Must be this flying thing was going to be a big surprise to everyone. Something he could accomplish that would set him apart from his two older brothers. But he quit that, too, I understand. We were told he never did finish his flying lessons and get a license."

Avery Lindahl, Tradewind FBO chief pilot, ex-FAA examiner "I checked Billie out in the Skywagon back in early May, right after he moved up here from Lubbock. He wasn't any great shakes as a pilot but he was passable. It took more than three hours before we were both satisfied with the checkride, but that was understandable. He had never flown anything larger than a 172 before then.

"I was impressed that he didn't care how long it took because it told me he wasn't a hotshot or anything. We get plenty of those in here. And he wasn't drunk, either. I would have spotted that in 10 seconds as soon as we closed the door of that Skywagon. Airplane cabins are close quarters, and you can smell alcohol on someone's breath instantly. Billie's eyes were clear, too, so he wasn't on marijuana or coke or drugs of any kind. In this business, you learn to look for those things.

"No, Billie was clean. From what I've learned since, though, he must have worked extra hard to get that way because he sure fooled me. And everyone else around here, too. Even on the day he got killed. Our cashier, Andrea, she would have noticed something. And the fuel attendant, Jimmy—who idolized Billie because he always let Jimmy do part of his preflight for him and then gave him a big tip each time—he for sure would have noticed it if Billie had alcohol on his breath. You get close enough when you're checking oil and draining fuel sumps together.

"The FAA and the state police came in here asking all of us a bunch of questions about Billie, how he was able to rent the airplane, how he paid for it. They made a big deal about that, by the way—the fact that he would drop $500 in cash and then settle up later. Like it was drug money or something. And they more than implied that we were overanxious to rent him or anyone the airplane—that we would compromise safety and good sense because someone would come in here flashing big bucks at us. But we shot that nonsense down in a hurry when we showed them that we had a preferred insurance rate and put them in touch with our agent. After they checked with him, we didn't hear any more about it."

FAA district office representative "The two people from our office who were on accident call that day got the shock of their lives. They never saw anything like that much beer on an airplane before. And the shotguns . . . Whooh! That was somethin' else. Can you imagine? Shootin' birds from an airplane? Man, what some of these jerks won't think of!

"We found out about that from the one passenger who lived for awhile. Otherwise, I doubt anyone could have figured out how those shotguns figured in. That airplane hit so hard and crunched up so bad, it would have been darn near impossible to spot that the left wing had been torn open from buckshot just before they crashed.

"When this story hit the newspapers here and in most of Texas, we got plenty of nasty inquiries about how we let a guy who was a known alcoholic into an airplane. Like it was us that put him up there. We just referred everyone to OK City, because that's where all the licenses and medicals are controlled. Man, was that a mistake!

"After two or three days, and 100 or more phone calls they must've gotten up there, we got chewed out by everyone. OK City chewed on us for not handling it locally—but we never did figure out what they expected us to tell everyone. The media reported that we were stonewalling them—man, was that a crock! And the families of those four fliers practically accused us of killing their loved ones.

"I can tell you this about the FAA here in Amarillo: We are a district service office. Our job is to supervise the airports and operators in our district, see to it that the pilots and airplanes are airworthy, and investigate accidents. We do our job well and we're proud of it. But we don't make the rules. We don't issue pilot's licenses or medicals. We don't check on people's driving records. And we are not policemen.

"I hope that last point is clear. Because the Texas State Police criticized us on TV for not keeping those people out of the sky. Now tell me, how were we supposed to do that? We have no enforcement authority. Even if we knew what they were going to do in that airplane—shootin' at birds an' all—we couldn't have stopped them.

"If the police who shooed them off that little airport down near Canyon couldn't stop them, what could we or anyone else have done? You know, it's funny—and none of us around here have ever been able to understand it—the local police could have legally stopped them from driving . . . but not from flying. There's somethin' wrong with that!"

Binham T. (Bam) Riggs, 43, Billie's older brother "It was a helluva shock to us when Billie got killed. And when we got the details of what happened, it made all of us sick. But I'm sure you've heard all about that by now. So, I'll just tell you what I know, which ain't much.

"Billie was an alcoholic. He got that way shortly after his wife became pregnant while they were still in college, before they got married. Then he dropped out to get a job after Dad got all out of joint over it. He wanted them to get rid of the baby—you know, have an abortion—and start their lives prim and proper, like the rest of us. But Billie was headstrong and decided to do it his own way.

"Then the worst thing of all happened. Dad died. And left his three sons and two daughters all a lot of money. Billie just quit everything after that, after he got the money from dad's estate. He didn't really have to work anymore, so he didn't. That's when he started drinking and hanging around with the wrong kind of people. I guess he needed something to hate, after he screwed up his life the way he did.

"Before that, we were the Riggs brothers: Biff, Bam, and Billie. The way dad and everyone else made us out to be, we were going to conquer the world. But Billie just couldn't get it back together and he turned to alcohol.

"I was surprised when the investigators told us he had a medical certificate of some sort because he was a student pilot. I couldn't imagine Billie being able to get one of those, being as how he was an alcoholic and all. But they said it wouldn't show up unless he had told their doctor about it. Huh? That sounded like some kind of worthless procedure to me. I mean, if it couldn't filter out a chronic alcoholic like Billie, what good was it?"

FAA headquarters representative "This was such a bizarre accident that it very quickly became a high-profile news event. We must have had over 50 requests for the pilot's flight history, medical file, and the likes. Much of which we don't normally release without a formal written request. But some of the calls were so threatening, and from such important sources that we figured we'd better make some exceptions. That turned out to be a good decision because it took the heat off of us and the local FSDO. I think if we hadn't, we'd have been accused of dodging the issues and given the media license to report all kinds of distortions. The way it turned out, fortunately, we got a chance to feed them factual information. So, most of what got on TV and in the magazines and newspapers was close to the truth. Now we're hoping some good will come of it eventually because it shed some much needed light on a problem we've been wrestling with for years. That problem is that we, the FAA, the ATC system, and the National Transportation Safety Board as well, have no enforcement authority.

"Let me say that again so that, if you are putting this in some published form, it gets in there loud and clear. WE HAVE NO ENFORCEMENT AUTHORITY! None.

"We require and issue pilot's licenses. But have you ever heard of anyone going to jail for flying without one? The same thing applies to medicals. This is not the case with airlines because we and they maintain very stringent control and safety standards. Nonenforcement does apply to general aviation because we have no arrest authority or police backup, except in very few places. And even in those, the follow-up is abysmal. So there we are, a big, efficient organization with well-thought-out rules and regulations, but not one single ounce of muscle to make any of them stick, except on a voluntary basis.

"About the most we have going for us is the insurance industry. Our rules give them standards on which they base their claim requirements. And since money talks louder than anything else, that does give us some indirectly enforced compliance. The owner of an airplane, for instance, would be crazy to fly without a valid medical because they could never collect if they ever had an accident. It would be like paying for insurance you don't have.

"Insurance has an even greater deterring effect through FBOs, flight schools, corporations, and so forth, that actually account for the bulk of general aviation flying. They also have the most to lose. So, as could be expected, they screen and police their pilots and renters pretty carefully. Probably better than a city or state police force could do.

"Then we have the luckiest thing of all: A pilot population of responsible people who understand and respect the fact that we're there to protect them and make the system work. I say lucky because pilots, for the most part, are a cut above the general population: wealthier, smarter, more self-motivated, better general citizens. They take their own and other people's safety seriously. And the success of our country's general aviation system—which is the best in the world by a long shot—is a reflection of and a credit to them.

"Where we fail miserably is in our ability to get rid of the garbage and keep the system clean. By that I mean we need the teeth to prevent anyone from ever getting into an airplane who doesn't have proper certification. I think anyone would agree that we need that authority at least as much as the highway patrol does!

"Then we need procedural muscle. We and the ATC need to be able to tell pilots they can't take off from controlled fields in weather they're not certified to handle, or in equipment that isn't adequate for the conditions. We need to be able to check out who is filing a flight plan, or even using flight service for information. I don't mean we want or need to become a Gestapo organization. But we do need to be able to at least make a start at addressing many of these issues.

"In the case of those four bird hunters, for example, if they had faced arrest, conviction and jail, they might not have taken off in the condition they were in. After all, it worked to keep that pilot out of a motor vehicle on the ground."

NTSB representative "This is one of the most flagrant, most disgusting wastes of lives we've seen in general aviation. It comes close to being a case of mass suicide. But, no matter, general aviation gets blamed for it anyway and the clamor for preventative action will again be laid at our doorstep. And all the local, state, and national politicos and do-gooders will be awaiting some pontifical rhetoric that they can carry back to their constituents. Then in no time flat, case closed. Until the next deadly crisis.

"Well, this time, we may not close the case so fast. This time we've got enough black eyes in enough agencies to finally have a chance to do something concrete. We've got local police, state police, the FAA, us and all the media in Texas. And we're not going to say word one until they're all ready to listen to everything we have to say. Even if we have to take a lot of flak for it.

"But when we're ready, they're going to get an earful. Because we've just completed a full-blown study on this long-neglected situation and we're ready to make some very far-reaching recommendations. And these four crazy bird hunters may just have created the climate we need to get serious consideration from enough forces to make it happen.

"Let me give you some examples of where we'll be coming from. I can't give you anything specific to quote—not yet—but you'll be able to get the general idea.

"The first thing we have to do is be able to communicate outside the aviation universe. Would you believe that we really aren't set up to do that yet? We don't have any procedures established to receive data from law enforcement agencies, the court system, the prison system, states, and dozens of available computer data banks that can give us invaluable information about the people who already are pilots and those who want to be.

"The next thing we have to do is let the world out there know what our needs are and what our rules are so they can give us important information even before we ask for it. Police systems all over the country have been doing that routinely for years. Every licensed driver's file is automatically updated by computer. Have an accident in another city or state, and it's in your file before the ink is dry on the accident report. We need to know hundreds of things like that. For instance, if we'd have had routine reports on Billie Riggs over the past three years, he'd still be here, and so would his friends.

"Then, in obvious sequence, we need the capability to disseminate information out into the field quickly, cheaply, and conveniently. For example, if that FBO in Amarillo had the same information available to him that the state police did, that Skywagon never would have left the ground with Billie flying it. Not even for the checkride he took several months before the accident.

"Next—and this is a good one—we need to develop, in conjunction with the various national associations and organizations like the AOPA, the EAA, NAFI, the AG group and the state aviation officials, a program to encourage anyone connected with aviation to intervene whenever a general aviation pilot attempts to fly after consuming alcohol or using other drugs, or if conditions and circumstances are known to be beyond that pilot's capability and training. In order for that to be possible, rules and standards must first be set up.

"Then another 'next:' We have to disseminate, on a continual basis, posters, mailers, and a barrage of educational materials dealing with alcohol, substances, and drugs. I mean real-world stuff—easy-to-understand and down to earth—with all of the known facts about what those things can do to pilots at altitude, in turbulence, in the clouds, at night, and whatever else they may encounter in the unnatural environment of the sky.

"Then we need some legislation. National, state and local governments must enact comprehensive laws pertaining to alcohol and drug use in aviation, or amend existing laws as appropriate, to include implied consent provisions to obtain biological specimens for toxicological tests. If the police can require it of drivers, why not pilots?

"And finally, we need a new set of rules, regulations and recommendations dealing specifically with alcohol and drug use in aviation, written so they can be clearly understood and administered, and with enforcement provisions strong enough to deter potential violators, willful or otherwise. That will get everyone's attention, make them understand the seriousness of this subject, and give the appropriate law enforcement authorities adequate guidelines so they can help us get our house in order and keep it that way. Permanently.

"When these recommendations become reality—and we believe they all will eventually—they will play an important part in securing the long-term future of general aviation. Right now, we're moving as fast as we can because we realize that the present future of general aviation is short-term. It needs a quick fix to get it moving in the right direction before 'short-term' becomes too short."

Author comment Change in a universal system is always, and only, the end result of a catalyzing agent. A spark that triggers other forces. An instant and momentary event. Usually a chance opportunity.

Perhaps this grotesque distortion of the use of an airplane by a pilot with a suspended driving license and his aerial bird-hunting buddies will be all of the above and arouse enough indignation to create the spark that changes the way alcohol, substances, and drugs are dealt with in general aviation. If so, it will be a giant leap forward catapulted by one of the lowliest examples of irresponsibility—certainly a welcome conclusion.

10

A high time for ice

Preliminary report: January; Cessna Cardinal RG; private pilot, single-engine land, instrument rating, 1,280 hours. The pilot and three members of his family were seriously injured in a crash during an instrument approach to Yeager Airport in Charleston, West Virginia. On the IFR trip to Charleston from Atlanta, the pilot selected 11,000 feet as his cruising altitude to stay above an undercast at 9,000 feet. Rime ice had been forecast in the clouds, and the pilot wanted to remain clear of it for as long as possible. During his descent for the ILS 23 approach to Yeager, the pilot tried to keep his speed up in order to minimize ice buildup but noticed that the Cardinal's airspeed had dropped to 75 knots by the time he was intercepting the localizer course. The rear seat passengers told the pilot that ice was accumulating on the wings and the airframe. Shortly thereafter, the pilot was unable to maintain the glideslope descent rate and the Cardinal crashed into trees and a house. Two people on the ground were injured.

Further investigation revealed:
- Light to moderate icing had been forecast for the general area. The pilot was advised by approach control and the tower that several aircraft had diverted from Charleston to airports north and west of the area after encountering rime and clear ice.
- Weather at the time of the crash was 600 and 1 in light freezing rain.
- For the 2½ months preceding the flight, the pilot was taking a nonprescription diet pill, as part of a self-prescribed diet regimen, and had lost 18 pounds.
- The aircraft had no deicing equipment.

Official conclusion: Continued flight into known icing conditions. Failure to maintain flying speed. Loss of control due to ice accumulation on the airframe. Pilot error.

BURT AND MYRA ROBERTS WERE RETURNING HOME to Charleston with their two young children, Danny and Melanie, after a long weekend visit in Atlanta with Myra's parents and family. Burt, the heir-apparent of a successful automobile dealership in Charleston, had been flying for over 15 years. Myra, a practicing psychologist, was also a private pilot. She began flying three years prior to the accident, when they purchased their Cessna Cardinal RG and she was working on her instrument rating.

The first call to flight service on Sunday morning, the day of the flight, left the two pilots in limbo. An occluded front was parked over the central Appalachians and wasn't expected to begin moving out until late the next day. Weather associated with the front called for low ceilings and visibility, mixed rain and snow, a strong likelihood of icing in the clouds, tops at or below 10,000 feet. A typical January five-day weather cycle.

With important commitments in Charleston for all of the family members, the prospect of sitting around in Atlanta was not a happy one, despite the insistence of the grandparents that a prolonged visit would be most welcome. By midday, the news from flight service was hopeful: The front had begun swinging south. If it kept moving at the same speed, it would be south of the Charleston area by 8 p.m. Eastern Time. A second front was expected into the area early the next day and might become stationary.

Burt and Myra began making quick decisions. They did not like single-engine night flying. But the apparent access window into Charleston for the next two or three days was after 8 that evening. The next window might be late Wednesday, which was not acceptable to a highly motivated family. They started packing.

On their fourth hourly call to flight service, Burt filed a flight plan for a 6 p.m. departure. Their selected route of flight was Victor 267 to Knoxville and Victor 115 to Charleston, slightly west of a direct course, but one that would keep them clear of the heaviest weather and also passing over Knoxville and closer to Huntington, if a stop or diversion was necessary. He also selected 11,000 feet for their altitude, even though it was higher than they usually liked to fly. But it would keep them VFR on top, smooth and clear and with a helpful tailwind. The children would sleep in the thinner air. He and Myra would change off so they would both be well rested for what might be a tricky approach into Yeager Airport.

Grandma packed an in-flight supper of sandwiches and veggies for the travelers. Grandpa drove them to DeKalb-Peachtree Airport and waited while Burt and Myra loaded and preflighted the airplane, with ample help from Danny and Melanie, who were veteran passengers. One final call to flight service confirmed that the weather window would be open, and, after assuring grandpa that they would be careful, the Roberts family was taxiing out to Runway 20 for an on-time departure.

Because it was a night flight, Burt and Myra did an ultra careful engine runup and pretakeoff checklist. Then they repeated it. Off the ground at 6:08 p.m. and switched to departure control on 119.3, they were given a 020° heading and cleared: "Direct Harris when able, climb to and maintain one-one-thousand. Contact Atlanta Center on 127.05 passing through 5,000."

An hour-and-a-half later, over the Knoxville Vortac at 11,000 feet, with the full moon lighting the tops of the undercast 1,500 feet below them—especially pretty night flying—the report from flight watch required more decision making: PIREPs were coming in from the Charleston area reporting light to moderate icing in the clouds. Several corporate aircraft had diverted to Parkersburg, West Virginia, about 60 miles northeast of Charleston.

An in-flight conference began over a low altitude en route chart that was spread out between them on their laps. Many of the airports north and west of Charleston were receiving diverted flights. The Roberts' best option for an escape haven would still be Huntington, West Virginia, their already-on-file alternate. But there were several other airports with ILS approaches within half an hour of Charleston. It was nice to have several alternates considering the weather and with 1:10 of fuel remaining upon arrival.

The decision was easy: They would fly to the Charleston VOR, staying at 11,000 feet, make a quick descent to the GLAZE intersection for a sharp right turn onto the Runway 23 ILS, shoot the approach one time—and only one time—and then either land or divert immediately to Huntington or another alternate to be determined after they contacted Charleston Flight Watch. A very conservative plan, they thought, that would keep them out of the icing as long as possible.

Myra Roberts "It was such a perfect flight up to that point. The children were sound asleep. And Burt and I were enjoying the spectacular views from the moonlight on the clouds under us. We don't fly that much at night, so we were really appreciating it.

"But we were quite aware of the reality we were facing. Conditions in Charleston were not our cup of tea. Neither we nor our airplane were equipped for ice, and we had no illusions about that. We aren't daredevils, either. So, we thought we were making the most conservative decision possible.

"In hindsight, of course, we could not have made a worse one. But neither of us had ever been in bad ice before and we didn't realize that the airplane wouldn't be able to give us a second chance. We never learned that in our flight training and we haven't been able to find it in any manufacturer's aircraft operating manual, either. Believe me, since the accident, we have both researched it thoroughly, talked to the FAA about it and, as far as we know, we had done everything we should have done before the proverbial barn burned down.

"With something as dangerous and unforgiving as ice, I can't imagine why more isn't being done to warn pilots about it. And why the controllers didn't warn us to stay out of it, neither of us can understand. After all, they must have known how bad it was. Why, we found out afterward that we were the only airplane that had even attempted that approach after 8 p.m. Everyone else had been diverted. Were they using us as guinea pigs or something? No one will tell us.

"Since then, Burt and I bought a Centurion with partial deice capability. I have my instrument rating now, and we're doing a lot more flying. If all goes well, we'll get our multi-engine ratings and buy a cabin-class twin in a year or so. The children are older, and we need the room and the safety to travel as a family."

Reaching WHIRL, 17 miles southwest of Charleston, Myra took out the approach plates for six different airports, woke the kids, who were still asleep in the back seat, and tightened her seat belt and shoulder harness for the descent that would begin in 6–7 minutes. Burt was then handed off from Indianapolis Center to Charleston Approach on 124.1:

Approach "November . . . Victor, descend and maintain 4,000. Plan on the ILS 23 Approach. Kilo is current on the ATIS. Do you have it, sir?"

Burt (Embarrassed that he had forgotten to listen to the ATIS) "Uh . . . oh, sorry. I can get it and call back in."

Approach "Stay with me . . .. We have a SIGMET in effect for light to moderate icing in the clouds. Some sectors are reporting moderate to severe, and several light aircraft have diverted north. Parkersburg is reporting 1,200 over and 5 miles with no icing. Huntington is now 700 over and 3½. Only one report there of light rime by a Cessna 150 about an hour ago. Charleston is now 600 and 1½ in light freezing rain and drizzle."

Burt "Uh, . . . I would like to stay at 11,000 until the vortac, then make a quick letdown for GLAZE. We figure we'll try one approach. If that doesn't work, we'll head for Parkersburg. With a tailwind, it's only 25 minutes away."

Approach "Roger. Maintain one-one-thousand. Descend at your discretion to 2,600. You're cleared to GLAZE. Report reaching and plan a sharp right turn direct to MEEKY. We'll be able to get you in without delay. Wind is two-five-zero at 10, gusting to 15. Braking action on the runway is A-okay, last reported by a Citation about an hour ago."

Myra put the approach plates for Parkersburg on top of the several she was holding, glanced over and saw that Burt had the correct plate for the Runway 23 ILS approach at Charleston on his yoke clip, then settled back waiting for Burt to begin their rapid descent. Nobody had mentioned turbulence, but she knew it would be. The children were buckled in securely, too, waiting for what they considered to be the fun part of the trip. The routine part of flying was boring for them. But then, what do kids know?

Directly over the Charleston Vortac, Burt reluctantly pulled back the throttle and lowered the nose. It was a shame to leave that smooth, clear air for who knows what. He set up a 1,200 foot-per-minute descent and noticed that the airspeed indicator was 10–12 knots below the redline. A good number. He wanted to get through whatever ice there was going to be as quickly as possible. So far, so good.

By the time they reached 4,000 feet, they had a ½ inch of ice on the wings and empennage surfaces and the propeller was beginning to throw ice, making a cracking sound the likes of which no member of the Roberts family had ever heard before. It was unsettling for the children and nerve-racking for the pilot and copilot.

Danny and Melanie had been the first to visually notice the ice and they announced it with great glee and excitement. Burt had already felt vibrations in the controls. Myra was watching the airspeed declining. Both pilots knew their situation wasn't good. Both children were excited but beginning to sense their parents' disquietude. The Cardinal continued complaining with more vibrations and buffeting, and regular cracking noises as the propeller ice broke loose and slammed against the cabin.

At GLAZE, Burt dropped the nose as he began a sharp right turn to head toward MEEKY, the outer marker. The tower had already cleared them to land. They were 5 minutes from home.

Coming out of the turn at 2,500 feet, 100 feet below the glide-slope intercept, Burt pulled the nose up sharply and added power to keep the speed up. But the added power had no effect. The airspeed declined rapidly. Then full power. No help. The controls were getting mushy. Next was the shrill, piercing sound of the stall warning horn, followed by the shaking of the stall buffet.

Burt and Myra were frantic. The airplane was going out of control and into a full-power-on stall at 800 feet in the air. Just as they descended below the clouds, the right wing dropped. Burt did his best to stay straight and level, but then the nose started falling despite his heavy back pressure on the yoke.

When he felt and saw the nose go down, Burt reflexively released the back pressure. It saved their lives. Because he was able to regain just enough control to steer the falling Cardinal into the clearest area he could see in the split second of time he had.

The Cardinal's wheels touched down hard, bounced back into the air momentarily, and then the airplane careened forward. Burt and Myra were both on the brakes with all the strength their legs could muster. It was an exceptional, well-coordinated effort, but they had only 700 feet to work with. Their combined force could not have been enough to stop the Cardinal.

The right wing hit a small storage shed, which spun them around and threw them headlong into a small house. The crash was deafening. An older couple inside the home sustained serious injuries as the left wing of the Cardinal ripped through their living room window and collapsed the outer wall. They were thrown forward by the force of the impact, and the couch they were sitting on wound up on top of them. That was lucky. It protected them from the collapsing wall.

The Roberts family suffered a variety of minor and serious injuries. Miraculously, none fatal. The Cardinal was totaled.

Burt Roberts "The thought of spending two or three more days in Atlanta had all of us bordering on suicide. Myra's family, with all of their good intentions, never gave any of us a moment's peace. And the way everyone carried on about the 18 pounds I had lost. I was tempted to put on five or six just to shut everybody up.

"When flight service finally gave us some hope, after a morning of gloom and doom, we reached out and grabbed it. Obviously, we reached out too far. But we didn't think so at the time. Even the kids. They were actually anxious to get back to school.

"Myra and I had reservations about a night flight in bad weather, but it seemed to us to be our best alternative. By the time we got to Knoxville, at 11,000 feet, we were sure we had made the right choice. The air was super smooth, the moonlight on the clouds was overpowering pretty, and the thinner air made me feel better than I think I ever felt in my whole life. It was wonderful.

"Now I know what it really was. Hypoxia. I was in a state of euphoria. I had a feeling of well-being that was a total high. I felt like the Roberts family and the Cardinal could conquer the world. You know, I think if you could package hypoxia, you could sell it and make a fortune. That's how good it feels. That's also how dangerous it is.

"I've since learned that the diet pill I was taking, Dexatrim, is really phenylalanine—a form of speed that heightens the effects of low oxygen [thin air]. And I had taken one just before takeoff so I'd be able to control myself with all the food we had on the airplane. What I didn't know, of course, was that it also was causing me to lose control of my judgment and my ability to make intelligent decisions.

"But you know, looking back on it, I don't think the decisions we made at the time were all that bad. Besides, Myra wasn't on Dexatrim or anything else, and we both agreed completely on taking a shot at the approach at Charleston. Based on our mutual knowledge at that moment, we made a sound, practical, and conservative decision. What we didn't know, of course, was that the airplane could fill up with ice that fast, and that after it did, it wouldn't be able to fly us out of there. We were only in those clouds for a total of about 10 minutes, and when they found us, we had over an inch of clear ice on every surface. There must have been a thousand pounds of extra weight on the airplane.

"The other thing we couldn't have known was how horrible the weather can get for an airplane. Or how quickly it can happen. I doubt if a 747 with heated wings could have flown safely into Charleston that night. That's how fast the ice was piling on. (Pause) It was some lesson, I can tell you. When Myra and I hear the word 'ice,' we still shudder. And our new Centurion automatically turns itself around and runs whenever it hears that 'I' word, even though it's equipped with prop and windshield deice."

ATC representative "I really don't know what more any of our people could have done short of ordering them out of the sky, which we aren't authorized to do. We told them there was ice. That other airplanes were diverting north and west. That there was a SIGMET for the area. They just weren't listening.

"Anytime there's an accident like this one, we get all kinds of flak about our procedures. But what about their procedures? Aren't they supposed to know what a SIGMET is? 'Significant meteorological condition' does not mean a cool summer breeze.

"These people started getting serious warnings about the icing when they were over Knoxville, 180 miles away from Charleston. From that point on, every center controller they talked to told them what was going on. We don't keep severe icing conditions a secret.

"When they were finally handed off to Charleston Approach, they got a detailed report that the local weather was worse than terrible and were told that no other aircraft had landed at Charleston in the past hour. And the one that did, and gave a braking action report, was a Citation, no less. Not exactly an invitation for a Cardinal to come and land at Charleston, I'd say.

"You know, there are times when this 'pilot-in-command' business just doesn't work. All too often, low-time private pilots haven't got the experience or the knowledge to make some of the decisions they get faced with. Like the terrible call those two pilots made in that Cardinal.

"Every one of our people knew how dangerous those icing conditions were. But we couldn't do any more than advise them and then go along with their requests. Because we simply don't have the authority to stop them from hurting themselves and, like it was in this case, people on the ground, too. Can you imagine those two elderly folks in the house they crashed into? They'll never get over that shock!

"If you think seriously about it, ATC needs to be able to give orders in critical situations, without worrying about the pilot-in-command rules. After all, we can order an airplane to go around to avoid a potential collision on a runway because that's considered critical enough for us to take over. But we can't take over and order an airplane out of icing conditions, or to not take off in stinko weather without an instrument rating or a flight plan.

"Those situations, and several others like them, are every bit as dangerous as that potential runway mishap. But we're hog-tied. We have to sit at our scopes, biting our nails, and watch these tragedies unfold. Like the airplanes that we know are going to run out of gas. Or the drunks who call in so soused we can practically smell the alcohol on their breaths. Hell, a traffic cop can arrest a drunk driver. But we can't stop a drunk pilot who can do a hell of a lot more damage than any driver can. Next to a car or a truck, an out-of-control airplane is a lethal weapon, and much more feared by the public than any ground vehicle.

"Someday, these rules have to change. They have to give us the authority to stop some of these pilots from killing themselves. It just doesn't make any sense not to."

NTSB representative "There's always a lot of controversy about whether an icing accident is the pilot's fault or the weather's fault.

Nearly all of the time, the system relies on PIREPs from general aviation pilots to confirm the presence and the severity of ice. And it's become sort of a 'Wolf! Wolf!' situation because so many reports have come from inexperienced pilots who get hysterical over a trace of rime. People who fly enough listen to these PIREPs, find out for themselves that half the time they're grossly overstated, and then begin ignoring them altogether or, at the very least, not taking them seriously enough. And then they begin playing icing roulette.

"In this particular case, there wasn't any question at all. There was 'known ice' in Charleston. Flight service told them about it before they took off. Every controller after Knoxville told them about it, advised them to divert and told them where to go. The system performed perfectly.

"But the two pilots in that Cardinal sure didn't. They claimed that all of the icing reports they received were for light to moderate and were all nearly an hour old. That's their story after the fact because the transcripts and the interviews we conducted tell it differently. They had more than adequate warning.

"But, warning or not, they had no business even thinking about trying that approach into Charleston. The rules on icing are very clear, in fact, much clearer than most other FARs written: 'Any aircraft that is not equipped for *known-icing* may not enter an area which has been forecast or confirmed to have icing conditions.' There are no exceptions for how much or what kind of ice. The FAR says, 'icing conditions.' Period.

"In his written statement, the pilot said that none of the reports about icing were confirmed. We can't figure out what he meant by that because Charleston Approach told him flat out that there was a SIGMET for icing in the area. That is confirmation of 'known ice.'

"What we can figure out is that he was trying to blame the system for his lousy decision so he wouldn't have a problem with his insurance company or the FAA. Well, that didn't work. We recommended that his license be suspended. Maybe, with the time to think about it, he'll read the FARs more carefully and study up on icing. After all, it almost killed him and his whole family.

"We would have recommended pulling his wife's license, too, but that was beyond our jurisdiction. She told us that she was a passenger and not logging the time as copilot. We can't refute that, legally, but we sure don't believe it. All we can hope is that the two of them learned something from this accident and won't risk their lives again."

Burt Roberts "When the FAA told us they were suspending my license, that was like adding insult to injury. They said the NTSB's conclusion was that I knew there was known icing in the Charleston area and that I ignored all of the warnings and flew into it anyway. Well, I have plenty to say about that, none of which is fit to print!

"First of all, there were no warnings from anyone. Only advisories. Nobody, not even Charleston Approach or Yeager tower, ever said there was known-ice in the area. The only report I got was that a Citation had landed an hour before we arrived, with some light rime and a report that the braking action was okay. That didn't tell me anything significant about icing in the clouds. And neither controller bothered to tell me that the Citation was the only aircraft that had attempted to land at Charleston in the entire hour-and-a-half period before we showed up.

"Second, the approach guy told me there was a SIGMET for icing in the clouds and then proceeded to rattle off a list of nearby airports where people in light aircraft were landing with no problems. I remember him saying that some sectors were reporting light icing, but I'm sure he never said which ones. And for sure, he never said anything at all about moderate or severe icing in Charleston.

"And third, and the most important point of all: Right after he told me about the SIGMET and the fact that those nearby airports were all okay, I told him what our game plan was. And he cleared us for the approach!

"Now you tell me, if the area was closed to light aircraft because of the SIGMET, why did he do that? Why didn't he just say: 'No, you cannot do that, your game plan is unacceptable, you are *not* cleared for the approach'? What are pilots supposed to be, mind readers? How can they expect us to know what the hell is going on when everything they tell us is contradictory?

"When I pointed all of this out to the FAA, they were nice enough to restore my license. But it took over a month to happen, and I'm still not sure if the damned suspension has ever been deleted from my file."

NASA representative "After reading all of the transcripts and reports and statements on this case, it is safe to conclude that none of the involved parties learned nearly enough from the accident or the circumstances leading up to it.

"Let's start with the pilot. He made the point that he realized he was probably suffering from hypoxia, and that it may have been intensified by the phenylalanine he was taking. We're uncomfortable with 'probably' and 'may have been intensified.' He *was* hypoxic, as was his wife, and the phenylalanine *did intensify* the hypoxia, or perhaps better said, did intensify the effects of the reduced oxygen.

"Then, later in his statement, he alluded to the fact that his wife was okay, not affected by the altitude. That is where neither one of them learned enough. Because they were at 11,000 feet . . . *at night* which, at the time of their flight, would have been the equivalent of 14 or 15,000 feet. So, they were definitely hypoxic by the time they reached Knoxville. Not maybe.

"But . . . and here is the real misinformation . . . he said he now realizes that the phenylalanine made his condition worse. True. But not a factor here. It could have been if they were at 4 or 5,000 feet. But at 11,000 feet, it didn't make any difference. He was going to be dangerously hypoxic with or without the phenylalanine. And so was his wife.

"Now, let's look at the other participants in this case. Did you notice that both the NTSB and ATC made no mention at all about the probability of hypoxia? Like it wasn't even a possibility. Both agencies practically called these people stupid, arrogant, nonlistening jerks who foolishly ignored several warnings and deliberately tried to kill themselves and their children. That, in itself, is either a dumb oversight or a case of not wanting to deal with the problem. Neither agency even considered the fact that the pilot may have been impaired, even though they knew full well that the family had been flying at 11,000 feet for over 2½ hours—*at night*.

"That pilot was definitely impaired, and so was his wife. There isn't even any question about it. But for the people in charge of the system to continue turning a blind eye toward hypoxic impairment is a terrible and dangerous disservice to the pilots they are charged with protecting. Conscientious, capable pilots are being killed and injured because high-altitude hypoxic impairment is still an obscure, undealt-with subject that is deliberately being swept under official rugs."

Author comment This accident sheds some light on a few blatant flaws in an otherwise satisfactory system. The ATC needs much more authority to give direct orders when pilots are putting themselves, or are being put, in danger. It makes no sense at all to require controllers to dance around and make 'nice-nice' with pilots-in-command who either don't deserve to be, or are not capable of being in command. Straightforward, enforceable directions from controllers will serve the system better.

Considering the adverse weather conditions, perhaps it would have been beneficial for a controller to have notified the Cessna pilot that only a Citation had tried to land at Charleston for one and a half hours. Unfortunately, we all realize that controllers cannot and do not as a matter of course report how many airplanes have landed, or attempted to land, before we land.

Both the FAA and the NTSB are running out of time and excuses for not addressing the problems associated with altitude. Ignoring the subject is not a solution. It would also be a shame if another agency, or other forces, made the public aware that the FAA and the NTSB—in whose hands air safety and progress are entrusted—might have been recalcitrant in carrying out their responsibilities.

The general aviation industry is perhaps most responsible for its own deplorable situation. Manufacturers, FBOs, flight schools, and even the aviation trade press have unwittingly caused their own decline by allowing themselves and the public to believe that most general aviation accidents are caused by stupid, poorly trained pilots who have been turned loose to fall out of the sky like bombs when, in fact, those pilots were conscientiously trained and are anything but stupid. They were, however, made to seem that way and did many of the unexplainable things they did because of the effects of low oxygen, hypoxia, and disorientation—both spatial and general.

The result: General aviation is suffering from a bum rap it brought upon itself. And thousands of worthy people have suffered and died in the process.

11

Pressure leads to panic

Preliminary report: April; Piper Turbo Lance; private pilot, single-engine land, instrument rating, 580 hours. Damage to the aircraft was extensive after a precautionary landing, but the pilot and his three passengers were injured only slightly. The aircraft was taking off for an IFR flight when the pilot noticed that both fuel flow gauges were indicating nearly zero fuel flow. There was no apparent loss of engine power, but the pilot obtained an immediate clearance to make a VOR approach back to the airport, which was reporting 500 and ½. The aircraft stalled when the pilot prematurely flared for landing, and the Lance fell about 30 feet to the runway. Preliminary tests of the Lance's fuel system failed to disclose any anomalies.

Further investigation revealed:

- The pilot had received both his commercial and instrument ratings 2½ months earlier, but needed three checkrides to complete the process. His examiner on the second checkride cited him for overcontrolling during recoveries from unusual attitudes and recommended that he work on his confidence before trying again.
- After his second failed checkride, the pilot received 8 hours of dual, but from a different instructor. That instructor had suggested trying some low approaches in actual IMC before attempting another checkride, but the weather failed to cooperate.

- Two of the passengers were fellow employees of the pilot and had pressured him into leaving in weather conditions he felt were too close to his personal minimums.
- The pilot had 71 hours total time in the Lance but only 1 hour of IFR, other than during his training time. Of that, his actual IMC time was less than 10 minutes—up through a cloud deck to VFR on top, then flew 50 miles and was able to let down and land VFR.

Official conclusion: Spatial disorientation. Loss of control. Misjudged approach and landing flare. Pilot error.

A COMPANY SALES MEETING had brought the pilot, Jack Ferguson, 29, to Lake of the Ozarks, Missouri, in his Turbo Lance. His passengers on the trip were his fiance, Laura Brewer, 27, and two of his fellow employees, Phil Collins, 45, director of marketing, and Bert Nordstrom, 48, executive vice president and chief financial officer of Ferguson Electronics. Jack's father and older brother had flown to the meeting in the company's Citation, the airplane Jack hoped to fly someday.

The Lance was new in Jack's life. He owned it for only the past seven months, flying as often as he could find the time and the need to do so. His instrument rating, a necessary adjunct for a high-performance airplane intended primarily for business use, had not come easy. Jack was not a gifted athlete, nor was he particularly well coordinated. His claim to fame was a quick mind, an MBA from Ohio State University, and a family that owned a substantial business.

Mel Drexler, flight instructor "Jack was a determined, driven student. He had almost 500 hours of time in 172s and Warriors, all VFR, before he bought his Turbo Lance and started working on his instrument ticket. I'd have to say he was one of the best prepared students I ever worked with. He had already spent dozens of hours working with a complete IFR video training course, read every recommended workbook and IFR guide he could lay his hands on, and completed one of those weekend 'guaranteed-that-you'll-pass' ground schools. He also owned a desktop simulator.

"But he really wasn't ready for the Lance. Throughout his training, he always had trouble staying ahead of the airplane. I don't mean on instruments. I mean just flying it. He had never flown retractable before, or constant-speed prop, or handled a turbocharged engine. The Lance is a high-performance machine that requires more from its pilot than Jack was bringing to the party, what with his working on his instrument ticket at the same time he was trying to get used to the airplane. As a result, he didn't do either of them particularly well.

"After we had put in 30 hours or so—and as I mentioned about a quarter of that was spent on orientation in the airplane—Jack decided it was time to take his checkride. Against my better judgment. He wasn't near ready, and I told him so until I could tell that he was thinking I was just trying to sell him more instruction time. I guess rich guys like him think everybody's trying to work them for extra bucks. Believe me, I have no aversion to money, but I never worked Jack at all, except to teach him to fly better. I knew he'd be safe. He just needed more time than most to come up to speed. I also knew that if he didn't get the extra time and some TLC along the way, he'd never catch up to that Lance.

"You know, of course, that he flunked his first try. And then the second. Which wasn't all that bad a ride, except for his recoveries and some careless approach work. When he came back that second time, with his tail literally between his legs, I could tell that he needed a fresh start. You know, a new approach with a new instructor. The way he and I had been going at it, it was an easy read. I wouldn't compromise. And Jack really wasn't satisfied with himself.

"So, I recommended Abner Jung. He's an old-timer around here, with patience to spare. He was just what Jack needed. And the way it turned out, I was right, because he got his ticket within a couple of weeks.

"But he never did catch up to that Lance. And he knew it. You could tell by the way he flew. Always and only in good weather. Always with his fiance or a friend along for moral support. Never venturing into anything more severe than a thin cloud deck and mild turbulence.

"So, if you want a last word about my experience with Jack, I'd sum it up by saying that some people were never meant to fly sophisticated equipment. Jack is one of them. But I hear that he's thinking of moving up again. This time to a 340 or a Duke. Before he does that, he ought to be thinking about getting himself a good copilot."

Jack Ferguson "Mel Drexler is a good instructor, but he and I never hit it off. Our chemistry was wrong, or something. Most of the time, he was putting me down. You know, making me feel inadequate whenever I'd screw up, which wasn't all that often. But when I did, he'd come down on me so hard that I wanted to crawl out of my own airplane.

"After I flunked the second checkride, the examiner, Darrell Stevens, told me something that turned everything in flying around for me—in my head. While he was writing up the reasons why he was busting me, he said I had an attitude problem: I had no self-confidence. He said I seemed to be so afraid of making a mistake that I was being too timid handling the airplane. As a result, the airplane was handling me. He suggested I take a look at myself in the mirror and realize that I was just as capable as anyone else, and that I could fly an airplane just fine. He said he knew that from the way I did most everything else.

"So, I did. I thought about it and realized that what I needed was a fresh start, a new approach, a positive attitude. What I didn't need was more technical training accompanied by several knocks to my ego. Which made the solution come front and center: I needed a new instructor.

"This is a small aviation community here, and I didn't want to upset it. So, I decided to talk to Mel about what I wanted to do. And I must say, he was really great about it. He recommended Uncle Abner, Abner Jung, right away. Said he was sure we'd work well together and that Abner would be able to help me get my head straight about flying.

"Well, the proof is in the pudding. Uncle Abner and I got along great and I had my ticket in no time flat. He's the right kind of instructor for me. And I'm grateful as all get-out to Mel for touting me on to him."

The sales meeting ended on a high, but weather had moved into the central Missouri area just in time to spoil the golf outing planned for that afternoon. Thus the decision to leave early. Jack and Laura weren't in any particular hurry, but Phil and Bert were anxious to get home to their families.

Jack called flight service in St. Louis, via the 800 number, for a weather briefing and to file his flight plan. The news wasn't terrific for a recent IFR graduate: Low ceilings and visibility for most of Missouri and into Indiana. Rain and widely scattered thunderstorms, especially in the afternoon. May be embedded. Ohio weather VFR all day. Closest reporting station, Vichy, showing ceilings at 400 over, visibility 4 in steady, light rain. Temperature 55. Dewpoint 52. Wind 200° at 10 knots.

Notes in hand, Jack told flight service he would call back to file his flight plan. He wanted to have a conference with his passengers before deciding whether or not to take off. The low ceiling was definitely not his cup of tea.

And he told them so, explaining at the same time that the weather system would be in Missouri for at least two days and would be moving into Ohio later that same evening. Laura liked the idea of staying over in a pleasant resort area. Phil and Bert did not. They had family plans and business commitments in Youngstown. And Jack was their only way out of Lake of the Ozark.

The conference was short. Phil's logic was that because the weather in Ohio was still good, they should leave as soon as possible. After all, "Isn't landing the hard part?" His argument was too convincing for Jack to rebut without coming off like a wimp to Laura. So, with a hard swallow, he agreed and went out in the light rain to pre-flight the Lance. Worried.

Back in the flight office, ready to go, Jack called flight service to file his flight plan. The weather news was a tad better—Vichy was now reporting 600 and 3½—but then he was given something that was new to him: A time-off clearance and release time. Youngstown, where he was based, had a tower. All of Jack's IFR filings had been made through tower operators. This expiring departure time made him nervous. More so when he was further informed that he might not be able to make contact with center until he was airborne. His instant thought was that he might be in the clouds before he could talk to anyone. Tension gripped him.

In the airplane taxiing out, Jack was overly conscious of the time. He had only 7 minutes left on his release time and still had a runup to do. It only took 3 minutes. With the weather like it was, an experienced pilot would have done a double runup, even if it meant leaving the ground with only 30 seconds left on the release time clock. But Jack was intimidated by the finality of his time-off deadline and was off the ground 2½ minutes early. He had done a thorough runup but he wasn't sure of it.

Just as the Lance's nose climbed into the awaiting overcast, Jack had the uneasy feeling that he might have missed something during the runup. In a quick glance across the panel, he saw, or thought he saw, the fuel flow gauges reading zero. His call to Kansas City Center was frantic:

Jack "Center, this is Lance . . . Foxtrot. Just off 21 at Lee C. Fine with a problem. Need a clearance back in a hurry! We might be losing an engine."

Center "No contact, . . . Foxtrot. Say your altitude."

Jack "Just coming through 1,700, in the clouds, but we're going back down to get out of this stuff. Cloud bases were at 1,500 on the way up."

Center "Okay, you're cleared for the approach. Maintain 2,100 until established. No need for a procedure turn. Suggest you stay at approach altitude . . .. The ceilings have been reported ragged, and that's hill country you're in."

Jack "Don't know how long this engine is going to keep on running, sir. We're just passing the VOR now, and I want to get visual right close to the airport before we lose power."

Center "Roger . . .. You're cleared any altitude. Maintain VFR when able. You'll have a slight tailwind for landing on Runway 3. Shouldn't be a problem. That runway is 6,500 feet long. Call to cancel when you have the field in sight." (The controller sat frozen, staring at his screen. Waiting for the call back. He was transfixed.)

Jack (30 seconds later—an eternity for the controller) "Center, . . . Foxtrot has the runway. Raining awful hard. Uh . . . cancel IFR . . . thanks, uh . . . so long."

The Lance had come out of the clouds at 1,450 feet msl, 2 miles southeast of Sunshine VOR, the approach fix into runway 3 at Lee C. Fine Airport. Jack was excited and relieved to see the ground. It was raining harder than when they had taken off just a few minutes earlier, reducing visibility to about 2 miles. But Jack hardly noticed. He was concentrating on getting back on the approach and landing, still holding his breath, hoping the engine would run long enough to get them across the runway threshold. His grip on the wheel was too tight. He was in a cold, fearful sweat. But he was getting there.

Completing a shallow right turn, the navigation needle made a barely perceptible move off the left peg, then another, slightly more pronounced, and then started creeping toward center. They were on the 030° approach course at 1,450 on the altimeter, about 450 feet agl and 2½ miles on the DME. Jack let out a little breath and tried to relax.

They crossed the VOR dead center and Jack and Laura started looking straight ahead through the heavy rain for the flashers, the VASI, and the runway. Less than a minute later—bingo. Right on the nose. Jack let out another breath, picked up the mike, and called center, canceling IFR.

He put down the mike, went through his landing checklist—A-okay—looked out the window and froze. They were still at 400 feet agl and closing on the runway fast. It wasn't much of a tail wind, only 10–12 knots, but Jack had never before made a downwind landing in the Lance. Everything looked different and he wasn't prepared for it.

Over the runway threshold at 175 feet, with full flaps, wheels down, and no power, Jack cross-controlled to dump altitude in a hurry. The airspeed was okay at 100 knots. Too fast but okay. He could handle that.

What he could not handle was himself. His grip on the yoke was overpowering. He was sure he was going to land long or off the runway. His confidence had left him. He told himself he wasn't going to make it. He was talking himself into crashing. Past the midpoint down the runway and still 30 feet in the air, Jack hauled back on the yoke, pulling the nose up into a landing flare. The Lance did it's usual thing. It mushed, reaching for the runway that was too far below. Then it stalled and slammed down on the concrete on all three's, from over 20 feet in the air. The impact rammed the wheels up and through their wells, bending the wing spars and the engine housing and penetrating both fuel tanks. The Lance came to an abrupt halt after a short landing roll of 100 screeching feet, with its engine still running. Miraculously there was no fire, even though the tanks were almost full. The people fared pretty well, too, suffering only minor injuries.

Jack sat stunned. Bruised slightly and bewildered. His three passengers were in similar states of hurt and confusion. Finally, after 5 or 6 seconds that seemed like forever, Laura said something to Jack. It jolted him into reality and he reached for the switches and turned off the engine. They all sat for several more seconds and then began exiting the airplane. There was no conversation. They were all too much in shock to speak to each other.

Jack "I can't tell you how relieved I was when we crossed over that VOR dead center like we did. I was sure I had it made for an easy landing after that. But it was raining much harder than I had noticed, and when I looked out the front window, I was surprised that I couldn't see the runway from where we were. The VOR is only 3 miles or so from the touchdown point. That distracted me, and I forgot to fly the approach. I just stayed at the same altitude waiting to find the airport. I knew it would be coming up through the rain momentarily. When it did, a minute or so later, we were still at 400 feet and only a mile from the runway. And I hadn't yet lowered the flaps or the gear. With the 10-knot tailwind we had, I just couldn't get down fast enough.

"I think we were still at close to 200 feet crossing the front end of the runway. I tried to slip it in, but we were running out of room. When I got to midfield, I was sure I could slip it in some more and get down the rest of the way. That's when I lost it.

"I think what happened is that when I started to cross-control, I applied too much back pressure. The nose came up into what looked like a landing flare. But it was really just a control error on my part. I wasn't that much out of it that I wouldn't remember if I was trying to land or not."

FAA representative "This seemed to us like a classic case of an airplane that was way out ahead of a pilot. The best we can tell is that he took off in a state of semipanic. He was a low-timer in a sophisticated machine on a tough day. That doesn't make for a real safe combination.

"We checked the fuel system several times because the pilot claimed that he got zero fuel flow readings from both gauges. But they checked out fine. Anyway, it would have been unusual for them not to because about the only thing that could make them both read that way at the same time is when the fuel is shut off. And that couldn't have been the case, or the engine never would have run long enough for them to have taken off. So, we don't know what that pilot saw, or thought he saw, or *claimed* he thought he saw. For all we know, he may have just been looking for an excuse to get out of those low clouds and back on the ground.

"As far as the approach is concerned, from what he told us, and from what we were able to piece together from the other statements we took, that was what I said in the first place. He got behind the airplane and never did catch up. By the time he realized the predicament he was in, he then made the classic mistake of trying to force the landing. But he was probably too scared to think about making a go-around anyway. Not in that weather. And certainly not after he was so anxious to get back on the ground.

"Regarding the pilot's story about trying to slip it in when he was almost to midfield: It doesn't check out. We got an eyewitness report from the airport manager who said he watched them come charging down the runway, the wrong way, and then try to land after they were already too far along. We got the same report from a King Air that was sitting at the north end of the parallel waiting for a release time. They got the daylights scared out of them when they saw the Lance coming straight at them. They had no place to go. Their report confirms what the airport manager said: The Lance pilot tried to force it in after he'd run out of operating room.

"So, no matter how you slice it, this was a pilot error accident. The pilot just wasn't prepared for the conditions or the equipment he was flying in. It's a shame that his first real test of actual IMC on his own had to be such a tough one. Hopefully, his luck will be better from here on out. Or, better still, his judgment."

Laura Brewer "I wasn't going to say anything but, as long as you asked, I'll tell you that this whole affair has been a real eye opener for all of us. Jack never should have taken off in those conditions because he wasn't comfortable about it. He should have just told Phil and Bert to make other arrangements. But they're older than Jack and very forceful people. He didn't know how to turn them down without looking like he was wimping out.

"When he and I talked about it afterward, Jack told me he was somewhat flattered at the time that they were so sure he could handle it. Phil, especially, made light of the whole situation because he genuinely felt that taking off in bad weather was the easy part, and not at all dangerous. A lot of people apparently feel that way, but it's simply not true. I don't know how it shows up statistically, but Jack has shown me several accident reports where people were killed taking off into low clouds. That is exactly what we did, and Jack handled it very well.

"I remember that as soon as we went up into the clouds, Jack knocked on one or two of the gauges. They seemed to be stuck. But right after he hit them a couple of times, I saw the one that was closest to me move to somewhere in the middle. I didn't notice anything happen to the other one. But, whatever it was that was wrong with those instruments, Jack sure did get upset over it—so bad that he told us we had to go back to the airport because the engine could quit at any moment.

"When we finally did see the airport, after Jack brought us back out of those clouds, we were up too high and going too fast. But Jack was sure he could get us down quickly enough. And he almost did. If we weren't going so fast, I'm sure we would have made it.

"Just before we went down so hard, Bert or Phil, I can't remember which one it was, asked Jack if we were going to have to go around and try the approach again, since almost half the runway had already gone by. But Jack said he expected the engine to quit at any second and he didn't want us to wind up in the trees. Why they had to bother him at that precise moment I still don't understand because it distracted Jack and must have contributed to the accident."

Abner Jung "Jack Ferguson was one of the most difficult head cases I ever worked with. He had been mentally brutalized over that Turbo Lance he bought. It was the wrong airplane for him at the wrong time in his flying. And I'd have to say, in hindsight, that both Mel Drexler and I handled him poorly as well, under the circumstances. That was because Mel, who started with him on his instrument ticket, didn't realize at first just how badly Jack was intimidated by his airplane.

"By the time Jack got to me, the Lance was his nemesis and Jack had convinced himself that he would never be able to cope with instrument flying or the airplane. He said he was ready to give up, after having failed two checkrides. But what neither of us understood at the time was that he had already given up. He just hadn't told himself.

"I felt that it was my job to get him turned around psychologically so he could get his instrument ticket and then really begin to master aviation. I've worked with a number of borderline pilots, by the way, and I've always found that they don't really start to learn until after they get their instrument certificates. It must be the power of the paper, because it's a fact.

"What I didn't realize about Jack was that his was more a Turbo Lance problem than it was an instrument training and orientation problem. I had never seen anything like that before, so I didn't know how to deal with it. Consequently, the decisions I made were based on my own experiences with floundering IFR hopefuls. But those decisions were a disaster for Jack. I pushed him to get through his checkride so he could get that psychological barrier behind him and then begin in earnest to turn himself into a first-class pilot. But what I should have done was take him on two or three long cross-countries in the Lance so he could first become the master of his own airplane. Without that crucial step, he would take too long to get comfortable with his equipment and grow more and more discouraged as his IFR development stumbled because of it.

"After the accident, Jack was a mess. He wasn't sure he ever wanted to fly again. He was sure, however, that he did not ever want to see that Turbo Lance again. In fact, he was so emphatic about it that pretty soon we both came to realize that the damned airplane had to be mastered or Jack would never be able to count on himself to fly safely out of anything like a tough situation. So, that became our new challenge.

"It took nearly five months to put the Lance back together. When it was finally ferried back to Youngstown, the first thing Jack and I did was head out with his fiance on a weeklong trip to New York, Boston, and Philadelphia. We landed at La Guardia, Logan and Philadelphia International airports. Not a bad way to break in a local boy from the grand metropolis of Youngstown, Ohio. But it worked, and Jack is now as good a pilot as anyone flying instruments in a high-performance single-engine airplane.

"Oh, one last thing about the accident. A few weeks after Jack got the Turbo Lance back from the reconstructors, both of its fuel flow gauges went on the fritz. Apparently they had been installed wrong at the Piper factory. Jack had the mechanics here send a report of what they found directly to the FAA, but he never heard anything back from them. His file may have already been closed out."

NTSB representative "We are very aware that prejudicial junk occasionally finds its way into our official data. We call it 'junk' because that's what it is: Distorted factual material that represents an opinion, or only part of what occurred or caused an accident, leaving out brushed-aside details that could materially change the perspective toward the event. As you can imagine, we do everything humanly and 'computerly' possible to eliminate prejudiced reporting. But we're not perfect and we know that some of it slips through.

"Over the years, we have learned to watch for a tip-off that tends to show up in the written overview statements sent in by the field investigators: They don't give the pilot the benefit of the doubt.

"When a field person acts like a judge and jury, red flags go up here. Certain words and phrases like: 'Pilot failed to . . .', or 'pilot was not trained for . . .', or 'Pilot deliberately . . .'. They all indicate that the investigators might have decided in advance that it was pilot error, even before they arrived at the accident site.

"Having been a field investigator myself, I can tell you that it's not easy to always be impartial. After you've been to a few accidents where you've needed a crowbar and a blotter to untangle the bodies from the mangled airplanes . . . you start to feel a sense of anger over the outright foolishness that caused those needless deaths and injuries. In that state of mind, you want to point a finger and blame someone. And the pilot is usually the most convenient 'point-ee', especially if the pilot isn't around.

"In this case of the broken Lance, I'd have to say, unofficially of course, that a wee bit of prejudice did creep into the report. The pilot may have been grossly misled by faulty fuel gauges. If so, he certainly made the right decision to make a precautionary landing, in a hurry and downwind. If not, it was a clear case of panic. Since we can only go by what we can prove, we have to go with 'panic.' But either way, it doesn't excuse or explain why the pilot flared from 30 feet in the air after using up more than half the runway.

"Obviously, it would serve aviation better if we knew why the pilot made a mistake like that. But our mission is limited to investigating the accidents and reporting the provable facts. We have to leave deeper investigation and analysis to other agencies."

NASA representative "There are some accidents that are truly 'pilot error,' with no further explanation required. This one comes close to deserving that designation, at least on the surface. But consider some of the circumstances and, while you might come to the same conclusion, it may be for entirely different reasons than you thought or were led to believe.

"First of all, discount everything prior to the day of the accident. What his instructors said: the failed checkrides, his coordination, his personality—they're all of no significance. The FAA said he was qualified to fly and so did both of the instructors, despite their other remarks. What you're left with is an inexperienced IFR pilot who is suddenly put into a life-threatening situation, at least in his mind. It was probably the first time in his flying career, and may have been the first time in his entire life, that he ever experienced fear like that: The kind that grabs your gut and doesn't let go. You know what I'm talking about if you've been flying long enough.

"Then, everything turns nastier on him. Heavier rain. Reduced visibility. A downwind landing that he's never tried before. And before he knows it, he finds himself over the end of the runway threshold at 175 feet agl with a 110-knot ground speed. He knows he's in trouble and since he's had a considerable amount of recent training, it's safe to assume that his first thought is 'go-around.' But—and let me emphasize that but—he's expecting the engine to quit momentarily, so 'go-around' is out of the question. He simply has to land.

"Now put him into a steep cross-control slip that brings him to 30 or 40 feet agl, and a peak, with half the runway behind him. His next reflex is entirely correct: Put in another quick slip and get down in a hurry. But do it carefully. You're very close to the ground where slipping gets dangerous. In his case, it was another first. He had never before cross-controlled an airplane from 30 feet agl. And neither have 95 percent of the pilots flying because it's an unsafe maneuver from that close to the ground and reasonably intelligent flight instructors won't risk their own lives teaching something that's really a last ditch effort in a forced landing situation. Most pilots couldn't handle it. Jack Ferguson was no exception.

"The point I'm making here is that the official conclusion in this case was that the accident was caused by a poorly executed landing flare, even though the pilot and at least one of his passengers says otherwise. Well, we go with the pilot. His story is entirely plausible. While the rest of the accounts are suspect, especially since they are supported only by eyewitnesses on the ground. Have you ever seen what a slip looks like from the ground? It looks like a flare for landing because the first thing that happens when the wing is dropped and the opposite rudder is applied is that the nose rises momentarily. The way this Lance hit the ground on all three's also tends to confirm a slip rather than a stall after a landing flare.

"If I've made my point, permit me to emphasize that we still believe this to be a 'pilot error' accident. But not for the reason given as the probable cause in the official report.

"In our estimation, the errors took place on the approach, long before the airplane ever got near the runway. The first mistake the pilot made was forgetting to prepare the Lance for landing prior to intercepting the inbound course. Then, crossing the VOR and able to see the ground, he made the most fundamental, most common mistake of all: He went off the gauges and never went back on them.

"Had he followed normal approach procedures, when they first picked up the runway from a half-mile or so out, the Lance would have been at 450 feet with its flaps and wheels down for an easy landing on that 6497 foot runway.

"This rather inexperienced pilot did indeed make a classic 'pilot error.' But he was luckier than many. He lived to tell about it."

Author comment One thing this accident makes very clear is a pilot's need for experience and luck. You have to be lucky enough to learn from other people's experiences, experienced enough to be able to avoid experience-generating encounters, and lucky enough to survive the situations from which experience is derived.

Throughout the lifelong gathering of experience, it is better to be a teacher or a learner than an example.

12

It looked like an airport

Preliminary report: December; Piper Warrior; commercial pilot, single-engine land, 380 hours. The pilot and her passenger suffered minor injuries when they crashed into a truck terminal parking lot during a night VFR flight into IMC from Madison, Wisconsin, to Bloomington, Indiana. The pilot had transmitted on 121.5 MHz that she was low on fuel in the vicinity of her destination airport. Visibility in the area was 2–2½ miles in fog and haze, as forecast. The crash occurred while the pilot was trying to find the airport, which she claimed she saw once despite the fog.

Further investigation revealed:

- The pilot had received a thorough weather briefing and was advised that VFR night flying was not recommended because of reduced visibilities near the destination airport. Forecast for the Bloomington area was 1,200 overcast and 2–3 miles visibility in fog and haze.
- Of her 380 hours, only 12 were at night and none within the last 10 months.
- The pilot was a part-time flight instructor and had accumulated 260 hours of Piper Tomahawk time and 35 hours of Warrior time while teaching, plus 6 hours of recent instruction for an instrument rating.
- The crash occurred 3½ hours after takeoff of the scheduled 2½ hour trip. The pilot said there were many deviations around weather.
- A metropolitan area reporting 1,500 and 4, with three well-lit airports was overflown fewer than 30 minutes prior to the accident. The pilot admitted seeing at least one of the airports but was unable to contact the tower.

132

Official conclusion: Deliberate VMC into IMC. Fuel exhaustion. Violation of night flying currency requirement. Pilot error.

IT STARTED OUT AS A NOON DEPARTURE but turned into a night flight because of a scheduling mix-up. Terri Lynne Cunningham, 27, was a full-time lawyer and assistant states attorney for the state of Wisconsin in Madison. She was also a part-time flight instructor at Truax Field on weekends and early evenings during the summer. Most of her flying over the past three years was in Piper Tomahawks, primarily giving new-student orientation rides. Her boss, the largest FBO at Truax, felt that having an attractive, young woman take new students, mostly men, for their first few instruction flights would build their macho confidence and encourage them to complete their training.

At first, Terri had resented her role as "bait." But she loved to fly and the money was good. And her boss had convinced her that "Whatever it takes" was worth it because it was working and helping him build a bigger business. She was an easy sell. He also had sweetened the pot recently by giving her a bonus of one free hour per week of Warrior time to help her get her instrument rating. Terri was now happily ensconced in the role she had accepted tentatively three years earlier.

Today's trip was a time-builder's dream. Terri's closest friend, Jennifer Gray, 27, an accounting instructor at the University of Wisconsin, in Madison, had been offered an exciting career advancement by the University of Indiana, in Bloomington, Indiana. They were willing to pay $300 transportation cost for Terri to come for an interview. The 5-hour round trip in the Warrior, at $52 an hour, would net Jennifer a small profit, and Terri 5 hours of real cross-country time in the Warrior. They were both pleased and excited.

Arriving at the airport at 11 a.m. for their planned noon departure, there was a problem. The FBO's second Warrior was delayed in Rockford and would not return in time for a checkride that had been scheduled at 1 p.m. Terri and Jennifer would have to wait while their Warrior was used by the chief flight instructor and the student pilot.

Disappointed but undaunted, Terri called flight service to check weather again, for the third time, and reschedule her flight plan. She got some unsettling news: Night VFR into Bloomington was not recommended due to marginal ceilings and reduced visibility in fog and haze. She carefully wrote down all the numbers—1,200 over and 2–3 miles—and as much detail as she could jot down quickly—VFR out of Madison, some scattered to broken clouds over northern Illinois and northwestern Indiana, bases at 3,000, tops 5–6,000 variable, winds aloft at 6,000: 260° at 20. Not good, but not impossible either.

Terri shared her new knowledge with Jennifer, and they began evaluating their options: Jennifer could call ahead and reschedule. She could drive to Bloomington, but her car had just gone in for a new transmission. If she couldn't reschedule, it would delay her opportunity until after the Christmas holidays, or maybe kill it. Terri offered her car, but they both agreed that with 48,000 miles on the tires it would be too risky for two young women to take on a 6-hour trip at night.

Upset over the prospect that Jennifer might miss out on a major advance in her future, but even more so the disappointment of having to give up those 5 free cross-country hours in the Warrior, Terri looked over her notes more carefully and decided to get some fatherly counsel from Ollie Logan, head of operations at the FBO.

Ollie Logan "Terri and I checked over the weather notes she'd made, and it really wasn't a 'no-go' situation at all: Good VFR out of here. A few build-ups to go around on the way down, but with the almost full moon, no problem seeing them. Then marginal at Bloomington. But with plenty of decent-size airports available to run to, and over an hour of fuel reserve, I didn't think Terri would have any trouble getting in there.

"Actually, I was more concerned about her confidence and how she felt about making the trip. She was and still is a very good pilot, but I knew that most of her flying time had been in Tomahawks tooling around the local area. That was mostly what we talked about.

"She expressed some reservations about such a long night flight, because she'd never made one before. But never any fear. Just a healthy, professional attitude toward a new challenge, unlike many of the macho types we see around here who are looking for new notches to put in their guns. No, Terri was just fine. And she was looking forward to the trip. So, I advised her to go. And I reassured her that she'd be able to handle it easily."

Having decided to make the trip, and with several hours to kill, Terri made elaborate preparations to cover every possible contingency she could think of: flight routes, deviations around weather, alternate airports, sectionals and low altitude en route charts, approach plates—not that she was yet qualified to use them, but smart to have along just in case the weather folks had really blown it—two large flashlights, and the demonstrator hand-held communication transceiver from the counter—the Warrior had dual navcom, but you never know. In the process, she went over each item with Jennifer, carefully, turning her into a quasi copilot or, at the very least, an extra-helpful passenger.

At 3:10 p.m., Terri called flight service to get the latest weather and to file a new flight plan. Good news. The weather was holding, with a possibility of improvement, somewhat. She also obtained the weather everywhere on her route of flight, which was smart.

Then she decided on her routing and started to file, but because she could be illegal arriving VFR in Bloomington—it's a controlled area and requires 1,000 feet and 3 miles—Terri filed to Terre Haute, which is only 23 miles short of Bloomington but was forecasting 1,500 over and 4-5 miles visibility. Also smart.

At 4:10 p.m., a few minutes later than planned because Terri did the runup more than twice, the Warrior lifted off Runway 22 at Truax into the setting winter sun. It was clear as crystal and smooth as silk. A nice combination for the enthusiastic night flyers.

Picking up a 150° heading and climbing to 5,500 feet, Terri set the #2 nav at 150° FROM off the Madison VOR. She had already dialed in the Joliet VOR, 112.3, on #1, but that wouldn't be coming in for awhile. So far, they were on a straight-line course to Bloomington.

The first cloud build-ups they saw were in the vicinity of DeKalb and Aurora, Illinois. Nothing serious. And easy to spot in the reddish-purple sky on the right and the faint light from the first hint of the al-most full moon rising on the left. Pretty, too. Terri noticed a pronounced haze layer ahead at their altitude. A call to Chicago Center on 123.75 brought the welcome information that they would be able to overfly the weather ahead and let back down to 5,500 in 60 miles or so, just south of Kankakee. Five minutes later they were two euphoric flyers at 7,500 feet, enjoying a lovely airplane ride and talking about how they were going to maintain their many-year friendship after Jennifer landed her new job at IU.

Passing Joliet slightly behind schedule—thanks to the unkindlier-than-forecast winds aloft—Terri noticed another cloud build-up on their nose about 40–50 miles ahead. She called center again, this time on 132.95, and was advised that Champaign, Illinois, was on the west side of the small area of snow showers being reported near Kanka-kee. Terri dialed up 110.0 on the #1 VOR and began tracking the nee-dle to the Champaign VOR. Then she carefully measured the added distance they would be traversing and scribbled some numbers on her kneepad: 80 miles, about 40–45 minutes. Should be OK.

Over the Champaign VOR, the weather was still on their left and looked like it was continuous to the southeast, which would put it over Terre Haute and, of course, Bloomington. With clear sky around them and to the west, Terri elected to descend to 2,000 feet, which would put them just under the cloud bases reported at Terre Haute. She called Indianapolis Center to report their altitude change and was advised to pick up a 150° heading out of Champaign and fly it for about 20 miles to stay clear of the lingering snow showers to her east. She could then fly direct to the Terre Haute VOR and be back on course.

Terri was pleased with the advisory and herself, glad she and Jennifer had decided not to scrub the trip. They would be nearly an hour behind schedule arriving in Bloomington because of the weather deviations, but with ample time for a late supper and a good night's rest. She was confident, elated and self-satisfied as she checked her maps, recalculated the fuel remaining and thought about the rest of their trip. Terri considered the results of the recalculation: "1:20 left with 75 miles to go, or about 50 minutes total flying time, including 5 minutes to land and taxi in. Leaves about half an hour fuel reserve, plus or minus 10 minutes. Should be okay. The Bloomington VOR sits right on the Monroe County Airport, so it should be a cinch to find. The fuel gauges are showing under a quarter full on both sides, but those things are seldom accurate anyway. We're looking good."

Turning left toward Terre Haute at 2,000 feet msl, or about 1,400 feet agl, Terri noticed that she could not see the ground very clearly. She mentioned it to Jennifer who told her she was having the same problem. Together they decided it was either because of the haze or the windshield was diffusing the lights from the ground. But whatever, their combined visual capability was substantially reduced. Terri got her first pang of concern.

Terri "I began to notice that I was having trouble seeing things on the ground. It was like everything was getting a little fuzzy. Jenn said she was noticing the same thing. We figured it was the hazy air or maybe the plexiglass was doing something to the lights, like diffusing or refracting them. So, I just made off like it wasn't any big deal. I didn't want to upset Jenn. But I was plenty concerned about it. Where we were at that moment was being advertised as pretty good visibility. But I couldn't see anything, not clearly anyway. And Bloomington was supposed to be worse. The more I thought about it, the more worried I got. So I just turned my attention to flying the airplane and getting ready for Bloomington, to take my mind off of it. And looking out the window to see if it was getting any better. It wasn't."

Nearing Terre Haute, Terri began looking for the two airports she had noted on the sectional: Edgar County in Paris, Illinois, and Sky King on the northwest side of Terre Haute. They would both be on the left side of the airplane. Her side. And close enough to the Warrior's flight path to be seen easily at night. She spent most of the next 15 minutes looking out the window, scanning, waiting for the flashing green from Edgar and then from Sky King.

When the #1 nav needle began wavering, indicating impending station passage over the Terre Haute VOR, Terri's heart fluttered and then palpitated. She had not seen either airport, not even Sky King which they had practically kissed on the way in to the VOR. Carefully concealing her growing panic, Terri asked Jennifer to watch for a flashing green-and-white beacon at their 3 o'clock position as they crossed the VOR and turned right 20° to a 130° heading. Hulman Regional Airport would be only 3 miles away. Only 3 miles away.

Jennifer saw it first. The flasher from Hulman. She was excited as she pointed it out to Terri, who then instantly saw the lights from Runway 5-23. Terri felt a wave of relief as she dialed in 118.8 and called Hulman tower. They didn't respond. She waited 10 seconds and called again. Still no answer. By the fifth call her voice and her mike hand were shaking. Nothing. Hulman tower's frequency is 118.3. Terri had misread it on her sectional. The night tower operator saw the green and red flashers from the Warrior circling off the end of Runway 23.

Scanning the fuel gauges—now between ⅛ and EMPTY—Terri made a quick decision. They would fly on to Bloomington. It was only 23 miles away and Monroe County Airport would be on their nose when they arrived.

When there was no radio call from the unidentified aircraft at the approach end of his active runway, the tower operator tried his light gun several times. There was no response. Finally, after an anxious 3–4 minutes, the aircraft departed to the southeast.

Terri began looking for Monroe County Airport the moment she reluctantly turned away from Hulman. The visibility was getting worse, she was descending to remain beneath the lowering ceiling, and the airport would be coming up in less than 15 minutes. She wanted to see it before Jennifer did. She also wanted to make a straight-in landing on Runway 17 so she wouldn't need to circle and risk losing sight of the airport.

After 5 minutes of nervous scanning—left and right but mostly straight ahead—into the haze and fog, Terri called Monroe tower on 121.2 and listened to the taped announcement that the tower was closed. She had already dialed in Hulman Approach on 124.15 and keyed her mike to call. She waited 5 seconds for an answer that didn't come, looked at her fuel gauges just beginning to touch the EMPTY mark, and panicked. Quickly dialing 121.5, Terri announced their "N" number and frantically reported that they were low on fuel.

The Hulman Approach controller missed Terri's call on 125.45 by a split second. He was on his second call back to Terri when he heard her urgent call on 121.5. His response was immediate.

Terri heard the controller's reply and was about to answer when she saw a flashing white light and a row of lights right on her nose, less than 2 miles away. Dropping the mike in her lap, she pulled the throttle, lowered the flaps and dropped the nose. They were 550 feet agl, and this was one landing Terri Lynne Cunningham was not going to miss.

The controller kept calling, but Terri paid no attention to him. She was concentrating on her approach and landing. And watching the fuel gauges that were just then touching the EMPTY lines. Her heart was in her mouth and she was holding her breath. At 250 feet agl and a mile from touchdown, Terri relaxed a little, listened to the smooth purr of the slow-running—still-running—engine and relaxed a bit more. Her confidence was returning.

At ½ mile out, Terri and Jennifer got their first clear look at the flasher and the row of lights—both of them froze. It wasn't a runway. It wasn't even an airport. It was the parking area of a truck terminal and warehouse, 5½ miles northwest of Monroe County Airport, near the intersection of state roads 43 and 46 in the little town of Whitehall, Indiana. Terri swallowed hard as her brain went to warp speed, groping for a plan of action.

But the Warrior's engine made the decision for her with a short sputter, followed by a surge, and then silence.

From that moment forward, Terri did everything right. She was an excellent pilot, instinctively, and had a special knack for soft landings—the kind that gave nervous students a sense of safety and confidence that: "If she can do it, so can I, only better." They seldom did.

Terri's landing on the blacktop was picture perfect, a real greaser. They would have rolled out perfectly, too, if it hadn't been for a row of concrete tire barriers that were strung across the wide-open run down the row of lights.

Terri never saw the obstacles until almost on top of the barriers. Not that it would have made much difference to have seen them sooner. There was no place else to go. But she did have enough ground speed and reflex time to raise the nosewheel just enough to graze the bolted-down concrete barriers, which took up some of the impact shock as they hit, and hurled the Warrior skyward. After the mains struck, a split second later, Terri and Jennifer found themselves 20 feet in the air and stalling.

The Warrior dropped like a stone, collapsing its right main gear and then its right wing. It scraped and screeched along the hard surface for another 150 feet or so and finally came to rest just short of the truck terminal's main building. Except for those barriers, the Warrior never struck anything else on the ground—not the light poles, not the rows of parked trucks, nor any of the other vehicles and pieces of equipment in the lot. Terri had indeed threaded the needle. The Warrior would live to fly again. So would its occupants. Terri and Jennifer were not injured. Badly shaken, but okay.

The Bloomington Police Department arrived 5 minutes later and whisked Terri and Jennifer to the hospital, then to the police station, and finally to their motel, long after midnight.

This accident ended on happy notes. The folks at IU decided that anyone who would go to such extremes to show up for an interview was their kind of person. Jennifer beat out five other applicants for the job. And Terri, who spent the entire morning and part of the afternoon filling out accident report papers, was pleasantly surprised when Ollie Logan showed up in the company Baron to fly her and Jennifer back to Madison. It was Terri's first left-seat ride in a twin-engine airplane. Ollie had insisted that she fly in the pilot's seat—despite her protests that she was too weary from the whole episode—because he wanted to restore her faith in herself and as a pilot. He also filed an IFR flight plan at 10,000 feet, above all the weather, and they all enjoyed a delightful ride home. Another of Terri's excellent landings was icing on the cake.

FAA accident investigator "This was one of those accidents that defies logic. Intelligent people. A well-trained pilot, and I say that even though she was a low-timer and not current for night flying. But you should have seen where she brought that Warrior into. An ATP couldn't have done a better job. If those concrete separators hadn't been there, she would have been able to fly that thing out of there the next morning when the weather cleared up.

"You wonder how they could've run out of gas when there were at least a half dozen airports that they practically flew right over within 100 miles of here. In the report she gave us, the pilot stated that she hardly even considered the possibility that she could run out of fuel. She had planned to stop in either Champaign or Terre Haute if they got close to having a problem. But she didn't realize they had a problem until she couldn't land at Terre Haute. That really threw her. And it was really just a bad break, misreading that frequency and all. Could've happened to anyone.

"But then, she didn't see the light signals either, or maybe didn't know what they meant. She told us she had never lost comm capability at night before. And being from a large airport like Madison, she'd only seen light gun signals a couple of times. The tower operator at Terre Haute said he must have flashed (the light) at least 10 times. But he never got so much as a wing wiggle acknowledging any of them. It was like the pilot wasn't able to see anything. He tried alternating colors, too, because he kind of suspected it was them. Their flight plan was filed to his airport and, of course, they never showed up.

"Then mistaking that truck terminal for the airport. The pilot said she thought the flasher was a runway end identifier and that the row of street lights and the looks of the buildings was very convincing, especially through that haze and fog. I guess it could seem like an airport in 1½ mile visibility if you're expecting it to be about there, and you want it to be there awful bad. Your eyes and your mind can play some funny tricks on you in conditions like that. Especially at night when you're tired.

"None of what I just told you is in the record of this accident. We reported it straight, as what it was: 'Fuel exhaustion. Not current for night flying. Inadequate planning. Pilot error.' There's really not much more to say about it. Too bad though. That was one sharp young lady. You'd never imagine someone like her running an airplane bone dry."

Terri "You know, the more I think about the accident, the less sense it makes to me. I had a fail-safe flight plan worked out with checkpoints along the way for fuel, and alternate routings for weather, plus airports, frequencies, the whole shebang. The only thing that could go wrong is what I did. I never followed my own flight plan.

"I don't even remember where I gave up on it, Champaign or Terre Haute. It had to be one of those two. I had a fuel check to do at Kankakee, which I did and which turned out right on schedule. Then, with the deviation around the weather to Champaign, I was supposed to do another one. But I can't remember whether I did or not. And when we reached Terre Haute, the flight plan I had filed called for landing at Hulman. And I fully intended to do that unless there had been no weather deviations—which, of course, there had been—and unless the weather was above VFR minimums at Monroe County—which, again, it was not.

"I know I got very confused after we rounded the weather bend south of Champaign. And when we got near Terre Haute and I couldn't find my two checkpoint airports, I got rattled. Bad enough, I suppose, that I put in the wrong frequency to call Hulman. You know, I had the right one written down on my kneepad. But I had been checking the sectional to locate the airports and took the frequency off of there. In the low light, it was easy to mistake a 3 for an 8.

"After we circled around Hulman without being able to reach anyone, I decided we'd better get ourselves to Bloomington while we still had enough fuel. But we didn't have enough fuel, and, for the life of me, I still don't know why I thought we did. The gauges were telling me the truth, and I knew how long we had been flying and how far we had to go. It's just a mystery to me because I recall being quite certain of it at the time.

"When we saw that flashing strobe and those parking lot lights, we were both sure we were looking at the airport. It was exactly where it was supposed to be, right on our nose. Only it was 5 miles short of Monroe County, and I should have known that. But in that low visibility, which I wasn't comfortable with at night, and being so anxious to find the airport and get that Warrior put to bed, I must have simply made my mind up in advance that the first thing that looked like an airport would have to be Monroe County. I have no explanation other than that for what I did.

"Thinking about that parking lot sometimes gives me the willies. We ran out of gas about ¼ mile out. But what if we hadn't been that close to it, or hadn't seen it? We could have hit just about anything out there because we could hardly see where we were going. Jenn and I have talked about it a lot since and we both agree that there must have been someone watching over us that night."

NTSB representative "This is obviously much more than a simple fuel exhaustion accident. There were too many other contributing causes that belong on the record. Like spatial disorientation: This pilot got so confused that she failed to follow her own flight plan. Or maybe the pilot had a night vision problem that she didn't even know about, and which didn't show up on her medical. Or, how about failure to declare an emergency: That was just poor judgment, or lack of judgment altogether. If she had called Hulman on 121.5, they would have brought that Warrior in immediately, and those two ladies would have spent the night in Terre Haute. Safely. And, as the weather turned out, they could have easily flown to Bloomington the next morning in time for whatever it was they were planning to do there.

"That's why I said the 'probable causes' of this accident are so much more complex than just fuel exhaustion. And many times more frustrating as well—for us. Let me explain that so you understand what I mean: Because the two people survived, we can discover almost every detail of what happened. The key word there is 'what.'

We know 'what' happened. What we don't know is 'why' any of it happened. And that drives us crazy because there must be logical answers available.

"In fact, there are. The airlines find them all the time. If this had been an airliner that ran out of fuel and crashed into that parking lot, you can bet your tootsies there would be answers—lots of them. Because the airlines and the manufacturers of their airplanes would have gone over every detail with our airline division to find those answers, no matter how much it cost or how long it took to do so. And then, if it seemed like a good idea, rules and procedures would be changed to prevent an accident like it from ever happening again.

"But not on our side of the hall. We have very limited time and a fraction of the money we need. So, we're stuck sticking to the 'what's' without the 'why's.' And if, by accident, or by some quirk of fate, a 'why' falls into our laps every once in awhile, we can stand on our heads and can't get a rule changed. Because we don't have enough clout with the FAA. And they make all the rules.

"That's what I mean by frustrated. And accidents like this one make it worse."

NASA representative "An accident like this one gives every involved agency an opportunity to make a great leap forward in accident prevention. But all we can do is talk about it off the record. Because there are more constraints than we can deal with in getting information to each other.

"We're constrained because the pilots who report to our Aviation Safety Reporting System are guaranteed absolute confidentiality. The FAA is constrained because they can only report what they see and hear relating directly to an accident. And the NTSB is constrained because they can only report what they can prove after the fact, and mostly mechanically, with numbers.

"But here is a case where we can prove everything *before* the fact and we still can't get the information to where it belongs: to pilots, to the people who train them, to the airplane manufacturers, and to the rulemakers who control the system. We're not talking speculation here. These are cold, hard facts: Night vision is adversely affected as low as 5,000 feet. The longer you're up there, the worse it gets because the oxygen saturation in the blood decreases by more than 5 percentage points to as low as 92 percent, or even 90 percent at that altitude. That may not sound like a lot but it's more than enough to cause a measurable loss of direct vision in the retina of the eye. And peripheral vision, the panoramic part of sight, is even more affected.

"This pilot was at 5,500 feet or higher for 3 solid hours at night. Her blood oxygen level had to be at or below 90 percent by the time she began descending for Terre Haute. Now this is not speculation. This is fact we can prove and demonstrate on every human being we can test, except maybe for Sherpas who live at 15,000 feet in Nepal—but everyone else, even people from mountainous areas. Add 5,000 feet of altitude, starting at almost any elevation, and within half an hour we can measure oxygen saturation decline and vision loss. After 3 hours, the saturation level will be at 90 percent or less. In everyone. Even military pilots who are supposed to be in better shape than the average civilian.

"Other manifestations of low blood oxygen are harder to measure mechanically, but we can demonstrate and prove them just as conclusively. Things like manual dexterity, memory, judgment, the ability to perform simple mental exercises, they all go down the drain progressively when blood oxygen saturation remains at 90 percent, or declines further.

"Both of the women in that Warrior suffered from exactly what I just described. They couldn't see clearly. They couldn't think straight. They couldn't cope with finding an alternate communication channel, 121.5, to reach the tower at Hulman Airport. They miscalculated their remaining fuel. They used lousy judgment when they decided to leave Terre Haute with low fuel and an airport runway staring them in the face—one of the few things they could see clearly, by the way. And finally, they got fooled by a strobe and a row of street lights.

"All of the above are direct effects of their low oxygen bloodstream saturation, which we can prove beyond any doubt, reasonable or otherwise. Which then leads to one absolute, obvious conclusion: This was not pilot error at all. There are no 'probable causes' in this accident. There is only one direct cause: hypoxia—resulting from low blood/oxygen saturation of 90 percent or less. If anybody needs numbers, that '90 percent' is a number—a real, provable, measurable number. The fact that it can't be measured in a corpse a dozen hours after an accident doesn't make it any less real. And it will continue killing people in general aviation until it is taken seriously and dealt with appropriately.

"These two women were victims. Pilot error was not the cause of this accident. This was system error, procedure error, knowledge error, nobody-gives-a-damn error, and nobody-knows-what-to-do-about-it error. This was 'don't talk about high altitude and lack of oxygen error'—I could go on, but you get the idea. Every authoritative body involved in general aviation already knows enough about this problem to address it constructively and should be doing so. Otherwise, we will continue victimizing unsuspecting pilots and their passengers who believe we are protecting them."

Oxygen system manufacturer's representative "We do not provide primary oxygen equipment for small general aviation aircraft. The systems we sell are essentially for backup in pressurized airplanes operating at very high altitudes. So, since I don't have an axe to grind in communicating about this subject, I think I can give you some insights from an oxygen system manufacturer's viewpoint.

"Most of us in our business have done very little to educate the general pilot population about oxygen—the need for it and how to use it. We've pretty much left that responsibility to the FAA, the flying schools, and so forth. That's because there is a prevailing attitude among us that a little knowledge about it could be dangerous. And too much knowledge about it could scare away pilots, putting a further crimp in the aviation economy.

"At our company, we have our own perspective: We don't believe in primary oxygen systems. We believe that every aircraft, from trainers on up, should be pressurized. Let me put that another way: We believe that no unpressurized aircraft should ever be permitted to leave the ground. And when we say pressurized, we mean with some kind of fully automated system that is completely passive to the pilot. The unnatural third dimension of flying is enough for pilots to cope with. What and how they breathe and regulate their blood oxygen saturation should be taken care of for them.

"And why not? We already have existing technology that can be used to develop any number of acceptable systems, and at reasonable cost, given anticipated economies of scale. As a matter of fact, they could make airplanes and flying much cheaper than they are today because they would make such a dramatic difference in safety. That would then bring about equally dramatic reductions in direct insurance costs for pilots and aircraft owners. But, even more important, it would bring about major reductions in product liability insurance costs borne by aircraft manufacturers. That one single factor, product liability, has more than doubled the cost of a primary trainer and a four-seater family aircraft. It has, single-handedly, chased hundreds of thousands of pilots and prospective students out of aviation.

"Let me explain just how dramatic those cost savings would be and how we know that they are indeed probable: According to most expert estimates, the accident rate in general aviation would drop by more than 60 percent if all aircraft were pressurized, because it would eliminate most fuel exhaustion accidents; most alcohol, drug and substance accidents; most spatial disorientation accidents; most poor judgment accidents and most weather accidents. In other words, most 'pilot error' accidents. And those account for about 90 percent of all recorded accidents and incidents.

"These are not pie-in-the-sky estimates. They are real. And they can be easily verified by any space medicine laboratory or accredited university involved in high altitude technology and oxygen-related studies.

"I would like to make one final point: The primary oxygen industry would not benefit if pressurization became commonplace in general aviation and small aircraft. Not at first, anyway. But afterward, we would find ourselves in a much larger business supplying supplemental and backup oxygen systems to a greatly expanded and growing general aviation industry.

"Naturally, from a purely selfish standpoint, we hope it happens soon. Besides, it wouldn't hurt to save a few hundred lives a year in the process."

Author comment As the general aviation population dwindles to a precious few, the need to change "pilot error" into "pilot impairment" is finally getting the attention it deserves. And in places where changes can originate.

13

The great deice turnoff

Preliminary report: December; Cessna T303 Crusader; commercial pilot, single- and multi-engine land, instrument rating, 770 hours. The aircraft crashed while maneuvering for the approach to Greater Buffalo International Airport at 9:48 a.m. The aircraft was destroyed and the pilot and his passenger were killed. The Crusader was IFR and being vectored for an instrument approach when the pilot told approach control that he was "having icing problems." Radio and radar contact were then lost. A witness saw the Crusader flying at a very low altitude in a heavy snowfall. The aircraft banked to the right and left, then suddenly descended nose down.

Further investigation revealed:
- The businessman/pilot had 37 hours in type, having acquired the Crusader less than three months prior to the accident. He had previously flown a Cessna T210N Centurion.
- Although the Crusader was equipped for known ice, indications were that the boots had not been cycled properly.
- The pilot had a total of 55 hours of multi-engine time, all within the last five months.
- A SIGMET had been issued for the Buffalo area calling for moderate to severe icing in the clouds. The pilot was advised of the SIGMET by Cleveland Center and Buffalo Approach and responded that his aircraft was equipped for known ice.

Official conclusion: Improper use of deicing equipment. Failure to maintain flying speed. Loss of control. Possible spatial disorientation. Pilot error.

THE MORNING OF THE FLIGHT began on a happy note. Rod Granger, 30, and his girlfriend, Dawn Banks, 24, were finishing an early breakfast at Cincinnati's Lunken Airport with Rod's older brother, Ken, and preparing strategies for the mega-deal that Rod would be working on later that morning in Buffalo, New York. The two brothers had taken over their father's used machinery business earlier in the year and were hoping that a large single lot of heavy-duty cutting tools would become available to fill an important order they had been working on. This one in Buffalo, which had cropped up just the night before, could be theirs because Rod was going to get there first, before other dealers even knew about it—thanks to the company airplane.

Rod had been a renegade son ever since joining Granger Machinery Company right after graduating from the University of Ohio, where he had been a track star. Four years ago he learned to fly, convincing his father and brother that the efficiency of a company plane would far outweigh its cost because it would give them a distinct time advantage in important deals. This deal today would be the biggest notch on Rod's already successful gun. The company's business had more than doubled since Rod had done his convincing, and he had been personally responsible for most of the growth.

Rod's first airplane was a Cessna Skylane. A great learning airplane, but very limited as a long-distance business tool. Next came a Centurion because the FBO had done his homework and worked up a persuasive set of numbers showing why a faster, higher-flying machine was a better business tool. And now he flew, an all-weather, higher altitude, fast-enough twin-engine Cessna T303 Crusader— safer, more reliable, an even better business tool. A jet would come later. But for right now, Rod had his hands full getting comfortable with his new multi-engine rating and his new, much more complex airplane—all while feverishly buying and selling machinery in order to justify the substantial cost of the Crusader.

The weather forecast from flight service was troubling, but it barely phased Rod, a 765-hour instrument pilot who flew virtually every trip IFR. They were calling for moderately low ceilings leaving Cincinnati, tops at 15–16,000, winds aloft of no consequence—so far all as expected. But now, a new wrinkle: Buffalo had a possibility of heavy lake snow and/or freezing rain mixed with snow. Only a possibility, but if Rod had still been flying the Centurion, this would have been a scrubbed trip. Rod never took chances. He was as careful and cautious as he was aggressive. A quality he had learned from his coaches while he was developing his running skills in college.

The Crusader was going to prove itself on this trip, earn its keep, and help Granger Machinery Company reach new heights in business efficiency. This was going to be its first venture into heavy weather, a test for pilot and machine of its brand new "known icing" equipment. Rod, in particular, was going to get his first real taste of ice, something he had instinctively shied away from in his Skylane and Centurion. But the Crusader was equipped for ice, and he was confident of its capability. He was sure it was going to be a challenging flight and a brilliant business coup for him and Granger Machinery.

Rod filed the 2-hour trip at 21,000 feet on Victor airways to Youngstown, then direct to Dunkirk and Victor 14 straight in to Buffalo. Cincinnati was 400 over and 2½. No problems along the route of flight until about 50 miles shy of Buffalo. Then it was going to be a tossup, depending on what the surface winds did over Lake Erie: snow, rain, rain mixed with snow, all of the above, or nothing. He would know more over Youngstown and find out for sure over the Dunkirk VOR. It felt like a lucky day.

Dawn was a fairly regular copilot. She and Rod had met the day she started working at the FBO and they had been a number ever since. Because Rod was an important customer, Dawn's schedule was usually made flexible enough so that she could travel with him. Today was no exception and she was looking forward to the trip. She couldn't log the time because she was only a low-time single engine pilot, but she relished the experience and loved the way Rod handled himself and the airplane. She also loved Rod. They had already announced their engagement to their families and were going to do so publicly at a party at the end of the week. She felt like it was a lucky day, too.

Ken Granger "Rod and Dawn left here like they were going on a space mission for NASA. Like a couple of love birds but all business when it came to flying. Rod was like that. He could fool around, joke with everybody and have a better time than anyone. But when he got near an airplane, he was Mr. Meticulous and the best he could be.

"When he came back to finish his breakfast with their flight plan and the weather report, I didn't like what I was hearing. Neither did Dawn. But Rod went into a convincing description of how he would handle whatever problem came up, so we just settled back into our discussion about the cutting machines we were hoping to buy and the fact that the owner of the company up there was meeting them at the FBO flight lounge in Buffalo. Funny how impressed some people were when they found out Rod was a pilot and would be flying in to meet them in the company plane. I guess it made them feel important and us look like a Fortune 500 Company or something. Rod used to say that it gave them confidence that our checks wouldn't bounce. (Pause, then clearing his throat) He had some very sharp insights for a guy his age. (Another pause, more throat clearing) Excuse me. (Pause) With all of his nonsense as the young buck of the company, we all learned a lot from him. And when it came to the airplane, he was right about its value to the company. Most of the time, anyway.

"It's hard to imagine that someone like Rod could ever have let that airplane get away from him. He was so damned careful. So sure of what he was doing. And so good at it. But apparently that's what happened. The FAA people told us the airplane and the conditions got out in front of him and he just never did catch up. They said there was almost 2 inches of ice all over what was left of that airplane when they found it. It must have come up so fast that they never had a chance. (Long pause)

"There's nothing more I can say. He and Dawn were beautiful people with a great future ahead of them. And he was a great brother and partner. I miss him terribly."

Rod and Dawn took off from Lunken at 7:45 a.m., right on schedule, and were in the clouds at 400 feet, also right on schedule. Rod reported the cloud bases to departure and settled back for the 20-minute climb to on-top at 16,000. They actually broke out at 15,500 and then continued climbing to their assigned altitude of 21,000 feet. For the next hour, three calls to flight watch confirmed that the weather in Buffalo was still a big "if," but the surface winds were holding steady—300° at 12 knots. If they stayed that way, A-okay. No lake effect and less likelihood of serious problems when they arrived in another hour.

Over Youngstown at flight level 210, with 40 minutes to go, Cleveland Center announced the first inkling of trouble in Buffalo: The winds had shifted to 280° and light to moderate snow was falling in the area east of Lake Erie. Rod and Dawn could see the heavier cloud buildup moving from left to right across their flight path, about 80 miles ahead of them. The Crusader's color radar confirmed what they were looking at.

On his next handoff, Rod got an even clearer picture of the Buffalo weather—not good—and was told that a SIGMET was already in effect from Erie, Pennsylvania, to northeast of Dunkirk, New York, along the southeastern shore of Lake Erie. He was also advised that Rochester, New York, about 45 air miles east of Buffalo, was marginal VFR and expected to remain that way for at least another hour. It was decision time.

Rod and Dawn checked the en route chart, the radar, and out the window and requested a deviation to the right to bring them over

Jamestown, New York, then on to the COLDE intersection on Victor 33, and direct from there to the DALEE intersection on Victor 36. They were effectively staying southeast of the main weather area on a straight line heading for Rochester. At either COLDE or DALEE they would decide if they could make a run to the Greater Buffalo International Airport, only about 10 minutes from both intersections. Center cleared the Crusader as requested and soon afterward handed them off to the Dunkirk sector controller on 125.2.

Cleveland Center "Crusader . . ., the SIGMET has just been extended to the greater Buffalo area. You can remain at flight level two-one-zero, or descend to 6,000 after Jamestown—your discretion, sir."

Rod "(I) will descend to six after Jamestown. Have you got any PIREPs yet about icing?

Center "Not yet, sir. The SIGMET just came out. So far, the airlines are still making it in okay. We've had a couple of smaller airplanes diverted east. Not much else going on in this area. It's been very low IFR all morning."

Rod "Okay. We'll take a look when we get to COLDE. We're known-ice equipped and should be able to make it in. Just coming up on Jamestown. Out of 210 for 6,000."

Center (Five minutes later) "Attention all aircraft. A SIGMET is in effect for moderate to severe icing in the clouds along the southeastern shore of Lake Erie from Erie, Pennsylvania, extending northeast to 10 miles east of Buffalo and north to Niagara Falls." (The controller repeated the SIGMET notice)

Rod (Five miles southwest of the COLDE intersection) "(I am) five from COLDE, coming through 8,500. Wonder how conditions are holding in Buffalo?"

Center "Greater Buffalo is reporting 400 and 1½, snow starting to accumulate. Braking action on the runway is fair to good, according to a United 737 that landed about 10 minutes ago. We also have two PIREPs of moderate icing up around the Niagara area, and several from Dunkirk on up to the Buffalo area. A Mooney landed with ½ inch of rime at Orchard Park about 20 minutes ago. That's it so far. The airlines are still landing at Greater Buffalo, but the snow is starting to get heavy there."

Rod "Thanks for the report. Looks like we can take a shot at it after COLDE. If it gets too bad, we know Rochester's holding and only 15 minutes away. We're known-ice equipped, so we shouldn't have too much trouble. And we've been in the clouds for the last 15 minutes and haven't picked up any ice at all."

Center "Okay . . ., descend to 4,000 and call Buffalo Approach on 123.8. Better get the ATIS first on 135.35. It's been changing every 10 minutes or so. Good day, sir."

Dawn tuned in the ATIS and they listened to a cutoff report and then a brand new one. Buffalo was now 350 overcast and 2 miles in snow. Braking action on the runway reported fair to poor. The SIGMET for the area had been upgraded and was now calling for moderate to severe icing in the clouds.

Arriving at COLDE at 4,500 feet, Rod checked the wings for ice—just a trace of rime—and turned the windshield switch to ON. He glanced at the ammeter as he did so, noticing the needle dip momentarily—verification that the windshield deice was operating. He repeated the procedure with the prop deice switch and double checked the deice indicator needle—it was on, too. Then he pushed the wing deicer boot switch to full forward, looked out the window at the leading edge of the wing and watched the boots inflate. The results pleased him. It was the first time he had ever turned on the deice system in flight, and he felt a surge of confidence that he and Dawn were now protected from the nasty ice. The system was working. But he never cycled the boots, and they remained inflated.

Turning his attention back to the COLDE intersection and the radio, Rod called Buffalo Approach:

Rod "Buffalo Approach, Crusader . . . at 4,000 with Papa. We're just crossing COLDE and picking up only a trace of rime. Nothing serious so far."

Approach "Roger. Maintain 4,000 for now. Turn right heading 030°. We'll try to get you in as soon as possible. No other reported traffic. The SIGMET is still in effect calling for moderate to severe icing all sectors."

Rod "We've got all the deice working, sir. Looks like it's taking care of itself."

Approach (7 minutes later) ". . . You're 8 miles from KLUMP. Turn right heading 040° and descend to 2,200. We'll be turning you in about a mile outside the marker for a quick approach. The snow is getting heavier. Ceiling's down to 250 and the visibility is just over a mile—maybe."

Rod "Okay, heading 040 and out of 4 for 2 point 2."

As the Crusader descended through 3,000 feet, it flew into a temperature inversion and an area of severe icing. In less than a minute it accumulated nearly a full inch of ice. Rod felt it in the control wheel and saw it on the wings. The windshield deicer was cycling and winning, but not by much. The prop deicers were doing the same and the propellers were throwing ice against the sides of the cabin with resounding cracks each time they cycled.

But the wing boots were holding all the ice they were getting, and in roughly the shape of the inflated boots. The air foil was being dissipated at an alarming rate. Suddenly shaken into awareness of the problem, Rod tried the boot switch. Nothing happened. The boots were frozen solid with over an inch of clear and rime ice—and getting worse fast.

Rod saw the airspeed going down and applied more power. It stabilized the Crusader momentarily, giving him time to call approach:

Rod "Approach . . ., we're having real ice problems. Can't shake it all off. We'd like to go back up to 4,000 and over to Rochester."

Approach "That's approved. Climb to 4,000 and turn right heading 080°. You're cleared direct Rochester."

There was no reply. Rod was too busy. The Crusader was taking on more ice. Full power and they weren't climbing. They weren't maintaining altitude. The controls were sluggish. The airspeed was dropping. So was the Crusader. They were losing altitude. Going out of control. They couldn't see through the heavy snow. The controls were limp. The engine was surging. Rod and Dawn were frantic, terrified, sensing catastrophe. They were going down and they were helpless.

The final lurching dive was relentless. The ground was unyielding as the Crusader went down nose-first at high speed. There was nothing left of anything or anyone.

FAA accident investigator "The airplane came down about a mile outside the little town of Depew that sits on the highway 20 junction. Flew right over the intersection and a big semi before it crashed. Just lucky it missed everything there, or a lot of people would've been hurt or killed.

"A local police officer saw 'em go in and the officer was at the crash site in less than 5 minutes and on the way called the state police and they called us. Then they secured the area and did not let anybody touch anything before our people could get there. That was about a half hour later.

"What they found was an airplane that went in literally head first— nose down at high speed. And with about 2½ inches of ice on what was left of the wings and tail. As a matter of fact, they were able to determine very positively that the wing boots had been left inflated, because the ice that was on the wings had formed on the contours of the inflated ridges. That was unusual. It either meant that the ice formed so fast that the boots got frozen in that position, or that the pilot screwed up and forgot to cycle the boots altogether. They couldn't verify which because the console that held the boot switch was crushed too badly and the whole switch assembly had been torn loose.

"Before we wrote up the report, we were in touch with the manufacturer of the wing deice system, and they told us that the boots could not have been frozen over like that if the pilot had cycled them at all, not just correctly. Those boots are obviously made to deice, not to attract and gather ice. And in the inflated position they were found in, it was worse than having no boots at all. Because of what it did to the air flow and the lift under the wings. No airplane can fly like that, not even a jet.

"Another thing we were able to reconstruct from the radio transmissions was the pilot's attitude. He had the notion that his deicing system could handle any icing, even severe. Now where he got that idea, we'll never know. Every manual that's put out on icing says that a SIGMET that says *severe* is to be taken seriously and avoided like it can kill you because it can and will. But this pilot figured he could handle it.

"So, we had no choice. He was an excellent pilot in a well-equipped airplane, but he made a couple of critical mistakes. And that is 'pilot error.' We know that the suddenness of the icing played a big part in the accident. But he shouldn't have been in it in the first place. And then, when he saw the airplane icing up as fast as it apparently did, he should have been out of there lickity-split, climbing back up and out of the inversion. If he'd have done that as quickly as he should have, he and his girlfriend would have been sipping coffee in Rochester for an hour or so before flying back to Buffalo for whatever meeting it was they were in such a hurry to get to."

"You know, pilots in a hurry tend to make mistakes. In bad weather, they tend to make more mistakes. And in weather like that pilot flew into, they usually make deadly mistakes. We call them all 'pilot error.' But accidents like this one should be called 'pilot-in-a-hurry error.' It ought to be a special category."

Willard Granger, Rod's father "My son did not just die in an airplane crash. (Pause) He was murdered. (A longer pause) The FAA murdered him. The manufacturer of that deicing equipment murdered him. And the FBO who sold him the airplane and trained him to fly it murdered him.

"I'll take them one at a time so you get what I mean. I read the transcripts of the radio communications Rod had with the controllers. They knew how dangerous the icing was that day, especially the last two guys. But they never said so in ways that any reasonable person could understand clearly and without question. They told him there was a SIGMET—I've learned some of their fancy terms since the accident—but they also told him the airlines were still landing in Buffalo. Now what does that tell you? That the airplanes that are equipped for bad weather flying were able to handle it.

"But they really knew different. So, why didn't they just come out and say it in plain and simple language?: 'This area is closed. It is too dangerous to fly in. And we don't care what kind of an airplane you're flying, or how well it's equipped. Get out of here and go somewhere else, or just stay home.' If they were working for the highway patrol or the state police, that's what they'd say on dozens of radio and TV stations. (Short pause) I know that to be a fact because that is precisely what happened in Buffalo on the morning of the accident.

"And then the state police went a giant step further than the FAA did by closing I-90 and the rest of the beltway for over half the day. The airport never shut down at all, not officially anyway, even though nothing moved there for most of the late morning.

"But to make it even worse—and much more like a murder plot—they cleared him into the area and approved his attempt to land, even though they knew he'd never make it. In other words, they lured him into a death trap. If I'm not mistaken, in the criminal justice system of the United States, that is murder.

"Now take a look at the manufacturer of that deicing equipment—that we paid many thousands of dollars for. They call their system 'known ice'—that's another one of the fancy terms I've learned. 'Known ice.' Now what does that tell you? The truth? That it will only handle some of the ice some of the time? Hardly, because if they told the truth they'd never sell anything.

"And what about how to operate the stuff? After you've bought their system, you find out that it doesn't do its supposed magic by itself—automatically. No, you have to know when and how to cycle the boots—which, I understand, is no easy thing to learn. And you also have to know precisely when and how to turn on and off the rest of the system. Now, with those special requirements, you'd think they'd provide at least a little down and dirty training of some kind. Right? Hmmph . . . forget it. They barely give you a decent manual and spec sheet to work with.

"So, what you have is a very limited system that is advertised as *un*limited—and perceived that way by most pilots. No training on how to use equipment that is very complex and only works when it's used by experts. And a false sense of security foisted upon the users that can and does lead them into conditions that can kill them. Conditions, by the way, that they would otherwise avoid. Now, if that isn't murder, then we need a new definition of the word.

"Lastly, the people who actually sold him the deicing system. And who, according to the statements they've made since the accident, knew all about the limitations of the deicing system they sold him—and the fact that he wasn't adequately trained to use it. I'm talking about the FBO here at Lunken Airport. The excuse they gave was that he and they never got around to the training part because they spent so much time getting Rod his multi-engine license so he could fly the airplane. Now, what was that? A license to go out and kill himself? I mean, what kind of a sense of responsibility is that?

"They sold him a system that lured him into a situation that killed him, knowing full well that he would be unsafe using it without proper training. They knew that for sure because they didn't bother giving him the training he had coming with the purchase of the system. And they did that deliberately. It may have been because they were greedy to sell the damned system and make some extra bucks by not delivering the free training. But whatever their reason or excuse, they murdered Rod and Dawn just as surely as if they'd shot them.

"(Pause . . .. then in a subdued voice) I know you think I'm an angry, grieving father. Well, you're right. I am. I definitely am. My wife and I and our family lost our wonderful, talented son and his beautiful fiance because of a lousy air traffic system, a slipshod manufacturer, and an irresponsible FBO. So yes, I'm angry. Very angry. And I'll stay that way for the rest of my life."

Deicing system manufacturer "I can't say much about this case because we have been advised that the pilot's family is bringing suit against us for misrepresenting the deicing system that was sold to the pilot by one of our dealers. But I am happy to share some general information with you.

"To begin with, all of our literature, manuals, spec sheets, and so forth, state very clearly that none of our systems are designed to cope with severe icing. We do not know of any deicing system, not even hot-wing military systems, that can provide perfect protection in really severe icing conditions. In those very rare instances, the elements can overpower everything and everyone.

"As far as using our systems is concerned, everything about them is passive and self-controlled, except the boot cycling, which must be controlled manually by the pilot. There's a reason why that is the preferred method. It's because no two icing situations are ever the same, not even momentary ones. The applications vary from cycle to cycle during the same encounter. That's due to the variables of clouds and precipitation. Ice accumulates on a second-by-second basis and must be dislodged by inflating the boots after (the ice) builds up to an eighth or a quarter of an inch. Where the technique comes in—and it's really very simple to learn—is in judging the right amount of buildup. It doesn't involve any particular kind of skill either, just common sense. Most pilots master it easily after the first couple of cycles, which really boils down to a minute or two.

"Regarding so-called training on the use of any deicing system, it's really a misnomer. Reading any straightforward manual is usually adequate—and ours are certainly that because in many parts of the country it's no easy matter to find controllable conditions to practice in. Places like Tucson and Miami, for instance, would offer little or no opportunity for deicing training. And in other places, where icing conditions are available for at least part of the year, a flight instructor might be taking an uninsurable risk by deliberately flying into known icing conditions just to practice.

"In that regard, let me leave you with this final bit of information: Anti-icing equipment is intended to protect an airplane primarily from unexpected icing encounters. It is not a license to take on all icing conditions. Those two facts are communicated clearly to the general aviation community by us, by all of our counterparts in the deicing equipment business and, of course, by the FAA. As a result, we feel confident that every pilot who flies a 'known ice'-equipped airplane understands its limitations completely."

FBO representative (Cincinnati Municipal, Lunken Field) "When Rod Granger and Dawn Banks were killed in Buffalo, we lost a favorite employee, an important customer, and two very good friends. The Banks and Granger families have, understandably, been devastated by this tragedy, and our hearts certainly go out to them.

"You are probably aware that Rod's father, Willard Granger, is planning legal action against us, claiming that we were responsible for what appeared to be mishandling of the deicing boots. Mr. Granger is claiming that we sold Rod the anti-icing system under false pretenses and then failed to demonstrate it properly. He's also claiming that we failed to deliver some free training that was supposedly included with the equipment package. But he hasn't defined his claims in writing yet, or shown us anything indicating that we were obligated to provide any specific training with the anti-icing package—free or otherwise.

"As a matter of fact, and it's in the written statement we prepared for the FAA, Rod did receive quite a bit of free training in connection with his multi-engine rating and the purchase of the Crusader. Our chief pilot, Avery Judson, stated in his own written report that he did not demonstrate the deicing equipment to Rod because he had not been asked to do so. He also stated that there were no actual icing conditions in southwestern Ohio during July, August, and September while Rod was taking his training. Their last training flight was on September 28th.

"From what we were told by the FAA, the problem with the deicing system was probably only a minor contributing cause to the accident. The suddenness and severity of the icing would have overwhelmed the boots no matter how they were applied—right or wrong. Rod and Dawn just never had a chance."

NTSB representative "The facts, the circumstances and the conclusions relating to this accident seem to be coming from different directions. For the record, it's difficult, if not impossible, to dispute the official findings. The pilot did make mistakes, so the 'pilot error' label is definitely justified. The appearance of the ice on the leading edges of the wings was proof positive that the boots had been left inflated. That happening by itself, or because of a flaw in the boot system, however, is too remote to be considered possible. So, 'improper use' is certainly an appropriate call for the boot system.

"After that, the rest of the 'probable causes' are just logical parts of the sequence leading to the crash. Why 'spatial dis-' got thrown in, I can't say since the airplane was pressurized and the toxicology tests were all negative. Maybe the investigators felt that the pilot got so far behind his situation that he displayed signs of disorientation. Those would show up in the ATC transcripts and, I'd say, are more a matter of subjective interpretation than provable fact. But the field investigators are encouraged to express their opinions. You'd understand why if you ever had to separate body parts from airplane parts in order to conduct one of these investigations. It can do things to your head and your heart.

"The rest of this is strictly personal opinion. My first point of contention would be the pilot's preparation for the trip. From everything in the reports and the follow-ups, there wasn't anything unusual. I'd also say that the family's accusations are emotional rather than factual. To take the position that this very qualified pilot knew nothing about how the deice system worked is not believable. He did everything else too well and was much too thorough for that to be plausible. For sure, he would have read and understood what was in the operating instructions for that system. Those instructions, by the way, are written very clearly and conform to all required standards.

"On the subject of the FBO's performance, I'd say that their written statements, including the one from the chief pilot, are true accounts of what occurred. You don't tend to work on deicing techniques in midsummer. They also pointed out that the pilot was a quick and conscientious learner. Which would further confirm that he most likely read about and understood the deicing system.

"Moving on to the radio transcripts, you are now into a murky area. The center controllers definitely gave the pilot mixed signals about the conditions he would be flying into. They announced the SIGMET and told him that other aircraft had diverted. But then, in the next breath, they added that the airlines were getting into Greater Buffalo and reporting the braking action, without mentioning anything about icing on the way in. In a 'known ice' airplane and with an important customer waiting at the destination airport, I think most self-confident pilots would lean toward 'I can make it' rather than diverting.

"The approach controller had a better shot at sending the Crusader off to Rochester. But how was he supposed to know what the icing conditions actually were. He didn't have any PIREPs to go by, only the SIGMET which he did announce—and emphatically. From that point on, his job was to respond to the pilot in command who knew much more about his circumstances and capabilities than the controller did.

"Which brings us to a crossroad on this whole subject of ATC responsibility. Should an area and an airport be shut down every time a SIGMET is issued for moderate to severe icing? The airlines say 'no' because their pilots and their equipment are better prepared to deal with it. For most general aviation aircraft, it would definitely be logical to consider. But how would you implement something that would satisfy and intelligently protect both interests? And, I'd also offer, that contemplating a two-sided system, where an area was closed just for general aviation aircraft, would bring a firestorm of protest from the AOPA, the NBAA (professional pilots), and all of corporate America.

"Even if you were able to implement mandatory closings of areas and airports in connection with SIGMETs, it could cause a worse problem: Because of the seriousness of the decision to issue a SIGMET, it is safe to assume that fewer of them would be issued. And that could be even more dangerous than the system we have now.

"So, in conclusion, I would say that this accident was caused by one of those once-in-a-blue-moon crazy weather events that no one could have predicted with certainty—not unlike a microburst or clear

air turbulence or a lightning strike. This pilot and his passenger simply ran out of luck. And I don't believe that 'pilot error' played any
significant part in causing this accident. But again, that's strictly my
personal opinion."

Author comment More than the facts and the conclusions, the attitudes of the parties involved in this accident are both troubled and
troubling, and obviously coming from opposite ends of a wide spec-
trum. The Granger and Banks families are troubled, and justifiably so.
They suffered tragic personal losses from which they will never completely recover. But perhaps even worse for them will be the persistent feelings that this occurred needlessly because of, as they
perceive it, the negligence and indifference of the people and agencies that should have been protecting them.

The involved companies, as could be expected, are mostly troubled that the accident will be bad for business. Their positions might
seem like indifference because they cannot admit to anything but
perfect performance. But in reality, they will quickly and quietly do
whatever is necessary to correct anything in their products or services
that might have contributed to the accident. That is welcome forward
progress. Especially the FBO. They lost friends, people who they
knew and liked. Their corrections will be made on an emergency basis but, again, without any fanfare.

The government agencies are another story—troubling because
they answer to several masters. The first master is the American public, whose view of private pilots is: "A bunch of jocks who tool
around the skies and fly their little airplanes into the airliners we ride
on, endangering our lives." Forget the fact that it's usually the other
way around. The prevailing perception is that we little guys are running into and downing their big guys.

But change the context of the icing dilemma and an entirely different scenario emerges. Had this accident involved an airliner, the
hew and cry for corrective action would have been immediate, and
heard from coast to coast. And whatever in-depth studies and remedies were called for would be underway before the ink was dry on
the investigators' reports. But a few hundred private pilots being hurt
or killed every year by aircraft icing hardly raises an eyebrow. Unless
it happens to be someone they knew or loved, which is not likely to
be very often.

The second master is the airlines, who believe the sky is solely
theirs and everyone else is an intruder—a threat to them and the general public they serve. They also want fewer rules and restrictions so

they can fly more profitably. Shutting down an area or an airport because of icing conditions that barely affect them would inconvenience their passengers and counteract their quest for higher profits. And, once again, discount the fact that doing so could save the lives of private pilots. Their first and most demanding responsibility is to their stockholders. Do not think for one single moment that the airlines are indifferent to general aviation safety, because they are not. They care about it plenty. It's just that it is not in first position on their lists of priorities because profit must, does, and should come first, according to the rules of American business.

Remembering that, don't even suggest that a two-tier system of some sort be put in place to leave an open corridor for their heavy metal during an area icing alert because they will fight like tigers to prevent it. Why? Because if they ever, God forbid, had an accident during one of those alerts, they could be cited for willful negligence by every personal injury lawyer representing an injured passenger or passengers, or surviving family members. And then, worse yet, the public would demand that the airlines, from that moment forward, also abide by those more restrictive icing regulations. And that could have a negative effect on airline profitability.

The third master is the political bureaucracy itself. By its vested charter, it is the control mechanism, the stabilizing force and structure that maintains continuity and substance in what could otherwise be a chaotic environment. In fulfilling that mission and responsibility, the FAA, NTSB, ATC, and a myriad of government agencies resist the pressures for change in aviation. Most changes are better resisted because they represent the preferences of special interests, usually to the detriment of others and with little or no benefit to the overall system. But a few changes, like the ones that would improve safety in general aviation—this icing issue in particular—need to be addressed. Unfortunately, the resistance, or perhaps better said, the rejection mechanism, is nonselective—as it must be.

With that sobering reality in mind, and further realizing that change should not originate from within a controlling mechanism, it becomes clearly obvious that only the first master, the general public, can apply the necessary pressure to improve general aviation safety. There is hope, but not an immediate likelihood that badly needed adjustments in the system will be forthcoming. And that is troubling for the pilots who are active in general aviation today.

14

Mountain high and pilot low

Preliminary report: March; Cessna 402C; commercial pilot, multi- and single-engine land, 2,630 hours. All five occupants were killed when the aircraft flew into an escarpment 750 feet below the summit of Ruby Dome Mountain on a VFR flight into IMC. The flight had originated in Lake Tahoe, California, and was en route to Salt Lake City, Utah. Weather at the accident site was IFR, as forecast. Both the departure and destination airports were VFR, also as forecast.

Further investigation revealed:

- The pilot received a thorough weather briefing, which called for low cloud ceilings obscuring mountain tops, moderate turbulence and moderate icing in the clouds along his route of flight.
- A VFR flight plan was filed for 10,500 feet, via Victor 6 and Victor 32. Victor 32 had an MEA of 13,000 feet for 53 miles, but no altitude change was indicated in the flight plan.
- The pilot was a free-lance charter pilot who regularly rented the 402C from an FBO at Reno Cannon International Airport. Nearly all of his flying was as a semiprivate air taxi operator between Reno and Truckee-Tahoe Airport on the north shore of Lake Tahoe, an active ski resort and gambling casino area.
- A large bonus had been offered to the pilot by the four passengers, who were entertainers on their way to an important opening in Salt Lake City. The passengers had originally arranged for a chartered jet to pick them up at Truckee-Tahoe, but the jet was grounded for a mechanical problem in Denver and had left them stranded.

Official conclusion: Deliberate VMC into IMC. Poor flight planning. Spatial disorientation. Pilot error.

"HECTIC" COULD BARELY DESCRIBE the state of confusion and urgency that began at 11 o'clock on the morning of the flight. The three lead singers of the Mountain Rockers, a popular regional entertainment group, were about to begin their third day performing for a large dealer incentive meeting hosted by a major U.S. corporation, when they got some bad news: The jet they had chartered to take them to an important show opening was down with an engine problem and would not be able to leave Denver in time to pick up the singers at Truckee-Tahoe Airport and get them to Salt Lake City, Utah by 6 p.m.

The group's manager, Mike Rawlins, sprung into action. In 15 minutes he had the situation figured out. Friday was a difficult day to make last-minute travel arrangements. Ground transport wouldn't work because the trip was more than 560 road miles. Air was their only hope. But all the charter services contacted couldn't accommodate a pickup at 2 p.m. or later and delivery in Salt Lake City by 6:30 p.m. at the latest. The show opening was at 8 p.m.

Just as Mike was about to call ahead and cancel out for the opening, Rusty Barnes showed up with a group of seven skiers in the Cessna 402C he rented regularly from a Reno FBO. Rusty operated a gypsy air taxi service between Reno and the Lake Tahoe resort area. When Rusty walked into the pilots' lounge to gather up his passengers for the trip back to Reno, the counter girl suggested to Mike that Rusty might be able to help him.

After a short conversation and $3,000 later, it was agreed that Rusty would do one more round trip to Reno and back, find a friend who could take over his air taxi assignments for the rest of the day, and make the trip to Salt Lake City at 2 or 2:30. Mike was much relieved.

Rusty was excited about the money—almost $1,800 clear profit— and the prospect of a trip to a new place because he almost never flew any place but Reno and Truckee-Tahoe, his milk run for the past 11 years. That's why Rusty didn't finish his instrument training. He never went anywhere that required it. And when the weather was IFR on the milk run, limos were the preferred alternate.

His first call to flight service had good news and bad news: The weather in Salt Lake would be VFR all day—Reno, too, but he already knew that. En route could be a different story. There were cloud buildups throughout most of the mountain areas, and there were plenty of those. Along with the clouds, moderate turbulence was being reported and moderate to severe icing in the clouds was being forecasted. The turbulence he was used to; the icing would be a new experience—it was never a factor on the 14-minute trip between Reno and Truckee-Tahoe, which was always flown VFR, and always flown legally: clear of clouds. Rusty would never have put his thriving little business at risk.

Reno Flight Service specialist "Everybody around here knew Rusty. He was one of our very regulars because of the air taxi business he ran. Very well, by the way. He knew how to run his business and he knew how to fly, safely. Did everything in moderation. Never pushed his luck. I wouldn't call him a safety nut or anything. He just never did anything that was close to the edge, if you know what I mean. On the day of the flight to Salt Lake, I was on duty when he called in from Tahoe asking about weather in the Salt Lake area and everywhere else in between. It was strange for him to be making a trip like that, so I asked him about it, and he told me he had these hotshot singers who were paying him almost triple for a charter if he could get them to some show opening. He was excited about it.

"Anyway, I told him he'd better cool down a bit because the weather between here and there was plenty iffy and probably wouldn't improve much. Knowing how careful he was, I figured he'd forget about going after the report I gave him. I knew he wasn't IFR. Didn't need to be for the kind of flying he was doing. But I must have said 'VFR is not recommended' at least four times.

"When he called back awhile later checking again, I told him I was surprised to be hearing from him about that same trip. But I checked it all out for him and gave him a full and accurate briefing. The weather hadn't gotten any worse by that time, although it was forecast to bunch up some more. The turbulence was still moderate and the icing had been downgraded to light rime. Not bad, but still not good enough for him to go sticking his VFR nose into it, and I told him that, too.

"After all that, I nearly flipped when he said he wanted to file a flight plan. I asked him if he was on something, or if someone had a gun to his head. I even suggested he hang up, think about it awhile and then call me back. I wasn't going anywhere. But he insisted he wanted to try and asked me to help him figure out a way for him to either get through or around that weather without getting hurt.

"That, of course, is my job, so we went to work on it together. I rechecked everything and then some. He laid out five or six different routings with decision points in case they had to deviate. All in all, it was a good try. But we still came up with a 'no-go,' and I told him so. It didn't seem like it was worth the risk to me. Money or no money.

"But I had (very little influence). He was going and that was all there was to it. Nothing I could do except tell him again that VFR into those conditions was not recommended, and go ahead and file his flight plan."

Back in Reno, Rusty went to work. He got a briefing on what to do if he encountered severe icing—"Get the hell out of it." He assembled all the maps he would need—low altitude en route charts, Jepp charts for the entire Salt Lake and Reno areas, and sectionals, and got a quick lesson from a charter pilot friend on how to read the IFR stuff. With some help from the same friend, he ordered a fancy tray of hors d'oeuvres and a cooler full of soda and beer—for $3,000 his passengers were entitled to some first-class treatment. Besides, this could be a format trip for an expanded air charter business. Rusty was an entrepreneur.

Then it was back to flight service for a final look at the weather— about the same on both ends but a little worse up the middle. PIREPs were coming in about the turbulence. The icing wasn't being confirmed, but they knew it was there. Rusty didn't doubt it for a moment. He knew mountain weather. He also knew, or thought he knew, how to circumvent any cloud buildups except a system, and this was no system. Just mountain waves. Like the ones around his milk run. Rusty was respectfully concerned, but not worried. And his concern was being overshadowed by his excitement over the opportunity that the trip represented. It was definitely a "go" situation for him.

Rusty's flight plan was simple enough: VFR at 10,500 feet on V-6 to V-32 all the way. Or, if the cloud buildups were north of his course, he would track J-154 off the Battle Mountain VOR and fly that in instead—that last part was just showing off for the controller, who he knew quite well. Rusty had no business planning a "J" route and they both knew it. He also got a complete list of flight-following frequencies from the controller before noticing that they were clearly shown on the en route chart. So much for a short course in anything. But Rusty felt prepared and confident.

At 1:40 p.m., Mike Rawlins and his three singers showed up at the flight office at Truckee-Tahoe and found Rusty standing proudly next to the stair door of the airplane. Almost before strapping in, the singers were into the beer and the hors d'oeuvres. They were going to be happy passengers. Rusty welcomed the manager into the copilot's seat, taxied out, and took off without incident.

Climbing in clear skies over the Mustang VOR, Rusty spotted J-32 on the en route chart and decided to track a 045° heading out of Mustang and fly direct to Battle Mountain VOR. He was never averse to saving a little air time on a prepaid charter. That went directly into his pocket. Besides, it was elating to him to fly a high-altitude route.

Coming up on Battle Mountain VOR, the weather was building up ahead, closer at 11 o'clock, farther at 2 o'clock, with some semblance of a corridor at about 1 o'clock. Not terrific, but not hopeless either. Rusty decided to track J-154 out of Battle Mountain and took up a 070° heading, not quite accurate for the jetway, but close enough. It would keep him to the right of the nearer clouds for now. He would deal with whatever else later.

Later came sooner than he expected. Before they arrived in the vicinity of Elko, Nevada, only 54 miles from Battle Mountain, the 402 was on top of lower clouds and facing a wall of buildup. Rusty had a decision to make—fast: turn around and blow the trip or land at Elko; back at Battle Mountain and wait awhile; penetrate the clouds ahead and reach the VFR conditions promised at Salt Lake City. Circle and call flight watch for some advice. He did the latter.

The new information from flight watch was disturbing. The turbulence in and below the clouds was now moderate to severe from Elko to east of Wendover, Utah. And the buildups were higher, with tops in the 20s and 30s and growing, and coming together as a solid wall stretching from Boise, Idaho, to Ely, Nevada. There was no place to go but through it if they were going to get to Salt Lake City on time. A bit of better news influenced Rusty's decision: The icing that had been forecasted in the clouds had been downgraded to light rime and that had been confirmed by two recent PIREPs. But Rusty barely gave it a second thought. He had already decided to go for it.

Turning east and back onto J-154—the clouds still looked less troublesome to the south of Elko—Rusty and the 402 entered the clouds just as the aircraft crossed the 170° radial off of the Bullion VOR, just south of Elko. The first jolts of the turbulence were startling. The next jolts were worse. So were the next. They were taking a beating. Sudden panic took over the happy passengers. And Rusty. He thought about doing a 180.

But the turbulence didn't last that long and soon started to settle down. At least it felt that way to Rusty. Six minutes later, it didn't make a bit of difference. The flight was over. All over. The 402C, at 165 knots indicated airspeed and at 10,500 feet flew directly into a solid wall on the west side of Ruby Dome, the highest peak in the Ruby Mountain range. The wreckage was 749 feet below the summit. The explosion could be heard 20 miles away, but went unseen in the thick and churning clouds.

Several months would pass before the wreckage would be found in the rugged terrain 2,700 feet below the impact point.

ATC representative "This pilot asked for and received good flight following for the first third or so of the trip he was filed for. When they got to the Elko area, the clouds on the trouble side of the mountains ahead of them came into play. They hadn't been unexpected. They were in the forecast all day—*for* all day.

"Our people had extensive contact with the pilot when they were about 25 miles west of Elko. He had just called flight watch and got the bad news about the weather ahead of them that we were reading bright and clear. He asked for help if he had to pick his way through the buildups, which was refused. We don't make VFR pilots into instant IFR capable, and the pilot was told that. He was also warned several times to maintain VFR, and that we were showing precip in the clouds ahead of him.

"The transcripts verify that he got the first bad news from us as soon as he called 126.1 when they were about 30 southwest of Battle Mountain. He was back and forth a couple of times to flight watch, but we knew what was going on between the aircraft and Salt Lake City. All he was getting from flight watch was the Salt Lake weather.

"When it finally became obvious to our controller that this pilot just wasn't listening, in exasperation he told him that they would be entering an area of solid IMC, with heavy turbulence and icing reported in the clouds. He then advised them to turn around, or land at either Elko or Battle Mountain, but by all means to remain VFR. If you heard the transcripts, you'd realize that the instructions could not have been more emphatic."

NTSB representative "Occasionally there are circumstances where the clues are compelling but the opportunities to run any of them down are dead and buried with the bodies. This case is one of those. Because by the time the wreckage and the remains were found, toxicology tests were virtually impossible to run accurately, if at all.

"That was certainly a shame. This pilot displayed most unusual behavior for him, according to his background and the several inquiries that were made after the accident. He was an unreckless pilot who flew nothing but unreckless trips, and did so for many years. That wasn't the person we heard on the ATC transcripts.

"So, the obvious thing that comes to mind is substance abuse—and I don't mean drugs or alcohol—and I don't mean deliberate either. With a person like him, it would be inadvertent. Something he may have taken to pep him up for the trip, like a benny or a diet pill, or maybe a cold pill of some kind like an amphetamine or an antihistamine. Mixed with higher altitude, those things can play funny tricks.

"But we hardly suspect higher altitude in this accident. This pilot spent most of his life at 5,000- and 6,000-foot elevations. As a matter of fact, we suspect that he may have been too aware of altitude and hypoxia. Because he stayed at 10,500 feet and apparently never thought about going any higher, as if he was afraid to do so. If he did think about it, he didn't say anything to anyone.

"Ironically, if he had read his chart correctly and had been willing to climb to the 13,000 foot MEA level, he and his four passengers would most likely be alive today. I say that with a fair degree of certainty because this pilot had enough experience and a good autopilot. It's a safe bet that he would have been able to get through the buildup area, even though he wasn't IFR qualified. But that's all conjecture. We'll never know anything for sure about this accident or what happened to the pilot.

"That's too bad. We tend to learn the most from the strangest accidents. And this certainly qualifies as one of those."

Reno FBO representative "Since we lost Rusty and our 402, we've done plenty of soul searching about what may have gone wrong. Rusty was a good friend, a reliable customer and businessman, a very safe and careful pilot and just one helluva great guy. Everybody around here misses him. He was a fixture in this place.

"About the best we can come up with is that he just didn't want to disappoint those singers he was carting to Salt Lake City. That would be like him. That's why he was so successful. He'd accommodate everyone, anytime and anyplace, and put himself out like you can't imagine. Some of the favors he did for people are legendary around here. It was like if you needed something, call Rusty. And, sure enough, he'd be there with a smile on his face and raring to go. So much so that lots of people took advantage of him. But he never seemed to care.

"The accident investigators didn't believe us when we told them the kind of guy Rusty was and our theories about what caused the accident. They were nosing around to see if he took any drugs or smoked anything. But we set them straight on that. Rusty was a nonsmoker, who never drank anything more than a little wine to be sociable sometimes, and never within a full day of when he was going to fly. And he didn't have a cold on the day of the accident, so he wasn't taking any medications that anyone knew about. No, I'd stick to the theory we came up with. Rusty just couldn't say no. That kind of fits the way all of us want to remember him, and they'll never prove differently anyway. So, what the hell! Leave it at that and let him rest in peace."

NASA representative "Some accidents defy explanation because of circumstances beyond everyone's control. This case seems to be one of them. But if you're looking for preventable causes rather than blame, a different picture emerges.

"The most obvious direct cause of this accident was the altitude selection. Presumably, no matter whatever else was done wrong by anyone in the fatal sequence, if the altitude had conformed to the MEA, there would not have been an accident. Looking then at that one single factor, how could it have been corrected? By the pilot? Of course. It was his basic responsibility to select a safe altitude in the first place. But altitude is a secondary factor in a VFR flight plan. The 'V' stands for 'visual,' meaning you're supposed to be able to see everything at all times and, therefore, also be able to adjust your altitude as necessary. No argument about that. Or the fact that this pilot had no business entering those clouds. That was clearly 'pilot error.'

"But we're talking about prevention. So, the first question has to be: Could the system have saved those lives? If you check that out carefully, as we have, you get a 'yes' and a 'maybe.' Not very encouraging. Is it hard to believe it isn't a definite 'yes?' You bet. But what we learned is that there is no data base on altitude or MEAs in the flight service or air traffic control computers. None. The system relies entirely on the competence of the individual controllers and their personal diligence in spotting altitude errors. And that goes for IFR, too! Now isn't that a comforting thought?

"So, what you have in this case is flight service without altitude data available and ATC, with MEA data at hand but not expecting a VFR pilot to need it. But why not give that information to a VFR pilot anyway as long as there is radio contact? Especially in areas of mountainous terrain, it could easily be a routine part of a controller's regular comments to every VFR pilot, not unlike an altimeter setting or a precaution to maintain VFR. But it isn't. And five people died in this accident because it wasn't.

"Another interesting aspect of this case is the altitude itself, 10,500 feet. This pilot lived at elevations of 5,000 and 6,000 feet, which leads to the presumption that his altitude tolerance could comfortably accommodate the 5,000-foot difference. Unfortunately, the presumption can be and usually is wrong because other stress factors, like compulsion, play an important part in the effects of reduced blood oxygen saturation. This pilot felt strongly compelled to deliver his passengers to Salt Lake City. And the unusual behavior he exhibited resembled hypoxic symptoms. So, lack of oxygen cannot be dismissed as a possible cause, or even a probable cause of this accident."

Washington Flight Service representative "Service is our middle name, and that is essentially what we are: A service to pilots. We provide weather data and briefings as our primary service. And we relay flight plans to air traffic control as our secondary service. In some cases, we also assist with local airport traffic.

"But that's it. We are not regulatory, or supervisory, or controlling, or anything other than a service function. We don't edit flight plans. That's the pilot's job.

"Fortunately for the system, most of our people are conscientious enough to interpret the information they give to pilots. They also try to advise them how to use it, especially in changing weather situations. But we have no authoritative position or responsibility. Not even when we advise that VFR is not recommended. And not even when a destination area is socked in solid. We can't say: 'No, you can't go because you would be endangering your own and other people's lives.'

"Having just come from many years in the field, I can tell you that it's very frustrating to give a strong VFRNR—that's our acronym for 'not recommended'—and have the pilot in the very next breath ask us to file a VFR flight plan into the same IFR conditions we were just talking about. And it gets worse when that pilot then proceeds to have a weather related accident and we have to defend the briefing and the advice we gave. I can tell you that after going through that a number of times, controllers can get to the point where they're afraid to give any advice to anyone under any circumstances. And who can blame them? It's like they're presumed guilty until proven otherwise. Or blamed for the accident they tried to prevent. Talk about a 'lose-lose' situation!

"But, you know, all-in-all the system works pretty well. Nearly all of the pilots are reasonable people. And nearly all of the flight service people are competent and conscientious. That's why the system is as good as it is. Any enforcement authority we might get would be for the 'unreasonables,' those pilots who don't listen, who don't obey the rules, who think they're impervious to danger, who fight restraint of any kind, and who then go out and have accidents that the rest of us have to apologize for.

"So, yes, if you ask me, I definitely believe some limited amount of authority would be a good thing for flight service to have. I think the cooperating pilots and the concerned public deserve and should demand a system that requires every pilot to comply with common-sense rules of safety—on more than just a voluntary basis. But then, I've been fighting that battle ever since I lost my first pilot to a weather accident. It still haunts me because I had the knowledge but not the means to prevent it."

Author comment Over the years, a great many VFR into IMC accidents have involved encounters with obscured higher altitude terrain. Cloud enshrouded hilltops, mountainsides, and mountaintops have proven deadly to numerous pilots who have ventured deliberately or otherwise into atmospheric conditions where they were not supposed to be.

Without commenting on why VFR pilots do many of the illegal, imprudent and self-destructive things they do, but accepting the fact that, despite all reasonable efforts, they will continue to do them, the obvious alternative is to explore more effective methods of forewarning and preventing elevated terrain accidents.

Because every chart, sectional, and approach plate that might fall into a VFR pilot's hands already has clearly marked minimum en route altitudes on every Victor airway, it is obvious that some different or additional form of intervention should be considered in order to be absolutely certain that every pilot is aware of the minimum safe clearance altitudes of every area that they might fly in or through, VFR or otherwise.

Before any progress can be made, two things must first be agreed upon: First, enough people have died and it is time to save the ones who will surely die if something else isn't done to prevent their misadventures; second, the present system can, with the structure that is already in place, accommodate simple procedural changes that will provide effective intervention and prevention.

Once those basic premises are accepted, beneficial changes can be implemented. As for what those changes should be, that can and should be left to the FAA, flight service specialists and air traffic controllers. Their comments and suggestions regarding this accident are impressive. They know what to do and how to get it done.

15

Outsmarting the system

Preliminary report: March; Cessna Skylane; private pilot, single-engine land, 470 hours. The aircraft was destroyed when it went out of control and crashed during a flight from Watertown, New York, to Baltimore, Maryland. The pilot and his passenger were killed. Several weather briefings were given to the pilot, on the ground and airborne, all of which included "VFR not recommended" advisories. Just prior to the accident, the pilot was in contact with the New York ARTCC and was climbing from 3,400 feet to 4,200 feet, the minimum radar vectoring altitude, in order to receive flight-following service. The ground impact showed the airplane in a steep left turn at impact. Witnesses on the ground reported rain and fog. No evidence of a mechanical failure or malfunction was found.

Further investigation revealed:

- Two unscheduled stops had been made prior to the accident, at Syracuse and Binghamton, New York. The pilot received at least two detailed weather briefings at each airport.
- The Skylane had a loaded panel and a two-axis autopilot, but the pilot was not instrument rated, having started and stopped his instrument training twice.
- At his home base, Martin State Airport, in Baltimore, Maryland, the pilot was known as a scud-runner. He often proclaimed that he was safer and more efficient VFR than IFR, because "the system" was too cumbersome.
- The flight, a return from a long weekend, started out as a day flight and ran into night because of numerous weather delays. The pilot had only 9 hours of total night experience, none of which were cross-country.

Official conclusion: Inadvertent VMC into IMC. Self-induced pressure. Poor flight planning. Inadequate night currency. Loss of control due to spatial disorientation. Pilot error.

THE WEEKEND in Watertown, New York, had been a nice departure from a dreary mid-Atlantic winter, and a pleasant respite after a short but successful business trip. Jason Martin, 26, youngest son of a prominent Baltimore family, had arrived in Watertown on Thursday afternoon to meet with and set up a new distributorship that would sell industrial chemicals and lubricants for his family company.

Adding to the pleasure of his weekend was Gwen Davison, 23, Jason's latest heartthrob; he was a master at impressing young women with his expensive Skylane that he kept expensively hangared at Martin State Airport, just east of Baltimore. Gwen was no flying enthusiast, but she had grown up in Tyson, an upscale suburb north of Baltimore, and appreciated the good things in life that Jason represented.

Jason made his first call to Flight Service at 10:30 on the Sunday morning of the flight. The weather report was fair to poor: marginal VFR everywhere, ceilings 1,000–1,200 feet, 3–5 miles visibility, icing expected in the clouds above 6,000 feet, temperature and dewpoint spreads 2–3°, winds northeasterly at 8–12 knots, no improvement forecast until late the next day.

Disturbed but not dissuaded, Jason and Gwen took their time leaving their motel, had a leisurely brunch and arrived at the Watertown International Airport at 1:15 p.m. for their planned 2 p.m. departure. The 2½-hour flight to Baltimore would get them home before supper. Gwen wanted to be back early so she would have time to recover from the long weekend, get a good night's rest and be fresh and eager for the new job she was starting Monday morning. It was a "plum" job with an advertising agency that she had finally landed after a six-month, very competitive pursuit.

Before paying for his fuel and parking, Jason was on the phone to flight service. The weather picture was murky: low ceilings and visibilities prevailing; Watertown was now 1,100 and 2½–3. They would need a special VFR clearance to leave Watertown, which wasn't a serious problem, but not very encouraging either.

By 1:45, Jason had completed his preflight, loaded their luggage, paid his bill, sent Gwen off for ice and soda, and was back on the phone to flight service. Still yech. They could leave Watertown without the special VFR clearance, but Baltimore was worse. So were most places in between, except Syracuse, about 50 miles south. It had gone up a little, like Watertown.

Jason gave the complicated situation serious contemplative thought for about 2¼ seconds—demonstrating that he was also a master of lightning decision making, especially where life-threatening possibilities were involved—and filed his flight plan: V-29 to Binghamton, V-499 to Martin State Airport in Baltimore, 2½ hours en route with 4 hours of fuel, altitude variable to remain VFR.

Watertown Flight Service specialist "We had what I felt was a forthright discussion about the conditions that day. I told him he'd probably wind up spending the night in Syracuse, or maybe Binghamton, if he made the unwise decision to leave Watertown. Beyond there, the weather was turning worse all the way and into Baltimore, and was not expected to get any better. I must have repeated at least three times that VFR was definitely not recommended.

"From the conversation we had, I thought he bought my recommendations and was going to cancel the trip and stay over in Watertown. But he said they were going to try and get down as far as Wilkes-Barre or Lancaster because, from either place, he could rent a car and drive his girlfriend home in time for an important something-or-other the next morning. I checked everything over again and advised him that it was very unlikely they would make it that far and that he could have problems with the hilly terrain because the tops would probably be obscured.

"But there was no talking him out of it. He asked me to get him a 'special,' just in case, and to activate his flight plan. I think they were out of here right on schedule at 1400.

Off on time without needing the special VFR clearance, Jason climbed to just below the ceiling—about 1,400–1,500 msl—took up a heading of 200° and called Boston Center on 132.75 for flight following. He got a quick and positive response because there wasn't very much traffic. He also got some bad news: The weather south of Syracuse was not cooperating. They would be lucky to make it to Binghamton.

Jason explained the situation to Gwen, which she had already heard on the radio, and told her they would likely have to stop for awhile at Link Field in Binghamton, a nice airport with a comfortable restaurant. From there, he was sure the weather would improve enough for them to get closer to Baltimore for a reasonable road trip to home. Wishful thinking, but it sounded good to Gwen. It gave her hope and feelings of security and confidence in Jason.

The 48 miles to Syracuse was uneventful, although Jason had to maneuver around some hillsides to stay VFR. The weather was definitely not improving. Continuing south on a 190° heading after passing Syracuse, Jason and the Skylane were doing more dodging of hilltops and lowering clouds to remain legal VFR. It was getting very challenging. And not helped at all when Boston ARTCC handed them off to New York ARTCC, who immediately announced that Binghamton had just gone IFR.

Undaunted by the announcement, Jason asked if they could get a special VFR clearance to land at Binghamton, and was told that he would need to get that permission from Binghamton Approach on 118.6. The call to approach was even more disheartening. Ceilings had dropped to 800 feet and visibility was under 2 miles. Special VFR would not be permitted unless visibility came back up to at least 2 miles.

Jason didn't doubt the Binghamton weather one bit. He and Gwen were less than 30 miles north of there and already finding it more difficult to stay VFR. Conditions were deteriorating faster than Jason had expected. So was Gwen's comfort level as they both strained to see the next hilltop, which was coming up fast and partially obscured by the haze and fog. When they lost sight of the ground a moment later, Jason did a quick 180 to regain visual contact. A few minutes of circling followed by another attempt to find and traverse that same hilltop resulted in a more urgent 180. And a mutual decision to head back toward Syracuse. Where they landed 20 minutes later.

Leaving Gwen nursing a cup of hot chocolate in the airport restaurant, Jason made his first of three calls to flight service. There was a little hope. The weather at Binghamton had come back up a little, close to marginal VFR. South of there was still poor but hadn't gotten any worse. But Jason decided to wait awhile after listening to numerous warnings from the flight service specialist that VFR flight was not recommended.

By his third call to flight service an hour later, Jason was determined to have another try at getting through. The weather was holding—not any better, but holding. And Binghamton was then reporting 1,200 over and 3½ miles, which was much better than it had been and was expected to improve. Jason was cursing flight service and their flip-flop forecasts when he returned to the restaurant and hustled Gwen back to the Skylane, which had been topped off and chocked on the ramp. They were off the ground in fewer than 10 minutes.

At 2,200 feet and traveling south toward Binghamton, Jason could reach New York ARTCC. But they were unable to provide flight-following below 4,000 feet. He, Gwen, and the Skylane were on their own. Not a problem, though, because all of the hilltops were clearly visible. Conditions had improved and looked like they would hold or continue to improve, which Jason explained to Gwen was the way the weather usually behaved, and why he was safer than an IFR pilot. It sounded plausible to her.

Thirty-five miles south of Binghamton and 20 miles west of Wilkes-Barre, the weather did another dippy-do on the Skylane. This time, Jason did his 180s with less urgency. But after three tries, they still weren't able to pick their way across or around the hilly terrain. Calling Wilkes-Barre Scranton Approach, they got more bad news: "IFR with no 'specials' available." The weather was going down again.

With greater reluctance than the first time, Jason headed back north and found Binghamton's Link Field. A smooth landing, a new fuel order and a leg-stretching walk to the restaurant put Gwen behind another cup of hot chocolate and Jason back on the phone to flight service. He wasn't happy, and the forecasts weren't helping; the weather was still down and only a slight chance of any improvement by nightfall, which was coming up fast.

Over an early supper, Jason and Gwen discussed their options. A 5-hour road trip, requiring Jason to double back to pick up the airplane after the weather cleared out, didn't excite either of them, especially Jason. Staying over in Binghamton would cause Gwen to miss the grand entrance to her new job at the agency. Not a problem for Jason, but most disconcerting for her. They decided to wait an hour and review their situation then.

The final call to flight service had a little better news. Not terrific. But good enough to be enticing, especially for a pilot who wanted to impress his girlfriend. Paying little or no attention to the fact that night was coming on and his night flying experience was limited to touch-and-go patterns and some local sightseeing around Baltimore, Jason filed a VFR flight plan to Baltimore.

Binghamton Flight Service specialist "I was dealing with a determined, frustrated pilot. The weather was IFR or marginal everywhere, and I told him that VFR was definitely not recommended, especially night VFR. But he said they had to get closer to Baltimore, if not all the way, and that they were going to take a shot at it. Then he asked me some questions about flight-following service, and I gave him the frequencies. I also advised him that New York Center's radar didn't cover below 4,200 feet, and that he probably wouldn't be able to get up that high and be legal VFR. But that didn't seem to make any impression on him whatsoever.

"Before I took his flight plan, I made him wait while I went to recheck something, figuring it would give him some time to reconsider. That didn't work either, even though I repeated the part about center not being able to pick him up below 4,200 feet. He was hell bent to go, and all I could do was take his flight plan and wish him luck."

The conversation with flight service gave Jason an idea. He took his charts from the Skylane and spread them out on a table in the FBO's flight lounge. It took just a couple of minutes for him to determine that the highest point between Binghamton and Baltimore was 2,500 feet MSL. He quickly reasoned that if they remained at 3,000 feet or above, they would safely clear every obstruction. The fact that they would likely be in IMC illegally didn't bother him much because he correctly figured that there wouldn't be any other young hotshots up there in that kind of weather. So, who would know? And besides, he could handle the airplane on instruments in the clouds with help from the two-axis autopilot in the Skylane. Gwen was as good as home in Baltimore.

Departing Binghamton on a 195° heading, Jason climbed right to 3,200 feet after entering the clouds at 2,700 feet. He leveled off, sat back, and relaxed. This was going to be easy. There wasn't much turbulence and the altitude was easy to maintain with trim control. Next up, the Lancaster VOR.

After deliberately waiting 15 minutes, Jason called New York Center on 128.5:

Jason "New York Center, this is Skylane . . .. We're VFR at 3,200 feet, 35 south of Binghamton on Victor-499, squawking 1,200. Would appreciate advisories."

New York ARTCC "Squawk 4525 . . .. Did you say you were VFR, sir?"

Jason "That's affirm. It's patchy, but we've got good ground contact. We're on a VFR flight plan to Baltimore."

Center "Stand by one . . .. (Then, calling another aircraft on the same frequency.) Aztec . . ., say your altitude and your flight conditions."

Aztec pilot ". . . Just comin' through five-point-seven. We been solid ever since we reported the bases at two-point-eight out of Wilkes-Barre. Ride's okay. Nothin' more'n a little light chop. No ice so far."

Center "Thanks . . .. You can climb to and maintain 8,000. If you encounter any ice, we can clear you back to six. (Calling back to Jason.) . . . We've got an Aztec your vicinity heading northwest who's been solid IFR since leaving Wilkes-Barre. Suggest you descend now to 2,700 feet or below to remain VFR."

Jason (Swallowing hard but doing his best to sound like a pilot-in-command.) "Center, Skylane . . . has good ground contact. It's dark here, but the best I can tell, we're at least 500 feet below the clouds. And I'd call the visibility about 5 miles."

Center "Roger . . .. Our radar won't be able to pick you up below 4,200. If you can get up that high *VFR*, sir, we'll be happy to give you advisories. When you reach 4,000, turn right heading 280° for identification and report reaching 4,200."

Jason "Roger center. Climbing to four-point-two."

The center controller signalled to his supervisor, who came over to observe and got a quick explanation that the Skylane was a VFR hot-dog playing games on a lousy night. She plugged in her headset and waited for Jason's transponder blip to show up on the screen in front of them.

They didn't have to wait long. Jason reached 4,000 feet and turned the autopilot knob for a right turn. The airplane started turning as the call came from New York Center:

Center supervisor (In a stern voice) "Skylane . . ., this is the New York Center supervisor. Radar contact. Say your flight conditions, sir."

Jason (Rattled hearing a different, intimidating voice. Realizing instantly that they knew he was fudging.) "Uh . . ..VFR ma'am. We've had good ground contact all the way. But we're right under the clouds right now, ma'am. Might be better if we don't go any higher. We're turning right to 28 . . . oops . . . passed that . . . we're turning back to 280 . . . stand by . . .." (He turned the autopilot control to a full left turn.)

Center supervisor (In a softer, almost laughing voice.) "Okay, you can hold 4,000 and turn back on course. We'll let you know if we lose contact. Maintain VFR."

Jason never responded. The Skylane went into a hard left turn and the DG was through 280° and on its way to 195° in a hurry. Jason turned the autopilot control back to neutral and watched the DG slow down but continue past 195°. Frustrated with the lag in the system, he angrily shut off the autopilot, took the control wheel and began a heavy-handed turn back to 195°. The sudden pressure on the wheel overrode the trim and put the Skylane into a steep climb. Jason felt the sudden G-level change and saw the airplane climbing on the HSI. He quickly reversed the climb but, in doing so, overcontrolled the left turn, putting the Skylane into a sharp 60° bank and starting to roll.

With the DG spinning left and the nose coming down, Jason's head started doing a reverse spin. Fighting the controls and the false sensations, he went into vertigo as the Skylane went into a sharp left spiral. Out of control.

The center controller and supervisor watched their target doing flip-flop turns for about 20 seconds while they were waiting for a response from the pilot. It never came. The target went into a fast left turn and disappeared from the scope. The two controllers froze. Then, with a shaky hand, the supervisor unplugged her headset, picked up a phone and called the Pennsylvania State Police. She told them there might be an airplane down about 2 miles northwest of Wilkes-Barre—not for sure, but a strong possibility. She was hoping she was wrong, but she knew otherwise.

Four motorists and a truck driver on the Cross Valley Expressway saw the Skylane tumble out of the low overcast in a steep left spiral and slam into the ground within 100 yards of the expressway and the Susquehanna River. Amazingly, there was no explosion or fire. The truck driver notified the state police on his CB, telling them there was no need to rush.

The local TV stations had footage of the accident site on the 11 o'clock news that evening. Television coverage was limited to the few known facts: "Two people were killed in the crash of a small airplane, a Cessna. The flight originated in Binghamton, New York, and was en route to Baltimore, Maryland."

But a cub reporter working the graveyard shift for a local newspaper did a little further checking, found out a few more details unrelated to the accident, and submitted a sensationalized story that showed up prominently on the front page the next morning. The headline read "Sex weekend ends in Wilkes-Barre crash." The article vilified Jason and the Martin family, Gwen and her morality, the irresponsible controllers who supposedly dumped the airplane onto a populated area, and aviation in general for endangering the public with half-crazed pilots who shouldn't be allowed to fly if there's a cloud in the sky. The day editor quickly pulled the story after the first edition because he realized immediately that the story was mostly contrived and a gross disservice to his readers. But the damage was done.

A few weeks later, a formal complaint was made in Washington by a citizen's group citing the air traffic controllers for negligence because they allowed a small airplane to endanger a metropolitan area. They also demanded an explanation from the FAA as to why an untrained pilot was permitted to fly in bad weather near a city of more than 50,000 people.

Standard statements were released by both agencies. And the issue has quieted down to memory, albeit of distorted facts and presumptions. But several thousand more Americans were added to the growing list of general aviation opposers.

Air traffic control representative "These were unfortunate circumstances. A combination of bad timing and bad luck. The pilot was obviously where he didn't belong and killed himself and his passenger because of pilot error. The supervisor, just as obviously, should have been less confrontational. Not that doing anything different would have made any difference. She was still dealing with a pilot who was not IFR rated, in solid IMC, on a dark night, with rain and fog closing in. The chances of him making a safe trip that night were not real good.

"The pilot and his passenger, of course, paid with their lives for his defiance and indiscretion. But the supervisor was also a victim. She was so shaken by what happened—and by believing that she caused the pilot to lose control—that she had to take several weeks of rehabilitation time to get her head back to normal. She's fine now, and back on the job. But it took time, a lot of reassurance from her coworkers and several experts, and plenty of understanding from everyone else in her life. I can tell you, she was a mess for quite awhile.

"People tend to forget that while controllers are highly skilled professionals, they still have the same human feelings and emotions as everyone else. In some cases, more so. And when accidents like this one happen, they suffer.

"In two ways: They blame themselves for not having been able to prevent the accident. And they're frustrated because they're forced to operate with their hands tied behind their backs. Literally. You can't appreciate how frustrated controllers can get unless you sit behind a scope with them and watch pilots do themselves and their passengers in because those hotshot pilots-in-command don't have to take orders from ATC, even when the orders can and will save their lives. Like in this case.

"The controller and the supervisor had several pilot assists to their credit, so they knew exactly how to talk that pilot to an airport and help him land safely. But they never got the chance. He was too sure of himself. And they knew they couldn't force him to do anything. All they could do was try to coax him to listen, or sound authoritative enough so he would voluntarily cooperate. This time it backfired.

"Now, isn't that something? We're dealing with human lives in potentially dangerous situations. And we know exactly how to bring virtually every flight to a safe, successful conclusion. But all we can do is coax and sound authoritative.

"And then, to further complicate our situation—and I'm referring specifically to controller morale—we get bum-rapped by the media and a bunch of bleeding-heart citizen's groups who cry and complain but won't lift a finger to help us get the authority we need. And everyone wonders why being a controller is such a stressful job!"

FBO representative (Martin State Airport) "Jason was a person who always seemed to have something to prove. Being from a super-rich family made him that way, I suppose. And he was hard to reason with about rules and regulations. He treated the FARs like they were for all the other pilots but him.

"It's not that he wasn't likable. He was sort of a happy-go-lucky young guy who loved to fly and just wanted to do it his way. Which isn't a very good combination. Because it finally bit him. But then, it was probably inevitable. He took too many chances and he didn't take the weather seriously enough."

J. Frederick Martin, Jason's father "The loss of our son was a terrible thing for us. No parent should ever lose a child. It's like we've lost part of ourselves. My wife, Carol, and I will never be able to get over Jason's death.

"This whole tragedy has been made much worse for us by the media, the insurance company, the lawyers, and all of our friends, relatives, and associates who 'told us so'—that we never should have let Jason talk us into owning a company airplane. They've made us feel like we contributed to our own loss.

"But worst of all have been the government people, as well-meaning as they profess to be. They've blamed this whole thing on Jason. And on us, indirectly. For raising the kind of son we did—a brash 'yuppie' they called him, with too little respect for authority, too much money for his own good, and in too much of a hurry to succeed. Well, let me tell you something. We think those are damned good qualities, and I'm not ashamed to say so. It isn't exactly a sin to not be willing to settle for mediocrity—to have a hard-driven desire to really make something of yourself. That's what makes this country of ours great. The drive and ambition of people like Jason.

"The shame is that there aren't as many Jasons as there used to be. Because our country could sure use them. And if you're looking to pin a 'sin' label on something, pin it on all the highfalutin government systems that didn't work when it came to saving our son and his lovely girlfriend.

"You know, they said the accident was caused by pilot error. That's partly true. Jason pushed his luck too far and made a couple of mistakes. But what the hell were the flight service people doing? I understand he got several weather briefings and they were all bad. Why didn't they just tell him so? Instead of that 'not recommended' nonsense? They knew it was life-threatening weather for a pilot like him. Why did they let him file a flight plan and take off?

"And then that controller, or supervisor, or whatever she was. What was she trying to prove? That she caught him lying about what he could or couldn't see out the window? Was it so goddamned important that she had to kill them over it? (Pause . . . restraining himself)

"I'm sorry. I understand the woman was a seasoned pro doing her job the way she was trained. They said it was just bad luck that Jason was turning the airplane when she got on the radio and shook him up. I'll accept that because I'm sure she thought she was helping them. As a matter of fact, she called my wife a few weeks after the accident and expressed her condolences. Said she was having a hard time of it herself. It was nice of her to call, and we certainly wish her well.

"But tell me, how could a system that's supposed to protect pilots and people on the ground work that way? With no rules, no direct instructions, and the people in control pussyfooting around with semantics and a bunch of acronyms that nobody can understand? That's no way to save lives.

"Our son was very much at fault and he died for it, but it was a waste—a negligent waste. The flight service people and the controllers all knew how dangerous those conditions were. Jason apparently did not. So, they let him kill himself when they could have—and should have—prevented it. That's the real fault here. And it's a crime that something isn't being done about it."

NTSB representative "The primary issues of this accident have been obscured by emotions and complexities. There isn't much question that the New York Center supervisor did, in whatever way, contribute to the pilot losing control of the airplane at that unfortunate moment. But that could have—and likely would have—happened at some other point in the flight. He was a VFR pilot in IFR conditions that were getting worse, not better. How, for instance, was he going to shoot an approach into Baltimore, which was already IFR and forecast to be lower IFR when they arrived?

"As far as the kind of person he was, there's no doubt that he pushed himself over the brink, but not because he was trying to prove anything. It's much more likely that he was simply overconfident: too sure of himself and his ability to successfully handle the weather. And also self-compelled to complete the trip so as to not disappoint his passenger.

"Those, by the way, are a common combination in general aviation accidents. But we can never prove them factually enough to be able to call them anything beyond 'possible' or 'probable' causes. Remember, our responsibility is to investigate and report what happened—factually. We don't delve into the realms of possibility or speculation.

"Anyway, removing all the unprovables, we have a pilot who ignored the standard warnings, lied about his flight conditions, lost control of his airplane the first time he had to make an IMC turn, probably wound up with vertigo and, finally (crashed).

"That's a perfect definition of 'pilot error.' And, until somebody writes a different or more convincing one, our findings will stay as originally reported in this case. Whether or not it was preventable 'pilot error' is something else we can't speculate about, at least not officially. So, I'd rather not address that issue except to say that we at the NTSB believe that nearly all 'pilot error' accidents are preventable, but we also believe that it's primarily the pilots' responsibility to prevent them. Our job is to help intelligent pilots do that. It is not our job to be the policemen of the sky."

Author comment Regardless of their individual perspectives, all of the people touched by an aviation tragedy are victims. Whether or not accountability lies within "the system" or with pilots is arguable but certainly not tantamount; both could stand improvement.

Pilots need more and better training on how to *use* an airplane safely, not just fly one. They especially need to know more about weather—its unpredictability, its peculiarities and, for sure, its dangers—and why VFR pilots in particular should regard "not recommended" as "don't go," even if flight service and air traffic control refuse to say so.

The government agencies can do much more to prevent pilot-error accidents by shedding their obsolete procedures and technologies and accepting more hands-on responsibility for safety in the skies. A good start would be to apply airline attitudes and disciplines to general aviation. That means recognizing some basic facts: First, pilots are human and prone to make errors, especially in a complicated activity like flying; second, properly designed, implemented, and enforced systems can prevent and eliminate human error. The airlines have already proven that it works.

Unfortunately, this pilot was so busy trying to cope with a situation that demanded so much of his attention in the cockpit, that the ATC supervisor's tone of voice was a distraction that made controlling the airplane even more difficult. And we all know from personal experience in the left seat how quickly distractions multiply and make it difficult to concentrate on the task at hand: flying the airplane. Two controllers were on the ground and only one pilot was in the air; the pilot could not ask another pilot to take the controls.

16

Hearing is believing

Preliminary report: December; Piper Cherokee 140; private pilot, single-engine land, 270 hours. The aircraft entered an uncontrolled descent and crashed on a VFR night flight from Ardmore, Oklahoma, to Norman, Oklahoma. The pilot and his passenger were killed instantly. The pilot had encountered unexpected fog and was being vectored for an ILS approach at Will Rogers World Airport in Oklahoma City, an alternate agreed to by the pilot. Immediately after the controller issued heading and altitude instructions, the Cherokee started turning in the opposite direction and then descended rapidly. No further contact was made with the pilot.

Further investigation revealed:

- At 8:15 p.m., the pilot received a weather briefing. VFR conditions prevailed at his destination airport, but the temperature and dew point spread was only 1°.
- Takeoff was over an hour later, at 9:35. No flight plan was filed and no weather briefing was received at that time.
- The pilot contacted Oke City Approach Control and said he was VFR and had encountered fog. He was advised that two other flights had missed approaches at his destination, University of Oklahoma Westheimer Airport. But the pilot elected to continue on to Westheimer.
- The controller issued an IFR clearance to the pilot, who was not instrument rated, and began providing vectors to the Runway 3 localizer approach at Westheimer.
- When the pilot informed the controller that he did not have approach plates, the controller described the approach in detail and continued providing vectors for an intercept of the final approach course. Just before reaching the intercept

point, the Cherokee turned away and began heading northwest.

- After the turn away, the controller instructed the pilot to climb to 3,000 feet and asked him if he wanted vectors to Will Rogers World Airport for the full ILS Runway 35R Approach. The pilot accepted the offer.
- At no time did the pilot advise the controller that he was not instrument rated. Nor did the controller think to ask.

Official conclusion: VMC into IMC. Poor flight planning. Failure to obtain current weather briefing. Overconfidence in personal ability. Loss of control due to spatial disorientation. Pilot error.

IT HAD BEEN A PERFECTLY PLANNED DAY. Duane Carter, 25, and his youngest sister, Ellie, 20, rented a Cessna 150 at The University of Oklahoma Westheimer Airport at 3 p.m. CST and flew home to Ardmore, Oklahoma, to surprise their mother at her 50th birthday party. They had been home the past weekend and were not scheduled to return for the party because of school commitments. Duane was a grad student and instructor in the math department at the University of Oklahoma. Ellie was in premed. They were both honor students and both pilots—Duane for five plus years, Ellie got her private pilot's license two months ago. She had flown left seat for the trip to Ardmore and impressed her older, more experienced brother. The trip back to Norman would be his baby—a night flight with a full moon in decent weather.

At 8:15 p.m., with the party winding down, Duane called flight service from the restaurant and got a weather briefing. When he heard the magic word—"VFR"—prevailing at both Ardmore and Norman, he relaxed, made himself some mental notes and went back to finish the party. No need to rush with a happy forecast like that. He either didn't hear, didn't pay any attention to, or didn't realize the significance of a key part of the forecast: The temperature and dew point spread was only 1°.

Arriving at Downtown Ardmore Airport at 9:10, Duane and Ellie were pleased to find the sky reasonably clear except for some patchy clouds that were easily visible in the moonlight. Actual visibility was only about 4 miles in haze, but it looked better than that to them. Night air can be a fooler.

The 42° early December evening was bone-chilling to Ellie as she began preflighting the Piper. Duane had pulled rank on her and gone to the flight lounge to pay for their parking and a few gallons of gas. Neither of them called back to flight service for a rebriefing. They didn't think it was necessary because it was still very much VFR at Ardmore. And the trip to Norman was only 69 straight-line air miles, or about 42 minutes flying time in the Cherokee.

Airborne at 9:35, Duane turned to a heading of 335° and climbed to 3,000 feet. The air was smooth. The moonlight was intoxicating as it lit up the few clouds above them. It was a lovely night to fly. Too lovely. They barely noticed the creeping fog and haze intensifying all around them, silently obscuring their lateral and downward visibility.

Fifteen minutes later, they noticed it. Five minutes after that it got their full attention. Duane had 11 hours of IFR instruction time, all under the hood. His last lesson was three months ago. Ellie had 1:10 of hood time as part of her private pilot course. They were not prepared for an IFR night flight. Fortunately, the moonlit clouds above provided enough visual reference so they could maintain straight and level flight without total reliance on the non-IFR, very basic instruments in the 140's panel. Duane dialed in 120.45, Oke City Approach, on the single transceiver radio and picked up the mike:

Duane "Oke City Approach, this is Cherokee . . .. We're on a VFR flight to U of Oke Westheimer. About 40 south on Victor-163, at 3,000 feet and squawking twelve."

Oke City Approach "Roger 37 Hotel. The altimeter is 29.97 and falling. Say your request."

Duane "Uh, it's gotten pretty foggy and I don't think we can stay VFR much longer."

Approach "Okay . . .. Understand you're going IFR. Squawk 2347 and ident. (Ellie dialed 2347 on the mode C transponder and Duane touched the ident button. 4 seconds later, the controller's radar picked up the signal at the outer edge of its screen.) Radar contact . . .. Be advised that two small aircraft missed the approach at Westheimer within the past 10 minutes. Please say your intentions, sir."

Duane "Well . . . uh . . . I think we'd like to keep heading for Westheimer, sir. That's home and we need to get this bird back."

Approach "Roger . . .. Stay on your present heading and maintain 3,000. You can plan on the Runway 3 localizer approach. How much room will you need for your turn in at SOONR?"

Duane (Aware—because of his IFR training at Westheimer Airport—that SOONR was the identifier for the outer marker on the approach, Duane answered with a ring of confidence in his voice) "Uh, sir, I don't have any approach plates. This is a VFR flight, and we just got caught in this stuff. It came up all around us suddenly, with no warning. Wasn't even in the forecast we got."

Approach "No problem. The localizer frequency is 111.1. Intercept is at 2,500 feet and the MDA is 1,620. I can give you vectors for the intercept if you'll tell me how much room you'd like. Descend now your discretion to two-point-five and report reaching. SOONR will be coming up in 15 miles."

Duane signed off without giving the controller an answer about the distance he wanted for their turn to the outer marker. He was preoccupied with other things. Like keeping the wings level during the slow descent to 2,500 feet, now with less cloud definition to guide his peripheral vision. This was no practice session. There was no hood. He was flying instruments. This was the real thing. And he was scared stiff.

But he didn't want to upset Ellie any more than she already was. So he discussed the upcoming approach. To settle himself down, too. Then he set up the nav on 111.1 and watched the CDI needle deflect full left. That made him nervous. He could hardly take his eyes off that needle. Then more conversation.

After just a few minutes that seemed like an eternity, the controller called, telling them they were 4 miles from the marker and that another airplane had just missed the approach going into Westheimer. Duane's mind began racing. He did not know the missed approach procedure. The last missed approach he had practiced was more than three months ago. And he did not want to risk a real missed approach. So he decided right then and there that he was not going to try it. No way.

Duane picked up the mike to call the controller just as the controller called him, quickly told him to turn right to 030° for the intercept, and was off dealing with another airplane, and then another. Duane couldn't break in. And he wasn't going to turn onto that localizer approach that he could miss like the 3 other airplanes that did before him. He needed somewhere else to go; someplace with better weather; or somewhere with a full ILS approach and a lower altitude for the descent to landing.

The controller saw the Cherokee start to turn onto the approach and then turn back heading northwest. He called pronto:

Approach "Cherokee . . .. You just went through the localizer. Say your intentions . . .."

Duane (Fighting to maintain his composure) "Approach, (We) can't shoot the localizer approach. We have no plate for the miss. We'd rather find a VFR airport."

Approach "Say your fuel. The closest VFR with a full ILS approach is up north around Wichita. This fog has moved in and stayed in over a broad area. Your best bet for now is probably Will Rogers. They're showing 400 and 2. The ILS will get you in with 200 and ½, so you'd have room to spare. Everyone who missed at Westheimer got in okay."

Duane (Still fighting panic, calmed only slightly by the controller's matter-of-fact tone of voice) "Uh, sounds good. Uh, we'll need the ILS frequency over there."

Controller "It'll be the three-five-right approach. The frequency is 110.9. Turn left heading 250° and climb to 3,000. You're only 7 from the marker. That's GALLY. Expect a tight right turn in 4 miles."

The Cherokee started the left turn and began climbing. It reached 2,800 feet and continued turning past the 250° assigned heading. Noticing it immediately, because he had been paying special attention, the controller keyed his mike. But before he could say anything, the Cherokee's left turn suddenly tightened into a spiral and the altitude started falling. Then dropping. Then diving. The controller never said a word.

Duane was struggling, wrenching the control wheel. Ellie tried but couldn't overcome his frantic, overpowering strength. She was trying to push the yoke forward and to the right to stop the spiraling rotation. But he was winning, holding severe back pressure, aggravating the out-of-control stall, tightening the killer spiral. He was also losing the battle with his spinning head. Vertigo was destroying his equilibrium. Panic had taken over.

The controller watched helplessly as the Cherokee wound itself into a compressed spiral, dumped its altitude with increasing acceleration, and finally disappearing from the scope. The whole episode took 21 seconds.

Duane and Ellie were unconscious from the wild spinning and the lurching of the airplane. They were killed instantly when the Cherokee hit the ground.

The controller sat in trauma, staring at his screen in disbelief. He had heard about, read about, and had nightmares about what he had just seen—an airplane going down and off his radar. This was real and he might have unwittingly contributed to their deaths. He regained enough composure to signal to his supervisor, who relieved him.

That was the last airplane the controller handled. The day after the accident, he asked for a temporary leave of absence. Then a temporary reassignment. Followed by a permanent transfer to Washington. His nine-year career in a job he loved had come to an end.

ATC representative "We hate losing people in airplanes and we hate losing controllers. But it's part of this job. All the soul searching in the world won't change it that much. What's so unfortunate about this accident is that the controller blamed himself so totally, even though the pilot had very little chance of landing safely, based on his limited IFR experience and the conditions that prevailed that evening. As a matter of fact, the controller actually gave them their best option, the ILS at Will Rogers. So, if anything, he came closest to saving their lives.

"If you listen to the tapes and study the transcripts carefully, it isn't difficult to see where the confusion came in about the pilot's instrument capabilities. He'd had some IFR training. Not that much and not that recently. But enough to know the radio procedures. His tone of voice, the things he said, all sounded like they were coming from an IFR pilot. The acknowledgements, too. He accepted the vectors and agreed to both approaches. That was plenty convincing.

"If you think about it, you'll agree that the controller had only two possible choices anyway: He could handle the flight IFR or as an emergency situation requiring a flight assist. But because of the weather and the widespread low ceilings and visibilities, both procedures would have been very similar. The best alternative was still the ILS at Will Rogers, either by instruments or a talk-down.

"One other part of the transcripts could make you think the controller should have known right away that the pilot was not IFR rated. That was the business of the missing approach plates. But that's not all that uncommon or unusual either. Lots of IFR pilots fly VFR without hauling along their charts and plates. Especially on short trips like this one was. I'd venture that an average controller gives out approach plate information several times a year. We don't make a big deal out of it.

"That's about it. The NTSB spent a lot of time with the transcripts and focused on how the controller handled the flight, and whether or not anything he did contributed to the accident. When they got all through, they came to the conclusion that what the controller did, or tried to do, was the closest anyone or anything came to saving those two people. Now we wish we could convince the controller of that. He still blames himself and still doesn't want to go back to being a controller. That's a rather sad aftermath of this case."

Luanne Carter Perry, 23, a sister "My folks won't talk about the accident because it's only been two years and it still hurts too bad. I can't help a whole lot either except to tell you what we already told the government people from the FAA and the safety board.

"When Duane and Ellie flew in and called us from the airport the afternoon of the party, we were all surprised. They'd driven back to

Norman just two days before, so none of us ever dreamed they'd come home just for the party, what with finals and all. But there they were, showin' off Ellie's new pilot's license and braggin' how she'd been the pilot in charge, or whatever she called it, on the trip down from Norman. Them and their flying. That's about all the two of them ever talked about, and especially that day.

"Anyway, they weren't goin' to stay for the whole party because they were in a rented airplane and wanted to be sure they'd get it back on time. Besides, Duane didn't want to be flyin' around in a single-engine airplane too late at night. But mom and dad were havin' such a good time, and Ellie was such a hit with all the relatives and friends with her flyin' stories, that they decided that, if the weather was goin' to stay good enough, they'd be able to stay long enough to enjoy some more of the party.

"I remember Duane comin' back to the table from makin' a call to the flight weather people. He was smilin'. Gave Ellie a thumbs up and told her it was 'Vee-eff-n'-arr,' I guess meanin' it was good weather, and then they stayed for more of the party. My husband, Jack, and I didn't leave to take them to the airport until almost 9 o'clock.

"On the way out there, Duane was tellin' us that the weather was supposed to stay good for the rest of the night and that, with the full moon, it was goin' to be a really pretty flight. When we dropped them off, there was that moon shinin' full bloom and, except it was a little cold and damp feelin', the weather was just like Duane said it was goin' to be.

"And it stayed good, too. Jack got back from takin' the baby sitter home 'round a quarter-to-ten and didn't say nothin' about it bein' foggy or anythin'. In fact, we went to bed and didn't know there was any fog until we got woke up by the phone call about the accident. That was after 2 in the mornin'. They actually crashed at around 10:30, but it took that long for the police to figure out who to call.

"I don't know what else to tell you. Duane was a good pilot. Jack and I had flown with him several times and he always seemed real careful to us. Always checkin' up on everythin'. Always tellin' us how he never took chances with the weather. That's why this whole thing seemed so weird to us. And with Ellie along, who was miss prim, proper and perfectionist, it's even weirder that somethin' as crazy as that weather could have happened to the two of them. Makes you never want to fly again, not even on an airline.

"Oh, and one other thing. We got asked a whole bunch of questions about what Duane and Ellie ate and drank at the party that night. Well, I can tell you for sure it wasn't any alcohol. No one in our family ever touches it. But the investigators were sure persistent about it. Like they were lookin' for ways to blame Duane for causin' the accident. Which they did anyway. They came out with their official accident report, and it said it was 'pilot error.'

"But that's just a bunch of bull. They never had any proof that Duane did anythin' wrong. He got a weather report like he was supposed to. And it said the weather was okay. He called the controller like he was supposed to and instead of takin' them to a place where they could land safely, the controller started steerin' them all over the sky like Duane was a seasoned instrument pilot. Which he wasn't and never claimed to be. That's why he lost control of the airplane. They were havin' him do things he wasn't trained for. And they got the nerve to call that 'pilot error'? 'Controller error' would be more like it.

"I suppose they're just scared that we'll sue them for killin' my brother and sister. And they did kill them. But they don't have to worry none. We ain't suin' nobody. We just want to get this thing behind us and stop the hurtin'."

Flight service representative "The weather briefing the pilot got was complete, as far as we know, at least from what was shown on the report. There were a couple of things that we've never been completely comfortable with, though.

"When the pilot called in at 8:15, the first thing he was told was that the weather he'd be getting was over an hour old. There had been a system delay because of a major revision in the forecasts for that part of the country. The pilot was told all that and advised to call back later on. But the briefer went ahead and gave him the weather, knowing that it was being updated and likely would be very different from what he had then. He claimed that the pilot asked for it, and that's probably true, but in my opinion, he shouldn't have given it out. There were too many things about it that made it potentially dangerous for a VFR flight.

"For instance, the temperature and dew point spread was only 1°. That's much too close for comfort at night, in Oklahoma, and in December. Even seasoned IFR pilots take special precautions when they get a spread like that because they know that, if it comes together, they'll be looking at very low IFR, and very often conditions that are below IFR minimums. Especially in the early evening when the air is cooling down. And that's exactly what was happening on the night of the accident. In fact, that's probably why the area forecasts were being revised at the time.

"The briefer said he explained that to the pilot in detail. But we don't know how much of it the pilot actually understood, or why he apparently didn't take it seriously enough to call back for an update. Because according to what we've been able to learn about the pilot, that wouldn't have been like him at all. In fact, quite the contrary. He was a numbers guy—a grad student and math instructor at Oke U. If anything, a guy like him would probably have called twice, or just stayed home. He was anything but a daredevil fly boy.

"His sister, the passenger, was also a pilot. A new one but, from what we learned about her, a very good one, and also no hot rodder. So, between the two of them, if they had even slightly suspected that there was a weather problem, especially at night, they would certainly have made the decision to spend the night in Ardmore and let the airplane sit out the foggy night on the ground.

"Our official position is that the pilot received a complete briefing, should have called back but didn't, and took off on a VFR night flight in weather that was turning into IFR. That's for the record.

"Apparently, the briefer never told the pilot that VFR flight was 'not recommended.' That's our official language for a warning and should have been included with strong emphasis in the briefing, but it wasn't. And the fact that it wasn't makes us suspicious of the briefer's report. Because that pilot's actions spoke louder than the briefer's words. And we're absolutely certain that the pilot wasn't suicidal. So, in our book, he wins. It's just a shame that he isn't around to help us prove it.

"Now if you're wondering why I'm telling you all this, keep in mind that we run the best system of its kind in the world. And we take special pride in that. All of us. We also realize that we're human and that oversights can occasionally happen. And when they do, we want to correct them. All of us do. So, we hate cover-ups of any kind and from anyone, even from our own people. That's why you got this earful, and I hope you'll treat it with discretion in your report so it helps us improve our system."

NTSB representative "We can easily defend the 'pilot error' conclusion for this accident for two reasons. First, the pilot did not file a flight plan for a night cross-country trip. Even though it was only a 42-minute ride, a flight plan is proper discipline. Now think about that for a moment. If the pilot had filed a flight plan, it likely would have been a timely one—real close to takeoff. And what would he have gotten from the briefer if he had done that? Right. An updated briefing that would have told him to stay home.

"The second reason is that when he found himself getting into IFR conditions and accidently or deliberately misled the approach controller into thinking he was IFR rated, he knew he was in trouble. No one else did. Only him. So, what should he have done? He should have declared an emergency and let the system know his true situation. But he didn't do that. And that is definitely 'pilot error.'

"Having established that, let's look a little further because this particular accident had some interesting twists to it that warrant closer scrutiny. For instance, did the approach controller's wrong assumption contribute in any way toward causing the accident? How about a 'probably' on that one? The controller most likely would have treated an emergency or a VFR flight assist differently than he did that pilot, who he thought was IFR qualified. He'd have used kid gloves. Real gentle climbs and turns. Slow, soft instructions. None of the technical stuff like the names of markers, or what approach it was, or the MDA, or a choice of places to go, or anything else like that. In a flight assist, you talk 'em down nice 'n easy so they don't get excited and throw themselves out of the sky like that pilot did.

"Okay then, assuming that the controller's erroneous presumption did have some negative effect on the outcome, it's easy to agree that some procedure is needed that will prevent a controller from taking a convincing sounding pilot at voice value. And if you think about it a little, there's a very obvious preventer that's already in place, in every pilot's possession, that can instantly qualify the pilot and quantify his or her experience level—both in flying time and training. Know what it is? It's their pilot's licenses. With their own personal numbers on them. Which could be easily programmed to tell the system everything it needs to know about them. Starting with whether or not the pilot is IFR qualified, or night current, or current in type, or BFR current, or has a current medical, or if there is any record of alcohol or drug use, and so forth.

"It should be easy to do. Hell, if a parking meter attendant in any major city can access the parking ticket history of any one of 125 million drivers, by portable radio no less, it ought to be a snap to set up a data base on a mere 600,000 pilots. So, why don't we?

"Because nobody's asking us to. The public doesn't give a hoot about general aviation. Most pilots resist any rules or regulations that may restrict their freedom to bore holes in the sky—and sometimes the ground. In their macho mania they believe they are big-time 'pilots-in-command' who can take care of their own safety. And then there are the associations and unions who believe that a system capable of accessing that much information on a pilot would be an invasion of privacy.

"So, what you have is a standoff. At least for now and the near future. But think of what a system like that could do, starting at the flight service level. When pilots called in for weather briefings, the briefers would know what kinds of pilots they were dealing with—for real. They could then give some truly valuable advice and maybe head off most of the VMC into IMC accidents. They could also stop some of the drunks, drug users, and other nuts and fruitcakes who abuse the privilege to fly.

"A system like that would have saved the lives of the two very desirable people who died in this accident, which their families most certainly would have appreciated. And it could save the lives of hundreds of others every year. I'd call that a worthy endeavor that deserves some serious and immediate consideration."

NASA representative "The first real error in this accident was made by the flight service briefer. It was a mind-set error. By that we mean the result of a presumption without basis that led to a causal misunderstanding. If that sounds like gobbledygook, let me explain what happened.

"When the pilot first called flight service, he was told that the available weather data was over an hour old and that a significant change in the forecasts was in process. He was also told to call back later for an update before taking off. Then the pilot asked for the readings anyway. So the briefer gave him an abbreviated report of the current conditions, leaving out the usual warnings and precautions because he assumed that the pilot would be calling back. [Apparently the briefer never said 'VFR not recommended.']

"Of course, the pilot never did (call back) because he also had some preconditioned mind-sets: that the weather would remain VFR, as he had been told it would earlier in the day, before he left his home airport in Norman, Oklahoma. That the weather looked good visually when he called Ardmore flight service for the abbreviated reading he got and promptly misinterpreted. That the weather wouldn't change enough to ground him in such a short time.

"Putting the pilot and the briefer together for that particular discourse at that particular moment was unlucky. Then add the approach controller's false presumption, a terrible turn in the weather, a surprised and unprepared pilot, and you have the formula for an unavoidable accident. Too many things went wrong. Too many people made mistakes. Too many minds were astray at the same time.

"Any one of the mistakes could have led to the accident. But our choice for 'most critical' would go to the approach controller. There were actually two things that happened because of what he did: First, the initial assurances given to the pilot that he didn't need approach plates probably dissuaded him from declaring an emergency by giving him a false sense of well-being. After all, he was then in the care of the understanding, helpful controller who seemed to be treating the situation very routinely. How could the pilot second-guess such comforting, professional assistance?

"The second thing was the controller's final comments and instructions. Issued as they were just as the pilot was maneuvering away from the localizer at Westheimer, they came across as a barrage that rattled his cage and at precisely the moment when it couldn't stand being rattled because the pilot was already contending with as much as he could handle.

"You could lay odds on that last part because only seconds later the pilot lost control for no other apparent reason. Up to then, he had been flying competently and was not exhibiting any signs of spatial disorientation.

"In summarizing this accident, I would say that something useful could come of it. Because of the very unusual circumstances involved, it has helped shed some light on one other dangerous mind-set: The one that prevails at the investigative agencies. By limiting the 'probable causes' of an accident only to 'pilot error,' as they did in this case—and as they do in nearly every case, no matter how many errors come from other sources—they effectively sweep under the rug critical opportunities to implement changes that can make general aviation better and safer.

"Anything that illuminates the truth about that mind-set is a step in the right direction. It could lead to a break in the logjam that is stifling to general aviation."

Author comment Each commentary generated by this accident is the light at the end of so many long bureaucratic tunnels. It is refreshing and reassuring to discover that willing and caring people are progressing upward within the controlling government agencies a break who acknowledge that there are deficiencies in the system. The lives of the hundreds of pilots and their passengers who die every year because of those deficiencies are worth saving, now rather than later.

17

Flight training revamped

Preliminary report: April, American AA-1 Yankee; student pilot, single-engine land, 28 hours. The student pilot crashed on his first solo cross-country flight. He survived with serious injuries but died four days after the accident. No weather briefing was obtained and no flight plan was filed when the aircraft departed from Albany-Dougherty County Airport in Albany, Georgia. A large frontal system was approaching the airport but the departure airport was VFR at the time of takeoff. The pilot's instructor claimed that he had not authorized the flight, but the airplane was rented from the FBO that employed the instructor. Several people saw the pilot prior to his departure and noted nothing unusual about him.

Further investigation revealed:
- Weather at the accident site, which was fewer than 30 miles west of the departure airport, was reported by witnesses as foggy and rainy with visibility of about 1 mile.
- The pilot's training had been intermittent because of his business travel commitments, but he had just completed a weekend ground school program and passed his written.
- On the Sunday morning of the flight, the airplane had been reserved for the pilot by his instructor, who later claimed the flight was only tentative and also denied having signed-off the pilot for the solo trip.
- The pilot had not been trained to obtain his own weather briefing or file a flight plan. The FBO had a teletype and generally posted the local readings on its bulletin board. Witnesses stated that the posted teletype data was not always current.

Official conclusion: Inadequate preflight planning. VFR into IMC. Inadequate flight instructor supervision. Loss of control due to spatial disorientation. Pilot error.

A FULL WEEK HAD GONE INTO the planning for Kevin Jackson's first solo cross-country, right after he finished a two-day, high-powered ground school cramming course the weekend before. The 25-year-old student pilot had committed himself to catching up on a flight training schedule that had fallen far behind its game plan because his field auditing work had taken up so much time. Accounting firms are very demanding of their high-paid new hires and expect especially intense performance from a cum laude MBA Yale graduate like Kevin. They got it. But now the tax season had just ended and Kevin was determined to get on with his flying. It was part of his career plan, as was everything else in his life. Kevin was an obsessive planner.

That's why the flight planning for this trip had taken almost a full week. His sectional looked like an engineering schematic. Every frequency, every checkpoint, every elevation of note, every little detail he could think of was carefully marked. And then committed to memory. Kevin would have no trouble finding his way to Dothan, Alabama, 63 miles southwest of Albany.

Right after his last lesson, four days prior to the accident, he went over the whole trip with his instructor in minute detail. You'd have thought that Kevin was about to traverse the wilds of the Yukon on the way to Nome, Alaska. Chuck McCray, his 35-year-old instructor, did. He was definitely impressed with Kevin's planning ability. But less so with his flying skills. To his way of thinking, Kevin lacked some of the innate presence of a pilot and much of the confidence. It always seemed to him that Kevin wasn't really comfortable in the air. Like a sea lion out of the water, or a goose waddling along an embankment. Kevin was a graceful thinker and planner, but a lousy doer.

But Kevin was determined and demanding of himself. He expected to succeed at everything, and flying was no exception. Which is why he persuaded Chuck to sign him up for his first solo cross-country on Sunday morning—weather permitting, and with Chuck's final blessing just before takeoff. Or maybe they'd sneak in another ½ hour of dual to warm up. They would ponder on that, especially Chuck.

Four hours of sleep was all Kevin could muster against the anticipation of the flight. But it didn't show when he arrived at the airport raring to go at 8 a.m. Adrenalin can mask a lot of tiredness. His takeoff was scheduled for 9:30, but he wanted time to go over things with Chuck. To satisfy Chuck. Kevin was ready.

An anxious 20 minutes went by and Chuck never showed. No one at the airport had heard from him. But the flight log didn't show any change in Kevin's reservation, so he decided to get on with the preflight, which he did twice in 10 minutes. Chuck still hadn't arrived and the answering machine came on when Kevin called Chuck's home; Kevin left a detailed message that he would be taking off at 9:30, as scheduled.

The next 35 minutes were nerve wracking for Kevin. He must have checked the weather printout on the bulletin board five or six times at least. The same one. The teletype wasn't running. But no worry. Out the window was the same 3,000 broken and 10 miles that was on the printout. So Kevin's main concern at that moment was Chuck, not the weather.

Finally, at 0905, Kevin was going to Dothan, with or without the Yankee, and with or without Chuck McCray's final blessing. As far as he and Rita Collins, the counter manager, could figure, Chuck hadn't bothered to change the trip time, or showed up or called in to head Kevin off. So, in Chuck's mind it must have been a "go." The trip was already a "go" in Kevin's mind. And whatever Kevin wanted to do was okay with Rita, too. She had a lot of confidence in Kevin and liked him. More than he realized.

Rita Collins "That was a terrible morning for me. For everyone here at the airport. The weather came rolling in here about 30 minutes after Kevin took off, faster than the forecast said. Another pilot who left for the practice area, right after Kevin took off, barely made it back in.

"We all had this awful premonition that Kevin was in trouble. I must have made 10 calls to the FBO at Dothan. And five or six to flight service and air traffic control and the tower at Dothan. I could hardly talk on the phone. I was too upset. I knew he was down somewhere. I was praying he was okay. (Pause) I guess I wasn't praying right.

"Anyway, the day after the accident, I checked over the logs again and gave a complete report to the FAA people and Mr. Sheldon, my boss here. Kevin's instructor, Chuck, had set up the airplane for the flight the Thursday before. The log didn't say anything about it being a solo cross-country. Just a normal hour-and-a-half checkout, which usually means a local flight or to the practice area.

"Kevin was with him at the time because they had just come back from a lesson. Neither one of them mentioned that it wasn't going to be just another lesson or some solo touch-and-go work, or I would have marked it on the sheet. We always note anything that isn't routine, like a trip out of the area. And for sure, a first-time solo cross-country. But Chuck never said anything and never made any notation on the log. Which was his responsibility to take care of.

"I'll never completely forgive Chuck McCray for what happened. I don't care what his excuses were. He should have signed out the flight like he was supposed to. He should have showed up on time, not 2½ hours late like he did. By that time, Kevin was already down. And he should have made sure that Kevin knew how to check the weather and file a flight plan. Knowing how to do that was supposed to be part of every pilot's training here. Unfortunately, some of the flight instructors—especially the part-timers like Chuck—would check everything out themselves each morning and not bother their students with contacting flight service. They'd get to that later on in the training course, after the students knew how to handle the airplane and were ready to go out of the area by themselves. You can bet that procedure has been changed around here since the accident.

"You know, there was one other thing about that Sunday morning that was strange: Kevin never said a word to me or anyone that he was going to Dothan by himself. The only reason we knew that after he left was that he had written it on the log when he checked out the airplane. I never saw him do it. I get the shivers every time I think about it."

Out to the airplane for his usual perfect engine start, followed by a meticulous by-the-numbers run-up at the runway apron, Kevin was off the ground at 9:28. He eased the Yankee into a comfortable cruise climb, turned left to a 250° heading and looked out the window for his first familiar checkpoint, the little town of Pretoria.

Five minutes later Kevin was reading the name and the smile on the water tower in Pretoria. This was where he and Chuck always turned south to the practice area. From this point forward on his southwesterly heading, Kevin was leaving everything familiar behind—the purpose of the first very short solo cross-country flight.

Kevin felt the exhilaration as the Pretoria tower slipped behind him. So much so that he was somewhat startled when the ground suddenly disappeared below him as the Yankee climbed up and into the ragged base of the lowering overcast—at only 1,500 feet. As he quickly lowered the nose and descended, he wondered what happened to the 3,000 foot ceiling that was called for on the teletype printout.

The lowering overcast was a major weather system that was forecast to move into the area from the northwest. As luck would have it, there it was, ahead of schedule. The teletype report was from the day before. It hadn't been updated as it should have been, and almost always was. Except occasionally on Sunday mornings when most of the folks in Albany were in church. Ironically, the updated latest printout was posted just before Kevin taxied out. He obviously never saw it. And the newly arrived chief flight instructor who posted it had no idea that Kevin hadn't called flight service for a complete weather briefing before climbing into the Yankee. Nor did he know that Kevin was going on his first solo cross-country, because the flight log showed the Yankee checked out only until 11 a.m., the usual amount of block time for local solo practice flights.

The reason Kevin did not call flight service was that he had never before done so. Chuck always took care of clearing the weather, always decided whether they were "go" or "no-go." Kevin had never filed a flight plan either. They had never done that for their local flights. And they had only been cross-country two times before, with Chuck firmly in control and in command. This was Kevin's first time, his solo cross-country—all by himself. It was only a 37-minute trip out and a 32-minute trip back. With all of Kevin's meticulous planning, they had never talked about a weather briefing or filing a VFR flight plan. After all, Chuck was supposed to be there to see him off. That was always part of the plan.

Rob Russell, chief flight instructor, Albany FBO "So many things were out of synch that day that something was bound to go wrong. We almost lost two other airplanes in that weather. It got here about 2 hours earlier than the night before's forecast showed and swept in here like the creeping crud. Unusual for that time of the year. Thunderstorms and tornadoes would have been more typical.

"Since the accident, we've made some major procedural changes in the flight school and in the pilot's lounge here. Starting with the teletype printouts. We now mark the date and the time with a yellow highlighter and also write in the name of the day in big letters with a red pen. To the best of our knowledge, no one had ever before gotten confused over the date on the printout, but it was understandable that it could have been overlooked. It wasn't very prominent. And a pilot who was excited over his first solo cross-country could easily have missed it, or took for granted that it was up-to-date.

"We've also changed our training procedures so that our students get involved with flight service right from the start. We've made sure that all of our instructors and students understand that being a good pilot is more than just knowing how to handle an airplane. So we're stressing proper planning, good overall discipline, and thorough knowledge of the weather because this is Georgia and we get some mean and nasty atmospherics around here.

"Another thing that's changed is the instructor's participation in solo flights by students. Especially first solo flights, like the one Kevin was on. Now there has to be at least a half hour of dual given before any student can fly his first solo anything.

"I don't mean to bore you with details, but this has been a fatality-free flight school for over 20 years. And we intend to make sure that Kevin's death will be the last fatality we'll see around here for at least the next 20 and, hopefully, much longer."

Getting his nose out of the clouds wasn't easy for Kevin. He had never been in IMC before. In an airliner a number of times, but that was different. This was him, alone in a Yankee two-seater training airplane. He didn't like the feeling. And he had only a very scant idea of what the very limited instruments on the Yankee's equally sparse panel were telling him.

Seeing the ground was a great relief to Kevin. He wasn't going to let that happen to him again. He was going to follow the rules, remain VFR at all times, and stay well under those clouds and in 3 miles or more visibility. Unfortunately, the weather doesn't know the rules and has no concern for pilots. It does its thing, ready or not. And right then it was reaching down and around Kevin and the Yankee. Dropping the ceiling on them and reducing the visibility with fog and rain. Kevin felt like he was being sucked up into the clouds as he fought to stay beneath them and above the terrain, what he could see of it.

Panic can sneak up on a pilot. It snuck up on Kevin the instant he did a 180 to head back to Albany. Which was right after he had come to an astute conclusion that he wasn't going to be landing anywhere near Dothan. Not in that lowering weather. But he never figured that turning around might not be an escape route from the junk ahead of him. On that day, it wasn't. He was trapped.

Had he known the weather forecast, he may have thought to turn southeast and try to outrun the system. At that point, he had only been overrun by about 5–6 miles. With a little luck, he could have flown into better conditions in 3½ minutes and been able to land safely in Donaldson or Bainbridge, Georgia. They were only 10–12 minutes away and still very much VFR, about like Albany was when he left it just 18 minutes before. But that Georgia weather in the springtime can be plenty ornery, and Albany would soon be out of the question, heading that way was already out of the question. The hilltops were being obscured and visibility was down to a mile in fog and heavier rain.

Kevin wasn't ready for what he was dealing with. He knew it. And the thought of it gripped him like a vice. Finally, in order to stay clear of the rising terrain, he had no place to go but up. And that was no place for him to go or to be. He knew that, too. So did the Yankee as it lurched itself out of control under Kevin's incapable tutelage.

Kevin fought the wheel and the spinning sensations as best he could. Trying to get back in control. But it was hopeless and too late. Kevin was out of options and out of time.

The Yankee struck the trees in a 50° nose-low, right wing-low attitude, cutting an 80-yard swath into the trees and finally stopping at the trunk of a Georgia pine. A witness at the accident site later stated that the weather at the time of the crash was foggy and rainy, with less than a mile of visibility. Kevin never had a chance.

Joe Sheldon, FBO owner "I had the unhappy responsibility of dealing with Kevin's family. They were, of course, devastated by what happened. He was their pride and joy. A very talented young man with a terrific future ahead of him. And a loving, devoted son. Just a few months younger than my own son, Danny. They knew each other from here at the airport and had become friends, when Kevin had the time.

"The terrible part of this is that we were directly involved in killing Kevin. So many of our procedures had gotten so sloppy that something was bound to go wrong. It's just a damned shame that it had to be a fatal, and that a person as special as Kevin had to be the victim.

"I know you're wondering why I'm speaking so frankly and admitting our negligence because of product liability and all. But I've discussed it openly with the FAA, the NTSB and Burt Jackson, Kevin's father. I told him to go ahead and sue us if it would help. We wouldn't even attempt to defend ourselves. We'd let the insurance company worry about it, even if it wound up putting us out of business.

"The Jackson's are a pretty special family. They asked me what we could do to prevent what happened to Kevin from ever happening again and we've been working together on it ever since. The changes around here have been from start to finish. And everybody's been involved in making them. Even Chuck McCray, Kevin's instructor, who I fired that Sunday, right after we found out how badly he'd screwed up.

"Chuck was beside himself, too. He's a full-time Georgia State Trooper who's been a part-time flight instructor for the last 13 years. And a damned good one, I might add. That morning he was coming off the midnight shift and got hung up with an overturned semi on the north side of Albany. He didn't think to call in here because the way he and Kevin had planned it, they were going to make a decision about the trip after they talked it over. I guess the semi driver was hurt pretty bad or something and time kind of slipped away on Chuck. I can tell you that, from our experience, that was the first time anything like that ever happened to him. He was always Mr. Reliable Plus, and still is.

"Anyway, Chuck talked to Burt Jackson. Then they both talked to me and Rob Russell, our chief flight instructor, and we all agreed that I'd made a hasty, unfair decision. So we hired Chuck back. And it was the right thing to do. Since then, Chuck has kind of spearheaded most

of the improvements in our flight training, starting with our basic phi-
losophy. For instance, we've downgraded solo and the macho attitudes connected with rushing a student to fly by himself. No more
shirt-tail parties in this place. And we spend much more time on
teaching the system. Like dealing with flight service and air traffic
control for flight following and such.

"I can tell you that this whole thing has made us see some lights
and changed us in a hundred ways. We're a different kind of flight
school than we were, and getting better every day. I like to think that
Kevin knows that and forgives us for what happened. Maybe even
takes some pride in having brought about the changes we've made."

NTSB representative "Putting all of the pieces of this accident back
together took some doing because of the number of factors involved.
Obviously, we couldn't figure out what a student pilot was doing up in
that stuff on his first solo cross-country. And only 30 or so miles after
takeoff. We wondered if they'd started teaching scud running at Albany.

"When we got into it more, we realized that a whole series of human errors had taken place. And then they were compounded by
some crazy bad luck, which seems to be the case in many airplane
accidents. This particular one more so than most others I've seen.

"To begin with, there was that miscommunication between the
instructor and the student, made worse by whatever it was (that) delayed the instructor. Then there was the old teletype that never got
changed until just after the pilot was out the door. That was really
weird. But then, the way that weather moved in was something else.
Systems like that, with fog and steady rain, don't speed up. They
more likely slow down. Especially in springtime. This one apparently
got pushed ahead by a big cold front that moved in in back of it.
Fooled everybody at National Oceanics. They were at least two hours
behind that thing and didn't catch up until it was already coming
through. As far as I can remember, that was a first for them.

"All the way from Montgomery to Columbus and across to Atlanta,
everybody got surprised by the sudden speedup of that weather. So,
it may not have mattered much if the latest teletype was on that bulletin board, or if the student or the instructor had made a call to flight
service. They would have gotten poor information telling them that
the system wasn't due in the area for another few hours and that the
ceilings and visibilities associated with it were not all that terrible.

"But then, you have to look at it another way. Why in God's name
would anyone send a student pilot on a solo cross-country in marginal weather of any kind? Or when the weather is moving in—what-

ever kind it is? The answer is, you don't. And that's why we extended
the investigation of this accident way beyond normal. We wanted to
be sure that the flight school at Albany, which had a perfect safety
record up till then, hadn't flipped out.

"When we finished the reports, we were satisfied with everything
except one part. Our official findings did not say that the weather was
the ultimate culprit. That's because we have no classification for it, no
place in the computer that will say 'the weather did it.' So, everyone
and everything else gets blamed, and rightly so to some degree, but
the real cause of the accident gets left out.

"Which does a big disservice to pilots. It doesn't tell them that
sometimes the weather is beyond predicting and beyond their ability
to handle it. That's the truth for IFR pilots as well as VFR pilots. Our
reports should be reminding them of that fact, and they don't. They
don't tell them to give the weather plenty of extra room when it's
coming at you. They should be saying loud and clear that some
weather is too overpowering for military and airline heavies, so all of
you little guys should stay the hell away from it. But they don't.

"I just hope that someday they'll let us out of these straitjackets
and let us tell it the way it is. And in this particular accident, that's
the way it was. The weather did it. Everybody else was just a minor
contributor."

Chuck McCray, Kevin's flight instructor "I don't have to tell you
how badly Kevin's accident tore me up. I'm a state trooper, so I see
some pretty horrible accidents right up close. But I never cause any
of them and I never have to deal with the families and loved ones
who won't ever get completely over them. This one is my own cross
to bear.

"Kevin and I had kind of a special relationship. He was brighter
than most and a poorer pilot than most. By that I mean he was a whiz
when it came to flying knowledge, but (not equally able) when it
came to physical coordination. Oh, he always learned how to do
everything competently. It just took him longer and he had to work
at it harder. Nothing ever came natural to him. But when he did finally learn something, he did it as well as anyone. So I didn't really
worry about him. I just always knew he was going to require extra
time for every new skill and maneuver.

"He and I talked about that a lot. I know it bothered him more
than he ever admitted, to me or to himself. But we both knew there
was nothing either one of us could do about it, so we lived with it.
That's how it was when we scheduled the trip for that day. We were

going to fly a little first, see how it went, and then decide if we both felt he was ready to go off to Dothan by himself. We never talked about the weather or anything because that was kind of automatic. I always checked out the weather myself very carefully before I'd start my day. Then, depending on what stage my students were at in their training, I'd have them check with flight service and file their own flight plans. Kevin and I were going to do that if we decided he was ready for the trip that day.

"Since then, I realize what a dumb procedure that was. Now, every student learns to deal with flight service from day one. And I can tell you for sure that when they hear a briefer say 'VFR not recommended,' they know better than to get anywhere near an airplane. We show them pictures of what happened to that Yankee and Kevin. That works better than anything we could tell them, especially when they know it happened here. (Pause) God, I hate looking at those pictures. (Pause)

"The people I work for here, and the government people, too, have all been wonderful to me over this. We've made a bunch of changes around here. Tightened up most of our procedures. And we'll be doing more things, too, as we go along. We're making absolutely certain that no student ever slips through the cracks again. When we get all finished, this will be a better flying school than it ever was.

"I'm grateful that I've been given the opportunity to work on this project. It's helping me get over this thing. I hope the finished product helps everyone else get over it, too, and accept the fact that the accident was a combination of crazy circumstances and lousy luck, not carelessness or negligence on anyone's part. When that finally happens, it'll be better for everyone around here."

Burt Jackson, Kevin's father "Everything in life has a purpose, so we've decided that Kevin's death was meant to save others. Not just in Albany. But everywhere the FAA publishes its reports so pilots can learn from them. We have to think of it that way, or we'll never be able to get our grief behind us. Kevin was a very special son.

"After all the facts were finally in, we got the idea that everybody was a victim of Kevin's accident. Chuck McCray, Kevin's instructor was especially torn up over it—blamed himself for the whole thing—even thought about giving up flying. It took awhile and some doing to talk him out of it.

"Then Joe Sheldon, who owns the FBO at Albany Airport, he was ready to throw in the towel, too. Advised us to go ahead and sue him.

But money wouldn't bring Kevin back. It would only make every-thing worse for all of us. We're not among the majority of Americans who think a tragedy is a ticket to easy money and then wind up spending years in court making everyone else suffer with them. We'd rather find a way to make something useful come of the accident so Kevin's death won't have been wasted.

"My wife and I have visited some of the biggest and best flying schools in the country, including a couple of major universities. We've been learning all we can about their training methods, then passing it all along to the folks at Albany. They've been very good about it. Made a bunch of changes. Made us feel like we're making a difference. It all helps—them too, I think.

"But you know, we've come away so far with more questions than answers. More confusion than confidence. And more frustration than satisfaction over what the state-of-the-art in flight training is all about. We couldn't find any standards or enough rules to make stan-dards from. The career pilots learn it one way. Most of the others learn every which way. Career people invest considerable time and money, get all of the necessary ratings and go on to fly sophisticated equipment for large corporations, the airlines, and whatever. The pri-vate pilots seldom make much of a commitment of either time or money—like Kevin—and are turned loose long before they're even halfway prepared to deal with what they'll be facing up there, and usually in very old, poorly equipped machines. And they're all shar-ing the same airspace and airports.

"My wife and I will continue trying to improve things here at Al-bany. But we think some national changes are in order before any-thing significant can be accomplished. I wish we knew who to call or visit. Maybe some other people who've lost loved ones in small air-planes could help us get started?"

Author comment There are those who would argue that this acci-dent could not have been caused by pilot error because the pilot was only a student pilot, not a certificated private pilot. Technically, then, blame would fall back on the instructor and the school, or the FBO. Probably a better idea than the system that's in place at present.

The stated purpose of the accident reports is to inform pilots of the true causes of accidents so that similar accidents and incidents can be avoided in the future. It would certainly help to report *all* of the findings—without any restrictions or reservations. Especially when not to know can hurt so much.

18

Fixation flight

Preliminary report: March; Fan Jet Falcon; airline transport pilot, multi- and single-engine land, instrument rating, 5,680 hours. Less than 2 minutes after taking off from Allegheny County Airport in Pittsburgh, Pennsylvania, on a night cargo operation, the aircraft entered a steep right turn and crashed in an open field. The captain and first officer were both killed. Weather at the time of the accident was 300 overcast and 2 miles in light drizzle and fog. No preimpact malfunctions of the aircraft or engines were noted.

Further investigation revealed:

- The captain, flying right seat, was evaluating the first officer for possible upgrade to captain. The first officer had been employed by the scheduled air cargo company for 16 months.
- Both the cockpit data and voice recorders were recovered. The data recorder showed that the Falcon reached a maximum altitude of 473 feet agl, then entered a steep right turn and began descending at an accelerating rate. The voice recorder indicated that the captain was performing cockpit duties and giving departure information to the first officer, noting that they should climb to 1,750 feet msl— approximately 500 feet agl—before turning right to their assigned heading of 320°.
- As the aircraft descended below the overcast, the captain remarked to the first officer, "Don't go down . . . get up, up, up . . . up, oh!"
- During several prior training flights and at least two checkrides the first officer had difficulty performing instrument flight due to disorientation. He demonstrated a narrow focus of attention, or lack of instrument scan— instrument fixation—especially during high task work loads.
- The first officer's total instrument flying experience in actual IMC as pilot in command was less than 50 hours throughout his entire seven-year professional pilot career.

Official conclusion: Improper IFR procedure. Loss of control due to spatial disorientation. Inadequate supervision by pilot in command. Pilot error.

A FEW HOURS BEFORE his scheduled 10 p.m. departure time, Scott Crowley, 28, received a phone call at home from Dennis Markham, 51, chief pilot of the jet freight company they both worked for at Allegheny County Airport near Pittsburgh. Scott had recently failed a checkride and Dennis was going to ride along with him to see if he couldn't help Scott iron out any bugs in his technique. The company was anxious for Scott to move from first officer to captain.

Instead of being pleased with Dennis's offer to help him secure a higher position with an attendant increase in salary, Scott was suddenly scared stiff. Throughout his 10-year flying career, the last seven of which were as a professional pilot, Scott had never mastered instrument flying. He avoided it. He was afraid of it. He was sure he couldn't handle it.

Having grown up in Phoenix, Scott was able to pass his IFR checkride the same way he did all of his instrument training—by cheating under the hood—and by making sure his training flights and the check flight were made in VFR conditions. From that point forward, Scott advanced himself as a first officer and copilot and flew in areas of the world where IFR flying was a rare occurrence. Starting as a private pilot instructor in the Phoenix area, at the age of 18, he got his first copilot job in the Virgin Islands, working for the interisland charter service. From there he relocated two years later to a similar job in Hawaii, moving up to high-performance turbine twins and jets, still and always as a copilot.

Then it was back to Phoenix for marriage, a child, and a job with the jet charter service at Sky Harbor Airport. He would have spent the rest of his life and career there because he loved to fly. But after two years, numerous training flights and hood time, and three blown checkrides, Scott's employer was forced to give up on him. They needed left-seat pilots, not copilots.

Pittsburgh wasn't a happy choice for Scott and Pat, his wife of three years, but it was where Scott could land a job—with some help from a carefully worded reference letter that his Phoenix employer agreed to sign for him. That was 16 months ago, and the charade continued. But it was coming under scrutiny recently as his Pittsburgh employer wondered why a 5,500 hour copilot was content remaining a copilot. Scott's recently failed checkride added to their concern. And his. He wasn't making any progress overcoming his instrument fixation problem. He still couldn't scan the instruments properly when he was distracted by the radio, turbulence and anything else that increased his work load. And he was prone to spatial disorientation and vertigo. Much more than anyone suspected.

Pat Crowley "It was a terrible shock to Scottie that afternoon when Dennis Markham called. Scottie wasn't feeling all that well in the cold, damp weather we had been having. And he didn't want to be taking any checkride that evening on the bank run to New York. I remember him telling that to Dennis on the phone. But it had to do with somebody else being sick and Dennis having to fill in anyway. So, Scottie really had no choice.

"We had been in Pittsburgh for more than a year and we were hoping to be able to move back to the southwest near both of our families. Scottie had sent lots of feelers out to commuter airlines and charter services in Phoenix and Tucson and was following up on a couple of good leads. He was afraid that if he flunked another checkride, it would make it difficult to land another job in aviation. And we both knew he would have trouble with a checkride if he wasn't feeling well and if it was in real terrible weather, like it was that day.

"I know now that I should have stopped him from going. But we never thought about the danger. Only the problem with getting a new job. Scottie never told me about it in much detail, but I realized that he had a genuine fear of being on his own in bad weather. It was something he called instrument fixation. It made him dizzy when he had to fly without the autopilot for landings when the clouds were real low. He hated it. It was why he was so anxious to move back to the Sun Belt where the air is usually clearer and drier. He didn't want to have to fly in really bad weather any more."

Checking in at the flight office an hour before departure time, Scott and Dennis went over the details of the flight. The weather out of Pittsburgh was typical March—wet, low clouds and visibility. New York was fine—1,500 overcast and 6 miles. Their problem was going to be returning. Conditions were going down in Pittsburgh.

Dennis was also very reassuring to Scott. He and everyone else in the company liked Scott and wanted him to stay. They presumed that he was frustrated being stuck as a copilot because he had trouble taking checkrides. As far as they knew, his flying skills were fine. All of the captains who flew with him thought he was an excellent copilot and often requested him for extra trips. From their perspective, Scott had a fixation about taking tests, not an instrument fixation problem.

That's why Dennis was so sure he could fix Scott's problem with patience and a show of confidence in him.

The airplane loading and the preflight were routine. But when they started their prestartup checklist, Scott expressed some discomfort at being in left seat on an actual company trip, especially in such lousy weather. He had flown right seat for so long that everything seemed backward to him: the console, the radio talk button, all of the switches, even the position of the instruments. But his suggestion to Dennis that they change seats and put off the checkride until a less difficult day was met with a smile, a pat on the back, and solid reassurance that Scott could handle it. Dennis had genuine confidence in Scott.

Dennis also had a problem with first officer duties. He had been a captain for so long, flying left seat, that many things about right seat were also backward for him. And when he occasionally gave checkrides and had to take over first officer responsibilities, he would find himself engrossed in details and checklists. It just wasn't natural for him. The flight with Scott was no exception. Dennis was struggling with being a good copilot, while Scott was struggling with panic over the prospect of flunking another checkride and possibly disrupting his quest for another copilot job somewhere in the sun belt. They were not going to be a good cockpit resource management team.

Taxiing out to Runway 28, Scott took his time going over the checklists, expecting the usual 5–10 minute delay. It would give him time to settle down, get everything sorted out and in order, ready for the flight into the black night and the low hanging clouds, with bases reported at 300 feet. But before they reached the runup pad, ground control switched them to the tower, who promptly gave them "position and hold" instructions. Reluctant to give up their settle-down time, but afraid to look unprepared by asking for a 5-minute delay in their departure, Scott accepted the clearance and taxied into position for takeoff. That was a shame. They both could have used the extra time.

Cleared for takeoff and rolling, Dennis was still performing first officer cockpit duties at liftoff. Wheels up, a frequency change, and the first power reduction came just as the Falcon entered the low hanging overcast at 1,580 on the altimeter: 328 feet agl. Dennis reminded Scott to turn right at 1,750 indicated to their assigned heading of 320°. Scott acknowledged, gripping the wheel harder as the altimeter raced up the 170 feet to 500 feet agl. At 1,680, the tower told Falcon pilot to start the turn, climb to 5,000, and call departure. Scott touched the mike button, repeated the instructions and began the right turn with pressure on the wheel. Too much pressure. And he forgot to call departure control. He was already becoming disoriented.

Dennis looked up as he felt a surge in G forces—the Falcon was turning through the 320° heading and decreasing its climb. He reminded Scott that the heading was 320°, which Scott acknowledged as he reversed the wheel pressure to the left. Again too much. The Falcon began an accelerating left turn that Scott corrected quickly and harshly, also exerting more down force on the wheel. Topping out at 1,725 on the altimeter, they went into a sharper right turn and dive. When Dennis again looked up, the Falcon was charging out of the overcast heading toward the ground. He told Scott to pull up, grabbed his own wheel, and tried reversing the dive. But he couldn't overcome Scott's powerful grip and panic-driven strength. The Falcon leveled somewhat before contacting the ground. It then careened forward for more than ½ mile before striking a tree in a wooded area.

Both Scott and Dennis were killed by the force of the impact with the tree. The cockpit voice recorder and flight data recorder were recovered from the wreckage.

FAA accident investigator "This accident was so completely untypical of a professionally flown jet that we immediately suspected alcohol or drugs. But the toxicology tests all came up negative on both pilots.

"We knew it had to be spatial disorientation the way the airplane did an over-the-top dive right after it entered the clouds. That usually happens only in single-pilot flights where the pilot has limited experience in actual IMC. But these were two high-time pros with over 20,000 hours between them. And the captain had nearly 3,000 hours of actual IMC flying out of Allegheny County. So we didn't even suspect what came out in the follow-up investigation—that the left seat pilot had a serious hand/eye coordination deficiency and was literally incapable of flying IFR at all, let alone a very high-performance jet aircraft.

"Having learned that, and confirmed it, we next tried to find out how a professional pilot of over seven years could stay in the system that long with a problem like that and never be discovered. It was frightening to think it could happen. But happen it did, and under the most unusual circumstances. And what makes it so strange is that this guy knew he had an instrument fixation problem long before he ever became a career pilot. As far as we can tell, he must have known about it when he first started taking his instrument training.

"Now you'd think that with a handicap as serious as that, he'd have thrown in the towel. Just for his own safety. But he did exactly the opposite. He worked at covering up his deficiency by keeping himself out of pilot in command instrument situations. Apparently, all he wanted to be was a perennial copilot. The money was good enough and he loved to fly.

"We were able to trace back how he pulled it off by contacting everyone he ever worked for in aviation, starting with his first stint as a flight instructor in Phoenix. That's where he learned to fly, by the way. Anyway, he spent over a year in that first job and never saw a cloud. He taught only private pilots and never even started working toward a double "I" rating. But he was an excellent flight instructor and they hated losing him to his next job.

"That was a commuter airline in the Virgin Islands. He spent the next two years there as a copilot, and occasionally flew some single-engine interisland charters, but always in perfect weather. As far as they could tell us, he never flew the first hour of instruments in the whole time he was with them. That isn't all that unusual. The commuters down there seldom fly on the very few weather days they get because most of the places they fly to have strictly VFR airports.

"From there he was off to Hawaii. And again he flew nothing but VFR in the right seat of a Beech 99, and once in awhile in either a DC-3 or a Fairchild. He piled up over 2,400 hours flying back and forth between three close-by islands before they began insisting that he move up to captain. He apparently started doing that but then abruptly gave notice that he was going back to the states with his new wife and baby.

"Back in Phoenix, he repeated the same pattern. Right seat only for another 18 months, moving up to a Lear 35 by taking his check-ride on a perfect VFR day and without shooting any approaches. They never thought to include them in the checkout. Figured that with over 4,000 hours he only needed familiarization training and a ride. That was correct procedure, by the way. You don't have to demonstrate instrument proficiency when you qualify in a new type aircraft. Especially jets. It costs too much money. And the only people who move up to jets are long-time, experienced pilots, usually ATPs. So, his jet familiarization ride would not have been the appropriate place to confirm his instrument proficiency, even if they had thought to do so. He obviously knew that. It was part of the game he was playing.

"He would probably have stayed in Phoenix forever if the charter company didn't pressure him to become a captain. Their business was growing and they wanted to promote their own people. That's when his problem finally began to surface. Within a short time, the chief pilot, who was also a friend of his wife's family, spotted the scan problem during a routine BFR that the company required be given in actual IMC. They found some overcast conditions in Texas, easy conditions, by the way, about 900 over and 6. They flew into it on a trip to Brownsville, and he flunked cold. Another try a few days later under the hood was okay. But back in actually a week later and he stone cold blew it.

"What happened after that is a little fuzzy because the chief pilot wrote some kind of a recommendation letter that no one can find a copy of and that he doesn't want to talk about. He said it was just a verification of the pilot's employment and didn't discuss his proficiencies or qualifications. It did apparently verify the kind of aircraft he was flying, though, because it helped the pilot land the job in Pittsburgh, flying right seat in Falcons and Hawkers. From there, the pattern repeated itself until the day of the accident.

"What's so sad about it is that the captain who was giving him his checkride had only a couple of hints but no real suspicions about the monster he was flying with that night. He died because he assumed that a 5,500-hour ATP would for sure know how to handle a fairly routine IMC takeoff in an airplane he had been flying out of the same home airport for the past 16 months. To assume otherwise would have been insulting to the first-officer, a pilot who was held in high regard by everyone in the company, and especially by every other captain who had flown with him. I guess it just wasn't his lucky night.

"You know, there is one thing that is very disturbing about this whole affair: We found the loophole but we have no idea how to close it. It could happen again, and just as easily. Kind of scary, isn't it? When you think that this pilot spent five years flying passengers for the two commuters he worked for?"

Phoenix Sky Harbor flight school manager "Scott Crowley was a favorite around here. Kind of like the local boy who made good. He started his training here, got all of his ratings in the flight school, worked for us as a flight instructor for a year and then went on to become a pro pilot for the commuter in the Caribbean.

"When the FAA and the NTSB people talked with us about the accident, we got quite a surprise for ourselves. We couldn't imagine that a pilot as good as Scott could have faked his instrument checkride by cheating with the hood. It isn't hard to do, but why would anyone? I mean, who are they kidding? It's their own lives that are on the line. Once in a great while we suspect a student of fudging. You know, just a peek or two to maintain equilibrium. But it's usually only at first. Once they get basic confidence in the instruments, they seldom do it again. They don't need to. We even tell our instructors to ignore it in the first few lessons because we believe it helps build confidence quicker—you know, lets them confirm that the instruments are always telling them the truth. Which is really what IFR flying is all about.

"In Scott's case, we know now that the way he avoided IMC was deliberate for a reason. The reason was that he couldn't fly in it. But we didn't know it at the time. We used to kid him about being 'Mr. Clean' or 'Mr. Chicken' when it came to weather. But he would shrug it off and remind us that he didn't want any of his students to have any close calls or run-ins with IMC because it could scare them out of flying. And as far as I can remember, he had about the best completion rate of any instructor in the flight school. So, who could argue with him?

"Now that we know about it, it's easy to see how much trouble he went through concealing his problem. We talked about it here at the school, wondering if we could have helped him overcome it had we known about it. Our consensus was that we probably couldn't. Some people are just not meant to be instrument pilots. They probably shouldn't fly at all. Scott was obviously one of those. But we never had even the slightest inkling of that until after he had the accident and was killed."

Michael Wong, flight operations manager, Inter-Island Air Service, Maui, Hawaii "Scott Crowley left here shortly after I came on board, so I didn't get to know him very well. I may also have been instrumental in his decision to go back to the states because I implemented a system of quicker advancement for our copilots. It was intended to promote from within the company as we added aircraft.

"Our records indicate that Crowley flunked a BFR and checkride that we gave, then took his BFR somewhere else just before giving us notice that he was leaving. He never took a second checkride here because when he gave notice, he was history. We took him off of flight status almost immediately.

"When I was notified about his accident and asked to make a report about his performance at Inter-Island, I solicited comments from several of the people who had worked with Crowley. They were all very positive. Everyone liked him. And the pilots who flew with him thought he was more than competent. They enjoyed having him as their copilot and often sought him out when his schedule permitted.

"One thing that helped him conceal his handicap is that we fly very little IFR here in Hawaii. We have since found out, by checking our records more carefully, that he was able to avoid any confrontations by always taking his flight reviews and checkrides in perfect

VFR weather, which isn't particularly hard to find here at certain times of the year. And, as you can imagine, he always picked those times of the year.

"I sincerely doubt that we'll ever have another Scott Crowley at this company. Our screening and testing methods would certainly prevent it. After all, it did succeed in screening him out."

Lou Wilson, general manager, Southwestern Jet Express, Phoenix, Arizona "I got to know Scottie when he first became engaged to Pattie Andrews, who I knew from the time she was a little girl. Our families have been very close ever since my wife and I moved here as newlyweds 25 years ago. Pattie called me Uncle Lou until she was a teenager.

"At their wedding, Frank Andrews—he's Pattie's dad—asked me if I could help Scottie relocate back here in Phoenix. He and Pattie had met in Hawaii and the family wanted to try to get them back home. I was chief pilot at the time and would have hired Scottie in a wink, but we didn't have any openings.

"About a year later, after Pattie had her baby, the Andrews got more intense about getting the kids back to Phoenix. We still didn't have any full-time openings at Southwestern, but I was able to get Scottie in as a part-time relief pilot. It wasn't much of a job, but I remember him being anxious to move up to jet aircraft. He had been flying only prop stuff in Hawaii.

"After just a few months, we were able to move him into full-time status. He was a terrific copilot. Did everything well. Never had any problem that showed up while he was on duty. And if our business hadn't turned around the way it did, where we had to add a couple of new aircraft, Scottie would probably still be a copilot here. We never had any idea at all that he had an instrument fixation disability.

"It didn't show up until we decided to promote him to captain. I pulled some strings to get him the promotion because he didn't have as much seniority as some of our other copilots. But he was really better than they were and deserved it. Anyway, that's when his problem first came to light.

"He and I were on a trip to Texas and the marginal weather we were flying in turned into IFR. Not low IFR. I think it was about 900 or 1,000 over and 2. Really pretty easy stuff. But Scottie had trouble with it as soon as he had to do more than just fly the airplane. He started to lose it right after approach gave him a turn and descent to intercept. I remember him complaining of a bad headache at the time and him asking me to take over for a minute. I didn't think too much about it because something like that had happened to me a couple of times. I just shook it off. And that's what he did. He shook it off. And after I got the airplane squared up and heading for the localizer, he took over again and shot a perfect approach and landing.

"We talked about it afterward, and I got the surprise of my life when he told me about some of his previous experiences with fixation. I guess he figured I'd already spotted it when he asked me to take over. I hadn't, but he didn't know that. So he kind of leveled with me, since I was sort of his mentor at the company and so close to his wife's family. We both thought we could help him work it out if we did it together. I agreed to try.

"A few days later he took a BFR with another examiner and passed with flying colors. But that was in perfect VFR weather. And under a hood. I never asked him if he cheated on it, but it wouldn't have made any difference. Just knowing it's good weather can take a lot of the stress out of flying on instruments.

"Then about a week later, I signed on for one of his trips and we found ourselves in some real junk. I think it was about 250 and a mile in New Orleans that day. Scottie took over about a hundred miles out and did okay until we got in close, about the time we were switched to approach. I saw him staring at the HSI with the DG starting to move out from under him. He spotted it late, overcorrected bringing it back and then finally settled down, until the controller called with a tight turn and descent to the marker. That's when he overdid everything and apparently went into a mild vertigo.

"I was ready for it and brought us back to straight and level. We declared a miss and asked for another try with a bit more room outside the marker so we wouldn't have to make any tight turns. Scottie calmed down and said he was ready to try it again. He seemed confident to me. And I felt sure that if he did it once successfully, his problem would be over. I thought it was just a matter of confidence.

"But I was wrong. On the next try it was worse, and not any better on the third. By then we both realized that he had a real handicap, one that wasn't going to get cured no matter what we did. It took awhile for me to concede defeat because I don't give up on anything easily. But Scottie was really hopeless. He wasn't ever going to be able to fly instruments safely.

"We had a tough layover in New Orleans after I brought us in on the fourth try. ATC had a bunch of questions that we dodged around by telling them we were trying out some new procedures. I don't think they bought it completely, but they left us alone to talk about it. That's when we came to the conclusion that Scottie wouldn't be able to stay with Southwestern. And I agreed to help him get relocated by writing him a good send off letter and calling some people I knew who might be looking for copilots. Or flight engineers. We figured he could handle that okay.

"It was a shame that the only job Scottie could latch onto was in Pittsburgh. A bad weather area with cold winters. I knew Pattie would hate it, and she did. So did he. I think he must have kept on sending resumes to every Sun Belt job situation he heard about even before they moved to Pittsburgh. I must have had a hundred calls from him and the family asking me to help him find something nearby.

"But it wasn't to be. And I wasn't about to stick my neck out or put him over his head in something he couldn't handle. So he stayed in Pittsburgh. It was a frustrating year-and-a-half for everyone. I guess what happened was inevitable. Scottie should have gotten himself out of aviation."

Kirk Firestone, vice president of operations for Allegheny Jet Express "The tragedy of that accident was that we should have been able to prevent it. Scott Crowley was a good copilot and a very convincing and likable guy. But he had flunked all of his preliminary training flights and two checkrides. That should certainly have been enough to wash him out of here.

"But it didn't. Everybody just assumed that he was having some kind of a temporary problem. Like a ball player in a batting slump that he will eventually slug his way out of. Dennis Markham, who died in the crash with Scott, was a great believer in that. He was sure he could help Scott fly his way out of whatever problem he was having.

"Frankly, none of us had ever heard of a permanent instrument fixation disability. We thought it was only a temporary condition that resulted from stress, or a lack of confidence, or from a bad experience—like falling off a horse or something. And we never dreamed that a 5,500-hour professional pilot would have a problem like that. Besides, he had worked successfully, we believed, for three other outfits like ours, and had moved up in money and equipment each time he changed jobs. That didn't sound like a deficient or handicapped pilot to us.

"So, we just got blind-sided. Especially Dennis. He was sure he could fix the problem. But the problem fixed both him and Scott and cost us our perfect safety record. And a big kick in our insurance premiums along with it. We got an expensive lesson. Two nice people lost their lives. And a brand new Falcon went down the drain.

"And you know what? It could happen again— probably not to us because we already know it's possible, but to someone else who's like we were: unsuspecting and unaware and ready to give every one of their pilots the benefit of the doubt. It's like the man said: 'Nice guys finish last.' In this business, they sometimes don't finish at all and nice people get hurt because of it. That's what happened to us."

NTSB representative "Out of the hundreds of spatial disorientation accidents related to IMC weather conditions, this is the only one that is as well documented as it is. Where we pretty much know exactly what happened and why. But that's not to say that many more of the IMC accidents weren't possibly caused by instrument fixation, or lack of the ability to scan the panel properly in order to fly without external visual references. And I'm not talking about just VFR into IMC. Fully qualified instrument pilots have been known to lose it right after takeoff in low IFR conditions. In those accidents, we more often than not find alcohol or substance involvements, but not always. Sometimes they just hit the soup and fall out of the sky.

"The whole subject of instrument fixation is one big mystery. We don't know why it happens, who it's likely to happen to, or what to do about it when we're lucky enough to discover it before it causes an accident . . .. Most of the time it isn't a consistent deficiency. It may only occur, for instance, when there's stress, or an increased work load on the pilot, or because the pilot just doesn't feel well.

"That's the whole problem with it. If we washed out every IFR pilot who ever blew a checkride because of improper instrument scan, we'd have to reinvent the system or import military pilots from around the world just to staff our airlines. So that obviously is not the answer.

"Fortunately, there is no record of an instrument scan problem ever causing a commercial airline accident, at least not in recent years. There may have been some way back when, before we identified the condition, but those aren't in our official records. And we are seldom able to prove it in general aviation accidents, if the pilot survives, and if he or she remembers—or is willing to admit—exactly what led up to the disorientation and loss of control.

"Mostly, we just suspect it. And we try to head it off as best we can by making our IFR checkrides as demanding and as stringent as possible. But, as you can imagine, it's a long way from a fail-safe system. Lots of incapable pilots wind up getting IFR tickets by cheating under the hood, by taking numerous checkrides until they finally pass one, by taking their checkrides in easy VFR conditions with smooth air, and sometimes just by sheer luck. Our examiners do an overall excellent job. But they're human. Mistakes can and do happen. And probably will until somebody invents a better wheel."

Author "Are you saying then that this was not a pilot error accident?"

NTSB "Not at all. Both the captain and the first officer made errors that directly caused the accident. And that, by any definition, is pilot error. What I am saying, or trying to make clear, is that this accident happened in spite of influences that could have and absolutely should have prevented it. It happened directly because of pilot error. But what really caused it was the failure of many well-meaning professionals who were trying to help this pilot stay in the system, despite a known and very dangerous deficiency.

"Could it happen again? You bet. Because we're no closer to resolving this whole subject of instrument fixation than we were before that Falcon went down. We're just grateful that it's a very rare occurrence, at least as far as we know."

Author comment Many proponents of the use of simulators for developing the best possible IFR techniques would argue that instrument scan is a trained skill—it doesn't come naturally. They point to the airlines to support their position, overlooking one important factor: In an airline or commuter aircraft there are always two pilots who work as a team to handle the work load of flying the airplane, navigating, communicating, and making split-second decisions when called for. If an instrument scan problem were to show up in one pilot, the second pilot should be able to compensate and correct it. How often it happens is unknown because the NTSB only reports on accidents and incidents. And they claim that this Falcon accident is the first of its kind, at least in their official files.

For general aviation instrument pilots that fly mostly single-pilot IFR, the situation might be very different. They are required to do everything the two airline professionals do, but usually under much more difficult circumstances. Their equipment is usually inferior—less redundant and state-of-the-art—and not as helpful to them. As a result, they are far more likely to lose control of something in a stressful situation. How often instrument fixation is involved is anybody's guess because it isn't reported as such. Remember, it can't be proved.

But because it is known to happen and is strongly suspected in many accidents, it should be viewed in proper context: The Falcon did not go down because of instrument fixation by itself. The first officer pilot became disoriented, overcontrolled the aircraft, and literally flung it into the ground. Whether or not his lack of scan capability caused that is an important question because if it did, then training is necessary to unlink the cause-and-effect relationship between fixation and overcontrol.

It shouldn't be a difficult problem because it wouldn't be much different from learning the technique of recovering from unusual attitudes. That doesn't come naturally either. It's just a matter of recognizing the need to neutralize overcontrol tendencies and then making training such as that a standard part of the instrument curriculum.

Many instrument flight instructors would agree that teaching proper instrument scan is mostly a matter of training *out* fixation tendencies. Locking in on the HSI or the DG seems to come more naturally than scanning. Getting rid of that natural tendency is what IFR technique is all about.

19

Down with the weather

Preliminary report: March; Mooney M20C; private pilot, single-engine land, instrument rating, 1,770 hours. After a weather briefing at 5:50 a.m. ET, the pilot and three passengers departed from Vero Beach, Florida, on a flight to South Bend, Indiana, at 9:25 a.m. A refueling stop was made at Morristown, Tennessee, but there was no evidence of an updated weather briefing. No flight plan was filed for either leg of the trip. The aircraft crashed about 7 miles northeast of Kokomo Municipal Airport in Kokomo, Indiana. Both the pilot and his front seat passenger were killed. The rear seat passengers survived with serious injuries. No preimpact part failure or malfunction of the aircraft or engine was evident.

Further investigation revealed:

- The early morning weather briefing contained no warnings of deteriorating weather en route or at either the departure or destination airports. Subsequent forecasts, at approximately the departure time of the flight, showed slightly lower ceilings of 1,500 feet for the northern portion of the trip, with visibilities running 4–6 miles.
- At the fuel stop in Morristown, Tennessee, the pilot had access to a current weather printout that forecast only a possibility of lowering conditions along his route of flight. Worst expected was 1,000 and 3 in fog and light rainshowers.
- Reported weather at Kokomo Municipal Airport at the time of the crash was indefinite ceiling, visibility ¼ mile in fog, wind from 200° at 8 knots.
- Before impacting a tree and then the ground, the aircraft was heading 230°, apparently attempting to fly the Runway 23 ILS at Kokomo; however, no contact was made with Grissom Approach or Kokomo Municipal unicom.

- Although instrument rated, the pilot had not flown in any actual IMC in more than four years. Nor had he filed an IFR flight plan in the past three years.
- The Mooney had a full IFR panel, with dual navcom and a 2-axis autopilot. Loran had been added 10 weeks before the accident.

Official conclusion: VFR into IMC. Failure to obtain current weather information. Proper altitude not maintained. Lack of night currency and total instrument time. Pilot error.

CONTINUING CRUMMY WEATHER in eastern Florida prompted the Centella family to cut short their vacation in Vero Beach and head back home to South Bend, Indiana. It was Sunday, New Year's Day, clearer than it had been, but still unseasonably cold.

Bert Centella, 46, called flight service at 5:50 a.m. while his wife Marie, their daughter, Claire, 18, and their son, Victor, 15, remained snugly tucked in bed in the family's condo. Good news: ceilings en route generally 2,500 or higher; good visibility except for northern Indiana around nightfall; winds from 220°–230° at 8–15 knots. Comfortable VFR all the way, easy for an instrument rated pilot in a fully equipped Mooney. No matter that he hadn't flown instruments in four years. Bert relaxed and went back to bed. The trip he had made so many times since they purchased the condo three years ago was going to be a snap.

Reawakening at a more reasonable 7:30 a.m., the four Centellas finished their packing, drove the family's 8-year-old minivan to their assigned parking place in the FBO's parking lot at Vero Beach Municipal Airport, spent an hour having a leisurely repast at the airport restaurant and finally got to the business of loading and preflighting the Mooney, which was also eight years old. Weather at the airport was exactly as had been advertised during his early morning briefing, so Bert decided to dispense with another call to flight service. Not a smart choice but not critical either. The weather forecasts were holding with ceilings expected to be only slightly lower. It was still scheduled to be VFR all the way.

The Mooney was off the ground at 9:25 a.m., despite the few extra gallons Bert always insisted on. It put them at 30 pounds over gross. But it was a long flight and Bert wanted the luxury of choosing his en route fuel stop. A good trade-off, at least in his mind. Besides, Vero Beach Municipal had more than 7,000 feet of runway. No sweat for a well-maintained Mooney with good compression in all cylinders.

Reaching 6,500 feet and still 1,000 feet or more below the cloud bases, Bert engaged the autopilot, checked all of his instruments and gauges carefully, then leaned back in his seat and relaxed. It was going to be a long first leg—about 540 nautical miles—but only 3½ hours in the air, thanks to a slight tailwind, unusual for that time of year.

Bert was relishing the higher DME ground speed as he studied the low altitude en route charts. He didn't fly instruments anymore but he preferred navigating with en route charts rather than with sectionals. It was easier using the VORs and now his brand new loran for direct navigation. He was pleased with himself and his Mooney. They were working efficiently together.

Bert's attitudes toward IFR flying versus IFR capability are shared by many other middle time, lots-of-years pilots: Use your IFR ticket only as an insurance policy because single engine IFR by a private pilot who only flies occasional IFR is basically unsafe. Many others believe those attitudes to be a cop-out, an excuse to not maintain proper proficiency levels, to not invest enough time and money in their flying. There are substantial, valid arguments supporting both positions. Bert was satisfied with his choice, confident of his safety at all times.

The weather cooperated for about an hour, then the ceilings began to lower gradually. Subtly, hardly noticeable until the Mooney's nose began brushing some low hanging mist. After another hour they were at 2,500 feet indicated without much clearance beneath the persistently descending cloud bases. Bert was paying full attention while the rest of the family slept. It was a smooth and comfortable ride for them, but not for Bert. He was concerned about getting home VFR. Legal VFR. He didn't like to cheat. Scud running was against his better judgment.

For the next 45 minutes the ceilings and the visibilities remained stable at just above the MEAs along their route of flight. Bert was relieved and turned his attention to where and when to land for fuel and something to eat. Moore-Murrell Airport in Morristown, Tennessee, was among their favorite stopovers on the trip home from Florida. The flying service there was very accommodating, with courtesy cars always available to take their fuel-buying customers to an excellent restaurant only 2 miles from the airport. Bert set up a waypoint off of the Snowbird VOR and turned the Mooney toward Morristown, 32 minutes away on the DME. They arrived on time, placed their fuel order and were headed toward the restaurant within 10 minutes. The service was especially good that day.

Back from lunch at Moore-Murrell, Bert checked the weather printout on the bulletin board: local weather VFR, measured ceiling

1,500 overcast, visibility 5 miles in haze, temperature 42°, dewpoint 31°, wind southwest at 7; forecast called for improving conditions after 2000 Zulu. En route showed 1,500–2,000 overcast and 6 miles through Kentucky and southeastern Indiana, lowering to 1,200 overcast and 4 miles in fog and haze; forecast called for steady to lowering conditions after 2300 Zulu. The terminal forecast for South Bend called for VFR with ceilings of 1,500 overcast and visibility of 5 miles in haze, possibly lower in fog after 2400 Zulu, following frontal passage.

The printout was less than 30 minutes old when Bert read it. Satisfied but not pleased with the weather, the Centellas boarded their airplane and were off the ground at 2:05 p.m. local time. Within minutes, Bert was able to verify the ceiling at 1,600 feet agl by testing it with the Mooney's nose. He then descended to 2,700 indicated, engaged the autopilot and again sat back, relieved that the weather was slightly better than shown on the printout he had just read, confident that it would stay that way.

Through Cincinnati, the weather held as forecast, even a little better for the most part. The family was sleeping again, and Bert was content with their progress. Heading northwest toward Muncie, Indiana, the ceilings became somewhat ragged, the turbulence picked up a bit and Bert found himself dodging and descending to stay VFR. There was a definite change in the flight conditions that had not been forecast, but it was still VFR and Bert shrugged it off as a local en route situation that would improve just ahead.

It didn't. It kept getting worse. Very slowly. The bases were holding at about 1,100 overcast. But the visibility had gone down, probably to less than 2 miles. Still legal VFR, but not the kind of weather the Centellas liked flying in. They were all aware of it because the heavier turbulence just below the clouds had awakened the sleepers. All eyes were outside the airplane helping Bert identify the passing landmarks as their lateral visibility continued to decline, down to 1½ miles. Still legal VFR. But much too close for comfort.

When they were 25 DME miles southeast of Muncie, Bert dialed in the ATIS at Delaware County-Johnson Field. The news was startling and disheartening: 600 overcast, 1½ miles in fog and haze, wind 200° at 7, temperature 38, dewpoint 36. Definitely IFR. Bert knew that in order to land at Muncie, he would either have to request an IFR approach, for which he had no plates, or declare an emergency. Neither alternative appealed to him. And so far they were holding their own, under the clouds at 1,800 on the altimeter—260 feet better than the ATIS reported—and the visibility was slightly improved as well—as much as 2½ miles, by Bert's estimate. That was optimistic but it made him feel better.

Passing just 2½ miles west of Delaware-Johnson Field, none of the occupants of Mooney saw the airport. They were at 1,500 indicated and barely under the lowering overcast. Bert was noticeably uncomfortable but still confident that the weather at South Bend would be VFR when they arrived there. All they had to do was get through the unexpected, troublesome junk weather that nobody had predicted. But with the ceiling and visibility still going down, their safe passage was becoming questionable.

As a precaution, Bert decided to swing as close as possible to the Marion, Indiana, Airport, about 20 miles dead ahead. Then, studying his en route chart, he planned an improvised VOR approach into Kokomo, Indiana, another 15 or so miles up from Marion, if the weather was still declining. Bert liked to always be ahead of his situation. His plan was simple: Come in on the 050° radial off of the Kokomo VOR from 5 or 6 DME miles out. Based upon what he saw on the chart, that would pretty much follow what looked to him to be an ILS approach into a southwest runway. Actually it was an SDF approach into Runway 23, but SDFs are printed exactly the same as ILSs on en route charts. Then, because he thought it was an ILS, he figured the MDA would be 200 feet and ½ mile, fairly standard on most ILSs. That would work for them. They were at that moment clear of the ceiling at 1,200 indicated—about 340 feet agl—and getting used to their scant 1½ miles of visibility. If it got any worse, they could land at Kokomo, where there was no control tower and no one to report their very illegal VFR approach and landing. Bert was determined to not declare an emergency.

From 1½ miles out of Marion and not seeing the airport, Bert put his mind and his Kokomo plan into high gear. The ceiling had continued eroding to "indefinite" and visibility was reduced to a straining ½ mile. Much worse than he had expected. Too much to handle VFR. It was time to put his IFR insurance policy to work.

With his 2-axis autopilot engaged, Bert deftly climbed up into the gray IMC and leveled off at 2,000 feet indicated. He guessed that would be high enough to clear any obstructions, yet low enough to be under any other hapless soul who might be on a legal IFR approach into Kokomo. What he didn't know was that Grissom Approach, the approach control for Kokomo and also Marion, began tracking the Mooney as soon as they climbed through 1,500 feet msl. So, at least the legal IFRs in the area were safe.

Grissom would have assisted Bert with his landing, but he never called them, even though their frequency was printed on the information panel of the en route chart. He still didn't feel that he needed or wanted help. Because he wasn't about to spend the rest of his long day filling out papers explaining why he needed an emergency assist into Kokomo, or why he was flying illegal IFR without any approach plates and without contacting anyone. He swallowed hard as he thought about losing his pilot's license simply because he got in over his head.

Coming up on the 050° radial off of the Kokomo VOR, Bert turned inbound on a 230° heading, trying to track the radial. He missed it. The VOR needle went through center and pegged left in fewer than 15 seconds. They were only 3½ miles out, closer than Bert had planned, which didn't give him much room to become stabilized on his makeshift approach. Realizing his mistake almost immediately, Bert turned right heading 310°, flew for a long minute and then turned right again to 050° for an outbound leg.

When they were 8 miles out, he began what he thought was a normal procedure turn. But he hadn't made one in four years. So he botched it and turned too sharply, leaving them with the VOR needle still deflected left. He turned toward it, flew through it, repeated right and left three more times and used up 5 miles of the approach in the process—still at 2,000 feet indicated. He had forgotten to descend, having been so preoccupied with lining up on the approach course.

Another right turn and another outbound leg, this time to 10 DME miles out, set the Mooney up for its third try. This one was going to work. Bert was determined not to blow it. He started his turn and, at the same time, began descending. Which took some coordinating that he also hadn't attempted in four years, which was too long ago. Almost immediately, he began losing control, turning too sharply and descending nearly in a dive.

His recovery was commendable. They had lost nearly 950 feet, which put them just above the treetops before Bert regained control and began climbing back to 2,000 feet for yet another try. They never knew how close they came because the ceiling was by then that low and the visibility was down to ¼ mile, well below IFR minimums for any airport.

On his fourth try, Bert went farther outbound, lined up on the approach on his second turn and began tracking inbound—descending. This time using just his throttle and trim for up and down control, and the autopilot for directional control. He had it made. Or so he thought.

Continuing on his approach, Bert had calculated his MDA at 1,030 feet indicated, which would be exactly 200 feet agl at the runway threshold. But he had set his altimeter from the ATIS he had listened to at Muncie. It was exactly 170 feet lower than the setting Bert would have received from Grissom if he had called them. That was the last mistake he would ever make.

The Mooney struck its first treetop just as they came through 1,060 feet and began breaking up as it hit several more trees and then finally slammed head-on into a pole and then the ground. Debris and airplane parts were spread over a 600 foot swath.

The impact killed Bert and his wife instantly. The children in the back seat were seriously injured, saved by the cushioning of the tree branches that slowed the airplane considerably before impacting the pole and ground.

Claire Centella "My brother and I both woke up in the hospital. Neither one of us remembers much after we first hit the tree tops. We were both unconscious when they found us. I guess we were in pretty bad shape. Victor nearly lost his arm. I've had four surgeries since the accident.

"Dad used to call us 'the sleeping Centellas,' because that's what we mostly did on the airplane. He loved to fly and had no trouble staying awake. The rest of us would fall asleep right after takeoff and usually stay that way for most of every trip. But not that last one.

"When we left our fuel stop in Tennessee, dad seemed real happy about the weather and the tailwind. Coming back from Florida in the winter time, it was usually a headwind. So he was pleased about it. He kept talking about how lucky we were that the weather was holding and we would arrive home a little early for a change.

"But the weather didn't hold. I remember him waking us all up when we were somewhere around Muncie. He said he needed help watching out for things because we had to fly real low. And the visibility was bad, too. So, that's what we did. And it got a little scary. We came very close to some hills and one set of high tension wires that we didn't see until we were almost on top of them. Dad got very nervous after that. And when he did, we all did.

"Especially mom. She told him we ought to go back to Morristown—that's where we had stopped for fuel—but he told her the weather was fine farther up and that he could always fly on instruments, if he had to. It was right about then that he started doing that. I remember the airplane going up and into the clouds. And then we couldn't see anything at all. That was the first time my brother and I had ever been in the clouds in a small airplane. I didn't like the feeling. But my brother thought it was real cool.

"Anyway, dad told us we could either stay like we were and fly home that way, or we could land in either Marion or Kokomo. Mom said she would much rather land. She didn't like not being able to see anything. It was bumpy, too, and I think she might have been feeling it. I know I was.

"They argued about it for awhile, and then dad agreed. He said we shouldn't be flying IFR without a flight plan and he didn't know who to call to file one. So that was it. We were going to land at Marion. But then we missed it. Dad said we had flown within a mile or so of the airport and none of us ever saw it. That's when he got really upset.

"For the next 20 or 30 minutes we were completely in the clouds and it was very uncomfortable. Dad was making a lot of turns and going up and down. Sometimes suddenly. He said it was the turbulence. But I think it was at least partly because he kept missing some kind of an approach he said he had set up. He explained what he was trying to do to my mother, but my brother and I didn't hear much of it. Something about following a thing on the map that was lined up with the runway at Kokomo. What he wanted all of us to do was watch for the ground and the runway lights as we came down. Which I think he tried to do about four times.

"But each time, dad had to turn back because we never saw a thing. Not the ground and, for sure, not the runway. Until we hit that first tree. Then we saw an ocean of leaves and branches. We bounced off that first one, and dad tried to fly us out of there. I saw him throw the throttle forward and pull back on the wheel. But it was too late. We fell back into a whole bunch of trees, and the airplane started coming apart. That's the last thing I remember until I woke up in the hospital. They told me that my mother and father probably died instantly when the airplane crashed into something, and that my brother and I were alive because we were in the back. (Pause)

"You know, the government people from the FAA told us that the accident was dad's fault. That it was all pilot error. But how could that be? None of the weather reports dad got said anything about conditions being as bad as they were. He did everything he could to get us down. But it was impossible. Even an airliner wouldn't have been able to land in that stuff.

"They also said something about the altimeter being set wrong. I don't know what that meant but I did see dad turn the knob on the altimeter right after he heard the weather report from Muncie. So they must have given him a wrong setting that made him think we were higher than we actually were. That wasn't his fault. Why can't they admit it? Why do they want to make us live with thinking it was all dad's fault when it clearly wasn't? By their own admission.

"I know it's too late for my parents and for my brother and me, but I wish the government would do something to give other people who fly a better chance than they gave us. We got fooled by their bad weather reports, and maybe by a mistake that was made by someone at Muncie. They ought to fix those things. I thought it was their job to make aviation safe. The least they could do is tell the truth about what happened to us so other people could learn from it."

Grissom Approach representative "When we went back and checked the radar tapes and the voice transmissions from that night, we realized that the duty controller had his hands full with an unidentified VFR apparently attempting to shoot approaches into Kokomo. Everything in the area was closed at the time, even our air force base. Conditions were either zero-zero, or very close to it. Nothing was getting in anywhere within a hundred miles of Grissom.

"Weather like that is pretty typical around here in the middle of winter. We tend to get lots of dense fog that pops up from out of nowhere. That's what was happening that night. So when our controller saw their target show up from out of the blue, without warning, and without a call or anything, he figured he had a nut case out there or someone in real trouble. He assumed the latter and began trying every frequency he could think of to reach them and let them know they were never going to get into Kokomo or anywhere else nearby.

"While he was doing that and watching the target going back and forth on the 23 approach, he alerted what little other traffic there was about the stranger at Kokomo. Then he figured two things real quick: (First,) that the airplane had lost its comm—at least the ability to transmit—or that the airplane was flying very low since its Mode C signal was intermittent; (or second, that the target) might be some local turkey out of Kokomo playing weather roulette. They've been known to do that.

"Anyway, dealing with what he figured, he called for backup and got it immediately. He wanted witnesses because he was sure they weren't going to make it. Then he tried having other IFRs in the area call the aircraft with a general warning that conditions were on the deck and that all of the airports in the vicinity were closed. But that didn't work either. He had to just sit there and watch them go blanko off his scope. It was good that he had backup. Otherwise, he wouldn't have been assured that he had done everything possible to save them. That can be a tough thing for a controller to live with."

NTSB representative "In our conversations with the surviving passengers, the pilot's two children, several bits of information came out that gave us an interesting perspective of this case. It was 'pilot error,' for the most part, with some unusual circumstances that warrant plenty of thought and discussion. I say 'for the most part' because the weather that night was not correctly forecast. It went zero-zero over a wide area of central Indiana in 15 minutes. That can never be predicted and never is. Even the temperature/dewpoint spread didn't point to it getting as bad as it did. Unfortunately, (this is) not all that uncommon for that area in the middle of winter.

"As for those other circumstances, the first one is a common problem that should have been fixed 20 years ago. I'm talking about the weather printout the pilot saw at his fuel stop. It was a standard teletype. And when we checked it over, it was correct at the time. The trouble is that most private pilots, instrument or otherwise, can't or don't read them correctly or completely. Especially people who don't fly all that much. But with the simplest computers, the kind they have at nearly every airport in the country, those reports could be transmitted quicker and in plain English so they could be understood perfectly, and by everybody. But with the 60-year-old teletype system that only the National Weather Service is still using, we keep on delivering partial and often misunderstood information that is getting unsuspecting pilots in trouble.

"Take the case of this pilot, for instance. What he came away with when he looked at that teletype report was the fact that the local weather was VFR and so was the forecast weather at his destination airport. But in order to get a complete picture, he would have had to look at the strips on 10 or 15 other places, which he probably didn't do. Very few pilots do. They have enough trouble translating all the signs, symbols and abbreviations for the airports they're departing from and flying into. Now, if he had been able to punch a couple of airport designators into a plugged-in computer, he could have had a local, a terminal, and a complete en route weather forecast that would have told him to file an IFR flight plan, or stay on the ground at his fuel stop. He obviously never got that message from the teletype.

"The next tidbit we got was directly from the pilot's daughter. She told us that her father considered his instrument rating to be just an insurance policy, nothing more. He wouldn't consider flying IFR in a single-engine aircraft because it would be too dangerous. So he never flew instruments at all and hadn't done so since he got his ticket four years before the accident. Can you imagine that? No practice, no experience, no currency, no nothing in terms of real ability to fly instruments. What kind of an insurance policy was that if it couldn't work when he needed it? You might say he forgot to pay the premium, so the policy lapsed. Which is exactly what happened. That pilot killed himself and his wife because he thought he was covered when he wasn't.

"I wish I could say that this was an isolated case, but it wasn't. It happens all the time. And with equally deadly results. There are thousands of noncurrent IFR pilots who believe with complete confidence that they can handle IFR if they have to. Well, they're wrong. And it's just a shame that they pay such a high price to find that out.

"The last thing we learned is another disturbing common occurrence: A pilot in trouble who won't call anyone or declare an emergency because of fears of reprisal, or the inconvenience of filling out some paperwork. The daughter told us she heard her father telling his wife that he didn't want to let anyone know he was flying without a flight plan because he might have to fill out a bunch of papers, or put his license at risk for flying IFR illegally. Now think about what he did because of that cockamamie attitude. All he had to do was call anyone for an assist. Grissom would have gladly taken an air file, shooed them away from Kokomo and on up to South Bend, where it was easy VFR.

"Or [he could have called] flight watch. They would have given him a true picture of what his flight conditions were. Any of the center frequencies were printed clearly on the en route chart he was using. They would have put them in the system instantly and flown them right to the end of the runway at South Bend. But instead, he did it his way, kept his . . . secret and wound up killing himself and his wife and orphaning his two children after seriously injuring them. It wasn't worth it.

"But you know, that also happens with frightening regularity. Read enough accident reports where weather is involved and the same patterns emerge. No radio contact with anyone. Overflying available airports. No flight plan. No weather briefing. No turning around even if the weather is going down the drain on them.

"And, if they're lucky enough to survive, their excuses are always the same, too: 'The weather closed in on me. They didn't tell me it was going to be *that* bad. I didn't want to have to fill out all of those papers.' Hell, half the time they don't even know what 'those papers' really amount to. For your information, 'those papers' are seldom anything more than a simple explanation of what happened. And they almost never result in any action taken against the pilot, unless he or she is a multiple repeater of the same nonsense. Where everybody gets the idea that the FAA is some kind of bogeyman police organization, whose only purpose is to terrorize errant pilots, is something none of us here or at the FAA can understand. Our mission is safety and information. But we have obviously done a lousy job of letting the pilots of this country know that.

"About all I can say in conclusion about this case is that the pilot made a flock of errors, most of which should have been avoided. So, 'pilot error' is certainly appropriate. But the real cause of the accident was the weather itself and all of the errors and omissions in our weather reporting systems. They should be fixed. And they could be by applying some simple technology that already exists. All we need is the money and someone to give us a green light."

Author comment The weather was a primary cause of the accident, but only because the pilot was attempting to land in impossible conditions. He could have known that from any one of the several sources that were available to him—Grissom Approach, ATC, flight watch, probably even unicom at Kokomo—but instead, his decision was influenced otherwise without further inquiry, without knowing that no safe landing could be made at Kokomo that evening.

Had he opted to continue on to South Bend, legal IFR or otherwise, the likelihood of a successful conclusion to the flight was close to 100 percent. He was doing okay on the gauges; the autopilot was working and he wasn't disoriented in any way. So the 70-mile trip to South Bend, where the weather was VFR, would have been a breeze.

And that brings up the most important point: The idea of having an instrument rating as just an insurance policy. There is no question that Bert Centella was successfully flying his Mooney on instruments. After all, he shot four nonstandard, self-constructed instrument approaches and made three misses. He and his family wound up in the treetops because of an incorrect altimeter setting, not due to a flying or control problem. So, at least that part of his insurance policy was working.

What didn't work was his knowledge of the system. He had a mistaken notion of the procedures involved after declaring an emergency. He had unfounded fears of reprisals for being caught in the weather and flying illegal VFR and IFR. He had a lack of comfort using the system, demonstrated by the fact that he didn't think to air-file a flight plan. He had very limited skill in reading teletyped weather data. He was too accustomed to flying without the system: no flight plan, no communications, no accessing the abundance of information and help available free to every pilot. And he was too self-reliant for his own good.

None of which had any direct bearing on the value of his instrument rating as an insurance policy, but in combination, they rendered that insurance policy worthless by making it too complicated for him to implement. Too problematic for him to use comfortably within the system.

Two things can nullify an insurance policy. First, a failure to "pay the premium"—he let his IFR knowledge lapse. Second, a failure, inability, or unwillingness to "file a claim"—he never called anyone to activate his coverage. If the pilot had paid the premium and activated the coverage, there is no question that the IFR insurance policy would have saved their lives.

One last thing that is too often overlooked is the fact that the weather can and does occasionally become impossible for *any* pilot to deal with. And often without much warning. The airlines cope with unpredictable weather changes via constant checking and presence in and around the weather, coupled with continuous, routine communications.

General aviation pilots don't have that luxury. They have to take their own initiative to get the information and help they need to handle weather. Which means they first need adequate knowledge of the available systems. Knowledge that they often lack because their formal training usually leaves them far short of adequate. And that is only partially their own faults due to the constraints of time and money, versus the skills and knowledge they must acquire in order to get their licenses.

Therein lies the problem. The systems are there, but too many pilots don't know how or when to use them. So they don't. And the losers are . . .? All of us in general aviation.

20

Delay to darkness to disaster

Preliminary report: February; Rockwell 114TC; private pilot, single-engine land, 1,370 hours. On a VFR night flight from Memphis, Tennessee, to Huntsville, Alabama, the aircraft impacted the ground in cruise attitude at approximately 880 feet msl. The pilot was seriously injured, but his passenger was killed. During a weather briefing prior to departure, the noninstrument rated pilot was advised that possible IMC could be expected along his route of flight and that VFR was not recommended. The pilot was in contact with ATC throughout the entire flight and received several more weather advisories. Huntsville weather at the time of the accident was ceiling 1,000 broken, 4 miles in haze.

Further investigation revealed:
- The pilot had received 27 hours of instrument instruction over a 2½-year period and had passed his IFR written but had never completed his IFR training or taken a checkride.
- Huntsville Approach Control provided the local weather information and offered IFR clearance, which the pilot declined. The controller then instructed the pilot to maintain VFR, and he acknowledged the instruction.
- The pilot reported his altitude as 1,300 feet msl shortly before impacting the gently rising terrain at 880 feet msl. The altimeter setting had been entered correctly.
- It was an especially dark, moonless night. The pilot was not current for night flight, having made his last night landing 11 months prior to the accident.

Official conclusion: VMC into IMC. Lack of night currency. Failure to maintain reported altitude. Pilot error.

THE PILOT WAS ANGRY AT EVERYONE. Adam Lerner, 47, and his new girlfriend, Joy Franklin, 33, had been waiting in the flight lounge at Memphis International Airport for more than 3 hours. Adam's airplane, a Rockwell 114TC, began running rough when he and Joy taxied out at 3 p.m. for their flight to Huntsville, Alabama, that would last for more than an hour. At the runup pad, the engine spewed out a series of nasty pops when Adam tested the right magneto. So, it was back to the ramp for a quick fix. Except the fix wasn't so quick because it was Sunday and the maintenance shop was short staffed. At least that's what they told Adam.

Cooling his heels was only part of the problem. Beside a must-attend meeting the next morning, they would be making the entire flight at night. A dark night. Adam hadn't flown at night in several months. He was uncomfortable about night flying in a single-engine airplane. Even though his Rockwell had been a reliable machine for the five years he owned it, he was nervous. Especially after the way it had just blown a mag.

At 6:05 p.m., the FBO manager suggested that Adam and Joy head over to the terminal restaurant for some dinner because the shop needed another hour to finish installing the mag. Adam surmised that they were just starting on it but he was a captive customer, and it was take it or leave it. So he took Joy to dinner, cooled off as much as his anger would let him, and returned to the FBO's lounge at 7:20.

Finally, at 7:40 p.m., the Rockwell was ready to roll. Adam made his habitual final call to flight service and winced when the briefer told him that IMC was possible along their route of flight and that VFR was not recommended. That was very different than the earlier forecast, but it was then a winter night as opposed to a winter afternoon, and a dark night at that. There was no moon and mostly overcast skies.

Other than the dire warning from the weather briefer about *possible* IMC, VFR prevailed at both Memphis and Huntsville and was expected to stay that way. It was the in-between that could be a problem, but Adam wasn't too worried about that. With more than 25 hours of IFR training under his belt, he wasn't afraid of scud running, or even a little cheating now and then. Besides, the meeting he was going to was important. And having Joy along for moral support—or whatever—was even more compelling. They were definitely going to Huntsville.

After checking both mags three times, Adam was off the ground at 8:15 and heading east-southeast with the Muscle Shoals VOR dialed up. They wouldn't be receiving it for awhile because they were only at 2,000 feet msl—staying under the broken cloud bases—and the station was more than 120 miles away. At such a low altitude, it would be 40 minutes or so before they could track the signal from Muscle Shoals.

The air was smooth and Adam was pleased for Joy's sake. She wasn't exactly overjoyed about flying. He wished there was something for her to see of the pretty Tennessee countryside, but it was not to be. The busted mag had taken care of that. So he concentrated on the cloud bases, which he could see clearly by turning on his landing lights occasionally. He also began explaining to Joy the ease and simplicity of flying. At least the way an accomplished pilot like Adam Lerner did it.

After Memphis Departure Control turned them over to Memphis Center, Adam confirmed their heading to Muscle Shoals, made a heading adjustment that was suggested by the controller, and described every move he made and every instrument on the panel to his impressed passenger. So far so good.

Thirty miles west of Muscle Shoals, everything was not so good. The visibility was down considerably—Adam couldn't tell for sure because there were so few ground lights to follow—and they had been pushed to 1,500 feet msl by the lowering bases of the clouds. With an MEA of 3,000 feet along Victor 54—the nearby airway that was almost paralleling their course—Adam was getting uncomfortable. In the hope of regaining some confidence, he called the Memphis Center controller who had been providing flight following.

Adam "Center . . .. Wonder if you have any pireps for our vicinity? This ceiling seems to be getting lower. We're at one-point-four and having trouble staying clear of it."

Memphis Center "Sorry, not many VFRs out there tonight. If you'd like to file IFR, we can get you up to a better altitude so you wouldn't have to work so hard."

Adam "Thanks, but we're doing fine right here. Can you give us the current weather for Huntsville?"

Center "Sure can. What we have is almost 40 minutes old, but they're still calling for marginal VFR. Ceilings are running 1,200 to 1,500 with visibilities at 4 to 6 miles. Winds are northerly at 8 knots and the altimeter has been steady at 29.81 inches. Temperature is 40 and dewpoint is 38. That's been pretty steady, too. You'll be able to get an update on that when you call Huntsville Approach in about 20 miles."

Adam "Anything on Muscle Shoals?"

Center "Yes, sir. They're IFR and have been for the last couple of hours. Their ceilings are running about 400 feet, with 2½ miles visibility. That's a little worse than the last reading. And the barometer is 29.77 inches and falling. If you'd like, sir, you can try Huntsville Approach now on 125.6. You're a little far out but you may be able to reach them."

Adam "Will do and thanks for your help. Good night." (Switching to Huntsville Approach on 125.6.) "Approach, this is Rockwell . . .. We're at 1,300, squawking 1,200, about 40 west, landing Huntsville."

Huntsville Approach "Roger . . .. Squawk 4244 and ident please. Huntsville altimeter is 29.80 inches and steady. Ceiling is 1,100 over and 3½ in fog and haze. We had a pirep a few minutes ago that the tops of some of the hills were being obscured and that the higher terrain areas in your vicinity may be IFR already. If you'd like an approach, sir, it will be the 36 ILS. You can climb to 2,800 ft and turn right heading 130°. That will give you the marker with a couple of miles to spare. You're radar contact, 37 miles west of Huntsville International. Say your intentions, please."

Adam "We'll be fine at 1,300 but we're turning right to 130°. Would appreciate vectors all the way in and we'd like to expedite. We had a mechanical back at Memphis that's made us very late."

Approach "Understand you are remaining at 1,300 feet and turning 130°. Are you landing at Huntsville International, sir?"

Adam "That's affirm. Rockwell . . . is landing at Huntsville International."

Approach "Okay, ... Stay on the 130° heading, maintain VFR and climb to one-point-five. That's 1,500 feet. You're in a high terrain area, sir."

Adam "Uh . . . okay . . . climbing to one-point-five. Say again the altimeter, sir?"

Approach "29.80 and steady. Please say your present altitude, sir."

Adam (Starting the climb.) "We're just leaving one point three, climbing to one-point-five. That's 1,500, sir."

The controller caught Adam's final sarcasm but didn't think it was funny. He knew they were scud running and playing with fire. He watched their altitude readout carefully as they began to climb. Then he was diverted by a departure and two other inbounds, temporarily losing track of the target.

Adam had climbed less than 50 feet before he lost all ground contact. Quickly reversing the climb, they descended all the way to 1,150 indicated before Joy and then Adam finally saw some lights below. Ahead was pitch black. Just an empty void in the relentlessly dark night. A minute later, they were back in the overcast and descending. At 1,050 feet, more lights on Joy's side of the airplane. Ahead still the same. Nothing.

As they leveled off at 1,050 feet, the controller noticed the altitude readout on the "shrimp boat" of the radar screen and called immediately:

Approach "Rockwell . . .. Your altitude readout is 1,100 feet. Please say your altitude immediately." (There was a strong note of urgency.)

Adam "Uh, we're having some problem staying completely clear of the overcast. But it seems to be okay now. We're level one-one-thousand and VFR." (Adam was fudging on the altitude. But what's 50 feet? Anyway, it was easier to agree with the controller.)

Approach "You'll have to climb to 1,500 feet to stay legal VFR . . .. The minimum en route altitude in your vicinity is 3,000 feet. That means there are obstructions at 1,000 feet, and you'll have to stay at least 500 feet above them. If you can't do that, we'll have to declare you an emergency and bring you down at the nearest airport."

Adam "Okay. We're climbing back to one-point-five. I'll let you know if we have any problem remaining VFR. It's just very dark out here and we can't be real sure how much forward visibility we have."

Approach (Reluctantly, not believing Adam.) "Stay on your present heading . . .. You're 22 miles from the airport. No reported traffic. Maintain VFR and report reaching one-point-five."

Adam acknowledged the controller's instructions and climbed to 1,500 feet erratically. They were in total IMC at 1,100 feet. He leveled off at 1,500 feet msl, but continued having a problem controlling the aircraft. With all the instrument training he had received, he was having trouble flying straight and level in not-very-turbulent conditions. Perhaps because he was nervous because this wasn't hood flying, it was for real.

After 5 minutes of fighting, Adam decided he had had enough. Without informing the controller, he nudged the control wheel forward and watched the altimeter start down. Coming through 1,000 feet, lights from the ground came up on both sides of the airplane, but far away. Adam stopped the descent and edged back up to 1,100 feet. Then he called approach and reported his altitude, adding the comment that they were in good VFR. It was only a half truth, but he didn't want another confrontation with the controller.

The controller took his word for it, told him they were 20 miles southwest of the approach course, gave him a new heading of 150° to keep them clear of two other IFRs that would be entering the approach, and again warned Adam to maintain VFR. The controller also gave him the current weather at Huntsville: ceiling 1,000 broken to overcast with visibility 4 miles in haze. There had also been a pirep from a police helicopter that some of the higher elevations within 15 miles of the airport were in the clouds. He then turned his attention to one of the three other aircraft he was working.

Adam turned to the new heading, carefully. They were still brushing the clouds. He pushed the nose down again, looking for lights from the ground. At 950 feet indicated, still no lights. He stayed level for 20 seconds and then ventured lower. Just under 900 feet. That was enough. Joy saw lights off to the right side. Then Adam saw some on his side. But nothing on the nose. Just a void in front of them. But he relaxed a little. At least they were VFR.

The controller saw Adam's altitude readout at 950 feet and panicked when he couldn't get a long-winded inbound to clear the frequency. Then another aircraft called in just as Adam descended to below 900 feet. Finally, after an agonizing 18 seconds had passed, the controller advised all aircraft to stay clear of the frequency as he called the Rockwell. There was no reply. The controller waited 4 or 5 seconds and called again and a third time, anxiously waiting for the next sweep of the scope to come around to the Rockwell. When it did, the signal was gone. The controller kept trying until a new voice came on the frequency, inbound to Huntsville. On that pilot's second call, ATC told the new inbound to standby, then advised them to call the tower for the approach. The controller picked up the phone, dialed the emergency numbers, and waited for relief that came 1½ minutes later.

Adam and Joy heard only the first few words of the controller's call. It was interrupted by the crunch of the airplane as it collided with the slowly rising ground beneath them, careened forward, bouncing, off the terrain. Joy's neck broke and she died instantly. Adam, probably because he was holding on to the control wheel, was slammed forward against the panel with his head hitting the plastic windshield. He was knocked cold and seriously injured, but still alive as the Rockwell came to rest.

The fire from the fuel in the broken off wings made it easy for the authorities to locate the crash site. Adam was unconscious and bleeding. Paramedics were on the scene fewer than 30 minutes after the accident, in time to stop Adam's bleeding. Adam was badly disfigured and permanently crippled by the accident.

ATC representative "All of our senior people who heard the tapes relating to this accident have lived through similar experiences. When you put in 20 or more years as an active controller, you really see and hear it all.

"I'll never figure out who these pilots think they're fooling when they call in phony altitudes. Our Mode C readouts aren't perfect but they're never off by anything like 500 feet or more. You wonder why they'd risk their lives doing that. Hell, we don't care if they're scud running. Our job is to help them stay alive.

"This particular accident started happening way back upstream, about the time the pilot was still talking to Memphis Center, before the handoff to Huntsville Approach. The controller told him he would be flying into low IFR conditions at Muscle Shoals. And she offered to file an IFR flight plan for him. She knew they were on a VFR flight but, from the way the pilot handled himself on the radio, she assumed that he was either an instrument rated pilot, or at least had quite a bit of instrument training. If you were a controller, you'd assume the same thing from the way he sounded. He had the IFR lingo down pat.

"She also had no way of knowing whether or not he was telling the truth about being VFR. He may have been, at least the way he thought he was seeing it. Very dark nights can be foolers in marginal VFR. You can't tell how far away things are on the ground and you can't tell the clouds from the black sky. I'm a pilot myself and I can tell you, I avoid nights like that. They suck up single-engine scud runners . . ..

"When they connected with Huntsville Approach, that controller gave them even more emphatic warnings. He also knew the pilot was lying and as much as told him so. You know, we're limited in our authority and in what we can tell a pilot. We can't come right out and say, 'You're risking your life, you're a danger to everyone and you ought to get down, and now!' It would sure make us controllers feel better to be able to do that, but I doubt if it would do much for air safety. We'd end up having shouting and swearing matches with some of those determined machos who are up there . . .."

"Anyway, the approach controller did about as much as he could short of a confrontation. When the pilot climbed back up to 1,500 feet and stayed there for awhile, apparently not having too much trouble, the controller probably figured they were all right, at least he hoped so. But he was ready to give them an assist or vectors for the approach, and he kept hinting around at it. That's another thing we can't do is force a VFR pilot to accept vectors for an ILS. Even though that was effectively what was happening, the pilot could have told the controller to keep his vectors and just head straight for the airport, but (the pilot) didn't do that, which led the controller to believe that they were working together, that the pilot was flying safely, taking the vectors, and heading for what would have been an easy approach into a well-lit airport in VFR conditions.

"One thing in the tapes that got plenty of notice was the 20-second gap in communications. That's a pretty typical problem we sometimes run into because we're a party line system. Every once in awhile we can't get through to the airplane we need to talk to because of clutter. (Pilots) talking to much, or breaking in when they shouldn't. It isn't always bad procedure, or discourtesy, or anything like that. There can be too many airplanes on the same frequency with legitimate needs to talk to the controller. It's just an old, antiquated system that should have been upgraded years ago. Why it hasn't been, is a mystery to me and most of the people I work with, but frankly, after living with it for so many years, most of us don't give it much thought.

"But I'd have to admit, in this case the system added to the problems that pilot was having, and if the controller had been able to get through to (the pilot) right away and tell him to pull up in a hurry, maybe (the controller) would have done so and saved their lives, but that's not a sure thing. Most of what the controller told that pilot was ignored anyway, especially when it came to altitude. (The pilot) was doing his own thing and lying about it to boot.

"So, who knows? Maybe the bad luck that led to the communications gap made a difference. In my mind, and in the official position of ATC, it didn't. But it did put a spotlight on that glaring deficiency in the single-channel radio system we're living with. Maybe that will do some good. It may help somebody decide to do something about it. Let's hope so, and let's hope it's soon."

Adam Lerner "Most of what I remember about the accident was that it was the darkest night I'd ever seen in my life. Under a hood was all gray. This was, for the most part, all black. Nothing. Except occasional lights from towns and a few farm houses. Other than that it was unreal, like sitting in a darkroom with only the panel lights on. If (not) for some light turbulence, it would have been like flying a simulator. When you think about it, I guess, it was really an IFR trip for most of the way.

"That's what I don't understand about the FAA's position about whose fault it was. I made no secret about the fact that I was a VFR pilot on a VFR trip. There was a flight plan filed. The controllers all had to know that, but they kept asking me if I wanted to file for an IFR approach and I kept refusing them because I knew that would be illegal. I also wasn't too sure I could handle it by myself. Without approach plates, or knowing anything about what the approach even looked like, or how many turns I'd have to make, or altitude changes. Besides, every time we lost ground contact, I had trouble flying the airplane. Probably because I realized I was on my own, for the first time, and that the person sitting next to me was not an instructor.

"But whatever it was that was giving me a problem, I can tell you it was very real to me. To the point where I was afraid that somewhere along the line I was going to lose it and turn over and go into a spin. So I was determined to maintain some ground contact because I knew that the first thing I had to do was fly the airplane.

"That's when the controller started giving me such a hard time. He wanted me up into the stuff, and I wasn't about to stay up there, as queezy as I was. So I told him what he wanted to hear, hoping he'd buy it and leave us alone. I even thought about turning off the transponder and telling him I was having trouble with it. But I didn't bother because I knew it was VFR at Huntsville and we'd be there in 15 minutes or so anyway. Then it wouldn't matter.

"When we came down and saw lights out of both sides of the airplane, I felt better immediately, until I looked at the altimeter and realized how low we were. I hadn't intended to go below 1,100 feet. But we were under 900. I had leveled off and was just about to start back up when we hit.

"Whatever it was, we never saw it. I don't remember anything except being thrown forward and hearing a terrible noise, like an explosion in my head and crushing my body. I don't remember any pain. Only that noise. (Pause) I hope that's all Joy felt. They told me she must have died instantly. That her neck snapped. The FAA people said she probably never knew what hit her. That's how fast it happened. (Pause)

"So, here I am. With a torn up face that brings tears to my mother's eyes when she sees me. And a body that won't let me work or do anything useful. And a feeling of blame and shame over what I did to Joy. (Pause) She deserved better. (Pause) I think I did, too."

NTSB representative "Most pilots don't seem to realize that VFR on a very dark night, over water or sparsely populated rural areas, is really IFR, especially if there's some cloud cover or a ceiling. In marginal conditions it can be much more difficult because you tend to go on and off the gauges and that's tough even for experienced instrument pilots.

"After we finished analyzing the tapes and putting the pieces of this puzzle together, we realized that the most critical item was the 18 or 20 seconds when the controller couldn't call the pilot. Had a climb been initiated only 10 seconds earlier, the airplane would have cleared the rising hill it crashed into. They may have lost it later on—and I say that because the pilot wasn't doing too well flying the airplane—but for sure they would have missed that slowly rising hill.

"It's hard to pin the communications gap on anyone. It was un-usual for it to be that long but, in an antiquated system like the one ATC is stuck with, it happens now and then. You could call it incred-ibly bad luck that it happened right at that particular moment, but the way they were flying in those conditions, and in that terrain, they were an accident waiting to happen.

"Another thing that's drawn a lot of flak from the surviving pilot was the way he felt he was being badgered by the controllers. We've heard the tapes and we don't buy any of that. Controllers can't see and feel the conditions an airplane is flying in. They have to rely on what they're told by the pilot. If the pilot doesn't tell the truth, it can confuse the situation and lead the controller to give mixed signals and sometimes advice and instructions that contribute to an accident.

"In this case, the lies were compounded by the Mode C transpon-der that was reporting the airplane's altitude. The controller saw that the airplane was low from the reading on his scope, but he was be-ing told by the pilot that (the) actual altitude was different. Because the airplane was flying so low, the controller knew that its transpon-der signal could be unreliable, due to the hilly terrain it was flying in. So, he didn't know who or what to believe and in those kinds of sit-uations, he has to go with the pilot. (The controller is) trained that way, he's trained to accept the fact that the pilot is acting in his own best interest and won't do anything stupid enough to kill himself. Un-fortunately, that isn't always the case.

"Now, think about what an enormous difference the pilot's lying made. The center controller, who was a soft-speaking woman by the way, certainly never pressured him. She suspected he was scud run-ning because of the weather at Muscle Shoals. It was fairly low IFR, but she couldn't know for sure what the pilot was flying in, or what he could actually see. So she did the best she could by turning him over to Huntsville Approach as soon as possible, rather than offering him a flight assist to a VFR airport. Remember, he said he was VFR and okay. An assist would have been easy, by the way, because there were three airports reporting flyable VFR within a few minutes of where they were at the time.

"The approach controller then wound up inheriting the problem. Only it was much worse than he suspected because he wouldn't nec-essarily have known the weather at Muscle Shoals. He wasn't operat-ing out of Memphis Center where they knew Muscle Shoals was IFR. So, he was stuck looking at his scope and listening to the pilot, get-ting two different altitude numbers, one of which was critical. He and the pilot then proceeded to go back and forth, with the pilot saying one thing but doing something else. And while that was going on, the frequency suddenly got busy with other traffic, and the controller found himself helpless to do anything about his lying pilot. Talk about lousy timing! With a long-winded, drawling talker to boot! It was really a weird set of circumstances.

"We asked the pilot about his recollections of what happened and got mostly gibberish. Either he was really confused, or he wasn't ready to tell us the truth, but he did pretty much confirm that the controller's scope was giving accurate altitude readings, within a hundred feet or so. He also claimed that he had initiated a climb just before they hit the hill. But that isn't consistent with the investigators' reports. They believed the airplane was flying straight and level when it impacted because of the way they found the prop, the gear, and the separated wings. So again, two different stories. But for my money, I'll take the word of the professional investigators.

"Just one other issue warrants some comment. That's the question about the VFR flight plan that was filed by this pilot, and why both the center and approach controllers may have thought he was IFR qualified. First of all, he was out there on a very dark night in marginal if not IFR conditions and sounding like he knew what he was doing. Not that either of those things should have made any difference. He definitely should have been treated like a noninstrument rated, VFR pilot. But, if you'll take the time to listen to the tapes carefully, you'll agree that, from what he told both controllers, they couldn't know what to think. When he was offered IFR flight plans, he turned them down by saying he was VFR and didn't want to bother flying an IFR approach. He didn't say he was a VFR pilot and he didn't say that he couldn't accept an IFR flight plan because he wasn't instrument rated. If I recall, he even had an explanation for declining that he had gotten off late and was in a hurry.

"So what are controllers supposed to do? They're not mind readers and they don't have anything that tells them what kinds of pilots they're dealing with. They can only respond to what they're told and what they're asked for and I believe they have the right to expect those pilots to take at least some of the responsibility for their own safety."

Author comment: It isn't difficult to conclude that many factors contributed to this accident. 'Pilot error' was one of them, but it was by no means the sole cause, or even the primary cause. Several other things deserve distinction:

- The weather, of course, but that was a coin flip. Flight service did tell the pilot that VFR was not recommended, but "not recommended" is becoming a "wolf wolf" call and is being ignored by many pilots who have heard it too many times when the weather turned out to be just fine. It's not a smart or safe practice, to be sure, but it is a fact of life and in this case, the weather was forecast to be VFR at the destination airport.

- Both controllers needed to know if the pilot was actually IFR qualified and they should have asked. Just that simple question, "Are you IFR qualified?" would have led to an easy diversion to a VFR airport and the prevention of an unnecessary accident.

- The communications gap caused by the frequency overload could also have been caused by a stuck mike. Ask any controller who has had that happen, and they will tell you how frightening and frustrating it is watching the targets on their scopes coming together with no way to clear the frequency so they can talk to the pilots who are relying on them for their safety. ATC is working on a system that will enable controllers to clear a blocked frequency, but it isn't in place yet. Whether or not a warning from the controller would have prevented this accident is a moot question. It would be better not to have to ask it. This major flaw in the party-line radio system needs correction. In the meantime, every pilot should be aware of the potential dangers it can cause.

- One item that deserves repetition: There is no such thing as marginal VFR in a remote area on a dark, moonless night. That is *always* IFR because there are no reliable visual references outside the airplane. As a matter of fact, *any* moonless night with total cloud cover and no visible stars should be treated as IFR conditions. It isn't required by the FARs. It's just a smart idea.

21

You get what you pay for

Preliminary report: April; Piper Cherokee 6; commercial pilot, single-engine land, 520 hours. All five occupants of the aircraft were killed following an in-flight breakup during a night flight from Myrtle Beach, South Carolina, to Manassas, Virginia. Weather at the time of the accident at Blackstone AAF, about 35 miles northeast of the crash site, was (in part) 1,300 broken with 3 miles in rain and fog. Examination revealed that the aircraft's vacuum system and directional gyro were inoperative. Metallurgical examination showed that the wing separated from overload.

Further examination revealed:

- The flight was initiated later than planned even though the pilot had learned the weather was forecast to deteriorate. When the aircraft failed to arrive in Manassas, a search was initiated.
- Recorded radio information revealed that the pilot had encountered heavy rain and moderate to severe turbulence just prior to the accident.
- Radar data showed that before the accident the aircraft was heading northeast at 2,100 feet msl. The aircraft climbed to 2,400 feet, turned north, descended to 2,000 feet, turned west, and then descended to 1,500 feet before radar contact was lost. Radar contact ended less than 1 mile from the crash site in a remote area of the John Kerr Reservoir in northern North Carolina.
- The flight originated earlier in the day from Manassas, Virginia, and the rented Cherokee was scheduled to be returned before midnight or additional rental charges would have been incurred.

- The pilot had a total of 18 hours of instrument training and had not taken the IFR written. His last simulated instrument flight was eight months prior to the accident. Also, his night currency had elapsed 11 months earlier, although he had made one night flight and landing two months before the accident.

Official conclusion: VFR into IMC. Lack of night currency. Inoperative DG and vacuum system. Loss of control due to spatial disorientation. Wing overload and in-flight breakup. Pilot error.

ARRANGEMENTS FOR THE FLIGHT began two days in advance as a proposed charter from Pro-Charter, Inc., an aircraft charter and rental service based at Harry P. Davis Field in Manassas, Virginia. Haggling over the cost resulted in the following under-the-table, strictly off-the-record deal: The airplane would be rented on a personal basis by a part-time charter pilot who would then be reimbursed in cash—in advance by the four passengers who were going to Myrtle Beach for a one-day look at a resort property.

Because of the rock-bottom price agreed to, the aircraft assigned for the trip was a vintage Cherokee 6 that would be held back from scheduled maintenance for its 100-hour and annual—it was already 37 hours overdue—plus repair or replacement of its vacuum system and directional gyro. Also, the #1 comm and #2 nav had been inoperative for nearly six months, but neither radio was scheduled for repair. Pro-Charter was not doing very well and couldn't or wouldn't put out the money for the radios. Besides, comm #2 and nav #1 were working, as was a recently installed Mode C transponder—cannibalized from another Pro-Charter-owned aircraft that had been totalled. Pro-Charter wasn't an accident-free company, either, nor were its two owners, the Jarrett brothers, twins Ralph and Alf, in their mid-40s.

They had run a series of failed airplane brokerage, charter, and rental businesses, each time to the disappointment of several unsuspecting local investors. Both brothers were charming, very convincing and great salesmen. They just hadn't figured out how to deliver on what they promised and sold. Manassas was their latest venture and, typical of their unenviable track record, it wasn't going very well either. Their short tenure in Pro-Charter was tenuous, as was their questionable, low-cost insurance, which was on the verge of being canceled due to the accident that yielded the transponder.

One other glitch was unknown to the charterees: The pilot who had originally agreed to the unusual, surreptitious deal had backed out in favor of a more lucrative charter. In his place, after considerable frantic searching, was Greg Ellison, a 26-year-old part-time commercial pilot with no instrument rating, no night currency—although the return trip was planned to end well after dark—and only four hours of time in the Cherokee, none of it recent. As a precaution, Greg made two touch and go circuits the afternoon before the flight. Also, fortunately, the weather was forecast to be good VFR in Myrtle Beach, and okay in Manassas until after midnight.

Promptly at 8 a.m., Greg arrived at the airport to prepare for the trip. Flight service confirmed the good weather for the flight out and the iffy weather for the flight back—but not expected until around midnight. They also suggested checking carefully later in the day because the weather system that was heading toward the area had been moving erratically.

The four passengers arrived at 9:20 a.m.—a little late—the cash was paid to Greg and then to Pro-Charter, and the Cherokee was off the ground at 9:45 without a flight plan. Pro-Charter had advised Greg that they didn't want any official record of their out-of-annual, non-airworthy Cherokee 6 being rented by anyone, and especially by him carrying four passengers he didn't know. That could be construed as a clandestine charter in an illegal airplane flown by an unqualified pilot and they could be held responsible.

Nice weather and smooth skies prevailed for the 2-hour ride to Myrtle Beach. En route, unbeknownst to the passengers who were loving the scenery, Greg was familiarizing himself with the Cherokee's panel, discovering for the first time that comm #1 and nav #2 were not working. He already knew the DG was out, but he had no idea that the entire vacuum system was inoperative. It was a very old airplane and hadn't had a lot of tender loving care. None of its several owners had ever put much quality maintenance into it.

Following an almost-smooth landing at Grand Strand Airport in North Myrtle Beach, the four passengers deplaned happily and told Greg they would return to the airport for a 6:30 p.m. departure— which was an hour-and-a-half later than Greg had expected. The foursome rode off in a waiting van driven by an accommodating real estate agent. Greg was left to his own devices, which included studying the Cherokee's manual, something he had never done before, and calling flight service several times. The weather was moving in a little faster than forecast, but was not a problem. It wasn't expected to arrive in the area until three or more hours after they were back safely in Manassas; however, just as a precaution, he decided to call Pro-Charter to let them know he would be arriving late and for advice about dealing with the weather.

Ralph Jarrett, Pro-Charter former coowner "There were some things about Greg Ellison that we didn't find out until after the accident. We knew he wasn't IFR rated, but he told us he was taking instrument training and had also been flying copilot for another charter service. None of that was true. His IFR training was on and off and mostly off. And his copiloting was very once-in-a-while with a friend who flew occasional mail runs in an old Apache.

"When he called the first time from Myrtle Beach, my brother took the call and told him to let us know when the passengers were ready to go. We would then decide if it was okay after we checked the current weather. There was no point in making the decision in advance without knowing what time they'd be leaving. The second time he called, my brother and I were both gone. It was sometime after 6 p.m. The only person around was one of the charter pilots who just read him the note from the scheduling sheet that said the airplane had to be back for servicing early the next morning. Supposedly, Greg asked if there would be any extra charge if he brought the airplane back after midnight, or the next day, and the pilot told him he thought there would be. That wasn't true. We'd never have a rule like that, but the pilot was new and didn't know his way around very well. It was a shame that he was the only person there to take the call. Anyone else would have told Greg to stay put until the weather had cleared out.

"As you can imagine, the accident hurt us very badly. We lost Pro-Charter as a result of it but we managed to get back in business—barely—because one of our investors decided to keep us afloat. We also had a bad time with the FAA. But they couldn't prove anything, so all that happened was it wound up costing us a bunch of money that would be better spent on airplane maintenance, which is still a problem for us. We don't ever seem to have enough capital to buy decent equipment or keep what we have in good shape.

"Right now, things are a little better. We're still flying very old airplanes and we can't get an adequate insurance policy because of all the losses we've had. But we should be out of the woods pretty soon. My brother just landed a charter deal with a big casino over in Atlantic City. So, we're in the market for a Navajo or a 414 and two more pilots. If this deal brings in as much business as it's supposed to, we should be able to make this into a first-class operation and get rid of some of the junk we're flying."

At 6:10 p.m., Greg was paged in the pilot's lounge for a phone call from one of the passengers—they were going to be delayed by at least a couple of hours. Greg explained the possible problem from the approaching weather but all he could extract was a promise that they would try their best to be a little early. Hanging up with a heavy feeling in the pit of his stomach, Greg paced back and forth for several minutes assessing his situation and trying to decide what to do. His first call was to flight service. The news wasn't terrible but it wasn't good either. There was a chance of some rain, fog, and even a possible thunderstorm all through the northern half of North Carolina and up as far as central Virginia. Manassas would probably stay clear of it. If he could leave after midnight, or if he could fly about 150 miles west, he might be able to come in behind it, but that was only a maybe. The system was still moving erratically.

His next call was to Pro-Charter and not much help. The person he talked to, a new charter pilot he didn't know, told him the Jarrett brothers had already gone but had left word for him that he'd better get back before midnight or there would be an additional charge for the airplane. And as far as the weather was concerned, the pilot didn't think it was a big deal or anything he wouldn't be able to handle. Of course, the pilot didn't know Greg either, or the fact that he wasn't instrument rated. He merely assumed that every charter pilot would be. But then, he had never worked for anyone like the Jarretts before.

Reporting the entire situation to his passengers when they finally arrived at 8:15 p.m., they came to the following conclusions together: Greg could handle it because, at least in their opinion, he was an excellent pilot. If the weather got too tough, they could always land somewhere and wait it out. Anyway, they were looking forward to a night flight—with all the lights they would be able to see from a small airplane. And besides, it was a beautiful, clear night in Myrtle Beach, so how bad could it get?

Contrary to his slightly better judgment, which was tempered mostly by fear and uncertainty—he didn't share their confidence in him because he did know better—Greg agreed to take off and give it a whirl, again without a flight plan. He didn't want a problem with the Jarrett brothers. They were a couple of tough cookies.

Proceeding straight north out of Grand Strand with his one comm tuned to flight watch, Greg let the westerly crosswind keep them well east of V-136. At one point he called in to find out if any of the MOAs were active—they weren't—and also heard that rain was moving into the Raleigh, North Carolina, area and would probably be there to greet them. But it wasn't expected to be IFR except in a few areas of widely scattered thunderstorms, a few of which could be embedded in the thickening overcast. All of the passengers heard the report and agreed that all was well. They weren't afraid of a few small thunderstorms. Neither was Greg—he was *terrified* of them.

As luck would have it, when they reached 20 miles southeast of Raleigh, there was the rain, right on schedule. But the visibility was still good and they were able to hold 2,500 feet without being in the overcast. Greg's confidence swelled as they traversed the first 10 miles of the rain, dodging a few low spots in the overcast, but holding their own. The passengers were pleased and vocal about it.

Thirty miles farther, not so pleased and not so confident, it began raining harder. The Cherokee was quickly down to 2,100 feet to stay in the clear and Greg turned right 20° toward an area that looked lighter in the rapidly darkening sky. It was a good choice. Within a couple of minutes the Cherokee was back up to 2,400 feet and headed straight north on course. Greg relaxed a little, happy with himself but fearful of the next wave of rain or whatever.

He didn't have to wait long. Coming up on the southern end of the John Kerr Reservoir, the sky suddenly opened up on them as they flew under an embedded cell. Greg lowered the nose quickly in an attempt to get under the overcast, but it wasn't to be. He was solid IFR in the heavy rain with no outside references of any kind. And he wasn't ready for it. Neither were the passengers or the Cherokee with its inoperative DG and vacuum system. Greg was on needle-ball-and-airspeed and quickly losing control of the airplane and himself. Frantically, he grabbed the mike and announced the N number and the fact that they were in heavy rain and turbulence. The radio was tuned to flight watch, who responded immediately—several times. But Greg never replied. He couldn't. He was too busy trying to fly the airplane and a jolt of turbulence had knocked the mike out of his hand and onto the cabin floor.

With his head and the airplane beginning to spin to the left, Greg pulled hard on the control wheel to stop their rapid descent. Then it was hard right rudder, followed by sharp left pressure on the wheel as the airplane lurched right and out of control. Fighting hard, Greg and the Cherokee encountered the windshear of the small but potent cell. As the altimeter raced up, Greg applied hard down pressure on the yoke, not aware of the airspeed needle shooting past the redline and pegging itself at the top of the indicator.

The old wings of the dilapidated Cherokee couldn't handle the pressure and the G forces; the wings separated from the fuselage. Radar tracked the descending target through 1,500 feet and then lost it. The fuselage crashed in a remote area on the eastern side of the reservoir. The wings followed seconds later, impacting 700 feet east and nearly disintegrating.

There was no fire, perhaps because of the heavy rain squall and despite the fact that the crash site was less than a mile from where radar contact had been lost, it took several days and an exhaustive search to find the wreckage and the bodies.

FAA investigator's written report "So many things were wrong with the airplane that we immediately contacted the owners, a company in Manassas, Virginia named Pro-Charter, Inc., to get the maintenance records on the airplane. But they claimed they did not have any, that everything was destroyed in the crash. Field investigations turned up only the airplane's pink sheet but no other logs or records of any kind.

"Further attempts to get information from the owners, twin brothers Ralph and Alfred Jarrett, were met with denials and excuses and then outright refusals to talk with us. We have since been in touch with their attorney, who stated that the Jarretts would probably be forced to sell their business because of the financial loss from the accident. Apparently, their insurance did not cover everything.

"As far as we can tell, the airplane was severely out of annual, had a nonworking vacuum system, and several other instruments on the panel were inoperative. Also, at least two of the radios were not working.

"Information on the pilot was obtained from his mother, Mrs. Sarah Ellison, of Manassas Park, Virginia, who claimed his logbook must have been with him and lost in the crash. As far as she could recollect, her son had been flying for nearly eight years and worked for the Jarrett brothers only occasionally. The pilot's full-time job was as a money collector for a vending machine company, which required flexible hours. His mother also mentioned that her son did not particularly like the Jarretts because they were too demanding and he was afraid of them.

"From other sources, we learned that the pilot was not instrument rated, even though he had a commercial license and worked part-time for three licensed charter services. Our estimate of his flying time is 520 hours, based on data received from the flight school where he had taken some IFR training several months prior to the accident.

"The radar data available verified that the primary cause of the accident was spatial disorientation. This was a typical result of VFR into IMC by an inexperienced pilot. It was followed by a catastrophic failure of the entire wing assembly prior to impact. The wings were found 700 feet east of the main crash site. Also contributing to the accident was the condition of the airplane; however, the damage was so severe that only the vacuum system and the directional gyros could be confirmed as inoperative prior to the crash.

"Weather data confirmed that thunderstorms were present near the crash site at the time of the accident. It was also learned that the pilot had received a complete weather briefing just before takeoff, and had spoken to flight watch shortly before encountering the weather. No other contact was made with ATC and no flight plan had been filed in Myrtle Beach."

Harold Davidson, present owner of Pro-Charter, Inc. "About the only thing we actually bought from the Jarrett brothers was some maintenance equipment, some parts and the lease rights to our facility. Other than that, they didn't have anything to sell. Their airplanes would have cost more to bring up to our standards than they were worth.

"We were just anxious to find this location. And the airport management was glad to get rid of the Jarretts. I never really knew them but I have since learned that their leaving here was good riddance. I wish I could say that they've also left general aviation, but that's not the case. I understand they're back in business somewhere else and up to their old tricks.

"As far as the accident is concerned, most of what we know about it came from the FAA and the families of the people who were killed. Everyone was looking for records and maintenance logs, but we couldn't find any. Apparently, the Jarretts covered their tracks well. We did find out that the pilot wasn't instrument rated, which is pretty unthinkable in the charter business, and that the airplane he was flying was a pile of garbage, out of annual, with a busted vac and half the panel inoperative. Talk about a shoddy operation! Makes you wonder how any of those people ever got into the airplane, or why the pilot was willing to fly it on a trip like that and in those conditions.

"A couple of answers to those questions surfaced during the investigation. Somebody told the FAA that it was a gypsy charter: dirt cheap, strictly in cash and strictly off the record. The way they worked it was the pilot rented the airplane for the day, collected the money from the passengers and kept just his hourly rate, which couldn't have been very much, since he wasn't a qualified charter pilot. The whole deal was arranged by one of the Jarretts. As I'm sure you know, it was illegal as hell. But the word around here is they did a lot of their business that way.

"Other than that, I can't tell you very much. I wish we'd known before we bought this business the kind of reputation it had. We would have changed the name and done some other things different. But we've lived it down. We run a very clean operation, and the people around here have responded well to us. So, all in all, we're happy with how it's turned out."

Sarah Ellison "They killed my son. Plain and simple, they killed him. And nobody's doing anything about it. Those two animals are back in business doing the same things they did here in Manassas.

"I told Greg those Jarrett brothers were no good. I told the FAA the same thing. How they pushed Greg to take all kinds of chances. How their airplanes were always missing something or had something broken. Greg used to tell us about it. I never could figure out why he worked for them, but he used to say he sort of had to. They must have had something to do with his regular job. Otherwise, Greg wasn't into drugs or gambling or anything like that. He was a good clean kid who minded his own business and stayed out of trouble.

"I've written some letters and talked to a lot of those government people about what Greg told us, but they don't seem to care much about whether the Jarretts are out there killing more pilots and passengers. You'd think there was a way to stop them, but I haven't found one. And neither has anyone else I've talked to. Like the people who manage the airport. They thought the Jarretts should have been arrested for what they did. But they couldn't get anyone to do anything about it either.

"So they'll just go on cheating and hurting people, because the government either won't or can't do anything to stop it. I've about given up. But I hope somebody gives those Jarretts what they deserve. Maybe it will be up to God. That's fine with me because they'd have to die for that to happen."

NTSB representative "Nothing about this case is very clear. Our official position is that it was basically pilot error, complicated by several other factors. But in my book, the other factors had more to do with it than the pilot did. He was flying an airplane that shouldn't have been allowed off the ground. That's still part of pilot error. But the circumstances leading up to it involve a whole lot of other things. Like the people who owned the airplane and put some kind of pressure on him to start out way over his head in the first place. Or the passengers who probably goaded him into taking off from Myrtle Beach at night in questionable weather. Of course, they may not have guessed that he was unqualified to be a . . . charter pilot, or that he wasn't capable of flying instruments. I'm sure he never mentioned it.

The reason we think they must have put some pressure on him to leave was because none of them had brought along any luggage. It also had been a long day for everyone.

"Then there were some things the system did that didn't add up. So we checked them out and came up with a face full of egg. Flight service screwed up first and very badly. The briefer told the pilot the weather was expected to deteriorate but he never said how much or how soon. And he never used the magic words: 'VFR not recommended.' And he never said that embedded cells were likely, which they were, and which he knew about. As a matter of fact, he never even mentioned that IFR was a *possibility* along their route of flight, even though the information on the written report he had stated that it was a *probability*. All he said was that the weather would probably go down before they got to their destination. After the disciplinary action taken against him, you can be sure he'll never do that again.

"We also checked with flight watch and discovered another lapse: That briefer warned the pilot about precip ahead but didn't mention the thunderstorm that was building to a level 4 or 5 just north of Raleigh because the data on it was on a separate sheet—and somehow he forgot to look at the sheet. If he had told the pilot about the growing cell, that was probably embedded, SOP would have included a suggestion to call ahead to Blackstone, the military base, where they have wide-area radar coverage. As a matter of fact, Blackstone radar tracked the flight right up to and into the thunderstorm they were painting. They just had no way of contacting the pilot to tell him about it.

"Going back to the condition of the airplane, we'll never know for sure if it contributed directly to the accident. My guess would be that it did, very directly. I wouldn't have wanted to be up near that thunderstorm with no panel. And I've been flying instruments for 32 years. Think about how an inexperienced low-timer with no rating would do in it. Not very well, if at all. In fact, from what I've seen of partial panel capability, I'd venture that half the instrument pilots flying wouldn't have come through that encounter without tearing the wings off that crate.

"One last comment I'd like to make is about the owners of the airplane and the charter service—the ones who put those people up there illegally with their convoluted deal. They got beat up financially because their cheap insurance didn't cover much of the loss, but that's only part of what they deserved. They ought to be in jail. But you know what? They didn't even get sued by any of the surviving families. Probably because the attorneys figured they wouldn't be able to collect anything even if they won. And worse yet, I understand those characters are back in business at another airport, doing exactly the same things they were doing at Manassas.

"Now that's terrible. They break the law. Five people get killed because of it and there's no way to stop them from going right back in business. I have a real problem with that. But I haven't heard of anything being done to correct it. The FAA says it has no local authority and the states and cities say it's a national problem, something they can't deal with. So I guess all we can do is thank God [that] most of the FBOs out there are honest people running responsible businesses. Maybe we should post warnings in some of the bad places we know about, like the surgeon general does, warning pilots and renters that the use of poorly maintained airplanes could be dangerous to their health. It would be better than the 'nothing' that's being done now."

Author comment As the general aviation fleet becomes smaller and grows older because so few new aircraft are being built, the problems associated with the cost and quality of maintenance will intensify. Safety is being compromised as owners and operators find it more and more difficult to locate parts for the thousands of airplanes that long ago reached the vintage state. Mechanics who know how to service many of those very old airplanes, most of which already require the skills of artisans who can hand-make parts, are also a declining breed, with replacements nowhere in sight.

All of which leaves present and future aircraft owners and pilots with a strange dilemma: Do they learn to fix as they fly, or do they accept the risk of relying on questionable quality, harder-to-find maintenance? If nothing else, that perplexing choice will continue to plague the used airplane business by further dissuading potential buyers—especially the ones with real money because they are less likely to be do-it-yourselfers.

The anger and emotions this accident stirred up toward the shoddy practices of the irresponsible charter operators caused the various experts to overlook what was undoubtedly the single most important contributor to this accident—the weather itself, the embedded cell that crippled the Cherokee. But then, the weather's sometimes rapidly developing thunderstorms are prone to do that to the unsuspecting. What those baby cells can do to an airplane quickly dispels any false notion that because they are relatively small, they are also less dangerous. Quite the contrary. The speed at which a storm cell develops plays a big part in determining its power. Actually, microbursts are often spawned by smaller cells or cells within cells. That's why they are so hard to predict or see.

So, the question in this accident remains: Did it make any difference how new or old, or how unairworthy the Cherokee was? Probably not. The storm they ran into would have bent up anything flying, even a C-5A. That then puts the blame back in at least two places: flight service and flight watch. Both entities blew their assignments to properly inform the pilot and neither is subject to any more censure or penalty than the charter service—actually, less because at least the charter operators suffered some financial loss as a result of what they did.

That, unfortunately, was not the case with either of the briefers; they were both suspended with pay while part of the investigation was going on, which sounds like a reward to me. And then they were reinstated and promoted on schedule for their fine, untarnished performance.

22

Gambling on the weather

Preliminary report: September; Piper Turbo Arrow; certified flight instructor, CFI instrument rating, single-engine land, 4,890 hours. On a VFR flight from Sheridan, Wyoming, to Bismarck, North Dakota, the pilot radioed that he had lost his gyros and declared an emergency. Flight service received a special VFR clearance to below minimum weather but was unable to issue it to the pilot due to lost radio communications. The airplane crashed in a remote area near the Powder River, 11 miles northeast of Moorehead, Montana. The pilot and his passenger were killed. Post-accident investigation revealed that the vacuum pump had been installed without the shear shaft coupling.

Further investigation revealed:

- A complete weather briefing was obtained indicating IFR along the intended route of flight. The pilot informed the briefer that he was conducting the flight VFR because he did not trust his instruments.
- About an hour after departure, the pilot called flight service and requested the Sheridan weather, explaining that he planned to return because he could no longer continue the flight VFR.
- The airframe and engine logbooks contained no entries of any work having been done on the vacuum pump. An annual had been performed and entered in the logs but had not been signed off by a properly certified mechanic or a certified shop.
- Witnesses at Sheridan County Airport, where the airplane was based, claimed that the pilot was a tinkerer who did most of the maintenance work on the airplane himself. They further stated that the pilot was not a trained mechanic but

frequently bragged about his ability to do better work himself and substitute auto parts for many items in the airplane "because they're the same thing and cost half as much."

- Although he was a licensed CFII, the pilot had not given any flight instruction in the past seven years. He also had not flown IFR in the past 3½ years, usually making the excuse that his panel needed work.

Official conclusion: Deliberate VFR into IMC. Weather condition below approach minimums. Inoperative vacuum system. Loss of control due to spatial disorientation. Pilot error.

AT THE RIPE YOUNG AGE of 59, Lowell Dawson was the best known, best liked businessman in Sheridan, Wyoming. His enterprises included insurance and real estate agencies, the best sit-down restaurant in town, interests in several other retail and service businesses and a chunk of the local bank, from which he spawned many of the businesses he backed. He was also a pilot and an ardent supporter of the Sheridan Municipal Airport, giving amply of his time and energy, but none of his money. Lowell was also—proudly—the self-proclaimed cheapest person in northeastern Wyoming. Maybe all of Wyoming.

But everyone loved him because Lowell gave of himself to every cause and person who needed help. That's what the flight to Bismarck was all about. Marianne Palmer, 56, a sometime employee, friend, and recent widow, had a middle-of-the-night call from her brother in Bismarck that their 89-year-old mother had taken a sudden turn for the worse. Sharply at dawn, Marianne called Lowell and the flight was on, with her paying for the gas and oil, of course. He wouldn't want Marianne to feel obligated.

Lowell's first call was to his close friend, Biff Barnes, manager of the flight service station conveniently located at Sheridan Airport. Biff was at home and would call back promptly after checking with the briefer on duty. Lowell's next call was to the airport flight office with instructions to pull his Turbo Arrow from the community hangar, which he owned so he wouldn't have to pay monthly storage fees, and on which he also made a decent profit—as he did on all of his businesses.

Biff's return call came in less than 10 minutes and it wasn't good news. The weather between Sheridan and Bismarck was going to be lousy all day—okay at Sheridan, IFR at Bismarck, and worse in between. He advised Lowell not to go, not even if it was an emergency, unless he wanted to become an emergency himself. Lowell hemmed and hawed, but Biff was adamant: The weather stunk and Lowell shouldn't go. Period.

For some reason, Lowell wasn't ready to give up. Which he always did when Biff told him to. They had been friends and barnstormers for 35 years, and Lowell had learned to trust Biff with his life. But Marianne was becoming special in Lowell's life—a first since his wife had been killed in an auto accident four years ago—and he didn't want to disappoint her, at least not without considering every possibility. He and a grumbling Biff would check the weather again as soon as Biff arrived at the airport at 9 a.m. That's what Lowell told a worried but grateful Marianne on the phone, while he told her to be ready in 20 minutes so he could pick her up for a leisurely breakfast and some extra time together.

As luck would have it, the weather news at 9:15 was better, not much better, but closer to flyable, at least at Bismarck. In between was still calling for IFR—not quite as low but still IFR. Biff's advice didn't change. He had two very persuasive arguments: First, the next forecast could be back in the tank and second, Lowell wasn't up to handling low IFR with his questionable IFR proficiency and in his even more questionably maintained Arrow.

Lowell bristled at Biff's honest reading, especially the second point, but he had no rebuttal because he knew Biff wouldn't change his mind. So he swallowed hard and decided on an end run—that Biff was waiting for with a hard frown and a one-sided half smile. He knew Lowell that well, as well as he knew where north was on every weather map he had read over the past 35 years. The end run was simple: Lowell and Marianne would take off, try out the in-between weather and, if it got too tough, they would turn back to Sheridan where the forecast was passable. And he wanted help from Biff, "the best weatherman in the territory."

Biff wasn't buying it, but Lowell wasn't taking "no" for an answer. After 10 minutes of friendly but dead serious wrangling, they agreed to wait for the next hour's forecast and decide then. Lowell was anxious to go. Biff was worried. He knew how fickle the weather was in the northern plains. He also knew that Lowell was pushing. And pushing isn't safe in an airplane.

The 10:15 weather came in and Biff wanted to throw it away before Lowell saw it because conditions had improved slightly. The forecasts were a little better, too. Just enough to get an anxious pilot in trouble, but Lowell wasn't about to be dissuaded, or let Biff out of their deal. He and Marianne were going to Bismarck and Biff was going to ride shotgun for them, at least as far as radio range would permit.

At 10:55 a.m., Lowell, Marianne, and the questionably maintained Turbo Arrow lifted off into the beckoning blue, climbed to 6,500 feet msl and settled down in the smooth, early fall air. Lowell had calculated 1:50 of flying time for the 300 nautical mile trip, thanks to a nice push from a so-far friendly tailwind. He picked up his mike and called Biff on 123.6 to report their pleasant flight conditions and to check on the latest weather, which wouldn't be in for another 10 minutes or so, and on pireps from the barren country they would be flying over. But there weren't any pireps that morning. They would have to wait for the official weather.

By the time it came in, only 15 minutes later, Lowell knew—based upon he couldn't see ahead—what the weather report was going to say. It was worse and going down, but only just a little. Biff didn't like the trend but he couldn't convince Lowell that it was time to turn around, that he shouldn't put himself and Marianne at risk rushing to see her dying mother.

Lowell was descending slowly and persistently but not saying anything to Marianne or Biff. The ceiling was coming down; so was the visibility; and the hills were coming up, slowly. The flight was 35 minutes out and the Arrow was down by more than 1,500 feet and still descending. Lowell was becoming concerned. And noticing the intermittent readings and wavering of his HSI and DG. This was not a time for panel problems.

Another 20 minutes and the self-maintained Arrow decided to even the score for its unprofessional maintenance. With Lowell in and out of the overcast to avoid the looming hills, the Arrow picked the worst possible moment to dump its vacuum system and disable the HSI and the other gyros. Caught between the clouds and the rising terrain, Lowell cursed as he realized their predicament and began flying "needle-ball-and-airspeed," the basic instrument scanning procedure that he learned 35 years ago but hadn't tried or practiced for as long as he could remember. It wasn't coming back easily. He was struggling for control, sorely missing a normal panel-scan to keep the airplane flying straight and level.

Finally getting under some semblance of control, Lowell called Biff, still barely within radio range, declared an emergency and requested a special VFR to anywhere, preferably back to Sheridan. He knew they were only a few miles from Harding County Airport in Buffalo, South Dakota, but he wasn't sure they could find it in the deteriorating visibility. Biff answered anxiously, told him to standby while he called in for the clearance, and picked up his phone immediately.

The clearance was granted in 30 seconds, but Biff was unable to reach Lowell and Marianne to deliver it because Lowell was still heading toward Bismarck, afraid to do anything until he heard from Biff.

Another 3 minutes went by before Lowell realized they were too low and too far for Biff to reach them. So he took matters into his own hands, did a 180° turn to head them back home and lowered the nose to get under the overcast. But his choice of places to "duck under" was unfortunate, putting them almost into a hillside just as they came out of the clouds.

Lowell did a quick pullback, steadied himself and the Arrow as best he could after their close call and climbed grudgingly into the overcast. He called Biff again when they were up a bit higher but couldn't get a reply. Biff heard the call and replied immediately, but they never made contact. Lowell and Marianne were on their own as the turbulence picked up and it began raining harder.

Lowell kept trying the radio. Biff heard on-and-off bits and pieces of Lowell's calls and then steeled himself as the calls became desperate, then frantic in the worsening turbulence and rain. Lowell was losing it and Biff was helplessly listening, unable to reach his friend who needed a calming voice, a point of reassurance.

For the next 10 minutes, Lowell struggled with the Arrow and the weather, both of which were ganging up on him. The higher he went the more turbulent it got. Lower and under the overcast was out of the question. He wasn't about to tangle with any more of those obscured hilltops, but then he checked his altimeter reading at 4,200 feet and realized that they were way below a safe en route altitude and would be better off trying for VFR than risking flying directly into something that was higher than they were and in the clouds like they were. Down came the nose.

This time they were luckier. They were under the overcast at 3,200 indicated with some room to spare between themselves and the ground, in a valley, surrounded by higher hills on all sides, at least as far as they could see. Lowell circled, looking for a road, a piece of flat ground, any place to land his sickly Arrow and wait for better weather. He kept circling. And calling Biff, who couldn't hear him. They were much too low for transmission from that far away in hill country.

Finally realizing there was no place to land and nowhere to go in their present VFR environment, Lowell made the only choice he could: Back into the overcast. Up went the nose and the power. Down came the bottom of the overcast; they were hit with a hard, twisting jolt of turbulence just as they entered the base at 3,600 feet.

The Arrow wasn't ready for it. Neither were Lowell and Marianne as they were thrown against the sides and ceiling of the cabin, hurting themselves. Marianne grabbed her control wheel as something to hold on to, further aggravating their out-of-control situation, fighting

Lowell without meaning to. His response was a tighter grip, a harder correction, a violent recovery. But a recovery, nevertheless. And then a climb to 4,500 feet, a turn to 250° and a reassuring hand on Marianne's arm to calm her down.

He called Biff again, describing their encounter, hoping for a response of some kind, any kind. Biff heard him partially and tried to reach him, almost screaming into his mike, trying to warn him that a minisquall line was developing along a straight track between Sheridan and Bismarck. Lowell caught "squall line" and tensed inwardly, but it was good to hear Biff's voice. For a savored moment he felt relieved to be back in contact.

But he never acknowledged Biff's call. Without warning they hit the leading edge of a developing cell, a nasty one, and were nearly flipped inverted. Lowell didn't know that because his instruments were bouncing and pegging from side to side, but he took what corrective action he could, again fighting Marianne for the wheel, desperately trying to regain control. Desperately holding on, applying pressures the wrong way, increasing the turn and climb until they went over the top, and down. Both of them holding on for dear life.

The accident investigators found them that way. Still holding on, locked in death grips on their control wheels. The cabin had been crushed around them from the impact into rising terrain. But mostly crushed from the top and one side, leaving the condition of the instruments and the vacuum system intact enough to verify which ones were and were not working prior to the crash. They found that the vacuum pump had been installed without its shear shaft coupling. Failure was inevitable. It could not have come at a worse time.

Biff Barnes, Sheridan, Wyoming Flight Service Station manager
"I had a bad feeling about that whole day the minute I heard Lowell on the phone at 6 a.m. He never did things like that, rushing and all. His style was to take his time, never push or pull, just sit back and let things come to him. That's why everybody thought he was so cheap around here, but I think that was why he had half the money in Wyoming.

"The weather wasn't really all that bad early on and for awhile it looked like it was going to get better, or at least not get any worse. That's the worst kind because you never know how to call it. I knew that and I tried to convince Lowell to scratch the trip and let Marianne talk to her mother by phone until the weather got good enough for a safe trip, but neither one of them were listening. They had a mind-set to go and nothing I said was going to make any difference to either one of them.

"I wasn't much worried about Lowell's flying. I knew he could handle most anything. It was that damned airplane I was worried about. Lowell wasn't a mechanic but he insisted on doing everything himself. Even the entire annual, or whatever he did and called it that. I remember him trying to get the FBO people to do his gear drop inspection, but they weren't about to touch that airplane. Probably figured they'd end up losing their license if anybody found their name in the log books and blamed them for screwing up an installation of some sort.

"You know, I don't think money had anything at all to do with Lowell's working on his own airplane. I think he just liked to tinker, figured he could work everything out for himself and do a better job than the mechanics could. Then, if he got something screwed up, he could always get it fixed. But he also got stubborn about it. Wouldn't admit when he couldn't do something or when he made a mistake. Then he'd just leave it and fly without it. I'll bet his DG hadn't worked in six months, from the way he talked about it. Like it would get better by itself.

"As a result, I think he turned the Arrow into a very dangerous airplane. The report I saw said the vac system was out when they found them. That ties in with what Lowell told me on the radio—that he'd lost his vac and his gyros. It couldn't have happened at a worse time. It was as if that Arrow was waiting to get even with him. And it sure did. Anyway, I know you want an official report, so I'll stop gabbing about Lowell. He was a close personal friend of my wife and I, and it was a tough loss for us but life goes on.

"Officially, the weather was up and down between marginal VFR and IFR for most of the day. Sheridan was supposed to stay pretty good, but Bismarck and en route were not good. Lowell knew all of that because I gave it to him in person and begged them not to go. I didn't say that VFR was not recommended or anything like that . . . lingo we use around here. He was my friend, and I could talk to him straight. So I told him the weather was (bad), don't go, scratch the trip and go back to bed.

"What happened later to the weather was pretty typical. It got a little better for awhile—sort of like when a fighter plays possum with you before he beats the hell out of you—and then turned into a monster after they were out in it. What finally got them was a quickly developing squall line that eventually turned into a level 5 (or worse) thunderstorm. We and the National Weather Service never saw it coming. When they flew into it with no panel, Lowell never really had a chance. Even with a panel it would have been tough because I know he hadn't been flying much IFR. Since his wife was killed four years ago, I can't remember him filing an instrument trip. He had already quit giving lessons, and I guess he kind of gave up on everything else after that.

"I heard that the official report on the accident was pilot error, but for my money, it was definitely that thunderhead. I know they shouldn't have been anywhere near that thing, but single-engine airplanes don't usually have radar to help them find those big cells when they're embedded like that one must have been. And I know Lowell didn't have a Stormscope. So he was just out there naked as a jaybird waiting for that storm to pounce on them. That's what it did and that's what caused the accident. Other than that, Lowell was doing all right. His instrument skills were coming back to him. I'm sure he'd have made it home here to Sheridan with no problem and our weather was okay way past the time they would have arrived."

Sheridan FBO representative "Lowell Dawson was one of the most unusual characters you'd ever want to meet. He was a big supporter of the airport and aviation in general. He bought his airplane from us and probably would have advanced up to a twin if his wife, Betty, hadn't died back in '85 or '86. That was a terrible setback for him.

"Up to the time his wife was killed, Lowell was a good customer, but a guy who always wanted something for nothing. Everyone knew he was rich because he owned half of Sheridan and maybe as much of the county, but he spent money like he was down to his last dollar. After he lost Betty, it got worse, to the point where he wouldn't spend anything for anything, even for things he really needed. Like repairs on his car and his airplane. He started doing them himself.

"He started with his car and messed up something when he changed his oil filter. One of our mechanics helped him out with that. Then it was changing a tire on his Arrow. He finally got it, but it must have cost him double what it was worth and took him all day to do it. Everything he touched on his airplane went like that. He'd start on it, screw it up, and then call for help.

"We were always there for him until we found out he was signing us off in his logbooks without our knowing about it. That was serious and I called him on it, told him we couldn't be held responsible and couldn't be misrepresented like that. He apologized, said he hadn't thought we'd mind since we did help him with what he signed off on, and he promised he wouldn't do it again. But we know he kept on doing his own work, and sometimes using auto parts to boot, like spark plugs and gaskets and such, and he must have been using somebody's name to sign off with. But, as far as I know, it wasn't our company.

"After the accident, the FAA came around to look at our shop records. They told us the Arrow had blown its vacuum pump because it was installed wrong. But we hadn't touched anything on Lowell's airplane in over a year. They checked that out, too, because the airplane's logs had an annual entered that wasn't signed off. They thought we might have done it and would be able to give them some information on the general condition of the airplane. We couldn't, of course, but we did tell them about our experience with Lowell. I'm sure they thought it was bizarre, especially when they found out how wealthy he was.

"Since then, we haven't heard much about Lowell or the accident. His son came in a couple of times to inquire about taking lessons, but nothing ever came of it. And Biff Barnes over at flight service talks about him every now and then. But, other than that, we're just sticking to business hoping we don't run into any more do-it-yourselfers.

"People have to realize that airplanes are not cars. Not that maintenance mistakes in cars aren't dangerous, but in airplanes they're usually fatal, and sometimes to people on the ground as well. In a small community like this, we don't need another eccentric millionaire terrorizing the local folks by tinkering with his own airplane."

FAA representative "We're running into more situations where pilots are doing their own maintenance and causing some king-size problems in the process. It's gotten so bad, in fact, that we've begun including do-it-yourself maintenance tips in our Accident Prevention Program seminars; they've been well received, which leads us to believe that there may be more people out there doing their own thing than we thought there were.

"A lot of routine stuff like oil changes, spark plugs, tires, batteries, and things like that can be safely handled by many pilots. The hangup there comes from the parts they buy and the lubricants, oils, and fluids they use. Airplanes operate in a different environment than cars do and require special care because of it. Oils and fluids have to have specific viscosities, or they won't flow right at high altitude or when they're subjected to temperature extremes. Spark plugs, gaskets, filters, and many other things also must be made for the peculiarities of airplane engines. So, when those people undertake to save money by doing their own work, or do it because they like playing mechanic—since many of them can barely afford to fly these days—they have to be damn careful about how they go about it.

"This accident is a perfect case in point. The pilot apparently did some work on the vacuum system. He probably installed a new pump and when he did, he either forgot or misplaced the shear shaft coupling. But whatever happened, it didn't get put back on, so eventually, engine vibration worked everything loose and blew the whole system. It was just unfortunate that it waited until they were in solid IFR, but it usually works that way. Things like that tend to bite you when you're the most vulnerable.

"There was some consideration given to the weather factors and the thunderstorm they ran into, but several things overshadowed that. First, of course, was the fact that the pilot wasn't current IFR. He knew what the weather was going to be, so what was he doing there? Then the airplane wasn't totally airworthy, at least the panel wasn't. He had to know that since he did his own repairs on it. That was illegal. And finally, when he first got caught up in the weather, why didn't he just turn around and go back to Sheridan? The time to turn around is before you're in over your head. He had to know that, too, because he had been a flight instructor for many years.

"I suppose if you were to analyze all of the deep psychological parts of this puzzle, you'd come up with an equally deep—and confusing—justification for the pilot's actions. But the way we see it, it was still pilot error. Some of the other factors contributed to the accident, but they wouldn't have if the pilot hadn't made the mistakes he did. That thunderstorm wouldn't have done them in if they'd been back on the ground in Sheridan where they belonged."

NTSB representative "We have lots of partial panel accidents in our files and they all follow the same pattern, as does this one. The pilot does all right for awhile, usually a very short while, and then loses it. And that usually happens as soon as they begin to get comfortable enough to deal with other responsibilities, like the radio, or navigating.

"Apparently, the amount of concentration it takes to fly with only basic instruments is about all an average pilot can handle. After all, none of them are really trained on partial panel flying, except for some very rudimentary familiarization with it. That's especially true for VFR pilots; I doubt that more than 10 percent of them have ever had any exposure to partial panel flying at all and most IFR pilots don't get much more, for sure not enough to fly that way routinely.

"So, when the panel, or part of it, goes out, you have a pilot who's instantly over his or her head. Throw in a call from a controller and down they go. Or any little thing that diverts them ever so slightly and they're out of control. We're able to reconstruct those exact scenarios with the very few survivors of these types of accidents. They start out okay, get the hang of it, or at least they think they've got the hang of it, and then lose their concentration as soon as they start doing something else.

"Keep in mind that most partial panel situations arise during IFR flights and happen to experienced pilots in sophisticated aircraft, the kind with autopilots and HSIs and so forth. And on those flights, there's usually a lot for a single pilot to do, like following a precise flight plan, finding intersections and markers and doing quite a bit of communicating with ATC. Take away some of their crutches, especially an autopilot, an HSI, and maybe the DG, too, and many of them are helpless. From what we can tell, they usually panic and then become disoriented. If they survive by some miracle, half the time they can't remember what happened. They just found themselves in the clear, pulled out and lived to tell about it. But most of the time they're not that lucky.

"Partial panel situations happen to VFR guys, too. But most of those involve night flying—VFR, of course—and a high percentage of them survive. That's primarily because they're not really relying on the panel to begin with. So they're not losing a crutch or a vital support mechanism when the panel goes out.

"In the case of this accident, you have an element of both: A former IFR pilot flying VFR, suddenly losing his panel just as he was confronted with IMC. Up to that point he had presumably been flying VFR, meaning he was looking out the window at where they were going. If he had lost his panel at that point, he probably would have turned around and made it home safely. The panel situation wouldn't have made any difference. But put him in a little deeper, scud running for real, for instance, and the circumstances change abruptly. Now he's in and out of IMC, on and off the gauges, and relying on his panel. Take all or part of it away and he's out in left field. He's not talking to anyone. He's not on a flight plan. And he probably hasn't even got a decent chart with him. In that condition, panic is almost a given. Then add some turbulence from a developing cell and Chuck Yeager couldn't have handled it.

"So what you're left with in analyzing this accident is three separate probable causes: the thunderstorm, the partial panel, and pilot error. Except for the thunderstorm, neither of the other two would have resulted in an accident, as best we can tell. He did all right for quite awhile in IMC with most of his panel out. And the pilot error really applies mostly to the condition of the airplane and the faulty maintenance he did by himself. Other than that, he didn't make any accident-causing decisions, he got a complete weather briefing and had a game plan to return if it got too tough. And he wasn't physically impaired in any way.

"The fact that he didn't turn around immediately was anybody's call. From what he and the [ATC] system knew at that moment, there was nothing wrong with it. Those storm cells didn't start showing up until 10 or 15 minutes later. Flight service never predicted them and radar never saw them until they turned up from out of nowhere. By then he wasn't talking to anyone, so he had no way of knowing what the true picture was. He just got caught, and with his panel (partially functioning).

"So, while our official position—like it usually is—was 'pilot error,' I'd bestow that dubious honor instead on the thunderstorm, with a close runner-up position to the partial panel."

Author comment Self-maintained airplanes might fall into the category of experimental aircraft because there can be so many deviations from FAA-approved standards. In which cases, they can then be expected to crash with the same unacceptable frequency as experimental aircraft do, or about three times more often than commercially built, nonexperimental aircraft.

That is not to say that pilots should never fix their own airplanes, but it is to say that when they do, they must be aware of certain specific considerations that are unique only to aircraft. And pilots must be extra diligent as well because mistakes in airplane maintenance can be much more dangerous to the users and the public than faulty automotive repairs.

There isn't much question that the sudden development of the thunderstorm was the direct cause of this accident, whether or not pilot error was involved at all. The fact that the National Weather Service hadn't predicted it raises plenty of questions, because they never even called for "possible thunderstorms" on the day of the accident for anywhere near the area. Which should give every northern plains pilot great cause for concern.

But don't feel complacent because you live and fly elsewhere. The National Weather Service advises that many other parts of the country are subject to "sudden convective development"—that's their terminology for unpredicted squall lines and thunderstorms—at certain times of the year. Now isn't that comforting!

23

The gotta go's

Preliminary report: August; Cessna 210; private pilot, single-engine land, 2,520 hours. The aircraft was destroyed and both occupants were killed on a VFR flight from Salt Lake City to Hutchinson, Kansas. A VFR flight plan had been filed, and the pilot also received two in-flight weather briefings advising him of a convective SIGMET concerning embedded thunderstorms. The first controller provided current weather for Denver, Hutchinson, and several other cities. Radar data showed that an aircraft in the area had made a spiraling dive from 11,900 feet before radar contact was lost. Examination at the crash site revealed that the aircraft had impacted in a nose-down attitude. No preimpact part failure or malfunction was found. According to witnesses, the sky condition in the accident area was obscured.

Further investigation revealed:
- During the first in-flight briefing, the controller also suggested a routing around the thunderstorm area, which was over eastern Colorado and western Kansas at the time, moving eastward at 20 knots. But the pilot said he did not have a map for the new routing and requested the frequencies for several VORs. The controller provided the information and also added 128.3, the Salt Lake City Center frequency for flight following.
- After a hand-off to Denver Center on 124.8, the pilot was told that flight following would not be available due to heavy airline traffic in the area, but he was advised to try 125.8 after passing to the east of Denver. About 30 minutes later, the pilot checked in with Denver Center on 125.8, reporting his position and altitude, but did not request flight following service.
- The VFR flight plan called for an 11,500-foot cruising altitude for the entire trip, although the MEAs after Denver were only 8,000 feet or lower.

- During the second flight watch weather briefing, in the vicinity of Liberal, Kansas, approximately 80 miles south of the originally planned course, the pilot reported that he had been "chased south" because of weather. A new routing farther south was suggested to avoid the frontal area and the pilot was advised to call Kansas City Center on 134.0 for help in traversing the build-ups.
- Upon calling 134.0, the pilot was advised of a convective SIGMET covering his present position and was also told to call 125.2 for flight following. He checked in with the new controller, reported his altitude at 11,900 feet and asked for assistance around the thunderstorms, but not flight following. The controller pointed out where the storms were heaviest and suggested that the pilot fly farther east for another 50 miles before attempting to reach Hutchinson.

Official conclusion: Inadvertent VFR into IMC. Failure to observe SIGMET advisory received. Loss of control due to spatial disorientation. Pilot error.

EARL JENSEN, 57, WAS A SENIOR PARTNER in the accounting firm of Jensen, Kilbourn, and Lewis, a prominent CPA group in Salt Lake City. JKL's key clients were successful businessmen who were deeply involved in the Mormon Church of Jesus Christ of Latter-Day Saints, also headquartered in Salt Lake City. Alice Parker, 51, was a senior associate of JKL and a specialist in the church's international business and financial relationships. They were on their way to an important church fund-raiser in Hutchinson, Kansas, where Alice was the featured speaker. She was especially affective in her presentations to older couples, and widows in particular.

Earl had been a pilot for more than 20 years, and for the past eight years the proud owner of a Cessna 210. Although the 210 was elaborately equipped with a full IFR panel and a 3-axis autopilot, Earl was not an instrument pilot, because, "God meant for me to see where I'm going." He flew for sport, business, and church affairs, which he did at his own expense and in addition to his personal tithe to the church.

On the morning of the flight, Earl's early call to flight service left him troubled. Thunderstorms were predicted in Colorado and Kansas for most of the day and there was no way to get from Salt Lake City to anywhere near Hutchinson, Kansas, by commercial transport in time for the early evening fund-raiser. The 210 was it or they stayed home and disappointed more than 200 people who were looking forward to meeting and hearing Alice, who had recently returned from an extensive worldwide fact-finding trip.

Reluctantly, Earl reported the situation to Alice and also to Rupert Jones, the primary contact in Hutchinson, promising each of them an update in an hour and a half when the next forecast was due. Their chagrin was quite vocal, especially Rupert's—he had more than 100 phone calls to make if the event had to be called off.

The next briefing offered some hope. The thunderstorm area was moving eastward at only 20 knots and was probably traversable to the south. It would mean flying as much as 100 miles out of the way, turning the 4-hour trip into a 4.6-hour trip, but the 210 carried 5¼ hours of fuel, so their reserve was legal. And the 45-knot tailwind at 12,000 feet, which was figured in, could increase slightly when they were south of the storm area, the likely route they would take. Only two questions remained: One, would the movement of the storm stay the same? If not, the storm could reach Hutchinson before they did; two, would the tailwind remain at 45 knots or greater? Flight service gave Earl "a definite maybe" to both questions, leaning more toward "yes."

After his call to Alice telling her they would be leaving early, Earl called Rupert in Hutchinson and outlined his game plan: They would leave 2½ hours earlier than originally planned, fly the extra distance to go around the weather and then, depending on how fast the system moved eastward, land at either Hutchinson or Wichita. Rupert agreed to arrange ground transport back from Wichita, if necessary. And they were off.

Following a final weather check and a VFR flight plan filed with flight service, they took off on schedule, cruise climbed for 17 minutes and leveled off at 11,500 feet. Backing off to cruise power, Earl watched the airspeed climb and the ground speed on the DME reach 185, right on the nose. With a little luck from the weather, they'd be landing in Hutchinson in exactly 4 hours and 40 minutes. He leaned back, relaxed, and began a 45-minute conversation with Alice, talking about the fundraiser and the virtues of flying. There was nothing else to do. The autopilot was flying the 210 in the crystal blue Utah and Colorado sky.

Coming up southwest of Denver, Earl could see the towering clouds of the already-identified storm system way off in the distance. His call to flight watch was about as expected: The system was just reaching Dodge City, Kansas, 100 miles west of Hutchinson, and carried a convective SIGMET. The controller suggested diverting 50 miles south to Liberal, Kansas, because Dodge City was right at the southern tip of the system, which was moving southeast at 25. It had picked up some speed in the hour since Earl's last briefing.

Earl did some fast calculating: With 3:30 to go and the leading edge of the system moving at 25 knots, they would beat it to Hutchinson by at least half-an-hour. Close but safe. They also had an hour on top of that if they had to go to Wichita. He turned the 210 to a 105° heading for the southerly diversion to Liberal and resumed his conversation with Alice. It was turning out to be a smooth, pleasant and efficient flight.

Reaching Liberal with an hour or so to go, still at 11,500 feet and looking at the beautiful, billowing clouds at their 10–11 o'clock position, Earl called flight watch to hear the good news he was expecting. What he got was so-so. The storm had picked up some speed—to 30 knots—and was moving farther south than had been predicted. Its present track would bring it over Hutchinson in about an hour—and across his route of flight before then. The flight watch briefer also suggested a call to Kansas City Center on 126.95 for flight following and help in staying clear of the storm system, which was expanding and becoming more intense.

After calculating their remaining fuel at 1:40, Earl called Kansas City Center:

Earl "Kansas City Center, this is Cessna . . . .. We're 12 east of Liberal, squawking 1200.

Center ". . . This is Kansas City. Liberal altimeter is 29.75 inches and falling. Say your altitude and your request, sir."

Earl "Uh . . . .. We're a Cessna 210, sir. We're inbound to Hutchinson. Right now we're at 11,500 feet but I think we'll be going up some to stay above a build-up ahead."

Center "Cessna . . ., you're radar contact, 13 east of Liberal. The build-up in front of you is part of that big system you're looking at off to your left. Suggest you remain well south of it. Did you say you were inbound to Hutchinson?"

Earl "That's affirm, sir. After we get by this one little cloud area, we'll be starting down. Thanks for your help, sir."

Center ". . . The Vance One A MOA is hot. You'd need to descend below 10,000 or turn left to 060° to stay clear of it. When you get closer in toward Wichita, you can call the center on 118.35. They'll be able to give you a good reading on where the weather's at."

Earl "Okay, 118.5, got it. Thanks."

Center "That was one-one-eight point *three-five* . . . .. One eighteen *thirty-five*."

Earl "Uh . . . okay, 118.35. We got it." (Then, switching immediately to the new frequency, without signing off or waiting to get closer to Wichita, still 35 miles outside the new controller's coverage area.) "Uh . . . this is Cessna . . .. Wonder if you could give us an update on the storm situation? We're heading for Hutchinson."

Center (118.35) (Studying his scope, looking for a new target, not finding one.) "Cessna . . ., if you're coming from anywhere west, you'll have to come south to Anthony and swing up north from there. We're showing the leading edge of the system about 30 west of Hutchinson, moving fast and gaining strength. There's a SIGMET in effect calling for tops to 60,000, with golf-ball size hail and gale-force winds. No tornadoes associated with it yet, but they're definitely a possibility. Please say your location and your type aircraft, sir."

Earl "Uh . . . I think we're somewhere around Meade, but some clouds have moved in under us so I'm not real sure. We passed Liberal about 10 minutes ago. Uh . . ..we're going to have to climb to stay VFR. We've got a build-up in front of us. Thanks for your help, sir."

Center "If you're over Meade, sir, you're still outside my coverage area. I should be able to pick you up about 50 miles west of Anthony."

Earl "Uh . . . sir. Uh . . . I don't have Anthony on my map. Uh . . . Is that a VOR?"

Center "That's A-ffirm . . .. The Anthony VOR frequency is 112.9. That's one-twelve point niner. As soon as you start receiving it, I should be able to pick you up."

Earl "Uh . . . okay. We have 116.8 dialed up for Hutchinson and we're climbing now. The storm area is still well to our left. We should be able to go right over the clouds ahead, and it looks clear after that. I think we'll be okay holding the heading we're on. Uh . . ..We'll call you if we have a problem. Uh . . . thanks for your help."

Center "If you're coming in from Meade . . ., we're showing rapid buildup ahead of you around Pratt. Let us know when you see it. We'll appreciate a pilot report on it. That'll be about 75 miles or so from Meade, right on Victor 234."

Earl "Uh . . . Okay. We'll let you know . . . (garbled)."

The 210 climbed to 12,800 and barely cleared the puffs of clouds that were on its nose. A little dodging helped, too. The storm was definitely moving south, farther than Earl expected. Farther and faster than anyone expected. But they were still in the clear at 12,800, looking at pretty white clouds, enjoying the spectacular view and the smooth air. It was a wonderful feeling. Like being close to God.

For the next 20 minutes, the clouds settled down, and they were able to descend back to 11,500, heading straight for the Hutchinson VOR. The build-ups ahead weren't menacing. Just very harmless looking, almost enticing. Earl barely gave any thought to the fact that the tops of the clouds in front of them were climbing above the horizon. There were also several areas of blue sky in between, mostly to the south. He wasn't concerned. He and Alice were basking in the beauty of the clear blue sky and the clean white clouds ahead.

Ten minutes later, everything was not so clear, not so smooth, not so pretty, and not at all enticing. The clouds were all around and coming up under them; bouncing them; twisting them; jolting the 210 and its occupants. Earl had two thoughts at once: climb and turn south. The 210 responded immediately when he released the altitude hold, put back-pressure on the wheel, and increased the power. It was a good airplane. The turn south was started and stopped almost immediately as Earl realized that a giant and soaring cloud was blocking their escape route. Straight ahead was the only place to go.

Or back. So he thought as he did a quick 180°, only to find that they were in a valley of blue with clouds surrounding them, charging upward and closing up. And then coming up from directly beneath them. They were trapped. Another 180° put them back on course but heading directly toward a surging cloud. A turn to the right toward some blue helped a little, but only for a minute or so. It was a sucker hole. Another turn and they were in a cloud. It was instantly gray all around them.

Earl had no IFR training at all, except for an hour or so of instrument familiarization during his private pilot training. That was years ago. Since then, he avoided clouds and weather. This time he couldn't. He had gambled too far, ventured too close. They were in it, and he was helpless. The first updraft caught their left wing and threw the 210 up and to the right. Earl and Alice felt the shock as their bodies slammed against the cabin walls and ceiling and the control wheels, throwing the nose forward and the right wing farther down. Earl recovered momentarily and pulled himself and Alice off their wheels just in time for the next updraft to hurl the nose upward again—this time over the top—and throw the right wing into a spiral.

Kansas City Center radar recorded that an aircraft had made a spiraling dive from 11,900 feet until radar contact was lost, approximately 9 miles southeast of Pratt Municipal Airport. Two witnesses saw the aircraft spin out of the overcast and crash into the ground. They reported that the engine was running at high speed just before the crash.

ATC representative "Examination of all the tapes relating to this accident verify that the pilot had complete and accurate weather briefings from flight service, flight watch, and all of the center controllers he spoke to. (If he had) listened to them and done what they suggested—to stay well south of the system and then circle back to Hutchinson from the southeast—the accident wouldn't have happened.

"But the pilot acknowledged one thing and then did the opposite, or maybe just did what he had planned to do in the first place. He operated as if he had already made up his mind to everything and wasn't going to change it, no matter what. We see that every now and then. It's kind of like a macho attitude, but we get it from women, too. They call in real authoritative, trying to sound like airline pilots, trying to impress us and their passengers and half the time they don't know what the hell they're doing; they don't know what to ask for; they don't give us complete or correct information, which makes it hard for us to give them and everybody else proper service.

"I'd say the last conversations the pilot in this case had with our controllers followed that pattern. He asked for information and then ignored it completely, even telling the controllers he was going to [do so]. He never asked for flight following, which would have been provided (because) the traffic was light at the time. And he never called anyone after they got boxed in by the quickly rising clouds. At that point, a flight assist would have made the right decisions for the pilot and helped them get down and out of that stuff.

"The ground-based radar was painting clear pictures of the cells, which would have made it easy for the controller to keep them away from the heavier build-ups and, presumably, under control. A letdown with an autopilot is usually easy and their airplane had a good one. So, the odds were very high for a successful flight assist letdown and safe landing.

"But, of course, it never happened because the pilot never let anyone know they needed an assist. He never even asked for flight following, which he could have had long before they got anywhere near the storm area, and which would have kept them well clear of trouble.

"It might be, though, that the most damaging part of the whole episode came about when the pilot checked out of the first Kansas City frequency without telling the controller he was leaving. The controller had no idea he was off the frequency and didn't realize it until 15 or 20 minutes later when he tried to call him to tell him his position relative to the storm system—that he was getting too close and would be flying right into it on his present heading, but by then it was too late. They were already in trouble.

"The second controller—who he checked in with way too soon, long before they were anywhere close to his scope range—that poor

guy really had his hands full. After he told the pilot to head for Anthony, which the pilot acknowledged, by the way, the controller had
no way of knowing that they were instead heading direct Hutchinson
right into the leading edge of the storm system. (If he had) known
that—been able to see it on his scope—he would have advised them
accordingly and diverted the flight to safety. Presuming, of course,
that the pilot would have complied with the instructions he was
given, something he hadn't done up to that point. So, it's anybody's
guess as to whether or not anything could have been done by ATC or
anyone else to bring that flight to a successful conclusion.

"When all of the circumstances are as clear cut as they were in this
case, it isn't a question of whether or not this was a 'pilot error' accident. The only question left is how *many* errors did that pilot make?"

NTSB representative "With all the warnings pilots get about thunderstorms, you'd think they'd have the good sense to stay away from
them. Far away. This pilot gave that storm what he thought was about
20 miles of clearance distance that turned out to be none. The reason
for it is fairly simple: The leading edge of a thunderstorm is like the
razor-sharp blade of a saber. It charges in at low altitude and throws
the warmer air [that] it's displacing straight up. The faster the horizontal movement, the more violent is the upward movement of the
warmer air, and the more deceiving because by the time you can see
it as a cloud, it can be surrounding you with strong enough updrafts
to tear you and your airplane apart.

"There isn't much doubt that this was a 'pilot error' accident.
Those people shouldn't have been anywhere near the approaching
edge of a storm like that. And the pilot made a series of errors in both
procedures and judgment that put them there and left them with no
place to go and with no escape route. And at the worst possible altitude to deal with a speeding up, expanding thunderstorm. It's a wonder the airplane came down in one piece, that it didn't suffer a
catastrophic failure and lose its wings and tail when it hit what could
have been a 200 mile-an-hour vertical updraft. Staying in one piece
after encountering a violent force of that intensity is a profound testi-
monial to the structural integrity of the Cessna 210. Unfortunately, it
didn't do those two people any good.

"But think beyond the pilot and the (poor judgment) and some
other glaring faults come into focus. I'm referring to the fact that the
[weather reporting] system blew its call on the storm. That wasn't any
100-year phenomenon. Rapidly forming, high intensity storms happen
all the time in that part of the country. They're not all that easy to pre-

dict very far in advance, but once they get under way, they are *very* predictable. Especially when they start speeding up . . . and the storm those people encountered was definitely one of those. It should have been called for them at least an hour before it was. And they should have been taken around it with 50 miles or more to spare.

"Now every controller they talked to east of Denver had to know what the storm was doing—it was speeding up—and how bad it was going to get because it was speeding up, but not one word of real warning was issued by anyone. Instead of saying, 'Sir, that is a killer storm. Stay at least 50 miles away from it. Don't even think about going direct Hutchinson from your present position because you and your passenger will surely die if you do,' the pilot was advised to divert to the south so he could come up from the east and beat that monster into Hutchinson. 'Beat that monster into Hutchinson?' Hell, from where they were at the time, they could barely have beaten it into Wichita. Besides, trying to 'beat' those monsters into anywhere is like trying to outrun an avalanche on cross-country skis, or a high-speed train to a crossing on a bicycle. Even if by some miracle you win, you're still a loser because of the dumb risk you took.

"Then there was some questionable judgment on the part of both Kansas City Center controllers that compounded the errors the pilot was making. They should have known he was partially disoriented by the nature of their conversations with him. He didn't ask for flight following, but they never offered it either—not that they could have known that the pilot's first request for flight following had been turned down earlier in the flight, leaving him skeptical about being able to get it from any of the ATC frequencies that day. But, given all of the circumstances and the signals they were getting from the pilot, plus the fact that they had a VFR pilot who had already been in the air for over 3 hours, they should have insisted on providing flight following because by the things he was doing, they had to know immediately that he was making dangerous judgments.

"Understandably, ATC doesn't agree that their people did anything wrong. And they've got a mountain of tapes, transcripts and rule books on procedure to prove it. The trouble, though, is that while they didn't do anything wrong, they also didn't do everything they could have done to help that pilot—rule book or no rule book. And therein lies the problem. They could have saved those two people but they didn't. No, let me rephrase that: 'They *should* have saved those two people.' And having *not* done so is, in my way of thinking, a far bigger 'error' than any of the ones that pilot committed because they [ATC] knew what he was faced with, and he didn't. They knew exactly what the storm was doing and how bad it was going to get, but they never communicated that information to the pilot—at least not in terms that made him understand the seriousness of what he and his passenger were flying into. That it was definitely life-threatening.

"The official word on this accident is 'pilot error,' with references to VFR into IMC and spatial disorientation. But those are really symptomatic results of negligence by the system that failed to prevent those errors—the system that could have averted the tragedy but didn't. The pilot was a victim, not a perpetrator. He shouldn't have been expected to perform any better than he did by any of the experts he dealt with because he was on a VFR flight plan, wandering dangerously close to a killer storm. All of those experts knew that and should have taken steps to save their lives."

NASA representative "It amazes us when the real causes of an accident aren't even mentioned in the official findings, especially when they are classic, as they were in this case. I'm talking about human factors—several of them.

"The first one, of course, is lack of oxygen. They flew for 4 straight hours at 11,500 feet or higher without any supplemental oxygen. Using the most optimistic part of the blood oxygen saturation scales—because both the pilot and the passenger were from Salt Lake City, a relatively high-altitude area—the number you get is at or under 90 percent. That's low enough to guarantee some spatial disorientation, which was obvious if you took the time to listen to all of the tapes. The pilot's initial conversations were normal. His later ones were confused. The way he screwed up the frequency he was given for a handoff was typical of what we get in altitude chamber experiences—almost every time. Short-term memory loss and mixing up numbers are the first things to go as oxygen saturation levels decline.

"Then the instant, continuous spiral from almost 12,000 feet until impact. It indicates vertigo, the extreme form of spatial disorientation. Our guess would be that the pilot lost control on his first encounter with IMC, within a few seconds of entering a fast-building convective cloud. That would also be typical. Vertigo is sudden. It strikes without warning and hangs on like a pit bull. Until there's nothing left to hang onto. And its suddenness and persistence are directly relative to the pilot's blood oxygen saturation level, which in this case was quite low.

"A couple of other human factors must also have been involved. I say 'must have been' because we have no numbers on them like we do with oxygen and hypoxia. So we can't prove them. About the best we can do is speculate with some authority. I'm talking about the basic needs of the human body. The pilot was a man in his late 50s; the passenger was a woman in her early 50s. There was no indication in any of the reports that they were romantically involved. So when it came to the sensitive issue of bodily elimination, which most certainly had to be a problem for at least one of the people after 4 plus hours of isolation in an airplane cabin, we can only imagine the circumstances. Having to relieve oneself and not being able to do so because of socially driven embarrassment doesn't bring on spatial disorientation, but it can lead to lousy judgments and poor decision making. And in this case, there were plenty of both. So, our speculation is probably accurate.

"Finally, there's dehydration and lack of nourishment, neither of which are measurable or provable but we do know that both conditions, especially in combination, cause the brain and the body to function less efficiently. How much so is anybody's guess. In this case, probably a lot. For sure, enough to account for some of the things that went wrong with the pilot.

"What you have then is an accident officially caused by 'pilot error,' spatial disorientation, and a thunderstorm. But we know with absolute certainty that the causes behind the official causes were human factors. We can never tell what the outcome might have been without those human factors, but we do know for sure that the pilot could not have been as airworthy as he should have been or thought he was. And that puts the odds on the human factors."

Author comment The various government agencies almost never disagree officially about the cause or causes of an accident. Unofficially, it's a different story much of the time, but seldom are the disagreements by as much as they were in this accident. Their unofficial positions weren't even close.

It's a fascinating process in itself how they go about arriving at and then proving or justifying those positions. Take ATC for example. They did everything right—by the book. But the book was written by the FAA and the NTSB, who purport that ATC didn't do enough. That they should have known the pilot's mental and physical condition—from how he sounded and by what he did—and then taken more forceful action to provide proper options for safe passage. They didn't bother considering that the pilot might not have been *able* to respond to or comply with more forceful action, as NASA implies. But talk is cheap and when it's not part of an official report, talk doesn't go on the scorecard anyway.

This insight is informative, however, because it can reduce and prevent future accidents. Insights should be given a forum and careful, attentive consideration because they are coming from experts—real experts; the people who see and hear aviation accidents up close, firsthand; the people who haul away the wreckage and tend to the bodies—they know what they are talking about and the rest of us can learn from them.

About the only thing that seems to have been overlooked as a possible cause of this accident is the "gotta go" syndrome. That insidious self-compulsion that can be extremely dangerous in aviation. The pilot and his passenger had to be in Hutchinson in time for their fund-raiser; more than 200 people were waiting for them; to be late or not arrive was unthinkable. Besides, the pilot undoubtedly had made some assurances to his passenger and the contact in Hutchinson that his Cessna 210, piloted by himself, was just as reliable as commercial airline service between Salt Lake City and Hutchinson. Perhaps so, but not on that particular day.

24

Over the water
and into the trees

Preliminary report: May; Cessna 310; private pilot, single-engine land, 1,930 hours. On an IFR night flight from Bedford, Massachusetts, to Martha's Vineyard Island, the aircraft crashed into a single-family dwelling while attempting an approach to Martha's Vineyard Airport. The pilot and his passenger were killed. Although the pilot held neither a multi-engine nor an instrument rating, an IFR flight plan had been filed. Low instrument conditions prevailed at the time, and the flight service briefer informed the pilot that both his departure and destination airports were below IFR landing minimums. Postimpact fire destroyed the cabin and cockpit. Wreckage examination did not disclose any component failure or system malfunction.

Further investigation revealed:

- The pilot owned a finance company and recently acquired the 310 in a repossession swap. He took a total of 1½ hours of multi-engine instruction.
- After admitting to a flight instructor that he had flown several hundred hours on instruments, the pilot began taking formal instrument training because he was "fed up with the hassle of being illegal" and wanted more help from the system when he flew. But he was a disinterested student and withdrew from training after 17 hours of instruction. He discontinued the ground school portion of his instrument training after three sessions totalling 9 hours. His last instructor rated him "poor, probably incapable of ever flying instruments safely."
- The pilot's medical had a night flight prohibition due to repeated failures to identify numbers embedded in the color patterns on Ishihara cards. He was confirmed as color blind following a light gun test administered by the FAA.

- Prior to acquiring the 310, the pilot flew a Centurion for six years. He often bragged about filing IFR flight plans whenever it suited him because "flight service doesn't know its left hand from its right." He was also a champion hangar talker, topping all participants with his escapades, imagined if necessary.
- Unbeknown to the pilot, his wife had appealed in writing to the FAA to suspend his pilot's license. She said he was "irresponsible and dangerous to himself and others."
- When the IFR flight plan was filed, the closest legal alternate was Albany, New York, 113 miles from Bedford, and 163 miles from Martha's Vineyard—and against a 20-knot headwind. Even though the trip from Bedford to Martha's Vineyard was only 70 miles—about 25 minutes in the 310—the pilot accepted Albany.

Official conclusion: Deliberate VFR into IMC. Unauthorized night operation: license restricted. Illegal filing of IFR flight plan. Lack of multi-engine rating. Failure to maintain terrain clearance. Pilot error.

KNOWN AS A "MOVER AND A SHAKER," Buddy Polin—formerly Stanley Polinski—44, drove himself relentlessly but did most things with careless abandon. He flew the same way: always in a hurry and by his own rules. The FAA's rules were for "the other guys." He also enjoyed describing himself as a seat-of-the-pants pilot who could fly any airplane in any and all weather. By his own modest admission he was infinitely better than the system, a top gun who could handle anything.

The morning of the flight was typical for Buddy. He and a new employee, John Sutton, 26, were scheduled to meet a Boston banker at Bedford's Laurence G. Hanscom Field, just off the northwest beltway ringing Boston. From there they were going first to Waltham, then on to Lawrence, and finally finishing up at Lowell. After a wrap-up with the banker back at Hanscom, Buddy and John would fly back to Martha's Vineyard, where Buddy and his wife, Meg, resided from May 1 through September 30. John would spend the night—again—and he and Buddy would be off the next day for a series of meetings in New York, home for John and his new bride, Pattie, and Sunshine Finance, Inc., the company Buddy and his older brother, Vince, had taken over from their father 12 years ago. Buddy thrived on a break-neck schedule. It's what made him tick—and more than reasonably wealthy.

The disheartening weather report from flight service at 6:00 a.m. didn't phase Buddy. His company had recently repossessed a like-new, fully IFR equipped Cessna 310 that he was flying until the company decided whether to keep the 310 or Buddy's older and lesser equipped Cessna Centurion. With its 3-axis autopilot and top rated panel instrumentation, Buddy was sure he and the 310 could deal with anything the weathermen threw at them. No matter that the forecast was for very marginal VFR on the way to Hanscom, then turning to down-the-drain for the rest of the day. An occluded warm front would be coming through that could last until late the following evening; VFR was not recommended: IFR might not be possible for the trip back.

Buddy listened inattentively, didn't bother filing a flight plan, and declined impatiently when the briefer offered weather data for several nearby cities—"just in case." His next call was to the airport to get the 310 ready—the Centurion would stay in the hangar—after which he told John to "hustle up" and his wife to "step on the gas in the kitchen." The rush was on!

Their flight to Bedford/Hanscom was routine for Buddy—it would have been a thriller for most other pilots. They were marginal or much less all the way, but Buddy was an old hand at scud running; 750 feet agl over a highly populated, high-density air traffic area was duck soup for him. He never even bothered to turn off his Mode C, the altitude reporting function on the 310's transponder. He just let the controllers fret over having an "unidentified" flying all over their approach and departure routes. Creating havoc was something else Buddy relished.

Back at Hanscom Field at 6:30 p.m. after their day of meetings on the fly, Buddy left John and the banker in the terminal restaurant while he went to the phone to call flight service. The news was terrible, as he knew it would be from their drive to the airport. The occluded front had moved into the area and slowed to a crawl. It could be there for the next 36–48 hours. Everything in southern New England, especially the Cape Cod area, was at or below IFR minimums. Hanscom was reporting sky obscured and ⅜ of a mile. Martha's Vineyard was worse, under ¼-mile visibility in dense fog.

Buddy was undaunted. He told the briefer they would leave after dinner, at 8 p.m., but he wanted to file his IFR flight plan then—"to get it in without a hassle." He said he would call back just before departure time for a final weather briefing, and that a go-no-go decision would be made then.

The briefer checked every airport in New England in search of an alternate while Buddy kept insisting that anything close to legal would do for him. Finally, the briefer spotted Albany, New York, on the back side of the weather system. But it was more than 160 nautical miles the wrong way from Martha's Vineyard and about 113 nautical miles from Hanscom, an awfully tough alternate for a 71-mile flight. But Buddy accepted it without protest or further discussion. He had already made up his mind that he really didn't need an alternate. And, even if he did, it wouldn't be as far away as Albany. He could always find something closer by, legal or otherwise. After all, what does a nonpilot briefer know about the real world of flying anyway?

Finishing their leisurely meal on Buddy's schedule—less than an hour—the banker departed and the pilot and passenger prepared to do the same. Buddy didn't bother calling flight service for a final briefing. He knew what they were going to tell him by looking out the window—the visibility couldn't have been more than ¼ mile. Besides, he had made up his mind long ago: He and John would be spending the night in Martha's Vineyard.

With the 310's engines started and running smoothly, Buddy called clearance delivery for his flight plan and got some better news: There had been a couple of PIREPs stating that tops of the ground fog were at 1,500 feet msl and there was good visibility in the moonlight between 1,500 and 8,000 feet. Satisfied with his decision to not let the dire forecasts from flight service talk him out of making the trip, Buddy began rolling the 310 toward the taxiway as the controller read their clearance: "As filed, maintain 2,000, Hanscom Five Departure, departure is 124.4 and squawk 2535." There was no need to write anything down. Buddy had been to Hanscom Field many times. He knew the routine well.

Taxiing out, Buddy did a rolling mag check, his usual procedure before any takeoff after the first one of the day, and switched to the tower frequency, reporting that the 310 was ready to go. That was the extent of his pretakeoff runup, about as brief as his preflight inspection, which amounted to nothing more than checking the oil. Buddy had oceans of confidence in line crews, mechanics, and airplane manufacturers. He was sure they were as concerned as he was about his safety. In his case, he was probably right.

Off the ground from Runway 23, Buddy engaged the preset autopilot before he retracted the 310's gear. He was glad he did because they were IMC as they felt the wheels lock in their wells. He adjusted the rate of climb, pulled the power back to cruise climb, signed off with the tower and called departure control. So far, nice 'n easy.

Fifteen minutes later, Buddy was listening to the ATIS at Martha's Vineyard Airport: "Indefinite ceiling, visibility ½ mile or less. Temperature 54°. Dewpoint 54°. Altimeter 29.66 and steady. Wind calm. ILS

24 approach in use. Landing and departing Runway 24. Advise on initial contact that you have information Uniform."

When approach control answered his check-in call, Buddy had already begun their descent to 1,500 feet, the instructions he knew were coming. The controller noticed the early letdown and gave Buddy a vector to CHOPY, the initial approach fix. But Buddy rejected that, requesting instead a heading direct to BORST, the outer marker. His plan was simple: He would try one ILS approach; if that didn't work, he would circle back, cancel IFR and scud run back in from over Nantucket Sound. That way he could go as low as 100 feet above the water and find the airport from 10 or 20 feet higher than treetop level after making land contact. It wasn't legal; it wasn't safe; it wasn't smart, but Buddy had done it many times—mostly in daylight.

Using the autopilot coupler to turn onto the ILS 24 localizer, the 310 bumped slightly as it reached BORST and intercepted the glideslope. Buddy told John to look out his side window and let him know when he saw the ground or the runway. He stayed on the gauges until the altimeter read 250 feet, a few feet lower than the MDA. John saw and said nothing as Buddy leveled off, sneaked a peak himself, and then initiated a missed approach.

The controller asked Buddy if they wanted to try again and was surprised when Buddy told him they wanted to cancel IFR. He was even more surprised, and concerned, when the 310 circled back toward CHOPY, began what was apparently a 180° turn and disappeared from his scope. Buddy had climbed to 800 feet and turned the 310 toward Nantucket Sound. Upon reaching the 12-mile point from the Martha's Vineyard VOR, he began a turn back toward the airport and, at the same time, began a descent to just above the water. The controller's scope lost the 310 as they descended below 300 feet.

With his landing lights on, Buddy found the water. He had no way of judging exactly how high they were because he seldom did his scud running landing routine at night, but it looked different than usual, maybe a tad lower. If he had checked his altimeter, he would have known that they were just under 50 feet above the water. That was the altitude as determined by the accident investigators who calculated the first impact point in the trees nearest to the shoreline.

The 310 cut a swath through the trees about 650 feet long until it crashed into a tree and a house. An elderly couple in the single family dwelling suffered minor but traumatic injuries as the 310 tore into their home and burst into flames. They were luckier than the pilot and his passenger who both perished in the conflagration. The 310 and the home were beyond repair.

Margaret "Meg" Polin Wolinski "I knew Buddy and John had gone down less than 15 minutes after it happened. The tower knew they were on the approach somewhere out over the water when they lost track of them. They thought they went down about 10 or 12 miles out in the Sound. But a police report came in right after the airplane hit the Powell's house, out by the beach, and they knew it was Buddy. They called me from the airport right away.

"We lived only a mile from there, so I drove over and saw the mess. It was horrible. The house was burning. You couldn't even make out that an airplane was there, burning up like everything was. I talked to Sam and Dotty Powell, just before the ambulance took them to the hospital, but they were shaking so bad they hardly made sense. It was a terrible experience for them. They'll never be the same. But then again, who would be?

"It all happened so fast, I can't remember if I was surprised or not at the time. Buddy took so many chances in his airplanes that I had kind of resigned myself to expect the worst. In my mind it wasn't a matter of 'if' it was going to happen, it was 'when.' I was so sure of it that I wrote to the FAA asking for their help to save Buddy before he killed himself, and maybe others.

"I knew he shouldn't have been flying the airplane they repossessed, but it was the same as the way he used to brag about how he could always beat the weather. How chicken everybody else was about it. How the weather people had their heads in the sand and didn't know what they were talking about, scaring the daylights out of half the pilots they were supposed to be serving. Intimidating everybody to the point where most pilots were afraid of weather.

"He was dead wrong in his own attitude, of course, but there was never any talking to him about it. That's why I finally wrote the letter. I was desperate. The people at the airport couldn't—or wouldn't help. Buddy was too good a customer for them to want to slow him down. And the FAA people up in the Bedford regional office couldn't do anything about it, even though I told them the way Buddy was about flying and the chances he took. All they did was tell me where to write in Washington.

"You know, it was funny. The day of the funeral, Buddy got a letter from the government advising him . . . .. Can you imagine that? *Advising* him . . . .. that his license would be in jeopardy if he continued breaking the rules. There was a circular enclosed with some of the rules in it. But that was the last I ever heard about it. They never answered my letter. Just the dumb advisory they sent to Buddy. As if a letter was going to slow down a lunatic like him.

"It's just a shame he had to take a sweet young boy like John along with him. And just very lucky that Sam and Dotty got scared half to death instead of being burned to death. It could have been worse, but they'll never be the same.

"You know, it shouldn't be that way. People like Buddy spoil a good thing for everyone. There should be some rule or some way to stop people like him. To keep them on the ground and not flying over people's houses in machines they can't handle because those machines are lethal weapons when pilots like Buddy fly them."

George Hayden, flight instructor "Actually, I was Buddy Polin's second instructor. He had started working on his instrument ticket with Ralph Squires, a free-lancer who works out of New Bedford. A very good instructor, by the way. Anyway, I found out after the accident that Buddy had given Ralph such a bad time that he refused to fly with him anymore. He told me Buddy needed much more discipline and was dangerous without it.

"Here at Hyannis, we're a real flight school, with a set program for IFR training. We've got a simulator, full ground school, and a complete video course for our students.

"But Buddy wasn't interested in any of that. He just wanted to fly and shoot his mouth off about how poor the system was—overly cautious and too slow to be efficient, at least for him—and about his various escapades, most of which sounded like BS to me. Man, could he tell stories!

"As you've probably guessed, Buddy didn't do very well here either. He hated regimentation and following rules and that's what this place is all about: following rules and regimentation. We teach flying discipline as well as flying skills. We insist that our graduates know how to use an airplane safely as well as fly it. So Buddy's attitude just didn't fit in here—not with me or with the school. He was going to do it his way or not at all and after he had taken about 12 total hours of instruction, we both decided to call it quits—with plenty of hard feelings because I told him he was an accident waiting to happen, plus a few other warnings and observations about his overall approach to flying. In other words, I told him he was a jerk who was going to kill himself in an airplane.

"But he never listened to anything I said. As a matter of fact, on the day he quit, the weather was turning bad and he was flying back out to Martha's Vineyard, where he lived and kept his Centurion. Well, I could hardly believe it when he picked up the phone right in the flight lounge and called in an IFR flight plan. I got mad when I heard that, so I called flight service myself and told them he wasn't an instrument pilot, that he had just been dumped out of here, and that they should refuse to let him take off. I was dumbfounded when the briefer told me flight service couldn't do that, couldn't stop him from filing the IFR, and couldn't tell the tower not to clear him for takeoff.

"Then I got even madder. After all, he was a danger to me and all of the other responsible pilots who flew out of Hyannis. I didn't give a hoot if he killed himself. Hell, I didn't like him anyway but I sure didn't want him out there getting his kicks and killing somebody else. So, I called the police. And do you know what they said? They said it was an FAA matter. That they had no jurisdiction on an airport. That they couldn't arrest him, even if he was flying without a medical, without a license, or even dead drunk. Can you imagine that? I'm still flabbergasted over it.

"The more I checked up on it, though, the more I found out how true it is. I think it's just total irresponsibility on the part of the government and the whole FAA system. No wonder the public thinks we're all a bunch of nuts and scared silly that we're going to fly our little airplanes into their houses the way Buddy did.

"You know, it isn't nice to say, but I'm glad Buddy Polin is dead. People like him make conscientious pilots look bad. And they hurt general aviation. He deserved to die—by himself. I'm sorry for the passenger he killed. Probably had no idea what a ding-dong pilot Buddy was. I'm also glad the house he crashed into didn't turn up any dead bodies after it burned to the ground. That would have turned half this area into wanting to get rid of us.

"Which makes me madder than ever at the FAA and all the government do-nothings who can't keep the Buddy Polins out of the sky. By the time they wake up and make some decent, enforceable rules, the public will have shut us down—and deservedly so because they're entitled to the assurance that every pilot who's flying over their heads is competent, responsible, and safe. Right now that applies to most of us, but not all of us. And that ain't good enough!"

FAA accident prevention program specialist "Accident circumstances like this give everyone fits because the FAA and every other government agency hasn't figured out how to stop suicide, or murder/suicide like it was in this case. When you think about it, it isn't much different than when some maniac gets mad at an ex-employer, buys a gun at any sporting goods store and blows away half the company. Without elaborating, you know what the National Rifle Association has to say about that, something like 'guns don't kill, people do.'

"Well, we have a similar situation in general aviation. Our NRA is the AOPA, an organization that supposedly promotes safety but fights every rule change, every attempt at enforcement and anything that threatens uncontrolled access to the skies by their members. That also goes for nearly every FBO, supplier, and pilot in general aviation. They all cry out for us to clear the skies of irresponsible, untrained pilots, but as soon as we take the first step to do that, they're all over us complaining that this is America and we have no right to take away their precious freedom.

"If you think it's easy living with that, forget it. Most of us in the FAA would like to put some real teeth in the rules and regulations we already have and implement several new systems we know will be great improvements. Like TCAs [Class B airspace]. It took years to put them in place because of all the opposition we ran into. But look what they've done for safety around our major airports. And then try to remember how ridiculous it was before we had TCAs—with 150s and 747s practically shaking hands with each other because there were no altitude restrictions.

"When things in general aviation finally get bad enough, and I think they will pretty soon, maybe all of the forces—and I'm talking about *all* of the forces, not just the government—will be willing to work together and address some of these very glaring deficiencies in the systems. We can't do it by ourselves because nobody will let us, but we'd sure love to be given the opportunity to try. It could be the rebirth of this industry."

ATC representative "Accidents like this one damage the credibility of every part of ATC because the public has a preconceived notion that it's our job to protect them from these nut cases who tear up the landscape. I think they honestly believe we can reach up and pull some of these pilots down before they cause the mayhem they do.

"What they don't realize is how hard we try to do just that and, at the same time, how helpless we actually are. This doozie of a set of circumstances is a perfect case in point. The flight service briefer he spoke to in Bedford gave the pilot a complete briefing, and I mean complete. He didn't pull any punches. He told him both airports were below IFR minimums. Then he spent a good 5 minutes looking for an alternate and came up with only Albany, completely unacceptable to anyone but a fruitcake or a daredevil who didn't care what he got because he wasn't going to use it anyway. I think the latter pretty much describes this pilot.

"Then after all of the discouragement the briefer could muster, the pilot told him to go ahead and enter an IFR flight plan for a flight from one below-minimum airport to another. Believe me, that wasn't something he relished doing, but he had no choice. Our briefers don't make those decisions, pilots do—right or wrong, smart or dumb, safe or deadly. They call their own shots. We only take orders.

"The tower operator had the same problem. He is not allowed to deny permission to take off unless the airport is below takeoff minimums. Landing minimums have nothing to do with it and Hanscom Field was above takeoff minimums when the 310 departed. The tower also is not allowed to deny takeoff clearance even if the controller knows that the destination airport has been blown away and isn't there anymore. That isn't within the realm of the controller's discretion or authority.

"The same thing goes for the approach controller at Martha's Vineyard. He knew the field was below IFR minimums from where he was making his observation, but he couldn't know for sure what the pilot could see. The rule says that the pilot has the right to try the approach no matter what the ground observations are, unless the field is equipped with RVR measuring equipment, which was not the case at Martha's Vineyard. It is then the pilot's responsibility to execute a missed approach if the airport is not in sight at the MDA and that's exactly what happened. The pilot tried the approach, couldn't sight the airport and started to make a missed approach. Perfectly normal procedure.

"But then he shocked the controller by canceling IFR. Now at that point, the controller knew for sure that the pilot couldn't have been in VFR conditions. Everything within a 100 miles in all directions was socked in. But again, the controller was completely helpless to object or do anything about it. His only option at that moment was to turn off his scope—or walk away from it—so he wouldn't have to watch them drop off his radar and into the drink or the trees. He chose to watch, hoping the pilot might change his mind and head for his alternate, or at least not be crazy enough to try to scud run in, as he had seen many of them do, but not in conditions as bad as he knew they were that night.

"(Situations that are similar to what) I just described make controllers wish they had ray guns and skyhooks to zap some of those clowns out of the sky. Short of that, I can tell you this: It would help a lot if (controllers) could turn N numbers over to the state or local police and have them arrested as soon as they landed—later would be okay, too. Just so they didn't get away with the cheating they do, snubbing their noses at the system, endangering their own and everybody else's lives and giving general aviation a black eye. In other words: Give us the tools and the rules to do our job and we'll keep the skies squeaky clean. We'll also save lots of lives in the process."

NTSB representative "Although it certainly looked like it, there wasn't anything turned up in the investigation that indicated the pilot was in any way suicidal. Impetuous, rash, a swaggering braggart, compulsive, disrespectful, irresponsible: All of those describe him appropriately. He was the worst possible kind of pilot flying in the worst possible conditions. But you know what? He almost got away with it.

"That's the frightening part. If he *had* survived, he undoubtedly would have entertained the whole airport for months to come, encouraging other pilots like himself to defy the system and do it his way. Putting themselves in greater danger until, like him, they eventually piled in and killed themselves.

"Don't scoff at that last part because it happens all the time. We investigate many fatal accidents every year where compulsive, high-powered businessmen followed the lead of another crazy just like themselves . . .. They seem to conform to a similar pattern: The more high-powered they are, the more impatient and careless they are, the more susceptible they are and the more likely they are to have an accident.

"But however these circumstances came into play, this was indeed a pilot error accident. It was aggravated by lousy judgment, terrible weather and a lying, cheating, untrained pilot who thought he was God. But it was a 'pilot error' accident, nevertheless. And that's how it belongs in the record book.

"With that decided, I'd like to make a side comment about this and similar accidents: Just like you'll never keep every drunk off the highways, you'll never achieve anything close to perfection in keeping lunatic pilots out of the sky either. No matter how hard you try, you don't ever get them all. So then, it's really just a matter of deciding how many deaths are acceptable.

"I realize that's a hard-nosed, callous way of looking at a very sensitive issue because the goal is zero deaths and zero danger to people on the ground. I also realize that we can do a whole lot better and a whole lot more about it than we're doing now, but I've been with the FAA and the NTSB for a long time and I know a little about how these things are dealt with and how much chance there is that any real change will take place.

"The usual procedure, if you want to call it that, is to shuffle new ideas around, or stonewall them altogether, until the hue and cry for change dies down. But if for some unusual reason it doesn't die down—which is very unlikely—then you go through the motions of seeking guidance and resources from the Department of Transportation to make the improvements you know are needed. Be assured, however, that nothing of any substance will ever come of it because it never has and never will until the public decides it's worth doing something concrete to save a few hundred lives every year.

"Right now, the public seems to enjoy the headlines about pilots killing themselves. For sure the media does. But if and when the prevailing public attitude ever acknowledges the value of general aviation—that it is a real transportation system, and not just for rich people who like boring holes in the sky—then there is a chance that some positive steps will be taken. I hope so and I hope I live long enough to see some of them."

Author comment This accident was not incorrectly classified. Pilot error was evident. But the accident was not *completely* classified because many other factors contributed to it in major ways.

The lack of federal, state, and local enforcement of aviation rules and regulations is appalling. No other human activity is treated with such indifference in this country. This pilot had *no* multi-engine rating, *no* instrument rating, and he was *not* qualified to fly at night. Yet the system allowed him to file an IFR flight plan and take off in a multi-engine airplane at night.

This happened for two reasons: First, the parts of the system that dealt directly with the pilot had no idea that he was lacking the appropriate ratings and the medical clearance for the flight he was undertaking. Second, even if they had known, the briefers and controllers had no authority to intercede and prevent the flight.

Then there are the law enforcement agencies, all of whom claim lack of jurisdiction—it's always somebody else's turf. If the pilot had been hauling a planeload of pot, an army of state and local policemen, the narc squad, and the FBI all would have been there with reinforcements. But, absent a controlled substance or contraband of some sort, the police would not even have asked the pilot to show them his pilot's license or his medical certificate, both of which he was required *by law* to carry, and not even if they had been asked to do so by the briefers, the controllers, or even the pilot's wife.

Think about that a moment. A planeload of pot or stolen goods is typically not an immediate threat to anyone, but an airplane in the hands of an incompetent pilot is lethal and dangerous to anyone it flies near or over. A person driving a car without a valid driver's license can be arrested, but a pilot is not even required to present the certificate to any state or local police officer. A drunk driver can be forced to take a breath-o-lizer test and can be restrained from operating a car or truck. But in most states, a drunken pilot cannot be legally stopped by anyone.

The risks he took in his airplane—flying without proper licenses and ratings and ignoring a medical restriction—Buddy Polin would not have taken in his car because he would have been in trouble with the law if he had been caught driving without a valid driver's license, or driving at night with a medical restriction because he was color blind. He never did either.

General aviation gave him a free and untethered opportunity to exploit authority, but Buddy and his unfortunate passenger paid with their lives—it wasn't entirely free. The rest of us are also paying for Buddy's exploits and so is the system that let him kill himself. It was one more costly setback for general aviation.

25

Top secret wires

Preliminary report: May; Beech V35C Bonanza, private pilot, airplane single-engine land, instrument rating, 2,160 hours. The aircraft was destroyed and the pilot and his two passengers were killed during a night approach to the Barstow-Daggett Airport in Barstow, California. The flight was returning to its home base after an extended six-day trip. During that time, military electric transmission lines, spanning two hills and rising 385 feet agl, were installed crossing an east-west interstate highway 7½ miles east of the airport. Local pilots reported that when clouds or fog covered the airport, common practice was to fly outbound from the Daggett VOR on a 060° heading, descend until ground contact was made and then reverse course following the interstate to the airport. The main wreckage was found 400 yards west of the lines on the north side of the highway. A large section of the left wing was found directly under the lines. Ground witnesses stated the sky was overcast and estimated the ceiling at 300–400 feet at the time of the accident.

Further investigation revealed:

- As soon as the power lines were installed, 4 days prior to the accident, notices were sent to Barstow-Daggett and another airport in the area. Until the day of the installation, no one at either airport or the Riverside Flight Service Station knew about the planned power line installation.

- The FAA had been notified of the plans to install the new transmission lines, connecting the Marine Corps Training Center and the Goldstone Deep Space Tracking Station, but start and completion dates had not been finalized at the time of the notification. As a result, no NOTAM was issued, nor were any charts modified to indicate the location or the height of the lines until after the accident.

- There were no markers or lights on either the wires crossing the highway or the towers on either side at the time of the accident. Markers and lights were installed several days later.

- Originating as an IFR flight from San Jose International Airport, IFR was canceled by the pilot after a missed approach into Barstow-Daggett Airport. The flight then continued VFR until the aircraft struck the wires.
- Both passengers were instrument rated pilots. All three occupants of the airplane had flown approaches into the Barstow-Daggett Airport many times, VFR and IFR.
- Because the lines were more than 7 miles from the nearest airport, and less than 500 feet agl, they were not at first deemed an obstruction by the FAA. The designation was changed as a result of the accident investigation.

Official conclusion: VMC into IMC. Failure to maintain terrain and obstruction clearance. Pilot error.

SYSTEMS, LTD. was a computer/electronics design boutique nestled in Barstow, California, 50 miles east of Edwards Air Force Base. It was far away from but intimately tied to the Silicon Valley south of San Francisco and doing business with the major aerospace and computer hardware manufacturers on the West Coast. Three of the Systems, Ltd. partners had left on an extended trip in the company's Bonanza, which took them to Seattle and San Jose over a six-day period. Late Friday night, they were returning home to Barstow on an IFR flight plan. The weather, which had just moved into the area, was lousy—unusual for midsummer in that part of the country.

Phil Hendricks, 51, was the pilot on the final leg of the long trip. David Burns, 39, had flown the Seattle leg nearly a week ago. And Carol Harding, 37, had flown from Seattle to San Jose. They had departed from San Jose International Airport at 8:30 p.m., flown for just less than 2 hours at 13,000 feet—with oxygen—and were approaching the BASAL intersection and V-394, their last 18-mile run to the Daggett VOR for the approach into Barstow-Daggett Airport. Their letdown to the 5,000-foot approach altitude was routine, and ATC had cooperated nicely by giving them a convenient vector to a point 5 miles northeast of the VOR. No procedure turn would be necessary from there for the VOR-22 approach. Nice and easy.

Only two small problems: The weather at the airport was 400 and 2½. But the lowest MDA on the approach was 1,243 feet agl—no way that was going to work. They knew it before they began the approach and they weren't surprised or disappointed—it was standard operating procedure for the home folks at Barstow-Daggett. The airport had an unusually high MDA. So an off-the-record procedure had been worked out by most of the local pilots.

It was fairly simple and relatively safe. Done precisely, it was completely safe. The instrument pilots would fly the VOR-22 approach one time—to keep the FAA happy and not wanting to discontinue the impractical approach altogether—miss it, and cancel IFR on the way back to the VOR. They would then descend, passing Daggett VOR on a 060° heading until they were able to make ground contact and find Interstate 15, which would be directly under them. A 180° turn and 350 feet or so over the highway led right back to the airport and a safe landing on either runway. If they reached 2,250 msl, or 300 feet agl, over the interstate and still had no ground contact, they would immediately divert to an alternate. There was never a second try on the "Barstow-Daggett I-15 Scud Run Approach."

The VFR pilots had an equally practical plan. They would find the interstate from either side of the airport and track it in. They would then overfly the field and follow the highway eastbound for a mile or so, then turn back and land on Runway 22 or Runway 26. If they began losing ground contact, some of them had been known to track the interstate as low as 50 feet agl. No one ever verified that except the few who actually landed on the roadway. Fortunately, not very often. And even more fortunately, not recently because the weather had been excellent for the past two weeks until just before sundown— there had been no need for anyone to shoot the illegal approach.

The military had installed a new electric transmission system linking the Marine Corp Training Center and the Goldstone Deep Space Tracking Station, but the installation went unannounced until it was completed late the prior Monday. Everyone who read the bulletin board at the airport found out about it a few hours before the Corp of Engineers strung eight high-tension wires across I-15 7½ miles east of Barstow-Daggett Airport. The travelers from Systems, Ltd., had no idea the wires were there because they departed two days prior to installation. They were also going to be the first to try a real IFR approach into the airport in two weeks.

Phil brought the Bonanza across the VOR perfectly at 5,000 feet, turned to a 223° heading and started down to 3,500. They flew the approach precisely, reached the MDA and the MAP at almost the same time and declared the miss. Neither Phil nor Carol, who was flying right seat, had seen a thing.

Halfway back to the VOR, Phil canceled the IFR flight plan and told the controller they would be able to maintain VFR because they had just come under the overcast. The controller almost laughed, knowing the Bonanza would fly back over the VOR and outbound on the familiar 060° heading. He himself had flown to Barstow-Daggett many times and knew the routine well. But he didn't know about the wires that were stretched across the interstate 7½ miles out.

Descending quickly after station passage, Phil brought the Bonanza down to 2,400 feet msl and broke out of the overcast, 8 miles east of the VOR, which was 19.6 miles from the airport. With Carol confirming the highway and the rolling terrain beneath them, he made a swing to the right and then a left turn back to a heading of 220°, lining up on the highway for the 21 miles back to the airport.

Heading inbound, the Bonanza was in and out of the clouds, brushing the bases of the overcast. Phil lowered the nose to stay in the clear and keep the highway in sight. Finally able to level off at 2,300 feet, he remained partially on the gauges, letting Carol maintain the primary contact with the highway. At 385 feet agl, it was a joyride. They could see 5 miles down the roadway.

At the 10-mile point—right over a familiar exit ramp on the interstate—Carol verified their position. She picked up the mike, quickly dialed in 123.0, the unicom frequency at the airport, and announced that the Bonanza was 10 miles straight-in for Runway 22. A minute later, Phil reduced the power and put in 10° of flap to slow the airplane down to approach speed and he held their altitude at 2,300 on the altimeter, exactly 385 feet agl.

Unfortunately, that was the perfect altitude to encounter the wires. Twenty feet up or down and they would have found out about them after they had landed safely. As it was, they never did know that two steel-coiled high-tension wires sliced off a 5-foot section of the left wing as the Bonanza flew by at 100 knots. It happened so fast, it's more than likely that the aircraft tumbled and was thrown to the ground and the occupants died instantly. They died because they were so precise and so good at what they were doing; it's usually the other way around.

Barstow-Daggett Airport FBO representative "We've been trying to get those wires removed ever since they went up, but it's worse than fighting city hall. Between the Marine Corps, the FAA, the Department of Defense, and NASA, we can't even find out whose jurisdiction they come under. About the best we could get was bigger ball markers on the wires and strobes on the towers. And that took almost a year.

"Losing those three people from Systems, Ltd., took a lot of the wind out of everybody's sails around here. They were just getting ready to buy another airplane—a twin—and expand their operations here in Barstow. But with Hendricks and Harding out of the picture, it was like somebody put the brakes on. They were apparently the top designers in the operating unit and, without them, Systems, Ltd. had no other core people to build around. We're just happy they still base one airplane with us—another Bonanza the insurance company bought them.

"But that was only the half of it. We've had a major problem with all of our operations because those wires have made it a whole lot more dangerous for our pilots to do their special VFR thing. That's what it is, by the way, a special VFR. We're in uncontrolled airspace out here in the desert, so a mile and clear of clouds is legal VFR. When the field goes IFR, all the IFRs usually cancel and come in VFR. It's more efficient; I won't bore you with the details, but it is. They use the highway instead of the VOR approach, and it works better. It used to be safer, too, until they put up those wires.

"After the accident, we got asked a lot of questions by the Systems, Ltd., lawyers about how and when we were notified that the wires were being installed. It was the same day they strung them. Can you imagine that? No prior notice. No opportunity for us to discuss safety. No one to even talk about it with. They just wiped out three of the best people in this town and—poof—nothing. Like it never happened. And then they had the nerve to call it a 'pilot error' accident. None of us could believe it.

"But we're not through trying. We got the markers and the strobes. And we got the approach plate corrected so pilots outside the area are alerted. And flight service always issues a special warning. So, everybody locally is cooperating. It's the guys in charge we can't seem to reach, but we will. We'll do it for Systems, Ltd.; they're still our best customer. And we'll do it for the rest of our pilots, too. They deserve a safe environment to fly in."

Riverside Flight Service representative "You happen to be talking to the guy who was on duty that night, so I can tell you exactly what happened. I didn't actually see them go down, but I know what they did, because it used to be the standard approach procedure at Barstow-Daggett before those wires went in.

"It's desert out there so they don't get socked in very often. When they do, the VOR approach they have isn't worth much because it has one of the highest MDAs in the country and almost never gets anybody down to the runway. So most of the pilots based there had their own procedure. They'd fly either over the airport or the VOR, depending on how low the ceiling was. If it was real low, they'd go to the VOR, head out along where they knew the highway was right under them—about a 60° heading, if I'm remembering it right—and let down until they found it. Then they'd just turn back around and follow it on in to the airport. It used to be pretty clear out that way, without too many high-up things to run into. Not any more, of course.

"In better weather, they'd fly directly over the airport and then follow the highway east for a mile or so. It was then a left or right 180° for either runway. That's still okay, but it's strictly for the locals because of those wires. If you don't know the terrain real well, it's just too risky to venture too far out that way. Those lines cross the highway about 7 or 8 miles from the airport.

"When the Bonanza pilot called in, it was pretty late. I think about 11 p.m. or maybe later. He said he was going to shoot the VOR, but I knew what he meant to do. He'd shoot one try, miss it and go right to the 'I-15 Approach' that's what they used to call it. The ceiling was about 400 over that night, so I knew the scud run would work and I just forgot about them. About 45 minutes later I heard they had gone down. That's when I also heard about the wires for the first time.

"The FAA investigators were all over this place the next day, looking through all of our bulletins and NOTAMs. But we didn't have a thing on those wires. They were military, so whoever was in charge must have figured it was none of our civilian business. Besides, they crossed the interstate more than 7 miles east of the airport. Technically, that was legal but you'd sure think someone would have used some common sense and realized that something almost 400 feet high could be a problem for the nearby airports.

"They didn't, and three people were killed because of it. Since then, they put up lights and ball markers, and we've had a permanent NOTAM on it. It solved the problem. There hasn't been another accident there. But I'm sure the pilots at Barstow-Daggett are still plenty upset over it. They've lost a lot of their flexibility.

"I've heard that after the investigation was completed, they slapped a 'pilot error' primary cause on the accident. I'm probably not supposed to say anything but I have to tell you, that was the biggest pile of hogwash I'd ever heard in my life. That pilot never did anything wrong. When he canceled his IFR, as far as I knew, he was legal—a mile of visibility and clear of the clouds. And nobody can prove different. So saying that running into those wires—that he didn't know about—was 'pilot error' is just nonsense.

"I also found out afterward that they hadn't bothered marking or lighting the wires when they were first strung. Now tell me, how was that pilot supposed to see them on an overcast dark night like that one was. Not possible.

"No. This was no 'pilot error' accident, and I don't care who says it was. It was FAA error, if it was anybody's error, for having a dumb rule that allows a 400-foot set of wires to be strung right across a runway approach within 10 miles of an airport without telling anybody about it. That is really dumb, deadly, and dangerous.

"But what really galls me is that the rule hasn't been changed or, as far as I know, even been looked at. They just labeled the accident 'pilot error' and closed the book on the whole business. That hurts because I still feel like I was a part of the accident. That I could have saved those people if I'd just known about the wires. If somebody had used just one ounce of brain power and issued a simple notice. What would have been so difficult about that?"

FAA representative "There isn't any excuse at all for what happened in Barstow-Daggett that night. The pilot was technically responsible to visually avoid all objects and obstructions in his flight path. That's what VFR means: visual flight rules. But let's get real. How do you avoid something you can't see? And shouldn't be expected to see? That's (the first issue).

"(The second issue) is more complicated. It has to do with who has jurisdiction over ground and air rights within airport environments. In most cases, you're dealing with multiple levels of government: states, counties, cities, towns, villages, and whistle-stops—and most of those don't give two hoots about the local airport and the 'daredevil' pilots who don't care enough about their own lives anyway. You get the idea.

"So how do you, or should I say, how do _we_ deal with it? We try for as much room as we can get and hope and pray for some intelligent consideration, which isn't always what the other guys have in mind. Take the situation at Barstow, for instance. Our rules say nobody can build anything that obstructs a published approach to an airport without first obtaining FAA approval. The same thing goes for the 5-mile radius around the airport. We can limit the height of anything that obstructs any approach to a runway within the radius. But that's as much as we've been able to wrangle from the brilliant politicos who run those states, cities and so forth. Outside the radius, they can build anything they want to—skyscrapers if they can raise the money—and our only recourse is to beg for reasonable judgment and reasonable notice, which technically they don't have to give us. Fortunately, most of them do.

"The Marine Corps did in this case. They told us about the electric transmission installation several months before they started it.

They weren't required to do so, but (someone) must have realized (the installation) could affect the airport. So they sent us a detailed notice as a courtesy, also reminding us of their jurisdictional rights, but they didn't give us start or completion dates, probably because those hadn't been finalized. When construction actually started several months later, whoever had thought to tell us about it up front may not have been there anymore. We'll never know if that was the case, but for whatever reason, we were not informed until the day they strung the wires. Which obviously didn't give us nearly enough time to post the proper warnings or prepare the NOTAMs. Especially since the notice came in by mail and sat on someone's desk for a while because the person was away.

"By the time the envelope was looked at, five or six days had gone by. Emergency action was taken and everyone in our system was notified by phone, fax, and teletype. But it was too late for the people who tried the approach that night. They found out about the wires the hard way.

"One thing that was kicked around here was how it could have been that not one soul from the airport ever saw any work being done on the towers—the 200-footers that hold the wires. They would have stuck out like sore thumbs in that wide-open desert area and been a cinch to spot from any aircraft. Everyone who was interviewed at the airport pleaded ignorance, apparently because the weather had been so clear for so long that none of the locals had used the highway approach to land. And other pilots departing or arriving from over there wouldn't have paid much attention to it—they probably assumed the airport must have known about it.

"Going back to the first issue, visual flight rules and what a pilot should be expected to see, the regs make no distinction. The pilot is required to see and avoid everything, moving or stationary, big or little, easy-to-see or hard-to-see. It doesn't matter, but that's silly. It ignores the realities of human sight and reflex limitations. If you've ever experienced a bird strike, for instance, you'd know what I'm talking about. Birds and humans aren't built to see that well or react fast enough to avoid those encounters. Not at airplane speeds.

"High-tension lines are the same thing. In daylight, you sometimes get light reflections coming off the wires so you can see them from farther out. Even then it's tough to react fast enough to avoid them unless you know where they are and you're looking for them. At night, it's impossible even with landing lights. Try it sometime— you'll see what I mean. By the time you get a reflection or see the wires themselves, you can be history.

"But the rule is the rule, and it's what we're required to go by. So until somebody gets around to changing it to make some sense out of it—we're stuck applying it the way it was written. It gets a little embarrassing, though, calling an accident like this one 'pilot error.' It's about the same as calling a lightning-strike (accident) a suicide. Nobody in their right mind would call it that, because it would be absurd."

NTSB representative "After the preliminary investigation was completed, it became obvious that the circumstances relating to the transmission line installation needed further study, but when we began looking into it, we found ourselves involved in a comedy routine like in one of those old silent movies. Everyone was running and pointing and falling all over themselves protecting their butts.

"At the airport, nobody knew from nothing. They hadn't been notified, they hadn't seen anything from the ground or the air, and they found it impossible to believe that anyone could have been stupid enough to string those wires across the interstate the way they did without marking them or telling anyone in the local area about them. We checked it out and verified that they hadn't been notified. The rest of it we couldn't prove, so it was a wash. But, (from what I understand unofficially), the investigators said they tended to agree with the people from the airport—that it didn't make any sense to *not* put up strobes and ball markers as soon as the towers went up and the wires were strung.

"The Marine Corps people, to their credit, took quick action and got the identifiers up and operating. It may have been that they were concerned about their own choppers being affected—whatever it was, they didn't make any excuses. They just went ahead and took care of it and then clammed up like it was wartime. We never got another thing out of them except a referral to the Corps of Engineers, who handled the installation. Other than that, it was blanko from the Marines.

"Dealing with the Corps of Engineers was an entirely different story. They were waiting for us with reams of documentation—all of which protected every move they'd made, at least by the book—and a complete presentation of the project from start to finish. How they planned it, organized it, coordinated it, and beat their deadline for finishing it. All of which was (an impressive presentation) until we realized that the last part—beating the deadline—was probably what led to the accident.

"But they claimed (that beating the deadline was not the cause of the accident), that they never had any intention of marking the wires— because they were more than 7 miles away from the airport and not under or near any published approach—and that even the strobes were doubtful for the same reasons. Nobody had ever told them about how the pilots were using the highway to find the airport. And none of their people were from the local area, so they had no way of finding out about it in the short time they were there. It was a short time, by the way. Probably three times as fast as civilian construction. They made a special point of telling us about it in their presentation.

"And our people made a point of telling them how their super efficiency killed the three innocent people who should have known about the installation and been able to see the towers and the wires. We must have won because they didn't waste any time taking care of it. And we never heard another word about it not being required.

"That's about it. There hasn't been another incident at Barstow-Daggett, so we consider the situation resolved. I understand, though, that the airport people are trying to get the lines removed or buried, which probably should have been done in the first place. They've got an uphill climb, but I wish them luck."

Author comment One of the things you can't make into a rule is common sense. When pilots lack it, they usually pay a steep price for their indiscretions, after which the NTSB adds insult to their injuries by citing them for 'pilot error.'

But when the system doesn't make sense, or its operatives fail to use reasonable judgment, the pilots are still cited for 'pilot error.' It's obviously a cop-out, but the system calls its own shots, makes its own rules, blames the easiest (and) least defensible participant—invariably the pilot. Then hides behind its infallibility to perpetuate its own nonsense.

Take this case, for instance. It was a classical example of a void in the commonsense process within the system. When the Marine Corps notified the FAA of their plans to erect the towers and run power lines across the highway, start and completion dates were not included. The fact that there were no dates included did not make those plans contingent, but the FAA sat on them because their policy discourages premature notice of construction plans, especially when the structures to be erected are outside its jurisdictional boundaries. Such was the case here. The notice was a sensible courtesy by the Marine Corps, not technically required but it was not sensibly evaluated by the FAA. They stood by their rules or, perhaps better said, the FAA stood *behind* their rules.

Think what a difference it would have made if the FAA had sent a copy of the notice to the Barstow-Daggett Airport, or even to the

Riverside Flight Service Station. The people in either place would have taken immediate action to spread the word about the project. Someone in authority would then have had time to discuss it with the Marine Corps before the plans were finalized. A compromise could have been reached to lessen the threat to the pilots in the area. Or, if that wasn't possible, at least timely notice of the installation would have been posted and the three people from Systems, Ltd. would have known about the wires before the long business trip and been further reminded about the obstruction by flight service.

The government's position is practical because they can't alert the system prematurely to all of the numerous contingency plans they receive. There would be so many false alarms that people would eventually ignore all notifications completely, which would create an even greater problem.

There is, however, another possibility and it has nothing to do with the government's construction notification policy. It stems from the airport, the Barstow-Daggett Airport in this case, and its home-grown, self-created "I-15 VFR Approach." That became a valid approach procedure for all intents and purposes because of its widespread use by the local pilots. It became a valid approach that could be published like the Shore Visual Approach at Meigs Field in Chicago or the River Visual and Mt. Vernon Visual Approaches at Washington National Airport in Virginia, across the Potomac from the District of Columbia.

So why not? Why not publish the "I-15 VFR Approach" and others like it? When they were published, the FAA would have jurisdiction over the ground and airspace needed to maintain sensible obstruction clearance. It would also inject a measure of much needed control over some of the ad-hoc approach procedures in use—and abused—at many airports around the country.

26

He walked away

Preliminary report: August; Cessna 182; certified flight instructor (no instrument rating), single-engine land, 5,200 hours. On a VFR flight from Raleigh, North Carolina, to Sumter, South Carolina, the pilot reported that he diverted to Manning, South Carolina, after encountering marginal weather and thunderstorms. He obtained vectors from Shaw (AFB) Approach but was surrounded by heavy rain and IMC. Upon entering a thunderstorm, the aircraft went out of control and exited the clouds inverted. Recovering from the unusual attitude at treetop level, the pilot elected to land in a grass field. During the attempted landing, the right wingtip contacted the ground, and the aircraft was severely damaged. The pilot sustained only minor injuries. Police and medical personnel noted the odor of alcohol in the aircraft cabin and on the pilot's breath. A toxicology check of a blood sample drawn from the pilot 3½ hours after the accident showed a blood alcohol level of 0.17 percent. Also, the presence of Tenormin, a common blood pressure prescription drug, was noted, but not at a significant percent level.

Further investigation revealed:
- Just prior to departing from Raleigh, the pilot received a complete weather briefing advising him that visual conditions prevailed with possible thunderstorms. He was not told that VFR was not recommended.
- Communications with ATC were continuous throughout the flight but the pilot became less and less coherent as the flight progressed. The Shaw AFB Approach controller stated in his report that he believed the pilot was drunk.
- The pilot was denied a medical certificate after open-heart surgery 15 years prior to the accident. Despite numerous appeals, the FAA refused to grant a waiver and no medical certificate was ever issued.
- In his post-accident report, the pilot declared having more than 5,000 hours of flying time, including 180 hours of multi-

engine, 220 hours of actual instrument, and 35 hours of simulated instrument time. Yet he also stated that he had no multi-engine or instrument rating and had flown less than 15 hours in the most recent 90 days and only 70 hours in the past year. Nearly 3,000 of his total flying hours had been accumulated since his medical had been denied, according to his own estimate.

- One of the first people to arrive at the accident site was the pilot's brother-in-law, a South Carolina state trooper who was off duty at the time. He was seen removing unknown items from the cabin by two witnesses.
- The trooper's wife, a surgical nurse, arrived shortly afterward in a pickup truck. State troopers stopped her from leaving the area with the pilot, but she was allowed to ride in the ambulance that took him to the hospital in Sumter—not Manning, which was much closer to the crash site.
- A blood sample was drawn in the ambulance that showed zero blood alcohol when tested 2 hours later. Believing the sample might have been tampered with by the pilot's relatives, emergency room personnel drew a second sample 1½ hours later that showed a blood alcohol level that was four times the FAA legal limit and double the legal driving limit in South Carolina.
- Less than six weeks after the accident, the Cessna 182 was replaced by the pilot's insurance company, and the pilot resumed his flying—at a much more active level. He subsequently died of causes unrelated to any injuries sustained in the accident, or anything having to do with aviation. Prior to his death, but during the period since he lost his first 182, the pilot twice declared emergencies and was involved in two incidents and one minor accident. No one was hurt in any of them.

IT WAS A FARILY TYPICAL TUESDAY for Johnny Williams, 55. He had left his farm home, 8 miles north of Sumter, South Carolina, at 7 a.m. and arrived at Sumter Municipal Airport fewer than 5 minutes later. His Cessna 182 was fueled and waiting for him right outside the FBO's pilot lounge, as it was every Tuesday morning for Johnny's weekly trip to Raleigh, North Carolina. He owned a trucking business there that was run by his oldest daughter and her husband. It was one of several that Johnny and his two brothers operated in the Carolinas, along with multiple retail strip centers in places like Sumter. The Williams family had been understated wealthy for many years and Johnny was one of its driving forces, which was a primary reason for his heart attack and open-heart surgery at the age of 35.

Johnny had been a pilot for 14 years prior to his surgery and he immediately appealed to the FAA for reinstatement of his medical as soon as he had recovered. Flying was important to him, his family—his wife, Leila, 49, and his daughter, Bonnie Jean, 31, were both pilots and the other children loved to ride along—and his businesses, but Johnny Williams was not important enough to the FAA. They reviewed his request for a waiver and denied reinstatement of his medical certificate.

Their decision was not acceptable to Johnny or his very supportive family. He resumed flying almost immediately, at first always with family copilots but that didn't last long. Johnny was too impatient to wait for backup. His schedule was too demanding and his copilots were as busy as he was.

He was also an alcoholic, as were the rest of the men in the Williams family. They had been raised on backwoods moonshine. Johnny had started out careful about mixing booze and flying but over the years he had allowed mixing to take over until he was routinely mixing bottle, throttle, and VFR flying. His few attempts at IFR convinced him that the spirits wouldn't stay in the bottle if he couldn't see out the window. So he kept it that way, flying VFR only with his trusty bottle along and no medical in his pocket, piling up more than 3,000 hours over the next 15 years. He had his share of close calls and near-misses during that time, but nothing serious or life-threatening.

Only the FAA gave him a hard time every two or three years. They wouldn't renew his medical, not because of his alcoholism, which they didn't know about—although just about everybody else around the Sumter Airport did—but because of his heart condition. Johnny couldn't find a doctor who would perjure himself for the pride of the Williams family. So Johnny and the FAA maintained their status quo—they kept refusing and he kept on flying.

Johnny's call to flight service turned up no surprises. The weather was Carolina-typical for early summer: VFR all day with a chance of afternoon thundershowers developing. He felt well, the 182 was flying perfectly since its annual 12 hours ago, and the trucking business had been excellent. It was going to be a good day as Johnny poured the horses to the Cessna and turned left to a northeast heading after departing from Sumter's Runway 22. An hour-and-a-half later he was rolling up to his favorite FBO's ramp at Raleigh-Durham International

Airport just as his daughter and his 2-year-old grandson were arriving in their van. Johnny was a happy flier and grandfather that morning.

After a full day of business and family matters, Johnny was back at the Raleigh-Durham pilot lounge calling flight service. The news was fair: VFR with broken clouds at 4,500 feet, some thunderstorm activity noted south of Charlotte, building and then dissipating. That should be easy to see and traversable. Johnny didn't bother filing a flight plan—he seldom did—but he did call home to tell Leila he might be late if he had to skirt the thunderstorms that were definitely a possibility. She changed possibility to probability after looking out the window. She also turned on her scanner so she could listen to Shaw Approach and Johnny when the Cessna flew into the Sumter area.

Johnny departed without incident from Raleigh-Durham International, picked up the familiar 215° heading and climbed to 2,500 feet, just above the light turbulence. It was smooth, clear, and pleasant as he opened the full flask he always carried in his flight case and had his first swig since the three swigs that he had with an abbreviated lunch. Johnny didn't eat much because it interfered with his drinking. He also took the blood pressure pill he had forgotten about at noon because it had been a hectic day. The pill, plus another short swig, would settle him down. They did so quickly and completely as noted by the flight-following controllers who Johnny had contacted right after reaching altitude. Johnny and ATC had a progressively harder time communicating.

Fifty miles northeast of Sumter, Johnny found himself dodging rainshowers. Without signing off from ATC, he switched his radio to Sumter Approach and asked for a vector to the airport. The military controller that the air force base provides for the area's approach control services had difficulty understanding Johnny's request and was unable to locate the 182's target on his scope. Johnny hadn't bothered to tell ATC that he was 50 miles away, but did tell ATC that he was looking at big build-ups in front and to his right. The weather was definitely moving in and lining up. This was not Johnny's cup of tea; even in a stupor, he had a healthy respect for South Carolina thunderstorms because they are nasty and they don't treat airplanes well.

Leila heard the Shaw controller call Johnny's number, but Johnny was too far away for her scanner to pick up his signal. She listened to the controller's side of his conversation with Johnny for the next 10 minutes, finally realizing that Johnny was dealing first-hand with the thunder, lightning, wind, and rain that she was watching from the comfort of her family room. When she finally heard his voice, she sensed that Johnny was in trouble. She also could tell he had spent more time than usual with his flask. It wasn't a good combination.

Leila Williams "Some of those military controllers from Shaw aren't capable of working VFR pilots in bad weather. They treat us like we don't belong there. The one that day sounded young to me. Not too experienced either, but we get a lot of those.

"I heard him trying to talk to Johnny, having a problem hearing him from so far out. He said something about a vector and then about the thunderstorms in the area. That was before I could hear Johnny. When I finally did hear him, I knew he was in trouble. He wasn't making sense. It sounded like he was being bounced around, losing his grip on the mike button. You know, on and off and scratchy. He was hard to understand. He also sounded like he may have taken an extra blood pressure pill. Whenever he did that, it made him lethargic and he'd slur his words a little.

"After a couple of minutes, Johnny said the build-ups in front of him and to his right were getting worse and he asked for a vector to Manning. That's about 25 miles south of here and it's where we usually go when Sumter gets weathered in. My sister, Clarice, also lives just south of there, so it's real convenient. She or her husband can usually pick us up. Clarice works nights as a surgical nurse at the hospital down there and Chuck's a state trooper. He patrols the whole area around Manning, so one of them is almost always available. That day, Chuck was off duty. When I called to tell them Johnny was heading their way, Chuck said he would leave right away and meet him at the airport. He also told me the weather around there was pretty lousy. It worried me because I was listening to Johnny on the radio and he was having a hard time of it. I told that to Chuck and he told me he was on his way. He had his police radio with him and while he was driving he heard the report that an airplane was down right near where he was. I think he was the first person to get there. He called Clarice and she came over in the van. They live less than 2 miles from where Johnny crashed.

"Anyway, when Johnny finally got near Manning, I heard him ask the controller what he had on his radar. The controller told him it was pretty heavy around Manning but seemed to be getting a little better up here at Sumter. Johnny asked for a vector so he wouldn't accidently fly into any of the storm cells and the controller told him to turn right. I think he said to 350°. Then less than a minute later, Johnny's voice came on for just a second—it sounded like he was swearing and that was the last thing I heard.

"It happened so quickly after Johnny got the vector that it must have been the controller turned him right smack into a cell. He probably had the weather part of his scope turned off so he could see the airplanes better. Some of the inexperienced ones do that, even though they're not supposed to. But for whatever reason it was, that jerk put Johnny right into that storm. It's a wonder he came out of it and was able to land at all after he was thrown inverted like he was. It showed what a good pilot he was. But we all knew that.

"After the accident, we asked the FAA to check up on the controller because of what he did, but they came back with a bunch of lies and told us the radar was working just fine. They said they'd tracked Johnny till he was only 30 feet off the ground. When we told them that wasn't what we were talking about, that the weather function on the scope had been turned off or turned down, we never heard a peep from them after that. So the best we can figure is somebody's butt was on the line, and the rest of them were covering up for him.

"Anyway, Johnny passed away a few months ago. It wasn't from the accident, or anything like that. So you'll have to go by the statement he wrote out for the FAA. He told it like it really happened—the same way I heard it coming over the radio. But they went with the lies they got from the controllers and blamed the whole accident on Johnny. That gave us fits dealing with the insurance company. Johnny's brother, Biff, took care of it, and we finally made a settlement and got it squared away.

"I can tell you this about the accident. It spoiled Johnny's last two years of flying. He never trusted another controller again. His flying got more intense, but I could tell he never really enjoyed it anymore. My son and I still fly the 182, but it's not the same without Johnny carrying on and running the show the way he did. We're thinking of selling the airplane."

Finding himself in familiar territory near Florence, about 25 miles northeast of Sumter, Johnny told the Shaw controller he could see heavy rain at his 2 o'clock position and that he would be diverting to Clarendon Airport (renamed Santee Cooper Regional) at Manning. He made a left turn to 195°, flew directly over Huggins Memorial Airport at Timmonsville, and perhaps had a reinforcer from his flask as he began the 35-mile leg to Manning. Johnny knew every inch of terrain beneath him. Manning was the family's favorite alternate. The airport was just south of where his wife's sister and brother-in-law lived, and they were always happy to pick them up. His brother-in-law, Chuck Dowling, loved airplanes and flew in the 182 every chance he got. He wasn't a pilot because he couldn't free up enough dollars on his state trooper's salary, but he was hoping.

With the town of Manning at his 3 o'clock position, Johnny found himself looking down the throat of a powerful cell and a wall of rain right over where he knew the airport was located. He called the Shaw Approach controller and requested a vector to anywhere. The controller suggested Florence as a first choice and Sumter as a possible second. The weather had moved south and seemed to be letting up farther north.

Johnny never gave it a second thought because Florence would be inconvenient. He opted for Sumter and the controller told him to turn right to a heading of 350°, which looked like a clear track around the weather on his radarscope. Six sweeps of the radar later, the cell was right over the 182 on the scope. It was sudden, without warning, but not uncommon in South Carolina. Johnny knew it instantly. He was engulfed in rain and powerful turbulence. In his semistupor, he felt the airplane going out from under him and saw the instruments tumble. Four seconds later, the 182 was thrown out of the bottom of the cell, inverted but almost level.

With all the presence of mind and body he could gather, Johnny lurched the wheel and righted the airplane. Badly shaken, angry, and frightened, he grabbed his mike and swore at the controller, telling him he'd had enough of the garbage he was flying in and was going to land somewhere. Johnny's sudden outburst of four-letter words jolted the controller, who then watched the 182 descend to 30 feet agl and leave his scope. The controller's first call was to the state police with his best guess of where the airplane went down—he was off by less than a mile—and his second call was to the FAA's FSDO in West Columbia, South Carolina, about 40 miles away.

The field Johnny selected looked okay until he was right on top of it. From 15 feet off the ground he realized he would be landing across the furrows. Panicked and not functioning too well because of his half-empty flask, he threw the throttle forward and began a turn to the left, but it was too late to stop the sink rate. The 182's left main and wing hit together, followed by the nosewheel and then the right wing as the airplane bounced along. When it finally came to rest 650 feet later, Johnny was dazed, bleeding from cuts and bruises on his face and left arm, but otherwise okay. Nothing was broken on Johnny; the 182 fared less well, sustaining $33,000 worth of damage.

Without turning off any of the switches, Johnny exited the airplane and looked around. Barely able to walk—not as a result of the accident but because of his stupor—Johnny made his way toward a house at the far end of the field. As he approached it, he saw a car pull up and a tall man get out of it and start running toward him.

Johnny laughed and sat down on the wet ground as he recognized the man coming toward him. It was his brother-in-law, a state trooper who had heard a report that an airplane had gone down.

Two witnesses had seen Johnny fly over on his way into the field. They called the police and then made their way toward the airplane in a 4-wheel drive vehicle. As they were nearing the field where the Cessna was sitting, the witnesses saw a tall man leave the airplane carrying something. He never came back to the area and the witnesses did not see him again. When they arrived at the crash site, the witnesses found the airplane empty but with its strobes flashing and the radio squawking. They also noticed a strong smell of whiskey emanating from the cabin. It was an aroma that was quite familiar to them.

Kathy Bogart, Sumter/Clarendon County Ambulance Service

"We didn't get the call until half-an-hour after the plane went down. Two of the pilot's relatives were there with him and they wanted to treat him themselves, but the state police decided to call us instead. That's why there was a delay. But we were at the accident scene in less than 5 minutes after we got the first tone [the call for the ambulance].

"When we got there, the pilot wasn't anywhere near the airplane. He was in a van with his sister-in-law, who was a nurse. She had started treating him. We helped him out of the van and that's when we noticed a heavy smell of alcohol on his breath. He told us he wasn't drunk or anything, just shook up from the accident, but man, you could have gotten drunk from the fumes just from standing near that guy. He was really plastered.

"The sister-in-law insisted on coming with us in the ambulance. We were going to take him to the hospital in Manning, but she wanted to go on up to Sumter, which was closer to where he lived. We serve both places, so it didn't make any difference to us. Just more mileage that we got paid for.

"On the way, my partner, Randy, drew blood from the pilot—that's our usual procedure when we and the police suspect drinking—and I filled the 4 vials for the lab. At the hospital, we left the sister-in-law with the ambulance while we took the pilot into the emergency room. I guess we were gone about 15 minutes, with the paperwork and all. When we came back, someone had moved the ambulance, which was very unusual, and had also moved around the vials of blood. I knew that because they weren't the way I had left them. I didn't think much about it at the time and just took the four vials into the lab and got a receipt for them. But when I found out a couple of days later that the blood samples turned up negative, I couldn't believe it. That's when I realized someone must have tampered with them.

"I ain't accusing anyone, but that pilot was as drunk as a skunk, and no way his blood could have come up negative. I understand the emergency room people were just as shocked and took another sample and that one showed him totally pie-eyed, which he was. Other than that, he wasn't hurt bad. We see lots of his kind in highway accidents, but we don't get many airplane crashes to deal with. It surprised me because I thought pilots weren't supposed to drink any alcohol when they flew."

Johnny Lee Williams Jr. "I know what the reports said, and they were wrong. My dad wasn't drunk. He knew better than to drink and fly. What it must have been was that he was all sweaty from the warm, humid night, and the shock of the accident. They didn't find any alcohol in the airplane, and my dad was in Raleigh with my sister and her husband all that day, and they never saw him drink anything.

"We were told the first blood test came up negative, which is how it should have. Then the emergency room people took another blood sample that came up positive, but the lab lost that last sample for over a week and then came up with a number showing dad was practically stoned. Now that was totally ridiculous. After all, he had just flown the airplane through a blinding thunderstorm and landed himself in one piece in that field. He couldn't have done that if he was drunk. Hell, most pilots couldn't have done that at all, stone cold sober or whatever.

"What we think happened was that the controller from the air base knew someone at either the hospital or the state police and asked them to cover for him because he was the one who caused the accident by turning dad right into the thunderstorm that almost killed him. He wanted to make it look like dad was drunk, so nobody would check up on how he screwed up by giving him the wrong vector.

"Then the insurance company picked up on it, and we had a helluva time. They were trying to get out of paying the claim, but they never had a leg to stand on, and my uncle, he's a lawyer, he took care of them and got the airplane replaced within just a few weeks. Now you know they'd've never paid that claim if they could have proved dad was drunk. They couldn't, and neither could the FAA or the state police.

"About the only thing we do know for sure about that whole affair was that the Air Force transferred that controller out of Shaw awfully quick because we never heard anymore from him or about him after that. He was gone less than a week after the accident. That kind of tells you something, doesn't it?"

Shaw Approach Control supervisor "The accident at Manning caused more ruckus than it should have, probably because the pilot and his family were trying to blame us for what happened. Pilots and their lawyers try to do that so they can collect for their busted airplanes. In this case, I think they were trying to cover up a whole bunch of things.

"First off, the pilot had no medical and shouldn't have been flying at all. I don't know how they got that one past their insurance company but I'm not a lawyer. Then we checked the tapes from the whole flight, starting back at Raleigh. If you listen to all of them, you get the feeling that the pilot had a bottle of something with him because he got progressively fuzzier. By the time he called us, he was practically incoherent. When the controller could hear him at all, (the controller) had trouble making out what he was saying. Then he started dodging storm cells until he wound up way off course. At that point, the controller suggested some routings to him, which he ignored, and [the controller] finally tried giving him a vector. But by then the cells were all over him, and he just lost it. Our radar tracked him all the way down to about 30 feet or so above the ground. We pinpointed the location where he went off our scopes and called the state police.

"Everything I've told you is in the written reports. The tape transcripts from ATC and our radar trackings and audio communications were all turned over to the FAA and the NTSB. The controller who handled the flight also wrote out a complete report before he left here a few days later. By the way, the pilot's family made a big deal out of that, claiming we transferred him out to avoid questioning, but that was nonsense. He had requested his own transfer weeks earlier so he could be closer to his family . . .. As a matter of fact, he hung around here a couple of extra days to finish up the paperwork on the accident. We also had all of the transcripts anyway, and they very clearly told the story of what went on. That pilot was intoxicated, plain and simple. No other explanation could account for the way he acted."

FAA representative "If you saw the written reports this pilot submitted the day after the accident, you'd believe he was still drunk, or thinking we were. There were more discrepancies than there were facts. On the one hand, he said he had over 5,000 hours, but he had no logbook and wrote on the report that he had hardly flown in the last year or so. He also said he had lots of multi-engine and actual instrument time, but he had no rating for either of those. He even said he had about 20 or 30 hours of hood and simulator time, but then admitted he had never taken an IFR course anywhere. Which meant that all of his experience claims were baloney. Everything else probably was, too.

"The first thing our investigators noticed when they got to the wreckage, an hour or so after the accident, was a strong smell of whiskey in the cabin. He must have had a bottle with him that either broke or got spilled when the gear broke off. They never found a bottle or any other physical evidence of it, but they reported that the odor was strong and pungent. It was definitely alcohol, and that was later proven by the toxicology reports that came in. The pilot's BAC [blood alcohol content] was better than four times the legal limit. With that much alcohol in his body, it's a wonder he ever got off the ground at Raleigh. As you can see, it eventually caught up with him. It usually does.

"We pulled the pilot's medical file from Oke City and it was a lulu. He had open-heart surgery 15 years prior to the accident and several minor episodes afterward. He was on blood pressure and blood thinner medications and never did get a clean bill of health from any of his own doctors. In fact, his family internist's file on him showed that he was an alcoholic and had been for many years, but he still appealed for an FAA waiver every couple of years, like he was trying to prove something. I don't know what, though, because he continued to fly anyway. Having no medical and an invalid pilot's license didn't seem to bother him much. He probably treated everything else in his life the same way.

"And you wonder what he must have told his insurance company in order to collect anything on the airplane he piled up. They don't usually pay off when there's a medical missing or alcohol involved. That, by the way, was a crazy issue in this accident. Everyone who got anywhere near the pilot testified that he was too drunk to even stand up by himself. But the first blood test showed zero alcohol and the second one, which showed the very high BAC level, somehow got lost for more than a week at the hospital lab. We checked to see if there'd been a little hanky-panky going on because the pilot's sister-in-law was a nurse, but we couldn't prove anything. In general, the guy was sort of a flying time bomb. It was just lucky he didn't crash into a schoolyard or a shopping center.

"After the whole thing was over, we found out he was back flying about six weeks later: still no medical and still drinking. We notified the state police about it, but they said they couldn't do anything to stop him. His airplane was owned by his family's business, so we couldn't impound it for substance abuse. And we have no way of fining him or arresting him for not having a medical. The FARs don't provide for penalties. That's also true for his license and the ratings he doesn't have. We sent him a couple of notices and a threatening letter. But I'm sure that after so many years of ignoring the rules he just laughed at us and did all the flying he wanted to.

"There's nothing else we can do. It's a lousy situation that needs to be changed, but we haven't figured out how or what to start with. Every state has its own laws and expects us to do our own policing. But we don't have a police force. So we're dead in the water until someone figures out how to give us a set of teeth that will make our rules stick. In the meantime, we've been pretty lucky. There aren't a lot of Johnny Williams's out there flying airplanes."

Sumter FBO representative "Everybody around here knows the Williams family. They've been flying with us for years. And everybody knew Johnny was an alcoholic, but he handled it safely, so nobody ever paid much attention to it. As a matter of fact, when we heard about the accident—from him, his family, the FAA and the safety board—it sounded like he did a pretty good job of coming out of that thunderstorm, probably better than most. If you've ever been caught and trapped by one of our South Carolina summertime specials, you know what I mean. They're as ornery as anything in the whole country. Mostly, they tear airplanes apart.

"After the accident, Johnny got another Cessna 182. His wife, Leila, and Johnny junior still fly it. Johnny never liked the replacement airplane much. Said it didn't feel right, but he flew the wings off it like he was trying to prove something after the FAA cited him for a bunch of violations and pulled his license. He turned into an angry guy. I don't think he even liked flying anymore. Just did it to prove he was as mean and ornery as that storm cell he survived.

"(I don't know what he died from.) Somebody said he had a heart attack and dropped dead in his car but that's only a rumor. His family hasn't talked about it and nobody around here brings up the subject, so we just go about our business, happy they're such good customers and hope they stay that way."

NTSB representative "The whole issue of assessing blame for an accident has taken on distorted proportions. It starts with the underlying premise that something mechanical or human had to be at fault whenever an airplane gets busted up. And the emphasis is always on the 'someone'—usually the pilot—without even considering that circumstances can occasionally be completely beyond everyone's control.

"Our unenforceable FARs are a good example of what I'm talking about. No one at any of the government agencies likes the present situation, but we're stuck living with it. I can tell you, it can be very disheartening dealing with a flagrant violator knowing that, if push comes to shove, the violator is going to win. And frightening as hell realizing what a menace that person can be in an airplane, sharing the sky with the airlines and thousands of unwary pilots who expect everyone else to be as responsible and as conscientious as they are.

"You know, on the highway you have assurances that there are enforced laws to restrain the crazies, the drunks, the speeders, and the people without driver's licenses. We don't have those kinds of enforceable laws in aviation and the people who cause the problems are the first ones to find out how powerless we are, which encourages them to flaunt the rules and put themselves and everyone else in danger.

"That's exactly what happened in this case. The pilot had open-heart surgery and lost his medical—meaning he also lost his pilot's license and his flying privileges. He appealed for reinstatement, was refused, felt he was treated unfairly and then decided 'the hell with it—he'd fly until he got caught and deal with it then.' But he never did get caught or if he did, nothing ever came of it. As a result of whatever took place, he found out pretty quickly that it wouldn't make one damned bit of difference, except maybe with his insurance company and he figured his lawyer brother could deal with them. So, off he went and took off anytime and to anyplace he felt like going.

"He also used and abused the system with impunity—flight service briefings, flight-following, flight watch, and approach control— when it suited him. Otherwise, he just barged into the open skies like he owned them without regard for anyone. So, on your 'blame' scorecard, chalk up a big one for the system that couldn't keep this guy on the ground where he belonged.

"But that's only part of this accident. Mostly it was the weather and those thunderstorm cells that jumped on him. The National Weather Service never called them, so when he called flight service for a briefing, they didn't tell him VFR was not recommended because at the time, there were no warnings in effect. Which means that, when he took off, he had the best, most current weather data available. Score one 'no-blame' point for the pilot.

"En route he was discourteous at worst, but otherwise competent—I'm not talking about his drinking, which was unthinkable . . . that's another story. He flew his route well, maintained his altitude perfectly, and made all the right decisions when he ran into the weather. Remember, the first thing he did was divert to his alternate. He didn't hesitate or try plunging into the clouds first to see how bad they were. No, he turned and ran. Which is exactly what he should have done on a VFR trip. By the way, having the alternate up his sleeve and at the ready is an example of excellent planning. Better than we see in many VFR situations—some IFR ones, too. Give the pilot two more points for the en route portion.

"When his alternate blew up on him, he again made the right decision. He called in and asked for help. Choosing Sumter over Florence was a matter of convenience. The controller never pushed one over the other and the radar tapes showed that he made a perfect turn to his assigned heading and held his altitude at 2,500 feet, right on the money. Give him another point for the alternate switch.

"Then came the best part. The tumble and recovery after being thrown out of the storm cell—inverted. Both eyewitnesses verified the inverted part, by the way, otherwise we wouldn't have believed the pilot's story—not the way he lied about everything else. That part was real. He made a near-perfect recovery, in his condition no less, and then had the presence of mind to put the airplane down and not mess with the weather that could have killed him if he'd tried. He even called in his intentions to the approach controller while he circled a couple of times looking for the best possible place to land. Which he found.

"The only problem was that he landed according to the wind instead of according to the field conditions, but that was probably just bad luck. It was raining pretty hard, and he may not have been able to see ahead well enough. So, I say score a big home run for the pilot for the last part. He did everything right. And the proof is in the fact that he lived to tell about it.

". . . I consider (living to tell about it) to be a miracle unto itself. The man was dead drunk and on pills besides. He survived something that most stone-sober VFR and IFR pilots would not have. How he did that, we'll never know, but he must have had the constitution of a Mack truck.

"There is one final point of blame: his family and maybe throw the FBO in with them. They knew he was an alcoholic, that he had serious heart problems—the kind (of heart problems that) you can drop dead from—and that he was breaking the law every time he got into the left seat of an airplane. Yet they not only didn't try to stop him or report him to anyone who could, they actually covered for him and encouraged him to keep on doing it. In effect, they were sending a lethal weapon into the skies—a drunken heart attack candidate.

"So, if you're looking for what and who to blame for this one, I vote for the weather and the pilot's family. As for the pilot? If anything, his performance was either lucky as hell or impressive as hell. Personally, I'd vote for lucky . . .."

Author comment Whether or not this particular accident was "pilot error" is inconsequential and unfortunate because it sends the wrong signals to pilots who read about it. Given these exact same circumstances, 999 out of 1,000 pilots would have been killed or, at the very least, critically injured and probably crippled for life. This one miracle situation should not give false confidence to anyone who might be thinking about bending the rules on drinking. Alcohol kills pilots.

The same goes for heart patients whose medicals have been rejected or suspended. Flying causes stress and stress greatly increases the likelihood of a heart attack, fatal and otherwise. A pilot that has a heart attack while flying seldom, if ever, survives. The pilot also endangers everything around them and under them because they always crash. It is not possible to fly an airplane after suffering a coronary.

This accident also sends the wrong signals to nonpilot passengers and the general public. It tells them that the rules will not protect them and gives the impression that drunks and junkies and sickies are tolerated by the system. After all, the pilot's whole family participated in his misadventures; so did the FBO. And the FAA couldn't, and so didn't do anything about keeping him out of the sky.

Who else is there? In the public's eyes, that's everybody. Try explaining this one away to people who already think pilots are half crazy or worse and endangering their bodies and property.

The FAA and the entire aviation community owes itself and the public a greater sense of responsibility and commitment to safety. The laws and rules governing general aviation need to be revised and updated so they apply to the realities of the present and the future. And they must be honored without exception by the people involved in the system. Or else.

Epilogue

AS THE PILOT POPULATION of the nation continues its decline, some truths are surfacing that can no longer be ignored, denied, or overlooked:

- Product liability is not the sole reason for the decline in general aviation.
- "Macho" cannot be associated with flying.
- Pilot training and proficiency training need immediate rethinking so they can be made relevant to the needs of pilots, their equipment, and the environment in which they operate and coexist.
- The accident reporting and evaluating system must restore its credibility. Pilot error should be redefined and expanded to include "why," so the accident reports are truly educational, not just informational.
- General aviation needs active self-promotion and public relations in order to counter the sensationalism of the media and the deeply rooted negativism and lack of confidence of the public at large.

Air safety starts with education and training, which must begin with the awareness that human beings are land creatures. Our brains enable us to fly, not our God-given bodies; certain physical strengths and land adaptations are weaknesses in the three-dimensional environment of the sky. These human factors must first be addressed in their entirety before any real progress can be made.

The NTSB's accident reporting system plays a crucial role in identifying specific opportunities for improvement. The board needs to be unfettered and given wider latitude in order to accomplish its mission. So do the rest of the involved government agencies that have already demonstrated an exceptional level of competence and the willingness to hang in there, despite being hamstrung with obsolete equipment and antiquated operating systems. Turn them loose and air safety will make a quantum leap, which will then lower insurance rates, which will make flying more affordable, which will bring more people into aviation, and which will lead to improvements in equipment, facilities, and services. In other words, it's time to get our act together. And the accident investigation and evaluation process is a good place to start.

Glossary

automatic direction finder (ADF) An instrument that points to a nondirectional beacon, low frequency radio station.

Air Defense Identification Zone (ADIZ) An area of airspace that covers the entire perimeter of the United States.

air force base (AFB)

above ground level (agl) Height of an aircraft above the surface immediately below the aircraft.

Airman's Information Manual (AIM)

airman's meteorological information (AIRMET) A weather advisory bulletin pertaining to light twin and single-engine aircraft.

Air Line Pilots Association (ALPA) Labor union of professional pilots.

approach light system (ALS)

ALSF-1 Standard 2,400 ft. high-intensity approach lighting system with sequenced flashers.

altimeter setting Manual calibration of barometric pressure on an aircraft altimeter to read height above mean sea level. At 18,000 feet and above, constant setting is 29.92.

Aircraft Owners and Pilots Association (AOPA)

approach control Air traffic control in the area of an airport.

approach plate Chart depicting an instrument landing procedure for an airport.

airport radar service area (ARSA) Traffic separation service in a terminal area. Reclassified in 1993 as Class C airspace.

air route surveillance radar (ARSR)

air route traffic control center (ARTCC)

area navigation (*See* random area navigation.)

artificial horizon Instrument depicting the aircraft's position relative to the horizon. Critical for instrument flight.

Aviation Safety Reporting System (ASRS) Operated by NASA to accept and analyze voluntary reports of aircraft incidents submitted in strict confidence by pilots.

air traffic control (ATC)

automatic terminal information service (ATIS)

airline transport pilot certificate (ATP) Most advanced non-instructor license that can be held by a pilot.

autopilot Automatic aircraft control system; a 2-axis has turn and bank only; a 3-axis has turn, bank, and pitch (altitude) control.

avgas Aviation fuel for piston engines on aircraft. The fuel is not technically a gasoline. The fuel has a higher octane rating for reliable performance to ensure safety.

Civil Aeronautics Board (CAB) The defunct federal board that regulated the airline industry.

clear air turbulence (CAT) Sudden turbulence that is typically unexpected because the air is clear with no clouds to indicate the possibility of turbulence.

ceiling and visibility unlimited (CAVU) When the weather is clear and visibility is greater than 10 miles.

course deviation indicator (CDI) The readout instrument of a navigation receiver. The receiver converts a VOR's transmission into a directional guidance along a course that extends toward (TO) or away from (FROM) the VOR station.

Class A airspace All airspace above 18,000 ft.

Class B airspace A terminal control area (TCA) prior to airspace reclassification. A charted altitude separation system in a major airport terminal area.

Class C airspace An airport radar service area (ARSA) prior to airspace reclassification. Traffic separation service in a terminal area.

Class D airspace Formerly airport traffic areas and control zones prior to airspace reclassification.

Class E airspace General controlled airspace prior to airspace reclassification.

Class G airspace Uncontrolled airspace prior to airspace reclassification.

clearance delivery ATC's issuance of an instrument flight plan to the pilot of an aircraft preparing to depart.

certified flight instructor (CFI)

certified flight instructor-instruments (CFII)

departure ATC departure control in the vicinity of an airport.

directional gyro (DG) Gyro-driven device that provides the same guidance as a compass. A standard compass is susceptible to momentary errors when an aircraft is maneuvering; the DG is less prone to errors.

distance measuring equipment (DME) An instrument that displays distance to or from a VORTAC station plus displays the aircraft ground speed in knots. Many DME indicators also display elapsed time from a station or time to reach a station.

U.S. Department of Transportation (DOT)

en route flight advisory service (EFAS) This is commonly referred to as flight watch, which provides weather information to en route pilots.

en route chart Low- or high-altitude en route map for IFR flight.

estimated time of arrival (ETA)

estimated time of departure (ETD)

Federal Aviation Administration (FAA)

Federal Aviation Regulations (FARs)

fixed-base operator (FBO) A retail business selling fuel, maintenance, flight training, supplies, and general aviation services at an airport.

Federal Communications Commission (FCC)

flight following En route radar tracking and traffic separation service provided by ATC to the pilot of an airplane that is flying VFR, if the controller's workload permits.

flight watch Weather reporting service for aircraft in flight.

flight standards district office (FSDO) An FAA field office.

flight service station (FSS) Primary services, among other services, include dissemination of weather information and acceptance of flight plans filed by pilots.

glide slope The vertical guidance portion of a precision instrument landing system.

global positioning satellite (GPS) The abbreviation GPS has become a generic reference to aircraft navigation based upon signals from satellites that are primarily for military use, but are available for any form of transportation, including general aviation aircraft, a car or a truck, and more.

ground control Airport traffic control for taxiing aircraft.

horizontal situation indicator (HSI) An instrument depicting the aircraft's attitude, pitch, and bank relative to the horizon and ground-based navigation aids, usually displayed on a directional gyro. A crucial instrument for pilot reference during flight in instrument conditions when the ground and natural horizon are not visible.

hypoxia Physical condition caused by the lack of oxygen typically occurring near or above 10,000 feet. Hypoxia adversely affects judgment and performance and might lead to spatial disorientation and vertigo.

IDENT Identifier function of a transponder that transmits a momentary extra signal to help a controller locate that aircraft on a radarscope.

instrument flight rules (IFR) Rules governing the procedures for conducting instrument flight. Also used by pilots and controllers to indicate type of flight plan.

instrument landing system (ILS) Vertical and horizontal electronic guidance for the pilot to safely descend the aircraft and prepare for landing when visibility is reduced.

instrument meteorological conditions (IMC) When visibility, cloud distances, and cloud ceiling are reduced and do not permit VFR operations.

Jepp charts Navigational charts, airport approach procedures, and other aviation information prepared by Jeppesen Sanderson, Incorporated. (Company started by airmail pilot E.B. Jeppesen, who kept written records of the routes in a pocket notebook.)

jet route High-altitude airway route that is above 18,000 feet.

localizer The horizontal guidance portion of a precision instrument landing system.

LOM An electronic locating beacon that is typically a component of an instrument landing system.

loran A long-range electronic navigation system.

mach The ratio of true airspeed to the speed of sound.

MALSF (medium intensity approach lighting system with flashers) A configuration of lights at the approach end of a runway to help a pilot land an aircraft.

missed approach point (MAP) The point during an instrument approach at which the approach must be discontinued if the runway environment is not in sight for landing.

minimum crossing altitude (MCA) The lowest altitude at certain navigational fixes that an aircraft must cross at when proceeding in the direction of a higher minimum en route altitude when flying IFR.

minimum descent altitude (MDA) The lowest height that an aircraft can descend on a nonprecision approach without having the runway in sight.

minimum en route altitude (MEA) The lowest that an aircraft can safely fly through a certain area. Usually the MEA is 2,000 feet above the highest obstructions en route.

microwave landing system (MLS) An advanced instrument landing system.

military operations area (MOA) When active, must be avoided by all civilian aircraft.

minimum obstruction clearance altitude (MOCA)

mode-C Altitude reporting function of a transponder.

minimum reception altitude (MRA) Lowest altitude at which an intersection (of VOR radials) can be determined.

minimum safe altitude (MSA) Minimum altitude specified in regulations for various aircraft operations.

multi- and single-engine land (MSEL) A rating to fly multi-engine aircraft, as specified on a pilot certificate.

mean sea level (MSL) Altitude corrected with barometric pressure.

National Aeronautics and Space Administration (NASA)

navcom Combined navigation receiver and communications transceiver.

navaid Ground-based navigational aid.

nondirectional radio beacon (NDB) Low frequency AM station with audible identifier code.

National Ocean Service The U.S. government's aviation chart and information publisher.

notice to airmen (NOTAM) Flight advisory service.

National Transportation Safety Board (NTSB)

precision approach radar (PAR)

pilot in command (PIC)

pilot weather and flight conditions report (PIREP)

precip Visible rain, drizzle, sleet, or snow.

radar altimeter An instrument that measures an aircraft's altitude above the ground, typically accurate to within 5 feet.

runway alignment indicator lights (RAIL)

runway end identifier lights (REIL)

radio magnetic indicator (RMI) Navigation instrument that displays two VOR and/or ADF signals at once, usually on a gyro compass.

random area navigation (RNAV) Waypoint navigating system that electronically transposes VOR stations to desired locations, creating nonstandard routing that might save time and fuel plus increase safety.

runway visual range (RVR) Ground-based instrument that measures lateral visibility.

sectional An aeronautical chart for low altitude flight, typically in VFR conditions.

single-engine land (SEL) Pilot certificate rating for single engine airplanes.

standard instrument approach procedure (SIAP) Printed IFR procedure for approaching an airport.

standard instrument departure (SID) Printed procedure for departing IFR from an airport.

significant meteorological information (SIGMET) Severe weather warning for pilots.

spatial disorientation Human loss of sense of direction, position, or relationship with surroundings.

squawk A digital transponder code identifier.

short takeoff and landing aircraft (STOL)

tactical air navigational aid (TACAN) Specialized navigational information used by the military.

true air speed (TAS) Calibrated for air density at altitude.

terminal area surveillance radar (TASR)

terminal control area (TCA) Charted altitude separation system in a major airport terminal area. Reclassified in 1993 as Class B airspace.

terminal area A generic reference to the area that surrounds an airport, typically a large airport serving a large metropolitan area.

terminal radar approach control facility (TRACON) The building and equipment that comprise an approach control operation.

transponder Aircraft instrument that transmits a selectable coded signal for easier radarscope tracking by ATC. A mode-C transponder also transmits the aircraft altitude, which is processed by computers and displayed with the aircraft target on the radar display.

terminal radar service area (TRSA) A defunct type of airspace that surrounded an airport with a moderate amount of traffic.

transcribed weather broadcast (TWEB)

unicom Established radio frequencies for pilots to communicate with specific nongovernment airport facilities.

visual approach slope indicator (VASI) A glide path reference, typically lights, for landing.

vertigo Dizziness and the feeling that surroundings are whirling or spinning. A jumbled, disoriented state of mind.

visual flight rules (VFR) Rules governing the procedures for conducting flight in visual conditions (good weather). Also used by pilots and controllers to indicate type of flight plan.

visual meteorological conditions (VMC) When visibility, cloud distances, and cloud ceiling are better than specified minima; when VFR flight is permitted.

very high frequency (VHF)

Victor airway Low-altitude airway route, below 18,000 feet.

VOR (very high frequency omni-directional radio range) Ground-based VHF navigational aid station.

VORDME Collocated VOR and DME.

VORTAC Collocated VOR and TACAN.

will comply (wilco) Same as "roger."

Index

Index based on official conclusion information for each accident.

A

alcohol
  causing spatial disorientation, 306-320
  impairment, 1-13
altitude
  failure to maintain reported, 234-245
  proper, not maintained, 221-233
approach minimums, weather condition below, 258-269
approach, misjudged, 119-132

B

breakup, in-flight, 246-257
buzzing, unauthorized, 94-106

C

control, loss of, 67-70, 82-93, 94-106, 119-132, 146-160, 171-183, 196-206, 246-257
  due to ice accumulation on airframe, 107-118
  due to spatial disorientation, 184-195, 207-220, 258-269, 270-281
  structural failure, due to, 37-48
controls, overstressing of, 60-70

D

deicing equipment, improper use of, 146-160
DG, inoperative, 246-257
disorientation,
  alcohol, caused by, 1-13

spatial, 119-132, 161-170, 171-183, 196-206
  possible, 146-160

F

flight instructor supervision, inadequate, 196-206
flight plan
  intentional deviation from, 49-59
  misfiled, deliberate, 71-81
flight planning, poor, 161-170, 171-183, 184-195
flight, low, unauthorized, 94-106
flying speed, failure to maintain, 37-48, 94-106, 107-118, 146-160
fuel exhaustion, 14-24, 25-36, 49-59, 71-81, 132-145

I

ice accumulation on airframe, 107-118
icing conditions, continued flight into, 107-118
IFR flight plan, illegal filing of, 282-294
IFR procedure, improper, 207-220
impairment, alcohol, 1-13
  due to, 94-106
instrument approach procedures, improper, 60-70
instrument time, total, lack of, 221-233

J

judgment, poor, 94-106

L

landing flare, misjudged, 119-132
landing sight, poorly planned, 25-36
license restricted, 282-294

329

363.12
C   Cohn, Robe
         They ca

363.12
C
            Cohn, Robert L.   8
              They called it pilot
         error.

MAR 13
SEP 24   94-2118
SEP 10   9912

                          5835